Dark Ghettos

TOMMIE SHELBY

Dark Ghettos

Injustice, Dissent, and Reform

THE BELKNAP PRESS OF
HARVARD UNIVERSITY PRESS

Cambridge, Massachusetts
London, England   2016

First Printing

Library of Congress Cataloging-in-Publication Data

Names: Shelby, Tommie, 1967– author.
Title: Dark ghettos : injustice, dissent, and reform / Tommie Shelby.
Description: Cambridge, Massachusetts : The Belknap Press of Harvard
   University Press, 2016. | Includes bibliographical references and index.
Identifiers: LCCN 2016011715 | ISBN 9780674970502 (alk. paper)
Subjects: LCSH: Inner cities—United States. | Social justice—United States. |
   Racism in public welfare—United States. | African Americans—
   United States—Social conditions. | Inner cities—Government policy—
   United States.
Classification: LCC HV4045 .S44 2016 | DDC 304.3/3660973—dc23
LC record available at https://lccn.loc.gov/2016011715

For Jess

"Ghetto" was the name for the Jewish quarter in sixteenth-century Venice. Later, it came to mean any section of a city to which Jews were confined. America has contributed to the concept of the ghetto the restriction of persons to a special area and the limiting of their freedom of choice on the basis of color. The dark ghetto's invisible walls have been erected by the white society, by those who have power, both to confine those who have *no* power and to perpetuate their powerlessness. The dark ghettos are social, political, educational, and—above all—economic colonies. Their inhabitants are subject peoples, victims of the greed, cruelty, insensitivity, guilt, and fear of their masters.

—Kenneth B. Clark, *Dark Ghetto: Dilemmas of Social Power*

Unjust social arrangements are themselves a kind of extortion, even violence, and consent to them does not bind.

—John Rawls, *A Theory of Justice*

Now I can't pledge allegiance to your flag
Cause I can't find no reconciliation with your past
When there was nothing equal for my people in your math
You forced us in the ghetto and then you took our dads

—Lupe Fiasco, "Strange Fruition"

Contents

Dark Ghettos

Introduction

Rethinking the Problem
of the Ghetto

From New York City to Los Angeles, poor black neighborhoods blot the metropolitan landscapes of the United States. Social scientists, ordinary observers, and inhabitants of these stigmatized neighborhoods often refer to them as "ghettos."[1] In addition to concentrated poverty, these communities typically have a number of troubling characteristics—high rates of racial segregation, violence, street crime, joblessness, teenage pregnancy, family instability, school dropouts, welfare receipt, and drug abuse. Such neighborhoods emerged decades ago, after countless black Americans abandoned rural southern areas for industrializing cities in the wake of Reconstruction's collapse. Despite the efforts of the Civil Rights movement and various federal antipoverty initiatives over the years, ghettos are still a dreadful reality.

Why do ghettos persist? Some charge that the government has yet to create an opportunity structure that would enable those born or raised in ghettos to escape poverty. Others point to the attitudes and conduct of ghetto denizens, arguing that the black poor should make better choices and stop blaming the government or racism for hardships they have effectively imposed on themselves. Some split the difference, insisting that the public, through government action, should create more opportunity *and* that the urban poor should make more responsible choices.

This long-standing and contentious debate has reached an impasse over what best explains the persistence of ghetto conditions (the dysfunctional behavior of the black poor or structural obstacles to upward mobility) and over what kinds of state interventions (if any) would be most cost-effective in solving the problem. However, I urge that we reframe the debate, that we not view it primarily in terms of behavior versus structure or the strengths and weaknesses of particular antipoverty measures, but in terms of what justice requires and how we, individually and collectively, should respond to injustice.

Many view ghettos and their occupants as a "social problem" to be fixed, and they espouse policy approaches that take the following form. Describe some salient and disconcerting features of ghettos (the prevalence of impoverished single-mother families and youth violence). Identify the linchpin that keeps ghettos in place (joblessness or segregation). And then propose a cost-effective solution that would remove this linchpin (a jobs program or an integration initiative) with the expectation that ghettos will, eventually, fade away as a result. I call this the *medical model*. The primary aim of those working within this framework is to increase the material welfare of people living in ghettos through narrowly targeted and empirically grounded interventions into their lives.

Yet from the standpoint of justice, this approach has serious limitations and pitfalls. Just as physicians take basic human anatomy as given when treating patients, policymakers working within the medical model treat the background structure of society as given and focus only on alleviating the burdens of the disadvantaged. When it comes to the ghetto poor, this generally means attempting to integrate them into an existing social system rather than viewing their unwillingness to fully cooperate as a sign that the system itself needs fundamental reform. In short, features of society that could and should be altered often get little scrutiny. This is the problem of *status quo bias*.

In addition, the technocratic reasoning of the medical model marginalizes the political agency of those it aims to help. The ghetto poor are regarded as passive victims in need of assistance rather than as potential allies in what should be a collective effort to secure justice for all. The everyday, sometimes unusual, and often misunderstood choices of those in these disadvantaged communities are viewed, when seen through the lens of the medical model, as at best devoid of moral content or political intent and at worst pathological. Indeed, status quo bias invites us to see dysfunction where perhaps lies resistance to injustice. Call this the problem of *downgraded agency.*[2]

Furthermore, focusing on the problems of the disadvantaged can divert attention from or obscure the numerous ways in which the advantaged unfairly benefit from an unjust social structure. Keep in mind that the privileged have a tendency to believe that they have earned all their advantages while the disadvantaged have brought their hardships on themselves. Narrowly focusing on "fighting poverty" might seem progressive. But it can also serve to quiet the grievances of those most distressed while preserving a stratified social order that would still be marred by serious injustices, illegitimate privileges, and ill-gotten gains. Call this the *unjust-advantage blind spot* problem.

To avoid these limits and pitfalls, I advocate thinking about ghettos through a *systemic-injustice* framework. When we take up the problem using this model, both government and ordinary citizens are viewed as having a duty to ensure that the social system of cooperation we all participate in is just. The presence of ghettos in American cities is a strong indication that just background conditions do not prevail. Reflection on ghettos, then, serves not only to focus our energies on relieving the immense burdens the ghetto poor carry but also to make us think, as fellow citizens, about the fairness of the overall social structure we inhabit and maintain. Were the more affluent in society to think about the matter this way, they would view the ghetto poor, not simply as disadvantaged people in need of their help or government intervention, but as fellow citizens with an equal claim on a just social structure. They might then come to recognize that achieving social justice will require not only eschewing their paternalistic (and sometimes punitive) attitudes toward the black poor but also relinquishing their unjust advantages.

I do not object to the use of biological or medical metaphors in social inquiry or public policy (though these can sometimes mislead). The concern is substantive, not semantic. Nor do I oppose the medical model per se or the technocratic reasoning that usually accompanies it. It can be an appropriate way to think about and respond to a worrisome social problem when that problem is not a matter of basic justice. And, sometimes, the medical model is applied to ghettos because advocates of that approach don't believe they are addressing injustices. The tasks, then, would be to get proponents to see that matters of basic justice are at issue and to draw their attention to the pitfalls of uncritically invoking that model in the context of systemic injustice. But often those who are concerned to rectify a past or ongoing injustice still opt for the medical model. They think it is a suitable way to solve stubborn social problems even when these problems are a consequence of injustice. I aim to show that, from the standpoint of political morality, the systemic-injustice model is superior, particularly when thinking about and responding to the continuing presence of ghettos in U.S. cities.

Social Facts and Moral Principles

When social justice questions are raised, there is a common tendency to treat the answers as obvious or to regard disagreements about the answers as products of irresolvable "ideological" differences. Indeed, some are skeptical of the very idea of "social justice." Alternatively, some, though not in principle opposed to the discourse of justice, are content to rest their response to ghetto poverty almost entirely on empirical analyses of the social facts. Their assumption is that disagreements over empirical claims are more manageable than messy disputes over what justice requires. Thinking carefully through complex issues of political morality is thus taken to be unnecessary, unfruitful, or pointless, at best a mere academic exercise. There is, of course, profound disagreement, among philosophers and citizens alike, about what justice requires. The practical problems of ghettos cannot wait for consensus to form on such controversial questions. Still, questions of justice should not be avoided, downplayed, or ignored, as many of the sharp political clashes over ghetto poverty turn, I will show, on disagreements over values, not facts. Justice questions should therefore be a focal point of public policy, political activism, and civic discourse concerning the future of our cities and their most disadvantaged inhabitants. To that end, I have three main objectives.

First, I specify what it is about the social structure of the United States that justifies the claim that ghettos are a product and reliable sign of systemic injustice. Here I draw on influential contemporary writings in the liberal tradition that identify standards for judging the extent to which societies realize justice.[3] While these philosophical studies tackle basic liberties, distributive justice, and, to some extent, gender equality, research in this area is much less developed on race and on the confounding race–class nexus. I develop insights from liberal, feminist, and black radical thought to arrive at a systematic account of social injustices along the dimensions of race, gender, and class.

Second, though many accept that the state is obligated to ensure a just social structure, fewer appreciate the moral limits on what types of policies may be implemented while unjust conditions prevail. There are moral constraints both on how the state may treat those severely disadvantaged by injustice and on what means it may deploy to improve their circumstances. For example, if joblessness is a cause of urban poverty, as many contend, can government legitimately require work as a condition of subsistence support even when the employment opportunity structure is deeply unfair? I think the answer is "no" and aim to establish this. Thus, a second objective is to identify the normative limits on state antipoverty interventions.

Third, I explain what the unjustly disadvantaged are morally required and permitted to do in response to the unjust conditions that circumscribe their lives. Some of the conduct poor urban blacks engage in is harmful to others, self-destructive, or incompatible with self-respect. On the other hand, some of their actions are best seen as a moral response to injustice—that is, as a form of resistance or dissent. So I also explain what would constitute a responsible and dignified response on the part of the ghetto poor to their social conditions. This aspect of the book is a case study in the political ethics of the oppressed. There is abundant philosophical work explaining what a social system must be like if it is to be fully just. There is also a long tradition of writing on civil disobedience as a response to injustice. However, we have little work, comparatively speaking, that defines the duties of individuals living under unjust conditions or explains the virtues of political resistance.[4] And the work that does exist often focuses on the affluent or bystanders rather than on the oppressed.[5]

Some scholars and commentators who are sympathetic to the plight of the downtrodden do emphasize the agency of the oppressed, but only when the oppressed exhibit attitudes or take actions generally regarded as praiseworthy—for example, when they show resilience under hardship, defy their oppressors, or overcome tremendous obstacles. But not all responses to oppression are justified or virtuous. We must admit that the oppressed sometimes respond in ways that are wrong or blameworthy. There can be no *ethics* of the oppressed (and thus no point in emphasizing the *agency* of the oppressed) if those who are unjustly disadvantaged can do no wrong. In explaining the content and contours of the relevant principles and values, I therefore seek to avoid not only the tendency to view the ghetto poor as inert but also the tendencies to rush to blame them and to romantically celebrate them.

Some readers may feel that, as a matter of solidarity, the black intelligentsia should affirm the humanity of the black urban poor, defend them against false and insulting charges, and, most relevant, avoid publicly criticizing the way they respond to their oppression. They are, after all, simply trying to survive under trying circumstances not of their making. However, my articulation of an ethics of the oppressed is perfectly consistent with what might be called the *Stand and Fight* tradition in black political thought. This tradition counsels against suffering in silence and insists on fighting openly and assertively—in the press, in the legislative halls, in the courts, and in the streets—and not only quietly behind the scenes. For instance, Harriet Jacobs and Frederick Douglass, though born and raised under slavery, not only praised the solidarity and defiance of slaves but openly expressed contempt for slaves who were treacherous, servile, or apologists for slavery. Black abolitionists David Walker and Maria Stewart, though themselves never enslaved, maintained the same uncompromising moral stance. Walker insisted that slaves exhibit solidarity and self-respect, but also active resistance: "The man who would not fight under our Lord and Master Jesus Christ, in the glorious and heavenly cause of freedom and of God—to be delivered from the most wretched, abject and servile slavery, that ever a people was afflicted with since the foundations of the world, to the present day—ought to be kept with all of his children or family, in slavery, or in chains, to be butchered by his *cruel enemies*."[6] I have no greater conviction than the imperative to keep faith with this majestic and honorable tradition.

While this book engages with and draws on research in the social sciences, legal studies, urban studies, and African American studies, it is primarily a work of political theory and social philosophy. As a philosopher writing about ghetto poverty, my role is not to identify the causes of ghettos. Nor is it to propose policy prescriptions. Instead, I think systematically through the thorny conceptual and normative questions to which reflection on ghettos gives rise. Though this is a work in practical philosophy, one won't find herein concrete marching orders for activists and organizations seeking to improve the conditions of the ghetto poor. One will find, however, a detailed defense of the values and principles that I believe should (and sometimes do) guide grassroots reform efforts and policy prescriptions.

Social scientists tend not to make, or even to imply, value judgments about the subjects they study. In their role as empirical researchers, they do not presume to tell the poor (or anyone else) how they ought to live or what they should value. Though perhaps personally moved by a desire to reduce poverty or even by egalitarian concerns, in their vocation as scientists many take themselves to be doing no more than providing empirical analyses of ghetto poverty. There are, of course, some social scientists, particularly those making policy recommendations, who don't hesitate to make value claims or to rely on what they take to be widely held and sound moral judgments. But even here, the inferential links between analytical claims, empirical conclusions, moral assumptions, and policy prescriptions are often not explicitly or carefully articulated. Social-scientific studies of a social problem lead directly to specific proposals for how to fix it. Often missing is sufficient critical reflection on the values that should guide such proposals, in particular the basic justice considerations that should structure public policy. With notable exceptions, policy discussions of ghetto poverty don't explicitly state, let alone defend, the values upon which they rest.[7] *Dark Ghettos* addresses this normative gap.

Some readers may become impatient with the arguments to come, perhaps insisting that the only thing that matters is what would solve this urgent problem. But there are related, logically prior questions that also matter. For instance, it matters enormously how we conceptualize "the problem." While all agree that certain aspects of life in ghettos are troubling, what is it about ghetto poverty that calls for a solution? And what constitutes "fixing" the problem? That is, what standards are appropriate for judging progress or failure? Finally, even if we identify a set of actions that would bring about a desirable outcome (for example, a reduction in black poverty), we need to know whether these actions are justifiable to all concerned. These are questions of political morality that cannot be elided through pragmatism, no matter how urgently solutions are needed.

Contemporary debate (in the academy and beyond) centers on what caused ghetto conditions to arise and what best explains the persistence of these disadvantaged neighborhoods. Many point to racism and discrimination or to income and wealth inequities, and I discuss these factors. But I also consider seven other possible explanatory factors: residential segregation, cultural configurations, reproductive choices, single-mother families, joblessness, crime, and mass incarceration. The claim that these are central factors in explaining ghetto poverty is widely endorsed and has empirical support, but it is not my task to sort out which of these factors is *most* important for explaining ghetto conditions.

I have organized this book as a set of philosophical reflections on these possible factors. The argument is structured in this way, in part, to provide a better analytical and normative grip on ghetto poverty by keeping questions of justice always in view. I will consider questions like these: Should government attempt to foster integrated neighborhoods in order to reduce inequality? If there are cultural patterns in poor black communities that inhibit upward mobility, what, if anything, should be done about this? What responsibility does the public have to support vulnerable families in ghetto communities? What is the proper role of government in creating employment opportunities for jobless inner-city residents? What are the obligations of government to curb crime, and what limits should there be on crime-control measures that affect the unfairly disadvantaged?

Securing and maintaining justice is not only an obligation of state officials or a collective responsibility of the public. Justice also imposes duties on individuals, including disadvantaged citizens. These demands are valid even when government isn't doing all it should to bring about just conditions. Taking such moral requirements seriously leads to questions such as these: Should the ghetto poor welcome and seize opportunities for residential integration? Should they choose mainstream norms over deviant cultural norms even when their ambitions have been unfairly thwarted? Do they have a duty to work in legitimate jobs even when these are menial and low paying? What responsibilities do poor urban parents have to form and maintain well-functioning families despite socioeconomic hardship? Should the black poor respect and comply with the law even when civic equality isn't fully realized?

To the extent that lack of freedom, material deprivation, social stigma, and limited life prospects are the result of factors outside the control of individuals, no reasonable person could think that the plight of the ghetto poor is their own fault or that they don't merit assistance from their government or fellow citizens. If those born and raised in ghettos remain disadvantaged only because of racial discrimination, inadequate schools, unjust barriers that prevent them from leaving their impoverished and often violent communities, or some other circumstance not of their choosing, they cannot be blamed and are entitled to public interventions on their behalf.

However, when many look at America's ghettos and at the poor black people who reside in them, they don't see injustices (or only injustices). They see immorality, irresponsibility, and imprudence. They believe that the attitudes and conduct of the ghetto poor contribute to and even worsen their plight. After all, some of the factors that social scientists point to when explaining the persistence of ghettos—residential configurations, cultural dynamics, reproductive patterns and family structure, unemployment rates, crime and incarceration rates—are not wholly outside of the control of poor black people. These factors call out for critical reflection on structure and agency. We have to consider institutional constraint and individual choice.

Although my decision to focus on the seven factors turned on their empirical plausibility as explanatory factors, their relevance for thinking about justice and injustice, *and* the questions they raise about the responsibilities of the ghetto poor, it is this third dimension that makes the problem of ghettos so challenging and controversial. Many people, including some black people, believe that the ghetto poor are responsible for perpetuating their own poverty, and for this reason they don't view ghettos as unjust or a sign of injustice. But the ghetto poor often have good reason to think and act as they do. This becomes clear once we view ghettos from the standpoint of justice and take it seriously that their disadvantaged denizens are responding, as rational and moral agents, to sound reasons as they live their difficult and often tragic lives.

Liberalism and Nonideal Theory

How should we think about and respond to the persistence of ghettos in the post-civil-rights era? As a philosophical answer to that question, this book develops a liberal-egalitarian theory of black urban poverty. By "liberals" or "liberalism," I don't mean Americans' political self-descriptions or party affiliations. Nor am I referring to "neoliberalism"—an ideology that, for example, promotes the use of market rationality and business principles in all social institutions, prefers firms and private organizations (rather than state agencies) to carry out public functions, and views citizens primarily as economic agents (investors, entrepreneurs, workers, and consumers). Instead, I have in mind a political morality defined by a set of normative principles, a tradition developed by such thinkers as Immanuel Kant, John Stuart Mill, and John Rawls.

Liberal political morality regards the individual (rather than the family unit, social group, or nation) as the primary unit of moral concern and insists that each individual should be treated with equal respect by governing bodies. It denies that an individual's basic interest in self-governance can be legitimately sacrificed to promote the welfare of others. It opposes social hierarchies based on circumstances of birth (race, sex, caste, family background, or feudal rank) or on religious conviction and piety. Committed to democratic principles, it regards all members of society as equals, with the same claim to participate in public affairs. The kind of liberalism defended here takes seriously not only individual liberty and civic equality but also substantive economic fairness and so is better described as *liberal egalitarianism* to distinguish it from other variants in the broader liberal tradition. In this way, there are "liberals" (as defined by their self-description, Democratic Party membership, or confidence in markets and privatization) who are not liberals in my sense, because they are not liberal egalitarians.[8] And there are liberals in my sense who reject the label "liberal" altogether, though they endorse the principles of liberal political morality.

Also, the liberalism I defend is not grounded in utilitarianism or welfare economics. I don't think the promotion of happiness or preference satisfaction is the heart of morality. I embrace and defend a *nonconsequentialist* moral outlook (which draws on Kantian and contractualist ideas) and so reject the idea that the practical consequences of our actions are all that matters morally (which is not to deny that consequences are morally significant). This nonconsequentialism extends to political morality, even to principles of justice. For instance, individuals within a polity have a basic interest in being treated with equal concern and respect by the basic institutions of their society, even if upon reflection they don't value such treatment.[9]

The word "liberal" may put off some who believe that liberal philosophy has little or nothing to offer those who care deeply about racial injustices or the plight of black people in the United States. Some are convinced that liberalism (and the Enlightenment worldview with which it is associated) is itself an instrument of racial domination, a handmaiden of white supremacy. This judgment (widely held among black radicals) is mistaken, as I aim to show. The social and political philosophy that I defend is a version of what Michael Dawson has called "black radical egalitarianism" and what Charles Mills has recently dubbed "black radical liberalism."[10] Black radical liberalism, as a normative theory of state power, draws heavily from liberal-egalitarian thought. But in its broader social philosophy (which is not solely concerned with official state action), it embraces insights from black nationalism, feminism, and Marxism.

I don't offer a comprehensive account of the principles a society must satisfy to be fully just. That would be a project in ideal theory, and others have given liberal-egalitarian ideal theory detailed and, I believe, convincing defense.[11] In noting this, I am not suggesting that the enterprise of searching for a more profound and precise understanding of what social justice requires is worthless or without practical import. It is just that I believe we can rely on the wisdom and insights thus far attained to develop *nonideal theory*, which specifies and justifies the principles that should guide our responses to injustices.

Because some doubt the value of ideal theory altogether and the relationship between ideal and nonideal theorizing is hotly contested and often misunderstood, some preliminary remarks are in order. Ideal theory and nonideal theory are complementary components of an endeavor to devise a systematic account of social justice. In fact, nonideal theory logically depends on ideal theory, and the aims of nonideal theory give ideal theory its practical significance. For example, Rawls's famous principles of justice (equal liberty, fair equality of opportunity, and the difference principle) are the product of ideal theorizing and as such have two main functions: to serve as practical goals to work toward and as normative standards for judging the overall justice of particular social arrangements.[12] Ideal theory provides evaluative standards for judging when a social order is seriously unjust and an objective to strive for in our resistance to oppression. Injustices are conceptualized as deviations from the ideal principles of justice, in much the same way that fallacious reasoning is conceived as a deviation from the rules of logical inference. An injustice is a failure on the part of individuals, institutions, or social arrangements to satisfy what the principles of justice demand. Thus, charges of injustice presuppose ideals of justice, which particular individuals, institutions, or whole societies can and often do depart from. Such deviations can be small or great, minor or serious, and depending on the size and nature of the gap between ideals and practice (and also on whether these deviations are avoidable or blameworthy), different remedies will be required.

Nonideal theory includes four types of principles:

(1) Principles of *reform and revolution* are standards that should guide efforts to transform an unjust institutional arrangement into a more just one.

(2) Principles of *rectification* should guide attempts to remedy or make amends for the injuries and losses victims have suffered as a result of ongoing or past injustice.

(3) Principles of *crime control* should guide the policies a society relies on when attempting to minimize and deter individual noncompliance with what justice requires.

(4) *Political ethics* are the principles and values that should guide individuals as they respond to social injustices and that serve as the basis for criticizing the failure of individuals to promote just circumstances and to avoid complicity with injustice.

Together the principles of reform and revolution and the principles of rectification jointly constitute a theory of *corrective justice*. Type (1) principles have to do with altering the basic structure of a society so that it better approximates a fully just society. Type (2) principles address the need to lift or lighten the burdens on those disadvantaged because of injustice or to make amends to those harmed by injustice.

Type (1) principles are forward looking, oriented toward establishing a just society. Type (2) principles are backward looking, oriented toward repairing injury and settling unpaid moral debts. Theorizing about corrective justice is thus more than laying down principles for compensating the victims of past injustice or reducing their disadvantages. It also includes the philosophical arm of collective efforts to establish a society regulated by a mutual commitment to justice. Reformers and revolutionaries should be aiming to create a society in which the principles of justice are fully realized in its institutions and in which citizens comply with institutional rules because these are in accord with their shared conception of justice. It is in this way that ideal theory serves as a guide for nonideal theory.

We cannot develop a philosophically adequate theory of how to respond to social injustice without first knowing what makes a social scheme unjust. In the case of gross injustices, such as slavery or genocide, we may be able to judge confidently that a social arrangement is unjust simply by observing it or having it described to us, relying exclusively on our pretheoretic moral convictions. We don't need a theory for that. But with less manifest injustices, or when our political values seem to conflict, or when we're uncertain about what justice requires, or when there is great but honest disagreement about whether a practice is unjust, in the absence of a more systematic conception of justice we can't know which aspects of a society should be altered. Without a coherent set of principles that enables us to identify the unjust features of a social system, we could not be confident as to what direction social change should take.

Those living within a just and stable society presumably would, for the most part, comply with and respect the law. Yet even in a reasonably just polity, we can expect some individuals to break the law and violate the rights of others. Type (3) principles are designed to deal with these failures of individual compliance. When these principles are realized, they assure the law-abiding that others won't be allowed to take advantage of their goodwill and respect for justice. The normative theory of punishment falls within this domain. But within nonideal theory there is also the question of how a society should respond to lawbreaking when the society itself is seriously unjust. Any attempt to come to terms with the condition of the ghetto poor must address this issue.

Within a just society, individual citizens have various civic duties. For instance, they should do their part to uphold and maintain the social arrangements from which they benefit. This includes obeying the law, holding public officials accountable, paying their taxes, reporting crimes, serving on juries, and so on. However, when a society is unjust, individuals must decide how they should respond to this collective failing. A theory of political ethics explains and justifies the values that should figure in such deliberations. For instance, we each have a duty to help establish just institutions where they fail to exist and to improve the well-being of the oppressed when we can.

The ghetto poor are often viewed as either helpless victims of injustice or a menace to society. Their political acts of defiance are therefore generally regarded as posturing, treated as misguided, ignored altogether, or actively repressed. Yet some actions of the ghetto poor that are interpreted as deviant or pathological should instead be understood as moral responses to injustice. By looking at their conduct this way, we gain insight into the political ethics of the unjustly disadvantaged and can better evaluate when these responses are reasonable and permissible or blameworthy and self-defeating.

A New Theory of Ghettos

This book offers a normative nonideal theory of ghettos that emphasizes basic concerns of justice and highlights the political ethics of the oppressed. It is a liberal-egalitarian theory that takes economic fairness as seriously as it does individual liberty and formal equality. While my focus is on the plight of black people in the United States, this is not a book about race alone. I'm just as concerned about gender, class, and place. I discuss social structure *and* individual responsibility, avoiding the all-too-common tendency to emphasize one or the other, and I do so without devaluing the political agency of the ghetto poor. To that end, I advance a political morality of dissent appropriate to the ghetto context.

Systematic attempts to explain what justice requires are as old as Plato's *Republic*. Reflecting on modes of *injustice*, like the conditions ghetto poverty represents, can help us better understand the meaning and urgency of this perennial philosophical question. Throughout, *Dark Ghettos* moves back and forth between the sometimes esoteric, lofty, and abstract concerns of philosophy and the familiar, grim, and concrete realities of the contemporary urban landscape. I offer the resulting theory in the firm belief that careful philosophical reflection can assist in moving the public debate over black urban poverty in a more productive direction, pointing the way toward solutions that are fair to all concerned and that treat the truly disadvantaged among us with the respect they deserve.

PART I

Liberty, Equality, Fraternity

ONE

Injustice

Before offering arguments for my central claims, I define a few key terms and elucidate the content of some pertinent principles. Specifically, this chapter outlines a basic framework for asking and answering questions about social justice, a framework that, while not politically neutral, is ideologically capacious. The chapter also defends an account of "racism," distinguishing its three fundamental forms and making explicit the moral considerations that undergird apt charges of racism. It explains what "discrimination" is and what makes it wrong. And it provides an interpretation of "equal opportunity" that highlights how that ideal serves as a basis for condemning urban poverty and class-based stratification. In addition, this chapter specifies the relevant notion of "ghetto," which, though not uncontested, identifies the primary subject of the book. By combining these ideas with some basic and widely known empirical facts, I show that many blacks residing in ghettos in the United States today are not simply disadvantaged but *unjustly* disadvantaged.

Reciprocity and the Basic Structure of Society

Liberal-egalitarian philosophers disagree, sometimes sharply, about the precise content of political morality. For the most part the arguments I put forth don't turn on these philosophical fine points, and the theory I develop could fit comfortably within a number of liberal-egalitarian frameworks (justice as fairness, left libertarianism, luck egalitarianism, human capabilities approach, and civic republicanism). Besides the nonconsequentialism mentioned earlier, however, there are two ideas found in John Rawls's approach to thinking about justice that not all liberal egalitarians endorse but that are fundamental to the conclusions I defend.

Rawls has suggested that if we were to conceive of society as a *system of social cooperation over time* and took an impartial view of what the distribution of benefits and burdens of participating in this scheme ought to be, we could arrive at conclusions about what social justice requires that warrant our rational assent. The idea of society as a fair system of cooperation is a moral notion to be used in the evaluation of institutional arrangements. Social justice is constituted by the legitimate claims and responsibilities individuals have within a fair overall social arrangement. Thought about in this way, justice is a matter of *reciprocity* between persons who regard each other as equals.[1] Taking this approach to questions of social justice is particularly apt when considering criticisms often made against the ghetto poor. It provides a framework for settling whether the urban poor are *doing* their fair share in upholding the system of cooperation and whether they are *receiving* the fair share due them as equal participants in this system. Reciprocity, as a central value in liberal political morality, is the primary normative standpoint from which I reflect on family structure, joblessness, and crime in ghetto neighborhoods.

Rawls also emphasizes the paramount significance of the *basic structure* for social justice.[2] The basic structure is composed of the major political, economic, and social institutions that make fruitful social cooperation possible and that apportion the benefits and burdens of such cooperation. Within the political realm, the basic structure includes the constitution (which specifies the basic rights and duties of citizenship), the organization of government institutions, and the legal system (including the system of criminal law). Within the economic realm, the basic structure includes the organizational mechanisms (typically markets, firms, banks, and state agencies) that govern the production of goods and provision of services and also the system of private and public ownership that determines rights and responsibilities with respect to goods and resources. And in the social domain, the basic structure includes families and educational institutions, as these ensure that children are cared for and taught what they need to know so that they might eventually become equal participants in the system of social cooperation.

A well-organized and impartially administered basic structure may not be all that is needed to achieve or maintain social justice. Private citizens, attending to their civic duties, must do their part, too. Yet it should be clear why Rawls chooses to focus on the basic structure: its effects on the freedom and life prospects of individuals are immense and wide-ranging, and these effects have an impact on the quality of individuals' lives from birth until death.[3] Because each of us must make a life for ourselves under the dominion of the basic structure of some society or other, we each have a legitimate claim that these institutions treat us fairly. We live our individual lives, not in isolation, but with others in society, where these complex social relations are mediated by an institutional framework into which we are born. The basic structure fixes a person's initial position within society. Some individuals will be more, and some less, favored in the distribution of benefits and burdens—of liberties, duties, opportunities, and material advantages—of this association over the course of their lives, depending on their starting places within the social arrangement.

None of this means that a person's life prospects are completely determined by the particular social circumstances into which he or she is born. A person's choices, the good or bad will of other individuals, and brute luck will naturally have a significant impact as well. And, of course, in a liberal-democratic regime each should take primary responsibility for how his or her life goes. But at the same time, each individual's life prospects are profoundly shaped by a social structure that he or she could not have chosen. Moreover, it is largely through institutions—governments, schools, firms, markets, and families—that social, natural, and fortuitous contingencies impact our individual life chances. Thus, the social arrangement we participate in should be organized to give each of us a fair chance to flourish. We possess that fair chance only when the social scheme disadvantages us in ways that can be justified on impartial grounds.

One benefit of focusing on the basic structure of U.S. society is that it can help us avoid the pitfalls of the medical-model approach to ghetto poverty (in particular, its status quo bias and unjust-advantage blind spot). The background social arrangement is kept constantly in view, where it can be scrutinized for fairness and treated as a potential target of reform or even revolution (if things are bad enough). The illegitimate privileges of the advantaged in the social scheme are highlighted alongside the burdens of the oppressed. Centering public discussions of ghetto poverty on the justice of the institutional scheme as a whole is one way to highlight the need for the advantaged in the scheme to justify their privileged position to those at the bottom of the well.

Racism: Ideological, Institutional, and Structural

In the United States today, there would appear to be a consensus that "racism" and "discrimination" are wrong. Few seem to be inclined to describe themselves as "racists" or to be openly in favor of discriminating against others. The trouble is, there doesn't appear to be much agreement on just what constitutes racism and discrimination.[4] And even where people do seem to agree that the label "racism" or "discrimination" applies in a particular case, there's no reason to think that they attach the same normative significance to these terms—that is, that they have honed in on exactly the same wrong-making feature or moral principle. Some of the conclusions of this book rely on these two notions, so it is important to be explicit about how I intend them to be understood and why I construe their meanings as I do.

Perhaps the most hotly contested notion this book relies on is *racism*.[5] In its most basic form, racism is an *ideology:* a widely held set of associated beliefs and implicit judgments that misrepresent significant social realities and that function, through this distortion, to bring about or perpetuate unjust social relations.[6] These beliefs and judgments form a kind of system of thought, which influences how adherents understand their social life and identities. Ideologies purport to be forms of knowledge (factual and normative) and so are amenable to critique. They don't just contain false beliefs; more often they also obscure relevant information, organize facts in a misleading way, or rest on fallacious reasoning. Because of such epistemic flaws, ideologies constitute a distorted or biased outlook that conceals social injustices (even from those who accept these belief systems), thus inhibiting social reform.

Many in the grip of an ideology accept it while being ignorant of, or self-deceived about, the real motives for why they hold it. They would like to believe that they accept the belief system (solely) because of the considerations in favor of its truth. However, as a matter of fact, they accept it (primarily) because of the influence of noncognitive motives (for instance, a desire for social status or material advantages) that operate without their conscious awareness. This explains why various ideologies have had such longevity and popularity despite their epistemic flaws—they satisfy needs or promote interests apart from our interest in forming true beliefs. It also helps us understand why ideological beliefs are so often difficult to shake in the face of counter evidence and rational refutation.

In addition to racist ideologies, there are ideologies that center on religious notions, nationalist ideals, moral concepts, and ideas about sex and gender, and these often work together to legitimate unjust forms of hierarchy, exclusion, inequality, coercion, and violence. What is distinctive about racist ideologies is that they invoke or presuppose the problematic idea of *race*, a concept that attaches social meaning to visible inherited physical characteristics, continental origins, and biological ancestry.

An ideology's content can shift over time in response to changes in the sociopolitical context. So, for example, explicit beliefs about the inherent biological inferiority of nonwhite racial groups were more widespread in the past, during the eras of chattel slavery, Jim Crow segregation, and modern colonial subjugation. But social movements for justice and emancipation relentlessly attacked these ideas and the regimes they supported. Today, beliefs and implicit judgments about the cultural backwardness or behavioral pathology of nonwhite racial groups are more common but play essentially the same social function as biological racism.[7] These beliefs and assumptions are called upon to explain why disadvantaged groups persist in a low position within their societies. They are enlisted in defenses against charges that equal opportunity does not yet exist. They are invoked when people reject out of hand policies that would correct past injustices or reduce racial inequality.

Ideologies are those commonly held beliefs and implicit judgments that legitimate stratified social orders. Elites do sometimes espouse what we might call *ideological doctrines*, that is, developed theories. Most people, however, do not have sophisticated views about the relevant phenomena yet will have absorbed—through various media, schools, public rituals, or other revered institutions—many of the core assumptions propagated by elites. Indeed, the locus of ideology is common sense, that reservoir of background assumptions that agents draw on spontaneously as they navigate the complexities of social life and the demands of human existence. These assumptions are often held without full conscious awareness, creating various forms of cognitive and affective unconscious bias.[8] For this reason people can actually be surprised to learn that they harbor racial prejudices or implicitly accept degrading racial stereotypes.

Treating racial ideology as the paradigmatic form of racism does not preclude regarding things other than beliefs as racist. It simply means understanding these other forms or expressions of racism in terms of ideology's main characteristics or effects. In particular, racial ideology, like all ideologies, not only shapes thought but influences conduct and structures feeling and volition. So, for instance, someone who explicitly subscribes to a racist belief system is obviously a racist, but so is someone who is disposed to act on racist assumptions (even when the person does not fully know that such assumptions shape his or her conduct and attitudes). A racist action is one undertaken because of the agent's racist attitudes or an action the agent rationalizes in terms of racist beliefs.

The concept *institutional racism* was introduced into antiracist theory and practice because of the need to explain how ideological racism can operate in institutional contexts where the relevant agents do not consciously hold or openly express racist attitudes. Institutional racism can be *extrinsic* or *intrinsic*.[9] On the extrinsic conception, an institution's policies are regarded as racist, not by virtue of the policymakers' racist beliefs, but solely in virtue of the policies' effects.[10] Extrinsic institutional racism occurs when an institution employs a policy that is race-neutral in its content and public rationale but nevertheless has a significant or disproportionate negative impact on an unfairly disadvantaged racial group. Those who make and apply the policies need not intend this result and may not themselves be racists. What is nonetheless wrong with the institution's practices is that they perpetuate the negative effects of ongoing or past racist actions and thereby encourage racist attitudes and stereotypes. The underlying idea is that some groups in society are already disadvantaged by racism, and an institution that is not intrinsically racist may nevertheless play a role in keeping these groups in their disadvantaged condition, thus leading some to conclude that they occupy this low station because of the disadvantaged groups' culpable failings or inherent inferiority. Because the institution in question may not be responsible for the group's prior disadvantages, the racism with which it is implicated may be extrinsic to the institution itself. Nonetheless, considerations of corrective justice justify seeking to reverse or mitigate these negative institutional effects by requiring particular institutions (such as schools, corporations, or courts) to implement remedial policies or to opt for policies that have a less adverse effect on disadvantaged racial groups.

Take, for instance, the practice of racial profiling in policing. Suppose there is a significant correlation between racial group membership and the commission of certain crimes. Relying on race/crime statistics, the police could perhaps reduce crime if they were to stop, search, or investigate members of racial groups differentially—say, scrutinizing blacks more carefully than whites when trying to curb the illegal drug trade or prevent robberies in urban contexts. Further suppose that this policy was not instituted for racist reasons, that in practice it is not distorted by officers' prejudice or bias, and that the criminal justice system is not responsible for the prior disadvantages the targeted group faces.[11] Nevertheless, the practice of racial profiling would naturally cause great distress within the targeted group. The special scrutiny would stigmatize the group, leading others to view members in the group with suspicion or fear, and it might even brand the group as a bunch of criminals, thus reinforcing offensive stereotypes and perpetuating racist ideology. If the group is already disadvantaged because of ongoing or past racist practices, racial profiling (whatever its motivation) would likely make their situation worse. So they would be justified in demanding that crime control strategies be chosen that do not have these adverse effects or, if no alternative policy would reduce crime to tolerable levels, that group members be compensated for the extra burdens the policy imposes.

Assessments of intrinsic institutional racism focus on the constitutive features of institutions rather than merely their external effects. We can define an "institution" as a formal system of roles and rules that enable and regulate sustained cooperative action for some specified purpose. Within such a system, there are explicit criteria for assigning persons to specific roles, and each role requires its occupant to follow certain rules to remain in good standing. Institutions are not abstract entities but actual social practices: they are embodied by personnel who make, alter, and administer policy. Given this conception of an institution, we can think of racism as attaching to at least three features of institutions.

The *goals* of an institution might be racist—for example, to exterminate, subordinate, exploit, exclude, or otherwise harm the members of a racial group, where such actions are justified or rationalized in terms of racial ideology. Such goals may be the purposes for which the institution was designed or the aims of its current officials. These goals need not have been made explicit or public but can be covert. The rules and role criteria may be (or appear to be) race-neutral in content but may nonetheless be designed to achieve or sustain the subjugation of some racial group. The institution, even when ineffective in achieving its goals, can nonetheless be criticized for its aims. Thus, whether an institution embodies intrinsic institutional racism is not merely a matter of its actual effects.

Intrinsic institutional racism can also be a matter of the *content* of the rules and role criteria of an institution, where these rules and criteria contain racial bias or are racially discriminatory. (I return below to the question of what constitutes wrongful discrimination.) Those who administer the rules and criteria need not be racist themselves for the institution to operate according to racist principles, and administrators need not perceive the racial bias inherent in the rules they comply with.

Finally, intrinsic institutional racism can be implicated in the *application* of procedures. The goals of the institution may be legitimate. The content of the rules and role criteria, when viewed in the abstract, may be race-neutral and unbiased. Nevertheless, if administrators fail to impartially and consistently apply the institution's rules and criteria due to personal prejudice, conscious or unconscious, the institution may be criticized as intrinsically racist. Whatever the substantive content of institutional procedures, justice demands evenhandedness in their application. Institutional racism in application occurs when this distorting effect of prejudice is pervasive, thus leading to the systematic violation of the formal requirements of justice.

Of course, an institution can have all three of these features simultaneously—as exemplified by the institutions that constituted Jim Crow. Again, however, the point of the concept of institutional racism is to take account of the fact that unjust racial hierarchy and inequality can be systematically reproduced in the absence of explicit racist rules or overt racial animus.

It is useful to think of the controversial "disparate impact" standard in U.S. federal law in terms of institutional racism. At least since *Griggs v. Duke Power Co.* (1971), Title VII of the Civil Rights Act of 1964 has been interpreted such that an individual or a group has legal standing to sue an employer who relies on policies that, while perhaps not de- signed to discriminate, in fact have a disproportionately adverse effect on disadvantaged racial minorities. This charge of unjust treatment can be rebutted if the employer can show that the suspect policies serve a legitimate business purpose and the plaintiff cannot show that an al- ternative set of policies would adequately serve that business purpose with less disparate impact on the relevant racial group.

The disparate impact standard could then serve two distinct purposes: to constitute strong (if not conclusive) evidence of intentional (though covert) racial discrimination; or to protect unjustly disadvantaged ra- cial minorities from further marginalization by removing unnecessary barriers to equal opportunity. In the former case, the concern is with intrinsic institutional racism, and the disparate impact standard is employed to discover whether a policy that is race-neutral in content has actually been enacted to achieve a racist aim or is applied in a ra- cially biased fashion. Such standards of proof are necessary in a social context where discrimination is generally concealed and rationalized. In the latter case, the concern is with extrinsic institutional racism, and discriminatory intent is neither implied nor presumed. The focus is rather on the consequences for the unjustly disadvantaged.

Moreover, the legitimate business purpose condition could have two distinct roles, corresponding to the two objectives of the disparate im- pact standard. In one case, we demand that employers specify a legiti- mate purpose to allay our suspicion that the policy has been enacted on illegitimate grounds (that is, because of ideological racism). In the other case, we seek to protect the unjustly disadvantaged from policies that adversely affect them, allowing such policies only when a legiti- mate interest promoted by the policy outweighs our interest in removing obstacles to equal opportunity.

The principal institutions of a modern society are regulated by law, are causally linked, and interact in complex ways. Consequently, the negative effects of institutional racism can result from the combined force of two or more institutions. For instance, the life prospects of a black individual will depend on the treatment she receives from schools and employers. If, because of institutional racism in schools, she receives an education that is inferior to that of her peers, she will be disadvantaged in the competition for jobs even if she faces no employment discrimination. Institutional racism in either domain will, in turn, have effects on her ability to accumulate wealth, and so the consequences are far reaching. But her disadvantage could be a consequence of institutional racism in education *and* employment where this compound effect is neither coordinated nor sought by the relevant officials or policymakers. To highlight the significance of this combined effect of institutional racism, some refer to it as *structural racism*.[12] The terminology is useful and fits the focus on the basic structure of society. Yet the phenomenon at issue (which could also be called "inter-institutional racism") should be distinguished from another that sometimes goes by the same name.

The myriad injustices black Americans suffered in the past are among the sources of blacks' disadvantages in the present. Many racially marked contemporary social inequalities—for example, in wealth and educational achievement—are due, in part, to the history (including the recent history) of racial injustice in the United States. Because these disadvantages have been *caused* by racist practices, some refer to them as "structural racism."[13] Here the term refers more to an explanatory thesis than to a normative concept. Those who rely on it want to emphasize that contemporary racial inequality has been engendered by past racist practices. But there is an implicit moral concern: namely, that justice requires these handicaps to be remedied. The Great Society programs and affirmative action in hiring and education were, arguably, attempts to rectify the legacy of racism. However, many blacks remain deeply disadvantaged, which suggests that these remedial attempts were inadequate.

Some would insist that the existing disadvantages blacks face, including ghetto poverty, are not due to racism, whether ideological, institutional, or structural. They believe that enough has been done to make amends for the wrongs done to black people and that what racial prejudice remains is not so pervasive or powerful that it diminishes blacks' life chances or attenuates blacks' rights. Existing black disadvantages, they would argue, are now due to blacks' bad life choices and self-defeating attitudes. If this point of view is mistaken and widespread, as I think it is, then it represents an ideology that must be strongly resisted, for it contributes to sustaining unjust social arrangements by concealing the fact that these arrangements are unjust. And if this ideology is propagated or embraced in bad faith—say, because of veiled racial hostility, a desire to hold on to unjust privileges, or indifference toward black suffering—then its adherents are blameworthy for their reactionary stance, a disposition that some have termed *laissez-faire racism*.[14]

Thus, when "structural racism" is used as a normative concept, one that implies strong disapproval, the moral basis of the charge can take either of three forms. One might be objecting that principles of rectification have not been fully satisfied—that is, that amends for past racial injustices have not been adequately made or that harms done have not been properly remedied. Or one might be objecting to the effects of a new "postracial" ideology that represents existing racial inequality as if it were merely a consequence of disadvantaged racial groups' conduct and attitudes rather than a legacy of past racism. Or, finally, one might be alleging that racial ideology explains why effective remedial measures for past racial injustices are not instituted. When I use the expression "structural racism," I mean it in this value-laden way and will specify the normative basis of the charge.

Unjust Discrimination

Another contested concept that I use is *discrimination*. Most people use the label "discrimination" as a *thick* normative concept—not only to describe particular actions or policies but also to criticize them on moral or legal grounds. It is analytically useful, however, to classify certain actions or policies as "discrimination" without thereby assuming or implying that everything that falls into this category is impermissible or wrong, only then to go on to ask which actions or policies in the category are objectionable (that is, "wrongful discrimination") and to explain why. We should next note that discrimination necessarily involves, but is more than, judging two persons or two groups to be different (for instance, with respect to race, gender, or nationality) or valuing one type of person over another (the industrious over the lazy, and so on). The distinction or preference must also function, at least implicitly, as a basis for treating people differently—leaving aside, for the moment, whether the basis is sound. Discriminatory actions and policies favor some over others or benefit some while burdening others based on some distinction or preference. Not all discrimination, so understood, is morally wrong. Hiring as surgeons only those with steady hands is perfectly permissible even though it "discriminates" against those with shaky hands. Moreover, the fact that a form of discrimination is wrongful does not necessarily mean that the law should prohibit it. Refusal to befriend someone for no better reason than the person's race is wrongful discrimination, but it would be inappropriate to legally proscribe it. My concern will largely be with identifying wrongful forms of discrimination that are unjust and legitimately prohibited by government action.

So when is discrimination based on race unjust and permissibly proscribed? An influential view is that race-based discrimination is *always* unjust because it is a violation of the principle of *colorblindness*, according to which "race" should never be a consideration in determining how government institutions treat persons, regardless of the purpose of or rationale behind such race-conscious measures.[15] This principle is straightforward and easy to apply, but its validity is far from self-evident. What might justify it?

One argument is this: Race, as we have learned from history, is an invidious social distinction, so dangerous and divisive that the state, given its power, should be forbidden from using racial classification in policy and law and perhaps should be granted the authority to restrict the use of racial distinctions by private institutions. Here racial discrimination is considered unjust because of its propensity to produce negative social consequences (such as sowing social discord or to reducing human welfare). There is no doubt that treating people differently because of their race often causes great harm and can be a source of strife. For this reason it is legitimate to protect stigmatized and disadvantaged racial groups from further harm and abuse by restricting the use of race-based distinctions in certain contexts (such as employment and policing), even when such use is not motivated by racial prejudice.[16]

Consider, for instance, the case of "reaction qualifications" in hiring. Here race is treated as a basis for discrimination, not because the employer is racist, but because of the likely reactions of *others* to the race of her employees. The difficult question here is when reliance on reaction qualifications is consistent with racial justice. If one's customers do not want to be served by blacks, then it might hurt the profitability of one's business to hire blacks, and if this racist preference is sufficiently widespread in society, then hiring blacks could threaten the life of the business itself and perhaps one's livelihood. One reasonable response to this problem is to legally prohibit the use of reaction qualifications in employment when consumer reactions are based on racial animus or prejudice. Perhaps accommodating the prejudices of customers in order to ensure a profitable business isn't intrinsically unjust. However, when these preferences demean and burden the members of disadvantaged racial groups, the state can be justified in restricting the use of such preferences to protect already stigmatized groups from further disadvantage and humiliation. Considerations of corrective justice enjoin us to institute policies that lessen the burdens on the oppressed and that make it more difficult for employers and public officials to mistreat them.

But is the state's use of racial distinctions unjust no matter the purpose or context? There are good reasons to doubt this. Yet even if we were to grant that, on grounds of general welfare and administrative efficiency, it would be better if the state didn't treat people differently because of their racial classification, this thesis is distinct from the popular idea that all racial discrimination is *intrinsically* unjust, that people have a *right* not to have their race considered in public decision making, no matter the rationale. Can the colorblind principle make sense of this idea?

One approach used by advocates of colorblindness is to argue that persons should be treated not as representatives of their race but instead as individuals. There are no group rights—only rights of individuals to equal treatment. However, the use of classifications and generalizations in law and public policy is ubiquitous, absolutely necessary, and entirely legitimate. Imagine trying to make policy or laws without relying on broad categories such as "persons over the age of *y*" or "persons who scored at least *z* on the exam." These classifications treat persons "as individuals" no more than racial classifications do; and they do not presuppose that groups rather than individuals have rights.

A more plausible approach is to argue that public institutions should not advantage or disadvantage persons because of traits they possess for which they are not responsible. One's relative life prospects should depend solely on one's choices and effort. Because an individual's race, whether understood as a biological or a social difference, is an immutable characteristic that the individual is not responsible for having, the state should not allow it to affect the person's relative life chances. Bernard Boxill has objected to this argument on the grounds that, while perhaps one's *overall* life prospects (measured by, say, resources or welfare) should not be hampered by traits one is not responsible for, many opportunities, goods, and services are legitimately given to some persons and denied to others because of traits for which persons are not responsible.[17] For example, some people are given certain desirable jobs because of their aptitude or height. If such inherited and unchangeable traits allow those who possess them to provide important goods and services, then it is not unjust to prefer those persons for certain jobs despite the fact that they are not responsible for these traits. Thus, just because no one is responsible for his or her race, it doesn't follow that race should never be a consideration in how a person should be treated.

A more compelling account of unjust racial discrimination, one that does not rely on or attempt to justify the colorblind principle, focuses on *moral status.* On this account, racial discrimination is unjust when it treats race as relevant to basic human worth or moral standing.[18] Racial discrimination thus violates the principle that because all persons have inherent and equal moral worth, they should be treated with equal respect. No political morality worthy of consideration holds that the members of some race are moral inferiors or subpersons. If public officials treat the members of a racial group differently because these officials regard them as due less than equal consideration on account of their race, this is surely unjust discrimination. The question is whether all intrinsically unjust racial discrimination can be understood in this way.

Everyone is equal with respect to intrinsic worth and moral status. But individuals and groups do differ with respect to their needs and abilities, and such differences rightly bear on the way they should be treated. From the fact that one is owed equal respect as a human being, it does not follow that one should in all contexts be treated the same as others (for example, with regard to the distribution of scarce resources, social services, and valued positions). There is a difference between having a right to be *treated as an equal* and having a right to always receive the same goods, services, and opportunities as others.

Bernard Williams has argued that because all persons are owed equal respect, there is a standing presumption in favor of treating everyone equally unless there is a relevant difference between persons that rationally justifies differential treatment.[19] It is rational to give medicine to only those who are sick and jobs to only those competent to perform them, and so such differential treatment is consistent with equal respect for the sick and the healthy, the competent and the incompetent. But to grant voting rights to only those who are left-handed is to treat right-handed citizens without due respect. Such treatment is not rational, and thus it is arbitrary and naturally resented by those disfavored by such grounds. Armed with this idea, one might argue that because race, as a matter of scientific fact, does not determine a person's needs or abilities, race is *always* an immaterial criterion for benefiting or burdening someone.[20]

However, things are not that simple. The relevance of a selection criterion can't be determined without identifying the particular purposes the criterion is supposed to serve. Also, because a selection criterion might serve an institution's purposes well but these purposes might include such things as exploiting a vulnerable race, we must also assess whether these purposes are legitimate. Thus, a sound principle of differentiation must not only satisfy a condition of relevance and thus rationality—that is, the distinction must be rationally aligned with or likely to advance some policy or institutional goal—but the goal must be one that the discriminating agent is morally permitted to pursue. This analysis suggests that it is an open question whether differential treatment based on race might sometimes be justified (for example, if the goal is to increase racial diversity in public schools), contrary to what some advocates of colorblindness suppose.

In this connection, it is worth noting that the expressions "discrimination on the basis on race" and "discrimination because of race" are often used ambiguously. This ambiguity obscures the morally relevant distinction between treating a person differently (for example, denying her an important opportunity) on the grounds that she is a member of "an inferior race" and treating her differently (for instance, compensating her for an injustice she has suffered) on the grounds that she has been wronged because *others* believe she is a member of an inferior race. In both cases the treatment differed "on the basis of race," but the race-based considerations are different and the differences are morally important. In particular, the first form of treatment is always impermissible, but the second form of treatment may sometimes be morally justified or even required.

Similarly, people use the word "because" in "discrimination because of race" sometimes to mean a *normative reason* (a consideration in favor of doing something) and sometimes to mean an *explanatory cause*. Because reasons can (but need not) be causes, to remove the ambiguity we must distinguish between the *proffered* reason and the *operative* reason for an act, given that people can offer reasons in defense of their discriminatory acts that were not, in fact, the reasons they acted upon but are mere pretext or rationalization. Moreover, sometimes the cause of wrongful discrimination is not a reason at all but a mere bias (sometimes unconscious) that distorts judgment and decision making, often leading some to be denied opportunities or services to which they were entitled. Recall from the discussion of institutional racism that institutional rules that are otherwise justified can fail to be impartially and consistently applied due to administrative bias. For example, in cases of nepotism, employment procedures that are otherwise fair are misapplied because familial partiality improperly influences what should have been an impartial decision. Racial partiality can cause similar outcomes (and not only when the bias is *against* another group but also when the bias is *for* one's own group). When this happens, an injustice has occurred that we can rightly classify as wrongful discrimination.

With these distinctions in place, I can summarize in this way the conception of wrongful racial discrimination I've been defending: When a person or group is denied an opportunity, resource, or public benefit, this constitutes unjust racial discrimination if the unfavorable treatment (a) is based on the normative presumption (perhaps implicit) that one race has inferior moral status to another, (b) is based on racial considerations when race is not a relevant principle of differentiation that would further a legitimate end, or (c) has been caused by a racially biased application of institutional rules. Race-based discrimination that takes any of these forms is fundamentally unjust and intrinsically wrong.[21]

Notice that this account of unjust racial discrimination doesn't depend on the discriminator intentionally seeking to harm members of the disfavored racial group, nor, in the second form of discrimination, does it depend on the discriminator having racist beliefs or sentiments. Yet when malicious intent or racial prejudice is the source of the unjust discrimination, this creates an additional wrong from which the law might seek to protect certain groups, particularly those socially salient groups who suffer because these attitudes are widespread. This wrong is an *expressive harm*, a form of stigmatizing, insulting, or demeaning others.[22] Indeed, an expressive harm may occur even if the discriminator does not actually have malicious intent or prejudice toward those discriminated against. It is often enough if a suitably informed and impartial observer, given who the discriminator is and the social context, would *interpret* the action as conveying such intentions, beliefs, or sentiments.[23]

I believe that the account of unjust discrimination presented here also works *mutatis mutandis* for wrongful discrimination based on gender or class origins—two social categories that are especially relevant for thinking about ghetto poverty. For ease of exposition, I presented the account focusing on race. But it should be clear that men and women and individuals from different class backgrounds also possess equal moral status and should be treated as equals (that is, regarded with equal concern and respect) by the public institutions of society. Differential treatment based on gender or class origins is unjust unless it is based on a relevant principle of differentiation that would further a legitimate end. Gender and class biases can and often do upset the evenhanded application of institutional rules. And, of course, malicious intent and prejudice are often directed toward women and those of lower socioeconomic status, and these widespread attitudes are frequently the cause of unjust discrimination against members of these groups, creating expressive harms that need to be combatted if all are to have equal citizenship.

Poverty, Class, and Equal Opportunity

Although my subject is the condition of the black poor in ghettos, my central normative concern is not with *absolute poverty* (lacking access to basic necessities for long enough that it becomes health- or life-threatening) but with unjust disadvantage. The question I'm taking up is not whether the ghetto poor have adequate water, food, clothes, shelter, and medical care—though that is also an important a matter of justice. I'm addressing whether they are unjustly disadvantaged by an unfair basic structure, and if they are, what responses to this situation are called for. The question of their moral and political agency matters in this context. No matter how irresponsible or immoral persons are, they should not be left to starve, live on the streets, or suffer from treatable illnesses. But, assuming persons' basic needs are met, if their disadvantages flow from their own freely made choices and not from the social structure, then this would change the moral significance of the problem.

Relative poverty (defined, for example, as some percentage of average income) is problematic only if certain forms of inequality are objectionable. Because absolute poverty is defined independently of how well off others in society are, objections to it do not imply criticism of inequality as such. A wealthy society could manage to keep all its members above the absolute poverty line while otherwise troubling inequalities remain. Some liberals are primarily concerned with absolute poverty and its negative effects on children. They are not challenging the fairness of the opportunity structure or the distribution of wealth but simply trying to find measures that would secure a minimum standard of health and material well-being for all. For them the only question is what works, where the sole normative criterion is the cost-effectiveness of poverty-reduction policies. As I have stressed, though, one of my main tasks is to persuade readers that, when thinking about ghettos, we should move away from a technocratic "social problem" framework to a justice framework. This shift won't occur if "antipoverty" remains the sole focus. Our fundamental goal should not be merely to reduce poverty but also to bring about a just basic structure. This objective won't be secured unless substantive equal opportunity is realized.

Some think that equal opportunity exists if no important position or good afforded by the system of social cooperation is unfairly denied persons on account of their race, ethnicity, gender, sexual orientation, disability, religion, creed, or national origin. On this view, equal opportunity is simply the absence of unjust discrimination. However, within liberal-egalitarian thought, equal opportunity entails more than this. In particular, if equal opportunity is to be substantively fair (and not merely procedurally just), individuals must have equal life prospects. In other words, one should be able to expect that one's income and wealth, over a lifetime, will be similar to that of anyone else who has similar abilities and the same willingness to develop and use them, regardless of the social class one has been born into. There should be no class barriers to the acquisition of knowledge or the development of skills, which means that the educational system must be organized, administered, and funded so that each person has a similar chance to learn and cultivate his or her abilities regardless of class origins. Because many desirable jobs and valuable positions in public life require higher education, each person should have an adequate opportunity to acquire the necessary preparation for college and should have access to the means to pay for a quality college education.[24]

Lots of things affect our life chances. It is perhaps too much to ask that society arrange things so that only talent and effort determine which roles in social life will be available to each. But certain unfair obstacles to the pursuit of our ambitions can and should be removed, particularly those created by alterable features of the basic structure itself. Among these obstacles are an inequitable distribution of income and wealth, unjust discrimination in employment, and inadequate opportunities to learn and develop one's talents. Fair equality of opportunity, then, is an anticlass principle. In a system of social cooperation where each has equal standing and all are entitled to share equitably in its benefits, those born into affluent families shouldn't have better life prospects than those born into families with more limited material means. The classless society is one with fluid mobility between income groups across generations. The family you were born into does not seal your fate or ensure your success.

The point of equality of opportunity isn't simply to ensure a fair competition for jobs (antidiscrimination measures take care of that). It is to remove unfair obstacles to living a fulfilling life. One shouldn't be disadvantaged in the pursuit of one's ambitions because of one's class background. What makes differences in class background unfair? They are arbitrary handicaps or advantages (serving no moral purpose) that are created by the basic structure itself and so cannot be justified to those on the losing end. This structure is not an unchangeable fact of nature but the product of social practices that can be altered.

We can contrast this interpretation of the content of equal opportunity with a more radical vision, one rooted in socialist principles.[25] On this more strongly egalitarian interpretation (which we can call socialist equality of opportunity), socioeconomic inequalities that arise solely from differences in native talent are unjust. The fact that some are endowed with socially useful talents is not a sufficient ground to expect greater economic rewards from the system of social cooperation. One should be willing to use one's scarce abilities to improve the life prospects and welfare of others without demanding higher pay than others who work just as hard and long. No one can claim to be entitled to greater benefits from the social system simply on the basis of their native capacities, as these are gifts from nature, which no one deserves or is responsible for having. Accordingly, socialist equal opportunity means that each, regardless of ability, has the option to work for similar economic rewards provided they're willing to work the same number of hours. This would still allow *some* economic inequality, as individuals differ in their preferences for money and leisure. Yet this inequality is not unjust, as everyone is free to work more for greater rewards.

I'm not convinced that justice demands socialist equality of opportunity. I certainly agree that there is no "natural" division of income and wealth. We aren't forced to accept the outcomes of market exchanges and gift giving, whatever they happen to be. Material advantages are strongly shaped by the property regime and tax scheme, which a society controls through its laws. We could divide the material advantages of economic cooperation equally or in accordance with hours worked, but we probably shouldn't. Inequality in material rewards can sometimes serve a worthwhile purpose that is justifiable to those who have less than others. For instance, by allowing those with socially useful but rare talents to be more highly rewarded, we encourage the development and use of those talents, which benefits everyone, including those whose abilities are more common or less socially useful. Nor would it be unjust to allow some to have greater income or wealth than others insofar as this encourages and enables some to create valuable goods and services or to develop technology that increases productivity, saves time, or reduces burdensome labor. Moderate inequality can be a motor of innovation and boost to efficiency, which everyone could benefit from. But even if I am wrong and justice does require socialist equal opportunity, this should not affect the arguments to come, as the injustices that the ghetto represents are condemnable on even moderate egalitarian principles.[26]

What Is a Ghetto?

Ghettos are metropolitan neighborhoods visibly marked by racial segregation and multiple forms of disadvantage. When some insist that "segregation" is a principal cause of ghetto poverty, they often mean to include both the social processes that *cause* racially marked neighborhood patterns and the *patterns* themselves.[27] Unless we are talking about formal segregation regimes like Jim Crow or Apartheid, in which racial groups were forcibly separated and isolated by explicit laws, it is better, to avoid confusion, to speak of segregation as a neighborhood pattern. *Segregation* in the United States today is a residential pattern in which neighborhoods within a metropolitan region have strikingly different racial compositions, with one racial group in a given neighborhood far outstripping its percentage in the region as a whole, while other racial groups in the region are significantly underrepresented in the neighborhood. This uneven spread of racial groups across metropolitan space is sometimes combined with neighborhood *racial clustering*—where two or more similarly segregated neighborhoods are adjacent to one another, forming a racial band of segregated residential areas.[28] We can then distinguish segregation (including racial clustering) from the diverse social factors that contribute to bringing it about or maintaining it—discrimination, institutional racism, private residential choices, street crime, urban renewal policies, economic inequality, and so on.

I also treat "segregation" as a morally neutral term rather than as an expression of criticism.[29] We can then ask whether segregation causes injustices (for example, involuntary social isolation from mainstream institutions or lack of access to vital opportunities and public services)—and if so, what should be done about these. And we can examine segregation's causes to see which, if any, are morally objectionable (that is, "wrongful segregation"). Because in using the term "segregation" I am not thereby taking a position on segregation's causes (viewing it solely as a residential pattern), I am also not, on the basis of this terminology alone, attributing *unjust* causes to all forms of segregation.

Racial segregation is often discussed as if it were in itself a form of unjust disadvantage. It might be thought, for example, that segregated groups are, as such, stigmatized, and so segregation should be viewed as itself an unjust disadvantage. There remains an informal racial-status hierarchy, with whites on top and blacks on or near the bottom. If blacks as a group are stigmatized as inferior, then a black-majority neighborhood will also be stigmatized, "tainted" by the debasing black presence.[30] In this status hierarchy, the blacker the neighborhood (all else being equal), the lower its social status. But if there weren't antiblack prejudice (including its unconscious and implicit forms) or the ideological representations that encourage such prejudice, then the mere fact that blacks are significantly overrepresented in a neighborhood would not mean that the neighborhood is disadvantaged. Certainly few would maintain that white neighborhoods in multiracial metropolitan regions are stigmatized or inherently disadvantaged simply in virtue of being exclusively or predominantly white. Black segregation could be a form of disadvantage, not because blacks are numerically overrepresented in certain neighborhoods (which might be morally benign, as I later argue it sometimes is), but because of *where* blacks tend to be overrepresented—namely, in deeply deprived neighborhoods (those disadvantaged with respect to jobs, schools, crime rates, public services, and so on). However, this should turn our attention to neighborhood characteristics other than their mere racial composition.

To grasp fully the normative significance of contemporary racial segregation in the United States, we must also take into account class-based segregation. There is some moderate segregation between all income groupings, but the key justice issue with respect to class and neighborhood is the segregation of the poor from the nonpoor. Other classes are considerably more integrated than the poor. I reserve the term "segregation" for racial segregation and will speak of *concentrated poverty* (defined by neighborhood poverty rates of 40 percent or higher) when discussing the residential segregation of the poor.[31]

Concentrated poverty should be distinguished from *concentrated disadvantage*. Concentrated disadvantage has to do with more than the number of poor people in a neighborhood, as the well-being of residents in a community has to do with more than their access to income and wealth. Other relevant indices of disadvantage include low birth weight, abnormally low life expectancy, enduring physical and mental illnesses, disability, alcohol and drug addiction, homelessness and inadequate shelter, low educational attainment, dysfunctional family life, social isolation and unhealthy ties of affiliation, lack of self-esteem, unemployment and underemployment, chronic fatigue, inability to participate fully in public life, and high incarceration and felony-conviction rates.[32] Such disadvantages tend to cluster together and accumulate, so that the ghetto poor often suffer from multiple forms of deprivation, generally placing them at (or near) the bottom of the social order, sometimes extending across generations.[33] Some sociologists maintain that concentrated poverty is highly correlated with concentrated disadvantage; that is, where there are high rates of neighborhood poverty, one typically finds numerous other forms of disadvantage.[34] I follow their practice of using concentrated poverty as a proxy for concentrated disadvantage.

Concentrated disadvantage should be distinguished from the idea of a *disadvantaged neighborhood*. Concentrated disadvantage has to do with the percentage of *people* in a neighborhood who suffer from multiple deficits in well-being. A disadvantaged neighborhood is a *place* that suffers from a relative lack of nearby or readily accessible goods, services, and opportunities that are needed for human flourishing. Disadvantaged neighborhoods are ones with, for example, low-performing schools, high rates of crime and violence, dilapidated and insufficient housing stock, low property values, exposure to environmental toxins, limited employment opportunities, few good local grocery stores, visible signs of disorder, few recreational sites, and inefficient or expensive public transportation.

Of course, neighborhoods with concentrated disadvantage also tend to be disadvantaged neighborhoods. And many would explain high concentrations of disadvantaged residents by pointing to the fact that these neighborhoods are severely disadvantaged. But, as I will employ it, the concept of concentrated disadvantage (like the concept of segregation) is neutral with respect to the *causes* of such disadvantage. Use of the concept is, for example, consistent with the view that concentrated disadvantage is caused, not by the unavailability of opportunities, but by the moral failings and improvidence of the disadvantaged, who often, so it is said, don't take full advantage of the available opportunities and services that would enable their economic and spatial mobility.

One troubling fact about today's segregation patterns is that black segregation is strongly correlated with concentrated disadvantage. Blacks are in fact the only social group in the United States that experiences both high levels of metropolitan segregation and high levels of concentrated disadvantage.[35] The principal concern of this book is with that segment of the black poor that is both racially segregated and concentrated in neighborhoods in and around large cities.[36] I refer to these black, high-poverty metropolitan neighborhoods as *ghettos* and to the black poor who regularly reside in them as the *ghetto poor*. Within the category "ghetto poor" I include poor black individuals and families who effectively live in ghettos despite lacking a permanent residence in such communities. When speaking about any person or family who lives in a ghetto neighborhood (whether or not they are poor), I refer to them as ghetto *residents* or *denizens*. I should also emphasize that many segregated blacks live in neighborhoods that have moderate levels of poverty (20 to 30 percent) and yet their concentrated disadvantage is almost as severe as in ghetto neighborhoods.[37] We might think of these black neighborhoods as type II ghettos. Because much of what I go on to say applies equally to these neighborhoods, I refer to both types as "ghettos."[38]

The conception of ghetto relied on here contrasts with more theory-laden and thickly normative conceptions. For instance, Loïc Wacquant, invoking a structural-functionalist framework, conceives of a ghetto as a "social-organizational device that employs space to reconcile two antinomic purposes: to maximize the material profits extracted out of a group deemed defiled and defiling and to minimize intimate contact with its members so as to avert the threat of symbolic corrosion and contagion they carry."[39] Though sympathetic to his analysis, I'm not sure, and so do not assert, that ghettos serve the same social function wherever and whenever they exist. Indeed, I'm not certain that ghettos always serve a "purpose" or function, as opposed to sometimes being the (largely) unintended product of a complex and changing set of social practices, which might have different normative implications depending on the sociohistorical context. Moreover, given that my ultimate concerns are normative and not explanatory and that I don't want to beg any questions through my initial analytical choices, I have selected a more descriptive conception of ghettos. Contemporary American ghettos could of course be rooted in labor exploitation and racial stigmatization (as I believe they sometimes are), but they might reflect systemic injustice in ways other than through exploitation and stigma (as I shall attempt to show). However, such normative claims should be conclusions of social theorizing and normative analysis, not assumed at the start.

Injustice and Ghettos

From the standpoint of corrective justice, contemporary black segregation and concentrated disadvantage are best understood against the background of the hundred-year struggle to abolish Jim Crow and the nearly fifty-year effort to secure the equal civic status of blacks and to remove the group's disadvantages caused by the segregation regime. Under Jim Crow, law and custom prescribed residential segregation, thus violating the right of blacks to equal liberty. Blacks were not permitted to live wherever they could afford, as they faced severe housing and mortgage discrimination. Their rights to freedom of association were also violated, as the segregation regime restricted the liberty of individuals to form and sustain interracial relationships. Being morally concerned about barriers to interracial relationships needn't be rooted in a particular conception of the good life or a valorization of interracial community over intraracial community. The concern can be solely with individual liberty: laws should not impede individuals' pursuit of interracial association and intimacy.

Even apart from other related forms of mistreatment and unjust discrimination—intimidation, violence, destruction of property, union exclusion, and employment discrimination—Jim Crow residential segregation unfairly reduced blacks' chances for socioeconomic well-being. Because they were segregated in the same disadvantaged neighborhoods with few avenues of escape, blacks were vulnerable to economic exploitation and had limited access to quality schools. They were also severely hindered in acquiring property in neighborhoods with high and stable property values. Thus, it is important to remember that the segregation regime's violations of liberty had far-reaching consequences for black socioeconomic opportunity and black–white wealth inequality.

Jim Crow segregation laws also stigmatized blacks as social inferiors unworthy to associate with whites on equal terms. Communicating this sentiment through the voice of law was a grave insult to blacks, as it effectively denied that blacks should have equal moral and civic standing.[40] Blacks were not only forced to live without the secure conviction that their government regarded their interests as meriting equal concern. They were also subjected to explicit public dishonor and humiliation by de jure rules of segregation. This degradation was buttressed and exacerbated by the everyday informal disrespect and contempt that blacks endured at the hands of their white fellow citizens.

With segregation laws now abolished, "separate but equal" schooling ruled unconstitutional, and employment and housing discrimination illegal, it might be thought that the remaining tasks of corrective justice with respect to the Jim Crow regime are to repair the damage done to the victims (for example, to put them on an equal footing with their fellows in terms of resources and opportunities) and to contain and ultimately defeat any lingering racist attitudes so that they don't prevent blacks from taking full advantage of the resources and opportunities to which they are entitled. But this picture of post–Jim Crow racial realities is clearly too rosy, as many of the same wrongs perpetrated by the Jim Crow regime continued into the post-civil-rights era, after the state no longer engaged in explicit, de jure discrimination.

There have been housing policies that were race-neutral in their explicit content and in their proffered public justification but that have had a disproportionately negative impact on blacks (an example of extrinsic institutional racism). These policies contributed to the segregation of blacks, particularly the black urban poor.[41] For instance, the adoption of local governance over land use (zoning regulations) enables those in affluent areas to prohibit or limit multifamily housing units and rental property and to mandate minimum lot sizes and expensive amenities, effectively excluding the vast majority of blacks, who typically lack the economic resources to buy large single-family units in these expensive areas. For a time the Federal Housing Authority underwrote mortgages only in single-family, predominantly white neighborhoods (redlining) on the premise that neighborhood homogeneity was necessary to maintain stable housing values. Urban renewal projects displaced low-income residents in central cities without enabling their access to affordable housing in nondisadvantaged neighborhoods. The interstate highway program empowered whites to leave the cities for the suburbs and demolished housing units in low-income neighborhoods; and it effectively created a freeway wall between white and black neighborhoods in many large metropolitan areas. New government housing projects for low-income persons were located in black neighborhoods that already had high rates of poverty.

Some have argued that these and similar policies, whatever public justifications were offered in their defense, were actually adopted, at least in part, because of bias in favor of white interests, hostility toward or indifference to black interests, or both. One might interpret these policies as surreptitious attempts by advantaged whites to exclude blacks from gaining access to goods, resources, and opportunities so that these whites could hold on to and monopolize these advantages. To the extent that contemporary segregation owes its existence to these problematic biases and reprehensible motives, we should regard black segregation as due to intrinsic institutional racism.

Moreover, there continues to be private discrimination in housing that the state does not prevent or redress, and this discrimination also contributes to segregation.[42] Perhaps the discrimination continues despite the relevant government agencies and courts doing everything they reasonably can to prevent it. Or perhaps the enforcement mechanisms are too weak to sufficiently deter wrongful discrimination. Or maybe the enforcement mechanisms are adequate but not applied consistently, vigorously, or impartially. Whatever the details, a kind of informal and covert Jim Crow residential segregation could be sustained even though the law was prima facie race-neutral and nondiscrimination laws were given more than lip service. In addition to robbing blacks of freedoms and opportunities that should be theirs, the resulting segregation could also be said to be stigmatizing. Whites would still be communicating through their private actions (though not explicitly through law) that blacks are their social inferiors and as such don't merit equal treatment or respect.

As with Jim Crow segregation, one might object to the government policies and private practices that created and sustain contemporary segregation patterns because they wrongly restrict liberty, undermine equal opportunity, and disrespect black citizens. But one might also object to these policies and practices because they unfairly disadvantage blacks with respect to income and wealth, which only further limits their access to more advantaged neighborhoods. Some blacks find it difficult to exit ghettos because they can't afford to move out, and some ghetto residents can't afford the move because they've been denied a fair opportunity to acquire the necessary economic resources.

This lack of resources is not all due to unjust housing policies and housing discrimination. There is structural racism, that is, the legacy of slavery and Jim Crow: the accumulated socioeconomic handicaps and financial burdens transmitted across generations and never fully offset despite affirmative action policies and Great Society programs. There is employment discrimination, which inhibits blacks' ability to make a decent living and to acquire assets. There is also an unjust distribution of income and wealth—the inequitable allocation of the benefits of economic cooperation—that affects people of all races but blacks disproportionately.

This last consideration highlights one of the ways that racial injustice and economic injustice can combine to create and perpetuate ghetto poverty. I've mainly focused on race-based injustices that contribute to segregation, but class-based injustices are also important. Given black–white differences in socioeconomic status (whatever their causes), a higher percentage of whites than blacks are able to translate their higher incomes into better neighborhoods for themselves and their children. There are massive wealth inequalities between blacks and whites, which lead to homeownership differences.[43] And because the black poverty rate is more than 2.5 times the white (non-Hispanic) poverty rate, blacks as a group have more limited spatial mobility. Thus, rising economic inequality and other politico-economic dynamics that advantage the affluent over low-income people can exacerbate racial inequality and consequently limit the ability of blacks to improve or leave disadvantaged neighborhoods.

In the United States, economic mobility is often expressed as spatial mobility, where the affluent outbid others for the neighborhoods with the best schools, best amenities, lowest crime rates, lowest taxes, and most stable property values. In any major metropolitan area, there is a widely known hierarchy of neighborhoods that reflect economic inequality in America.[44] Given black–white economic inequality, blacks are at a serious disadvantage in these bidding wars even setting aside ongoing institutional racism and housing discrimination.

In fact, in addition to the possible racial prejudice lurking behind the urban housing policies, these prima facie race-neutral policies might reflect *class* prejudice against low-income families. Affluent families (with their large, single-family detached homes in quiet and safe neighborhoods with good schools) may seek to carve out enclaves that exclude poor persons, who are, again, disproportionately black. The affluent have the power to do this because of the institutional nexus of home-ownership rights, tax policy, local political autonomy, and the authority to restrict school district membership. They may not want to pay (in the form of higher taxes) for the public services that disadvantaged persons need, and they may want to avoid the social ills and nuisances associated with poor people (noise, blight, crime, violence).

There are complex questions about whether social justice is compatible with affluent self-segregation and residential exclusion of the poor. Is it unjust for affluent families to use their economic advantage to carve out enclaves for themselves that, due to high housing costs, effectively keep low-income people out?[45] But I won't pursue such questions. The question I'm addressing is whether self-segregation among the affluent can be justified to the ghetto poor given that racial and economic justice have not been secured. If the distribution of income and wealth in the United States is unjust, then these exclusionary practices don't simply reflect permissible differences in material resources but are instead instances of class subordination—institutionalized and unjust class-based exclusion. The underlying economic inequality that enables such exclusion should, at a minimum, be addressed through redistributive policies and the creation of greater educational and employment opportunity for the economically disadvantaged. And such redress is required quite apart from how economic segregation contributes to racial segregation and ghetto poverty. But if class subordination partly accounts for the concentrated disadvantage of blacks, then this is a further powerful reason to correct these economic injustices.

The racial and economic injustices that disfigure the basic structure of U.S. society not only create and perpetuate black urban poverty but also have other far-reaching and troubling effects. For example, because the segregated neighborhoods that the black poor inhabit are so often loci of concentrated disadvantage, whole communities become stigmatized.[46] The stigma of disadvantage is worsened through its association with familiar negative black stereotypes—the supposed lazy, criminal, violent, irresponsible, and imprudent tendencies of blacks—which rationalizes blaming the black poor for their plight. The combined stigmas of race, class, and place make the ghetto poor more vulnerable than better-situated blacks to unjust discrimination, political marginalization, public neglect, police surveillance and violence, and punitive action. And the stigma of ghettos comes to be associated with blacks as a group, downgrading black identity and attaching itself even to blacks who have never lived in a ghetto.

However, even if the familiar liberal-egalitarian claim that myriad structural injustices underlie the formation and reproduction of ghettos is true, this leaves open what corrective justice requires in response. In particular, there is the question of whether the policies that have been proposed and enacted to alleviate the burdens on the ghetto poor are appropriately rooted in principles of corrective justice and fully defensible to those they seek to help. There is also the question of whether the ghetto poor have responded in morally legitimate ways to their plight, grounding their conduct in sound political ethics, or whether, on the contrary, they have reacted in morally unacceptable and self-defeating ways and thus made their situation worse and their problems more intractable. It is to these questions of nonideal theory that I now turn.

TWO

Community

An influential political theory and policy orientation holds that racial segregation is unjust, views neighborhood racial segregation as a principal cause of ghetto poverty, and proposes residential integration as a cure.[1] This theory should not be confused with the traditional Civil Rights movement demand for an end to Jim Crow prohibitions and to racial discrimination in housing and employment. And the theory demands something other than, or in addition to, economic redistribution or educational and employment initiatives. The *new integrationists*, as I shall call proponents of this view, want to increase and foster interracial contact in neighborhoods, as they believe this is necessary to repair the damage done to the ghetto poor and to lift their unfair burdens. The intervention's aim is to restructure the demographics of ghettos and other neighborhoods in the hopes of ending (or at least attenuating) ghetto poverty.

In this chapter I consider, and ultimately reject, new integrationism. My criticisms are primarily directed not at the new integrationist diagnosis of the causes of ghettos but at how the theory conceptualizes the problem, its normative presuppositions, and the practical conclusions it draws from empirical findings about the effects of living in segregated communities. In particular, I show that residential integration is *not* a requirement of corrective justice and should not be viewed as a solution to ghetto poverty. I defend an alternative approach to thinking about unjust inequality and its relation to neighborhood dynamics, a view I call *egalitarian pluralism*.

No treatment of justice and ghettos would be complete without considering the widely held view that blacks are (at least partly) at fault for contemporary segregation patterns. I discuss two grounds for this charge.[2] According to one familiar view, *racial proxy discrimination* can be justified in residential choice. On this account, many blacks (though by no means all blacks) have characteristics that make them undesirable as neighbors (for example, criminal backgrounds, unattractive cultural traits, and weak labor attachment) and so whites reasonably avoid neighborhoods with a high percentage of blacks. A second response to the systemic-injustice framework I advocate insists that most blacks *prefer* to live among a substantial number of blacks (and consequently expose themselves to higher rates of poverty and it associated ills) rather than move to more advantaged neighborhoods that may contain few blacks and are perhaps predominantly white.

The full explanation for the persistence of ghettos has to do with more than the racial and economic barriers to entering whiter or more advantaged neighborhoods or the unjust barriers to leaving blacker or disadvantaged neighborhoods. There are also the practical reasons individuals have for choosing one neighborhood over another. Racial and economic injustices can and do constrain black spatial mobility. But neighborhoods will remain segregated, even in the absence of these unjust barriers, if individuals make certain residential choices. In particular, if whites avoid or leave neighborhoods with high concentrations of blacks and blacks won't join or stay in a neighborhood unless there is a significant black presence, then at least moderate segregation will continue. Thus, over the next three sections I address these concerns before turning to the new integrationist response to ghetto poverty.

Profiling Neighborhoods

Proxy discrimination (sometimes called "profiling" or "statistical discrimination") is a practice whereby a person makes a decision based on a proxy trait that he or she regards as sufficiently correlated with a relevant material trait. The otherwise irrelevant proxy functions as a reliable sign of the presence of the material trait. This can be rational when the proxy trait is easier, quicker, or cheaper to detect than the material trait. For instance, we use age as a proxy for responsibility when deciding whom to grant voting, drinking, or driving privileges. Age is easily, quickly, and cheaply discerned but responsibility is not. When deciding whether to buy or rent in a neighborhood, some people may use race as a proxy for some other relevant (desirable or undesirable) characteristic that would be difficult, costly, or time consuming to discover if race were not relied upon.

The racial profiling of neighborhoods should be distinguished from similar phenomena. For example, some might purposefully avoid high-poverty neighborhoods without relying on racial proxies and without seeking to avoid blacks. Low-income people, whatever their racial identity, often have lots of needs that can be satisfied only through a variety of expensive public services, which typically means (all else equal) higher local taxes. As discussed earlier, concentrated poverty is strongly associated with concentrated disadvantage. Those exposed to concentrated disadvantage for long periods (particularly those born and raised in such environments) are widely believed to exhibit higher rates of delinquency, criminal deviance, drug and alcohol abuse, mental and physical illness, teenage pregnancy, welfare receipt, and joblessness. The presence of lots of poor kids in a school may bring down the school's test scores, may slow the pace of instruction, and may hinder the development of more privileged children through negative peer effects. If whites avoid high-poverty neighborhoods, they will, as a consequence, often be avoiding black neighborhoods, thus contributing to segregation. But this practice, while perhaps otherwise problematic, is not an instance of racial profiling, because by hypothesis racial proxies aren't being relied upon. Indeed, some blacks and some among the poor may also seek to avoid high-poverty neighborhoods for similar reasons.

The proffered reason for avoiding concentrated poverty may of course be insincere or held in bad faith. Though justifying their neighborhood choices in terms of concerns about the negative consequences of concentrated poverty, some might actually be seeking to avoid blacks. Knowing that black neighborhoods are typically high-poverty neighborhoods, this ostensible avoidance of high-poverty areas could simply be a rationalization of antiblack bias. This phenomenon, though obviously deplorable, isn't neighborhood racial profiling.

Racial proxy discrimination also shouldn't be confused with the preference for class-based affiliation. Some people might use socioeconomic status as a proxy for lifestyle. People of the same class status or class background often have similar interests and values. Relying on this generalization, some affluent persons might avoid high-poverty neighborhoods because they seek to have neighbors with similar lifestyles.

They might desire class homogeneity because they want to live in a community of people with shared interests and values. This practice too would contribute to segregation patterns. But the proxy here is class, not race. Of course, such class proxy discrimination might also be insincere or in bad faith—a convenient and plausible cover for racism.

Some residential preferences are no more than an effort to benefit opportunistically from a racial-status hierarchy. Because of antiblack racism, metropolitan neighborhoods with no or few blacks have high prestige, and some people are willing to pay a premium to live in such neighborhoods to gain this dubious residential status. As a result of these racial-status differences between residential communities, white neighborhoods also have higher and more stable property values than black neighborhoods. Even people who don't affirm the racial-status hierarchy might nevertheless exploit it to gain financial advantages, such as inflated property values. Seeking to profit from injustice in this way is wrong, of course, but it is not the kind of racial profiling of neighborhoods at issue.

If the metropolitan neighborhoods where blacks are segregated tend to be places of concentrated disadvantage (ghettos), then neighborhoods with a high percentage of blacks might be a good proxy for low-quality neighborhoods.[3] Many black neighborhoods that do not themselves have high poverty rates are adjacent to such neighborhoods and thus experience spillover effects.[4] Moreover, residents of more advantaged neighborhoods (particularly those that already have moderate rates of poverty, say 20 to 30 percent) might worry that, were blacks to constitute a significant percentage of their neighbors, the problems associated with concentrated disadvantage would likely become prevalent, putting their neighborhood on a path toward decline. Persons with the financial means might therefore avoid black (or blackening) neighborhoods, not because they are hostile to blacks, but because they want to avoid living in or near a neighborhood with concentrated disadvantage and they see the large presence of blacks in a neighborhood as a reliable sign of such disadvantage.

Such racial profiling of neighborhoods relies on generalizations about racial demographic patterns. But it needn't rely on pernicious stereotypes. One doesn't have to believe, for example, that blacks tend to be lazy, criminal, or unintelligent to conclude that a high percentage of blacks in a neighborhood is a sign of a disadvantaged and thus undesirable neighborhood. And one doesn't have to believe that most blacks are poor to think that where lots of blacks reside, these neighborhoods will suffer from concentrated disadvantage and its negative effects. The person who relies on such generalizations when making housing decisions may even lament the fact that a high percentage of blacks usually means high rates of poverty and related forms of disadvantage.[5] Perhaps they believe that the connection between black neighborhoods and high concentrations of poverty is the result of racial and economic injustices, and perhaps they fight against these injustices in other ways. Still, the practice of profiling neighborhoods, while maybe not racist, does contribute to ghetto poverty by perpetuating segregation patterns. So, can the practice be justified to the ghetto poor?

If the generalizations that purport to justify such profiling aren't well grounded in the facts (for instance, if the proxy trait isn't highly correlated with the material traits), the proxy discrimination isn't rational. And we might thus suspect that racial bias (rather than simple cognitive error) undergirds the practice. If neighborhood profiling by race is based on factual errors and also harms the interests of blacks, this might be sufficient reason to object to the practice. But what if the generalizations are reasonably sound?

Analogies to the racial profiling of individuals may mislead here. For instance, one might think that even if race is a good proxy for a relevant disqualifying trait in employment decisions, we should not exclude from consideration individuals who have the proxy trait, because each individual should have an opportunity to compete for jobs on the basis of his or her merits. Using racial generalizations, one might conclude, unfairly denies individuals the chance to show that they possess the relevant traits of merit. This meritocratic principle is, however, irrelevant to the permissibility of profiling neighborhoods. Neighborhoods don't have the same right to fair treatment that individuals do, and using proxies to decide on the relative desirability of neighborhoods is not, in itself, unjust treatment. If a person relies on the presence of playgrounds in a neighborhood as a proxy for the concentration of school-age children (say, because he wants children around to play with his own child or because he doesn't like children and wants to avoid being around lots of them), this is not unfair treatment to the neighborhood that lacks playgrounds but has plenty of children or to the neighborhood that has several playgrounds but few children.

It might also be thought that the profiling of neighborhoods is relevantly similar to purposefully avoiding individual blacks in public places because (given crime statistics) one thinks they might be criminals or violent. When a person takes evasive action to avoid a black person on the street, the black person may feel humiliated by this public shunning. Yet when a person decides not to buy or rent in a residential neighborhood because the neighborhood has a large number of blacks, residents of the neighborhood rarely know that a decision has been made at all—let alone that racial proxies were used in making it. Of course, they may know that, in general, the practice of neighborhood profiling exists, and this fact may cause some resentment. But they are not generally subject to public humiliation, because the decision to *not* buy or rent in a neighborhood is not usually an act in public view.

Still, even if the practice of profiling neighborhoods by race isn't unfair to disfavored neighborhoods or humiliating for their residents, it is problematic on other grounds. Keep in mind that the rationale behind proxy discrimination is that the proxy trait is easier, less costly, or less time-consuming to detect than the material trait, such that it can be rational to rely on the proxy in decision making. But neighborhood facts like crime rates, school quality, and property values can be readily found on the Internet or through real estate agents. Even neighborhood poverty rates are relatively easy to discover without relying on racial proxies, as these facts are available through the U.S. Census data, which are also online. Given the pervasiveness of racial bias and the consequences of such bias for segregation, it would be morally irresponsible to resort to racial proxies when the information about concentrated disadvantage is readily available.

The fact that ghetto poverty has been caused by racial and economic injustices should also put a break on the racial profiling of neighborhoods. Our duty to foster just institutional arrangements gives us strong reason to avoid reinforcing injustices or perpetuating their negative consequences, particularly when this can be done with relatively little cost to ourselves. Some might deny that the permissibility of neighborhood profiling turns on the specific explanation for the connection between the proxy trait (race) and the material trait (socioeconomic status). That is, some may believe that the fact that injustices have caused blacks to be disproportionately poor and concentrated in ghettos is irrelevant to the permissibility of avoiding neighborhoods with high concentrations of blacks. I'm not sure that's right, but let's suppose it is. If the ills of concentrated black poverty are the result of an unjust basic structure, then these burdens should at least be more equitably shared. The issue here is the distribution of the disadvantages caused by injustice and the costs of corrective justice. All else being equal, these costs should be paid largely by those who have benefited most from the unjust basic structure, as they have profited most from the injustices of the social scheme. Their claim on these benefits is therefore weakest. And, when possible, we should seek to relieve the most oppressed from having to carry so much of the burdens of injustice as we work toward a more just society.

Now even if racial profiling of neighborhoods to avoid concentrated disadvantage is indefensible, this doesn't show that avoiding concentrated disadvantage is impermissible. The risks and costs of residing in such neighborhoods may be too high to reasonably expect people with other options to accept these burdens as their contribution to correcting injustice. The issues here are complex, and I'm not sure how best to resolve them. But it is worth noting that if the avoidance of high-poverty neighborhoods is morally defensible, then some practices that contribute to segregation are not unjust.

Not all racial profiling of neighborhoods, however, is a matter of preferring to avoid concentrated poverty. Some making residential choices might be interested in other material traits that are correlated with high concentrations of black residents. For instance, some might be concerned to avoid certain cultural patterns or the prevalence of particular political attitudes. These material traits are not so easily discerned in the absence of proxies, and it is not clear that the connection between black identity, on the one hand, and cultural traits or political attitudes, on the other, can be explained by injustice.

Some whites may dislike the cultural patterns typical of blacks (or typical of working-class or poor blacks)—or at least strongly prefer non-black cultural forms. They may be averse to the lifestyle or cultural tastes of the average black person.[6] This aversion needn't be premised on "culture of poverty" theory—the hypothesis that concentrated disadvantage leads to self-defeating and other problematic cultural patterns—and it needn't presuppose cultural essentialism. The assumption, not unreasonable, is that there are recognizable cultural patterns more typical of blacks than of other social groups such that race is a reliable proxy for these patterns. A high percentage of blacks in a neighborhood is likely to affect its cultural dynamics, which may in turn attract certain kinds of business establishments and cultural institutions that cater to black preferences. One consideration when choosing a neighborhood (indeed, when choosing a city or town) is its cultural patterns and associated commercial services—nearby restaurants, recreational facilities, music venues, art establishments, and clothing stores. Now if one dislikes black culture, not because of its intrinsic properties, but because one is prejudiced toward blacks, then that would obviously be racist. Or, because of racial bias, one might be led to make unjustified and unflattering generalizations about the cultural patterns of blacks. This too would be racist. But the desire to avoid a neighborhood where black culture is pervasive isn't necessarily racist. It may simply be a matter of taste. After all, some blacks choose black neighborhoods because they expect to find more agreeable cultural patterns there.

Many might also avoid a neighborhood because of the political attitudes that they expect to prevail there. Blacks and whites differ, on average, with respect to political ideology, particularly with respect to issues of crime control, poverty, and distributive justice.[7] A neighborhood with a high concentration of blacks will generally mean a neighborhood with a lot of liberals, radicals, and black nationalists, just as a neighborhood with a high percentage of whites will typically mean a lot of people who are conservative on redistributive taxation, antipoverty measures, and crime control. In fact, if voting patterns are a reliable indicator, then the correlation between black identity and political ideology is much tighter than the correlation between whiteness and political ideology (for example, it is not unusual for Democratic candidates to garner 90 percent of the black vote). Many might be less inclined to join a neighborhood where their political views are not dominant or where they would be politically marginalized. Some prefer not to socialize with people with whom they have fundamental political disagreements. And no one wants to be subject to the laws their political opponents favor.

Thus, using race as a proxy for cultural patterns or political attitudes is not irrational and needn't be a reflection of racial bias. Although the desire for agreeable neighborhood cultural and political dynamics may be less weighty than the reasons to avoid concentrated poverty, these preferences are, other things equal, legitimate bases for residential choice. Yet these preferences, while not intrinsically immoral, would, if acted upon, contribute to racial segregation and ghetto poverty. So if there is an obligation to reduce black concentrated poverty through residential integration, then these cultural and political preferences must be outweighed by the duty of justice.

The Duty of Justice

The duty of justice is a moral requirement all are bound by. It demands, most fundamentally, that each of us respect and support just institutions, particularly those that lay claim to our allegiance and from which we benefit.[8] When we fall under the jurisdiction of a just institutional framework, we fulfill this duty by complying with the institutions' rules and encouraging others to do the same. Just institutions could not remain stable and just if individuals did not regard themselves as bound to respect and support them. The very idea of social justice presupposes the duty of justice: no one can resent being treated unjustly by the basic structure of society yet consistently reject the duty of justice. In this way, the duty of justice is simply a corollary of the value of justice itself. Justice would be an empty ideal without it. Rawls argues for the validity of this duty by pointing out that the parties in the original position, seeing their common rational interest in the existence and stability of just institutions, would naturally agree that everyone should support and further such institutions.

When an institutional arrangement is seriously *unjust*, the duty of justice still has a claim on us. Perhaps its strongest demand is that we help to establish a just social order and to reform unjust institutions. Obviously, the principal perpetrators of injustice should cease their immoral actions, reform their ways, and provide compensation and issue sincere apologies to their victims. The burden to set things right naturally falls on them first and most heavily. Bystanders too, whether they are beneficiaries of the unjust regime or in no way complicit, should do their part to bring about justice. In addition, though, and contrary to what some might suppose, the oppressed should contribute to the reform effort, not simply out of self-interest but because the duty of justice enjoins them to do so. To be sure, conditions of oppression, by their very nature, are forcibly imposed on the oppressed, and the oppressed may bear no responsibility for the injustices they endure. Nevertheless, the oppressed do have some freedom to determine how they will *respond* to these conditions—for example, whether they will acquiesce or resist. And the duty to help correct injustices is binding regardless of who the victims are, whether others or oneself. The duty of justice, then, is a fundamental normative ground of the ethics of resistance.

Sometimes our circumstances are such that we can't do much to effectively reform unjust institutions, at least not without great personal sacrifice. Still, a somewhat weaker demand that we can often meet is that, as far as reasonably possible, we not actively lend support, by word or deed, to an unjust social structure. This isn't simply a matter of keeping one's hands clean. Supporting unjust institutions can give them legitimacy, effectively strengthening their power over the oppressed and enhancing their staying power. We should therefore do all we can to avoid complicity with oppressive structures, to refuse to cooperate with them. This duty is not absolute, however, because it may sometimes be practically impossible to reduce the suffering of the oppressed without inadvertently helping to perpetuate an unjust social system. Buying slaves to set them free lends legitimacy to a slave regime by suggesting that it is morally permissible to buy and sell human beings. Yet it may be the right thing to do, all things considered.

The weakest demand that the duty of justice imposes, a requirement that is all but inescapable regardless of one's circumstances, is that we not be indifferent to societal injustices. Even if we cannot make a positive contribution to social reform and cannot entirely avoid some complicity or compromises with an unjust system, we should at least care about injustice. When we show a lack of concern about ongoing injustices, we fail to value justice properly, fail to acknowledge the moral urgency and normative priority it should have in our lives. Apathy in the face of injustice is a serious vice, for it allows oppressive relations to go unchallenged, enabling their continued existence. Such apathy is also an affront to those who suffer from injustice, as it suggests that their pain isn't worthy of concern. Despite having a strong personal interest in not being treated unjustly, the oppressed can sometimes exhibit this vice—for example, when they resign themselves to living under unjust conditions, regarding these conditions as "just the way thing are" or, worse, developing an "if you can't beat them, join them" mentality. Even when pessimism about the prospects for positive social change is warranted and when the way forward with social reform is obscure, passive acceptance of the status quo is not the only remaining option. One can still publicly condemn the injustice by taking advantage of low-cost opportunities to openly express one's principled opposition to it—that is, one can *dissent*.

Black Self-Segregation

Now consider the residential preferences of blacks. Though integration is proposed as a remedy for black disadvantages, it is still regarded as an imperative *for* blacks (among others, of course). So, if residential integration is a requirement of justice, blacks' residential choices that are incompatible with integration are also contrary to their duty of justice. On the new integrationist vision, then, either generally blacks lack the moral prerogative to choose black neighborhoods when the option of integrated neighborhoods is available or considerations of corrective justice override blacks' otherwise permissible residential prerogatives. Against this vision of racial justice and political ethics, I argue that black self-segregation in neighborhoods need not violate blacks' duty of justice, and thus justice cannot require neighborhood integration.

Some blacks do, of course, desire to live in integrated communities, want to garner the advantages associated with white neighborhoods, or seek to avoid the disadvantages typical of ghettos. Despite discrimination and economic disadvantage, there are blacks, particularly those with higher incomes, who are able to act on such preferences and thus live in integrated or white neighborhoods.[9] But the residential choices of some blacks arguably increase or maintain segregation. For example, some blacks avoid residing in white neighborhoods to limit unpleasant experiences with whites. The main concern is to elude interpersonal discrimination, racist treatment, and hostile attitudes.[10] Another reason is to avoid interracial conflict, which can, and generally does, reflect the operation of stereotypes and implicit bias but needn't be motivated by hostility or animus.

There is also, I should emphasize, the positive preference for a black neighborhood. Group self-segregation need not be entirely voluntary, as it may be partly a response to unjust exclusion or economic disadvantage. But black self-segregation is still a choice, albeit a constrained one, when there are other acceptable options—for example, integrated neighborhoods or neighborhoods with few whites or blacks (which there sometimes are). We should also distinguish residential group self-segregation from *closing ranks*—the defensive tactics a group uses to strengthen its internal social ties and to exclude outsiders from (full) affiliation. Both whites and blacks, dominant groups and subordinate groups, can close ranks. And residential self-segregation can itself be a way of closing ranks. However, residential self-segregation and closing ranks need not coincide. Blacks, for instance, control some organizations and may assign blacks and whites to different roles within them or exclude whites altogether; but many who participate in black organizations may live in integrated neighborhoods. There can be closed social institutions and organizations within an otherwise integrated neighborhood. And there can be informal ranks closure in an integrated neighborhood.

If a social group largely controls an entire social domain (such as employment, education, government administration, or residential and commercial property) and equal access to this domain is necessary for citizens to have equal civic standing and fair prospects in life, then closing ranks in that domain will naturally lead to serious injustices. But the problem is not closing ranks per se. The problem is that no group should be permitted to prevent others from gaining access to these vital goods and positions. And this is why it is dangerous for a social group to have a virtual monopoly over these goods and positions, for they may be tempted to exclude others from access to them, keeping these advantages within the group, or may permit access but only on unfavorable terms. Blacks do sometimes engage in residential self-segregation and close their social networks to whites, including within black institutions and organizations. But they do not control sufficient resources or have enough power to prevent whites from gaining access to important goods and positions on fair terms.

Moreover, the permissibility of self-segregation and closing ranks depends not only on their actual or likely effects, but also on whether their *aims* can be given adequate justification. Blacks may sometimes engage in self-segregation or close ranks out of prejudice toward other groups. But often they engage in these practices to protect their shared interests in a society where they are deeply disadvantaged and vulnerable to mistreatment and political marginalization. When motivated by a sense of justice (rather than narrow group interest), these practices express political solidarity.[11] Acting on considerations of solidarity, some blacks might seek to live in black neighborhoods where they can expect to find high concentrations of politically like-minded individuals. This black-politico concentration could enable them to influence local policies and to elect officials who will listen to their concerns and so is, in principle, an important source of political empowerment.

It's difficult to see how practices of self-segregation and social closure among whites could be reasonably thought to promote justice or protect the vulnerable and marginalized. Yet black solidarity is different, because it can be defended as a group-based effort to fight for racial justice or to protect the group's members from race-based maltreatment. The point of this self-segregation is not, then, to hoard advantages or to prevent nonblacks from gaining access to the things they need. It is instead a component of an ethic of resistance to injustice.[12]

Still, one can be committed to black solidarity without preferring to live in a predominantly black neighborhood or seeking black communal independence. Black solidarity could be expressed as a desire to live in neighborhoods with a *black critical mass* (25 to 50 percent) and therefore shouldn't be equated with racial separatism.[13] Moderate concentrations of blacks in metropolitan neighborhoods could enable black social networks to flourish and black institutions to be sustained. Most whites, however, consider a neighborhood with a significant number of blacks to be intolerable or unappealing.[14] So blacks rarely have the opportunity to live in integrated neighborhoods with a black critical mass. They are usually forced to choose—when they have a choice at all—between segregated black neighborhoods and neighborhoods with very few or no blacks, and most, so it would seem, prefer the former.[15]

A commitment to black solidarity should be distinguished from a desire for black *community*. Blacks, like members of religious or ethnic groups, often have an affinity for one another, and these valuable social ties sometimes express themselves as a desire to live together in the same neighborhoods.[16] But this desire for black residential community needn't be politically motivated or conceived as resistance to injustice. It needn't (though it might) be based on shared heritage, culture, or lifestyle. Some blacks may simply desire the intrinsic pleasure and comfort that come from living among people with similar life experiences.[17] Some may have grown up in these neighborhoods and are just more comfortable in familiar surroundings. Or they may view black communities as places of refuge from unwelcoming, predominantly white work-places and schools.

Blacks sometimes prefer neighborhoods with a black critical mass, not only because they want to avoid white hostility and interracial conflict, practice political solidarity, sustain black institutions, or experience a sense of community. Where there is a greater residential concentration of blacks there will also be a greater array of establishments and associations that cater to blacks' preferences and interests—such as hair salons and barbershops, clothing stores, places of worship, restaurants, bookstores, cinemas, music and dance venues, art galleries and theaters, and retail outlets that sell black hair-care and skin-care products. Their status as a numerical minority (13 percent of the U.S. population) makes it rational for blacks to cluster in neighborhoods so that they can benefit from local organizations that cater to their distinctive tastes and needs.

These various reasons for choosing black neighborhoods, if acted upon by a sufficient number of blacks, would contribute to, and maybe even worsen, segregation patterns. When such choices are motivated by racial prejudice, they are clearly wrong and incompatible with political ethics. But many of these reasons are perfectly legitimate and therefore should not be dismissed or ignored in efforts to respond to ghetto poverty.

Integration and Corrective Justice

Let's distinguish the new integrationist vision from other influential conceptions of integration. In the fight against Jim Crow, many civil rights activists viewed their efforts as a struggle for *desegregation*. The goal was to abolish the unjust legal exclusions and prohibitions of the segregation regime, a social system that granted whites privileges and advantages they weren't entitled to, while depriving blacks of rights, opportunities, and resources they were owed, and that stigmatized blacks as inferior. To end discrimination in housing, education, employment, and lending, effective antidiscrimination laws were needed. There must be no race-based constraints on the use of public space, the receipt of public benefits, or access to social services. One's race must not be an impediment to receiving due process or the equal protection of the law. In the political sphere, desegregation meant granting blacks the unfettered right to vote and hold public office and to the equitable sharing of political power and participation in public decision making. But desegregation, so understood, is compatible with voluntary residential self-segregation. Thus, the new integrationists, while certainly favoring desegregation efforts, seek more than desegregation.

A second ideal has sometimes been described as *social equality* but is perhaps better understood as an application of the right to freedom of association: Every individual should be free to interact (both in public and in private) and form relationships with the members of any race without molestation or legal constraint. This is the liberty to form and sustain intimate interracial bonds without the state or private individuals interfering with the exercise of this freedom. But it, too, is compatible with residential self-segregation, because it includes the right *not* to seek such interracial bonds.

A third ideal is *national interracial solidarity*—a society in which the members of different races have a sense of goodwill toward one another and think of themselves as collectively constituting one people. According to this vision, we should strive for interracial civic friendship, a sense of fraternity among members of a multiracial society of equals. This unity is to be founded on mutual respect and understanding. It cannot be a matter of legal requirements alone but must be constituted by the shared and steadfast ethical commitment of individual members of society. Some new integrationists endorse this ideal. It is not, however, their main reason for favoring residential integration.

Residential diversity is a fourth ideal. According to this view, each neighborhood (or almost every neighborhood) should contain people from different racial groups in rough proportion to their presence in the region. Yet notice that a neighborhood could be diverse and still contain little, if any, friendly interracial interaction. Residential diversity, in the abstract, is more an aesthetic ideal than a moral one. However, the new integrationists see the worth of residential diversity in its potential to foster meaningful interracial relationships and cooperation. For them it has instrumental value.

The new integrationists view residential diversity as *a necessary instrument of corrective justice.* It is, they believe, the only viable remedy for the disadvantages from which the ghetto poor suffer. They think the state has the authority and the obligation to promote residential integration through the force of law. Yet they don't think it should stop at desegregation and social equality. In addition to helping to achieve the long-term goal of national interracial solidarity, residential integration is an attempt to reduce black–white inequality and to eliminate ghetto poverty by bringing blacks (particularly poor ones) into greater contact with advantaged whites. Integration, on this view, is a way of overcoming, or mitigating, unjust disadvantages that blacks experience. I discuss two variants of this vision—one emphasizes *racial* integration and the other *economic* integration.

Elizabeth Anderson has offered the most comprehensive philosophical defense of racial integration as corrective justice.[18] She, too, defends her conclusions within a liberal-egalitarian framework. But she is also a leading proponent of a nonideal political theory of racial inequality developed within the framework of the medical model. The differences between our approaches to segregation in ghettos are subtle but significant, and thus I give her views extended discussion.

Anderson is concerned with problems of group-based disadvantage, which she attributes to segregation. Her defense of integration rests on a detailed empirical account of the underlying causes of black disadvantages. She argues that today's residential segregation is the legacy of state-sponsored, overt housing discrimination and contemporary private (though sometimes covert) discrimination. Processes of race-based residential exclusion, formal and informal, are the principal cause of group inequality, and these processes are unjust. Integration is thus a principle (or rather a set of principles) for correcting injustices, for responding to existing social problems traceable to unjust practices.

According to Anderson, desegregation and social equality are insufficient to deal with unjust racial inequality, because blacks are deeply disadvantaged by social capital deficits, which can be remedied only by greater black–white interaction across multiple social domains, including neighborhoods.[19] *Social capital* is understood as the networks of associates through which knowledge of and access to opportunities are transmitted and norms of trust and reciprocity are enforced. It comes in two forms. *Bonding* social capital is ties between people who share an identity, while *bridging* social capital is ties between people who have different social identities. Anderson claims that segregation fosters strong intraracial bonding ties but undermines the building of interracial bridging ties. Indeed, she believes "the tendency of blacks and whites to associate within largely segregated social networks" has profound negative consequences for black opportunity.[20] This is a problem of justice, she argues, because access to jobs and educational opportunities is often gained by word of mouth, and blacks have limited access to white social networks. Anderson insists that unjust black–white inequality can be overcome fully only if blacks join white social networks so that their bridging capital can be increased, with the result that whites give blacks vital information about and thus access to employment and educational opportunities. It is the need to increase black social capital, she maintains, that makes integration beyond desegregation and social equality an imperative of justice.

Owen Fiss has defended *economic* integration as corrective justice.[21] He, too, is a liberal egalitarian working within a medical-model framework. Fiss believes that concentrated poverty creates a debilitating and destructive culture in ghettos, one that inhibits the black poor from taking advantage of any educational or employment opportunities that might be created. The only hope, he thinks, is to eliminate ghettos and thus their distinctive subculture. His proposal is to move the ghetto poor to middle-class or upper-class neighborhoods. This solution is premised on the idea that the black poor mustn't be too concentrated or else a culture of poverty will continue to flourish. These more advantaged neighborhoods already have high-quality schools, ample employment opportunities, low crime rates, and good public services, so these needn't be created by government action. Even if the black adults who move don't reap the socioeconomic benefits themselves, the cycle of poverty would be broken because their children would grow up in more enriching and safe environments, with good schools and positive role models.

Fiss thinks such economic integration is a requirement of justice. It is an effective remedy for a great injustice the state has actively perpetrated and been complicit in: "The inner-city ghetto stands before us as an instrument of subjugation and thus represents the most visible and perhaps most pernicious vestige of racial injustice in the United States—the successor to slavery and Jim Crow."[22] He argues that the state, by engaging in and acquiescing in a range of discriminatory practices, produced and maintained ghettos, and so the public has an obligation, not only to prevent racial discrimination, but also to remedy its negative consequences for the victims. This is a corrective justice argument, which Fiss distinguishes from a narrow compensatory justice argument. *Compensatory justice* demands that the victims of past injustice be brought to the level of well-being they would have attained had the injustice not occurred. By contrast, Fiss argues that ongoing unjust practices have created *a system of subordination* that the perpetrators have an obligation to dismantle. He is advocating economic integration as a principle of social reform, not as reparations.

For Fiss, this poverty-deconcentration strategy does not aim at racial integration. The ghetto poor should be enabled to move to whatever neighborhoods they like—black, white, integrated, or whatever—provided these neighborhoods have low poverty rates. His aim is to deconcentrate black poverty so as to avoid its associated ills. The trouble is, economic integration generally means racial integration, because there are very few black communities with low poverty rates, only enough to absorb a tiny percentage of the ghetto poor. And given racial clustering, those majority black neighborhoods with moderate poverty rates (say, 20 to 30 percent) that do exist are often adjacent to ghettos or would quickly reach unacceptable poverty concentrations (40 percent) if a significant number of the ghetto poor were to move to them, contrary to the corrective justice objective. Most advantaged neighborhoods are either already integrated or are majority white with few, if any, black families.

Racial integration and economic integration are two distinct approaches (in terms of rationale, if not practically speaking) for responding to spatially concentrated black disadvantage. These two related solutions to ghetto poverty can be used in combination, as they were in the Chicago Gautreaux program.[23] Both advocate addressing ghetto poverty by reengineering neighborhoods in an effort to bring poor blacks into greater contact with whites or the affluent. The two visions rest on the idea that racial inequality and ghetto poverty are explained, at least in part, by the patterns of informal social interaction and the cultural norms that people are exposed to in their residential communities. So it is not just that ghetto neighborhoods are disadvantaged—have few accessible decent jobs, lack affordable housing, are served by substandard schools, suffer from high crime rates, and so on (though this is clearly part of the problem). According to the new integrationist vision, concentrated black disadvantage is also perpetuated by how social networks and cultural dynamics within and across neighborhoods mediate access to goods, opportunities, and services.

Integration or Egalitarian Pluralism?

Desegregation and protecting freedom of association are clearly required by justice. National interracial solidarity is an attractive ideal
and perhaps should be a long-term goal. And the individual preference
for residential diversity is perfectly legitimate. However, I believe that
blacks, including poor blacks, should be free to self-segregate in neighborhoods and that this practice is not incompatible with justice. I also
maintain that we should not regard residential integration as a legitimate mechanism for correcting the unjust disadvantages the ghetto
poor face, where programs like Gautreaux and Moving to Opportunity
are the paradigm.[24]

The rest of this chapter details the limits of the social capital argument for integration. (I address the culture of poverty argument in
Chapter 3.) I do not deny that the social processes that cause segregation also contribute to spatially concentrated black disadvantage. Nor
is my principal objective to dispute that integration policies have worked
or, with suitable adjustments, could work to reduce poverty in ghettos.
My focus is on ethical ideals and on how nonideal theorizing about
social justice should be conceived and practiced. Even if we were confident that integration policies would reduce socioeconomic inequality
and black disadvantage, we would still need to know if they can be adequately justified to blacks in light of the costs and risks of such policies for the unjustly disadvantaged and the legitimate counteraims of
the oppressed. Any advocacy of integration as corrective justice must
be sensitive to the reasonable demands and concerns of blacks themselves. And it is here, I believe, that the new integrationist vision falls
short.

In the history of black political thought, questions of integration
versus separation and assimilation versus pluralism have been frequently
take up, particularly in the black nationalist tradition.[25] These debates
have been at the center of discussions about the place of blacks in U.S.
society from slavery to the present. Out of these debates a position
has emerged that is neither integrationist nor separatist. On this alternative *egalitarian pluralist* vision, racial justice requires desegregation,
social equality, and, importantly, economic fairness. It does not require
residential integration. Nor does it oppose it. It does not proscribe
voluntary self-segregation in neighborhoods. Nor does it call for it.

Unjust race-based residential exclusion demands an appropriate response, as do the socioeconomic disadvantages caused by racial injustice. Yet that response should be to prevent and rectify discriminatory treatment, to establish fair equality of opportunity, and to ensure an equitable distribution of income and economic assets. Consequently, blacks would be able to live in the neighborhoods of their choice constrained only by what they can afford given their fair share of material resources.

To the extent possible and in a way that is fair to all affected, we should work to improve the residential environment of the unjustly disadvantaged, that is, to make their *neighborhoods* less disadvantaged, but without aiming to rearrange neighborhood demographics by race. These corrective justice measures would inevitably require the investment of public funds and significant transfers of resources from the affluent to the disadvantaged. But this is perfectly consistent with, indeed required by, justice. And finally, egalitarian pluralists, in light of U.S. history (including the recent past), are generally skeptical that a sufficient number of whites are currently willing to relinquish their unjust social, material, and political advantages in order to secure racial equality. Thus, blacks must not only agitate for racial justice but, taking a realistic perspective on its prospects, organize as a group to protect their vital interests. In the history of black political thought, this outlook is perhaps most closely associated with thinkers such as W. E. B. Du Bois, Harold Cruse, and Derrick Bell.[26]

Anderson rejects this vision as inadequate, not because she regards it as too pessimistic, but because she believes it would likely lead to black self-segregation, which she argues would deprive disadvantaged blacks of opportunities to acquire needed bridging social capital. So let's examine the social capital argument to see if it justifies neighborhood integration programs as a requirement of justice and to determine if it gives us sufficient grounds to condemn black self-segregation.

There are several things to notice about the social capital argument that should give us pause. First, social relationships are treated, like other forms of capital, as a kind of resource to be used for socioeconomic advancement. No one can deny that people often rely on their relationships for information and favors that could improve their socioeconomic prospects. But properly conceived, this benefit is a *by-product* of social relationships, not the reason we cultivate them. Healthy relationships engender goodwill and special concern, which can lead to mutual favors, large and small. Outside of the marketplace, when people go out of their way to form relationships on the basis of the would-be associate's socioeconomic usefulness, this is a perversion of association and normally viewed as a sign of bad character. The social capital argument turns the old adage "It's not what you know but who you know" on its head, from a lamentable fact about social life to something we should positively embrace and foster. Perhaps urging the ghetto poor to cultivate relationships with the affluent is sound pragmatic advice in desperate times, but it hardly seems like an appropriate basis for public policy directed at correcting injustices.

Second, notice that the social capital argument treats social relationships not only as an economic resource (like money or property) but as a resource governed by principles of distributive justice. This suggests that the state has the standing to redistribute social relationships when some individuals have too few of high economic value. As a matter of basic liberty, individuals should of course be free to cultivate relationships with their neighbors with a view to leveraging these relationships for economic gain (however base the motive). But making an individual's success in building such relationships a condition for material well-being does not treat individuals (who might have a rather different conception of the value of community) with the respect to which they are entitled as free persons. They might reasonably reject this neoliberal conversion of personal relationships into economic assets, along with the state's presumption to play this role in the intimate lives of citizens. Moreover, even though, as practical matter, government policy can foster interracial relationships only indirectly (through incentives and penalties), this is nonetheless a roundabout way to bring about economic justice. Rather than call on the government to tax the affluent for purposes of transferring income and wealth to the poor, the new integrationist would have the state forge interracial mixed-income communities against the background of a highly economically stratified society. Skeptics could be forgiven if such a scheme struck them as a way for the affluent to hold on to their unjust economic advantages.

The social capital argument also makes integration a particularly distasteful remedy for ghetto poverty because of its racial dimensions. Such an approach to corrective justice would reinforce the symbolic power that whites hold over blacks by encouraging whites to see their relationships with blacks not as intrinsically valuable forms of interracial community but as an avenue for blacks to share in (not abolish) white privilege. Because such relationships cannot be coerced but must be entered into voluntarily, whites are free to dole out this dubious privilege to whomever they see fit and, crucially, to withhold it at their discretion. This puts blacks in an untenable supplicant position, which many naturally seek to avoid, and it does too little to weaken the illegitimate power that whites hold over black lives.

Yet even if we were to leave these concerns aside, there is still sufficient reason to prefer egalitarian pluralism over new integrationism. For one thing, in their desire to see black bridging capital increase, new integrationists often give too little weight to the bonding capital that disadvantaged blacks already possess, social ties that would likely be lost or weakened by moving away from their existing neighbors.[27] The ghetto poor, particularly black single mothers, are often dependent on their established social networks for childcare, transportation, and employment information and referrals; and these relationships are often sustained by frequent interaction in black neighborhoods. In response, Anderson would likely emphasize that many, if not most, good jobs are in or near white neighborhoods, and access to these jobs often depends on being in local white social networks.[28] The social capital argument assumes, however, that blacks will form economically useful bonds with whites when in more integrated neighborhoods.[29] But just because you live in the same neighborhood doesn't mean that your neighbors will invite you into their homes, vouch for you when it counts, share information with you that would advance your socioeconomic prospects, or even be friendly toward you. So blacks have little assurance that sacrificing their bonding social capital would lead to more valuable bridging social capital.

Anderson is relying on the hypothesis that increased social contact will reduce racial prejudice and thus improve the likelihood of social ties forming between whites and blacks, even between affluent whites and the ghetto poor.[30] Note, however, that conditions for prejudice reduction in interracial, mixed-income neighborhoods with a significant presence of the black poor are far from optimal.[31] In just about any neighborhood setting, residents can avoid sustained contact, limiting their interaction to greetings as they pass each other in apartment halls or on the street. Unlike in schools or the military, there is no overarching power with the authority to effectively demand cooperation across racial lines or between social classes. Affluent whites and poor blacks don't share the same social status or a similar lifestyle, and thus they often perceive their interests as at odds (particularly when whites are homeowners and blacks are renters). Perhaps these obstacles to reduced prejudice and interracial ties can be overcome eventually. But these unfavorable conditions will presumably slow the rate of prejudice reduction. Insofar as it is reasonable to expect a reduction in racial prejudice, this reduction will take time, and even then, it is not clear how long it would take to reach tolerable levels.

It would be reasonable to expect such interracial ties to form among neighbors where advantaged whites are willing to sacrifice to realize racial equality, are tolerant of those with a different lifestyle, and are patient with blacks' lack of trust in whites. But if affluent whites maintain exclusive enclaves in order to hoard resources, hold on to their advantages, and avoid poor blacks, as Anderson insists they do, why should we expect them to share information about job opportunities with new disadvantaged black neighbors? Wouldn't they also seek to limit contact with these former ghetto denizens? And if blacks perceive this lack of goodwill and weak commitment to racial justice, as they almost certainly would, shouldn't we expect them to shield themselves from its repercussions, perhaps closing their social network off to white neighbors or simply returning to a black neighborhood?

But let's suppose whites didn't practice employment and housing discrimination, adequate schools were available to everyone, and an equitable distribution of material resources existed. Why, under these more just circumstances, would it be so important that whites and blacks live together in the same neighborhoods? After all, opportunities for interracial contact would exist in workplaces, the marketplace, and educational contexts.[32] There would also be opportunities for interracial contact and communication in the broader public sphere, recreational contexts, and other public spaces. Nowadays many social networks are cultivated and sustained through social media. However, blacks might still have legitimate reasons to prefer living in black neighborhoods—to maintain long-standing community ties, to sustain black institutions and cultural practices, and to ensure access to establishments that serve black needs.

Anderson might nonetheless maintain that despite these other opportunities for interracial interaction, social capital deficits would remain if blacks self-segregate in neighborhoods and thus racial injustices would be left uncorrected. But would they? Let's suppose that, after the egalitarian pluralist vision had been realized and whites demonstrated their willingness to integrate on fair terms, material inequalities remain because some blacks forgo the social capital advantages that greater integration would afford them. Would this mean racial justice wasn't realized? No. Blacks would have the real option of joining racially diverse communities and, consequently, wouldn't have a justified complaint. There is, in short, a difference between saying that justice requires that obstacles to integration be removed so that individuals have the *option* to integrate (which is the demand for desegregation and social equality) and saying that justice requires that individuals *actually* integrate.

In response, Anderson might insist that the weight of the empirical evidence is on her side and that, in fact, blacks do need to integrate more fully with whites if unjust racial inequalities are to be entirely overcome. Perhaps she'd be correct. But while there is a great deal of agreement among social scientists that segregation processes (particularly discriminatory practices) create and worsen racial inequality, there is much disagreement about whether and how much integration efforts would reduce such inequality.[33] Given that there is conflicting empirical evidence, that the evidence is highly complex and thus difficult to assess, and that such empirical studies are rarely, if ever, conclusive, it would seem that Anderson should regard the prospects for success of her integration solution to racial inequality as, at best, probable. In light of this reasonable disagreement and ineradicable empirical uncertainty, her practical prescriptions should also be more tentative and qualified. Instead, she sometimes treats the evidence in favor of integration as decisive and suggests that this evidence entitles state officials and institutional authorities to override the residential preferences and associational prerogatives of blacks who reject integration as a solution to black disadvantage.

But let's assume that she puts her case directly to disadvantaged blacks (rather than solely to policymakers or state agency bureaucrats) and they reject her prescriptions. Even if she were *correct* about the weight of the evidence, these blacks would not be acting contrary to their duty of justice if, remaining skeptical, they nevertheless practiced self-segregation. Indeed, blacks would be acting under tremendous uncertainty even if they were mostly persuaded by her social analysis. They couldn't be confident that things would work out as she expects. Consequently, disadvantaged blacks would understandably want to take precautions, to protect themselves from potential costs or unforeseen consequences. If some blacks refuse to go along with integration efforts, this may be because of reasonable disagreement about whether these efforts would actually remedy the problem, and thus would reflect neither an unwillingness to honor their duty of justice nor unjustified hostility toward whites.[34]

One known cost of residential integration is greater racial conflict, which causes blacks to experience stress and alienation. With more interracial contact (which increases the chances that they will interact with whites who are racist), blacks also experience more racial discrimination, hostility, harassment, and even violence. The concern, then, is not just that integration won't, even with time, make interracial interaction smoother and less costly to blacks. The concern is that blacks, an already unjustly disadvantaged group, will have to carry these burdens in the meantime, particularly when a positive result from their sacrifice is far from certain. If a suitable alternative is available that does not entail these costs but is compatible with justice, then blacks would be right to insist that we experiment with that one first. Egalitarian pluralism, I maintain, is that alternative.

This conclusion might be rejected on the grounds that blacks, like everyone else, have a duty to resist racism and that such antiracist efforts won't succeed without greater integration than the egalitarian pluralist position requires. Anderson thinks that even if all (or almost all) whites were to sincerely reject conscious racism, they won't be able to overcome their implicit racial bias against blacks unless whites and blacks become more integrated.[35] Whites need to spend more sustained time interacting with blacks to fully overcome unconscious stigmatizing ideas. And so some subtle unjust discrimination would remain if blacks insist on residential self-segregation.

So would it be contrary to blacks' duty of justice if they were to refuse to play this role in the moral reform of whites? The answer depends, I think, on the conditions under which they would be expected to play it. If Anderson and other new integrationists think that blacks should play this role *now*, before they have assurances that their fellow citizens oppose and seek to rectify ideological, institutional, and structural racism and are committed to bringing about fair equality of opportunity, then the demand is unreasonable. Disadvantaged blacks are too vulnerable and the costs and risks too great to expect blacks to forgo the option of self-segregation. No plausible interpretation of the duty of justice requires such self-sacrifice and heroism on the part of the oppressed. But once it was clear that whites sought to live in a just society *even if this would mean losing some of their existing advantages*, I suspect that a great number of blacks would, in the spirit of reciprocity, seek out opportunities for greater interracial interaction.[36]

In the meantime, given that blacks are already concentrated in metropolitan neighborhoods and few whites are eager to join these communities on fair terms, why not simply attempt to create black communities that are not disadvantaged, working to correct the relevant injustices without insisting on residential integration? Anderson thinks this isn't possible. Part of her reason for thinking this is based on her social capital argument and worries about the persistence of white unconscious bias, considerations already discussed. But setting aside those arguments, is egalitarian pluralism unrealistic?

There is no doubt a sense in which thriving black communities might be a utopian fantasy: advantaged whites won't let it happen because it will cost them more than they want to pay and the forces of opposition aren't strong enough to overturn this reactionary preference. For instance, Anderson notes that state-sponsored K–12 school integration initiatives "consistently encounter massive white resistance and are not politically feasible."[37] However, this can't be the kind of feasibility Anderson has in mind when she insists that integration is the only viable path to racial justice, because on her account, white intransigence in the face of manifest racial inequality and severe black disadvantage is clearly unjust and unreasonable. The kind of "realism" in political philosophy that she favors does not entail capitulating to injustice.

Moreover, most whites are also unlikely to accept the demanding forms of integration that Anderson prescribes, for these too would cost them more than they are willing to pay. Indeed, there is some reason to think that most whites would prefer improving black communities to residential integration. After all, this would allow them to limit their contact with blacks. One lesson we might take from the intense fights over school busing is that while privileged whites may be reluctant to spend the necessary resources to improve schools and neighborhoods for blacks, they are even more resistant to what they see as threats to their own schools and neighborhoods. To be sure, an egalitarian pluralist American society is not on the immediate horizon. But Anderson rightly admits that the prospects for realizing her integrationist vision are also "gloomy."[38]

To return to the main point, even if there is no viable alternative to integration that would erase all unjust black disadvantages, as Anderson maintains, blacks don't have a duty to accept the burdens of integration, nor is the state justified in imposing them. A better response to the costs objection is to insist that integration be voluntary, with real freedom to choose one's residential community: those blacks who wish to bear the costs of integration should be enabled to integrate, but those who don't want to should neither be pushed into residential integration nor condemned for not integrating.[39]

If integration requires that blacks relinquish the benefits of self-segregation, endure the increased white hostility and interracial conflict that often accompanies integration, and, in order to have equal life prospects, work their way into white social networks, then blacks have just grounds for complaint. Blacks, as an unjustly disadvantaged group, should be the ones to decide if forgoing the returns to social capital that integration might provide is worth it to them. Policies that seek to end unjust racial inequality by pushing, or even nudging, blacks into residential integration or that make needed resources available only on condition that blacks are willing to integrate show a lack of respect for those they aim to assist. In response to such reform efforts blacks would be justified in refusing to move out of black communities—whether these be ghettos or not—as a form of political dissent.

When it comes to correcting injustices, some hold that our interventions should not add to the burdens of the oppressed.[40] Because integration would burden disadvantaged blacks, we shouldn't promote it, they maintain. I believe this principle is too strong, however. It would rule out activism against a group-based injustice if such activism would create a backlash against the disadvantaged group. It would also rule out state interventions that add to the burdens of the oppressed in some ways but relieve their burdens in others, creating a net gain for the oppressed. The principle I rely on is weaker and perfectly compatible with the oppressed having a duty to contribute to social reform even when this entails some costs and risks. I hold that the state should avoid adding to the burdens of the oppressed when the goals of corrective justice can be achieved without them. But when justice cannot be achieved without adding to their burdens, we should keep these costs to a minimum and, importantly, give the oppressed maximal freedom in choosing the form that these necessary burdens take. We should also be sure to share the burdens of redress equitably, with the "winners" in the unjust system paying the lion's share of the cost of reform. The duty to correct injustices falls to us all, the disadvantaged and the privileged, so it is reasonable to expect the oppressed to pay some of the costs of social reform. However, some costs, such as being made more vulnerable to unjust treatment, which integration would likely involve, should be imposed only when absolutely necessary, with provisions that allow the most oppressed to opt out without being left destitute.

Economic Integration?

Fiss acknowledges the costs to the ghetto poor of residential dispersal programs—the disruption in their lives caused by moving, the broken communities of support, the damage done to existing social networks, the loss of connection to place, and the sometimes difficult adjustment of moving to a new and unwelcoming community. Mitigating these costs may be part of the reason he insists only on economic integration, not racial integration. Yet he maintains that we must enable those who want to leave ghettos to do so or else damn them to a life of oppression. He also maintains that each ghetto family should be free to choose whether to leave or stay. Thus, his view is closer to an egalitarian pluralist philosophy than to a committed racial integrationism like Anderson's.

But why not also offer ghetto denizens the option of staying put but with renewed efforts at urban community development? Such urban planning should include the ghetto poor in the decision making, not leaving these community matters to politicians, more advantaged residents, and private developers. Then the ghetto poor would really have a meaningful choice.[41] If the only options are the ghetto as is or moving to a more advantaged but white neighborhood, then many (though not all) would of course "choose" the option of exit (assuming they can afford to move). Yet for those who find the hazards of ghetto life (such as the prevalence of street crime) intolerable this would effectively be a choice under duress.

Fiss thinks improving the lives of the ghetto poor without moving them out of their current neighborhoods won't work, because the ghetto itself is a "structure of subordination," as it creates destructive cultural dynamics that significantly reduce its inhabitants' life prospects. The only viable solution, he thinks, is to help the black poor leave ghettos for more advantaged neighborhoods. But these alleged destructive and self-defeating cultural dynamics occur, by hypothesis, only when there are high rates of poverty and joblessness. So if good local jobs were created, or if there were affordable and efficient transportation to existing jobs in surrounding areas, poverty should be significantly reduced and these dynamics would then not occur. If there were more affordable housing in or near black neighborhoods or more housing vouchers that offset the costs of higher rents, then the poor wouldn't have to spend so much of their already limited income on housing and consequently would be less poor. If schools were better, more would have an opportunity to attend and be successful in college or to compete for good jobs and so would be less likely to be poor. And where there is less poverty (say, due to generous income subsidies), there is less crime; and where there are decent jobs available, fewer people are tempted to turn to crime for economic reasons. Thus, leaving aside the social capital argument (which I have argued is inadequate to justify state-sponsored integration programs), the only grounds I can see for insisting on economic integration through the residential dispersal of the ghetto poor (and consequently racial integration) is political feasibility—which is *not* a requirement of justice but rather a compromise with injustice.

When considering the current trend toward urban development through creating mixed-income communities, liberal egalitarians should naturally ask: Instead of "integrating" stratified social classes, why not reduce socioeconomic inequality? We should be abolishing class hierarchy (so as to satisfy the requirements of fair equality of opportunity), not finding an efficient way for antagonistic social classes to live more peaceably among each other. Except for reasons of pragmatic compromise, the mixed-income neighborhood solution to ghetto poverty should be compelling only to those who accept that the current institutional mechanisms for distributing income (markets, the property regime, and the tax scheme) are justly structured and that the ghetto poor are not therefore unjustly disadvantaged but simply unfortunate victims of bad brute luck. Such a stance would be out of step with a corrective justice framework, which is a response to injustice, not misfortune. And the injustices at issue are not merely that the black poor are often "concentrated" in the same neighborhoods, but that they are needlessly poor and their neighborhoods are disadvantaged in ways that cannot be justified on impartial grounds.

It is worth noting that any poverty-deconcentration scheme (whether voluntary or not) that involves moving poor families to more advantaged neighborhoods would be progressively redistributive. So, redistributing people is also redistributing resources. Rental payments would have to be subsidized by public funds, and thus the poor would have more material resources as a result. And these subsidies would inevitably be funded by taxes on the more affluent or on private firms. Yet there are two key differences between Fiss's deconcentration scheme and the "pure" redistributive scheme of egalitarian pluralism. The first is their ultimate aims. One is concerned to create mixed-income communities and the other is concerned to ensure that everyone can find and afford adequate housing, whatever the demographics of the neighborhood. Second, although both schemes might rely on housing subsidies, a program that would place no restrictions on neighborhood type would give the ghetto poor greater overall freedom. In accordance with liberal-egalitarian principles, when correcting the negative consequences of injustice it is morally better to make required resource transfers to the unjustly disadvantaged in a way that gives them the most control over their lives. This might mean, for instance, providing cash payments instead of food stamps and a more generous earned income tax credit (preferably distributed biweekly or monthly rather than annually) over housing vouchers. In this way we avoid degrading forms of paternalism and we respect the agency of the oppressed.

On Interracial Solidarity

It might seem that in defending the legitimacy of black neighborhood self-segregation and rejecting residential integration as a requirement of justice I am also abandoning the ideal of interracial unity (the "beloved community") that Martin Luther King Jr. so eloquently defended.[42] However, if the basic structure of society is deeply unjust and the burdens of injustice have fallen heavily and disproportionately on a stigmatized racial group, then it is entirely appropriate for the members of that group to withhold some allegiance to the nation and to invest more in cultivating solidarity and mutual aid within the group, simply as a matter of self-defense and group survival. Full identification with and loyalty to the nation will naturally come as the public demonstrates a commitment to equal justice by removing the unfair burdens on the oppressed. The existence of black ghettos and exclusive white suburban communities across America's metropolises is a salient and painful reminder that this commitment has yet to be adequately undertaken. I believe that an integrationist ethos—a pervasive sense of interracial unity—would be a natural *by-product* of a just multiracial society of equals. While I doubt that residential integration is a necessary means to such a society, interracial unity would likely be a consequence of a just social structure and the manifest willingness of the citizenry to support and maintain it because it is just. Our emancipatory aim should be, therefore, to establish such a structure, not to artificially engineer multiracial or mixed-income neighborhoods in the name of national unity.[43]

THREE

Culture

Many think that ghettos persist mostly, if not only, because there are destructive and self-defeating cultural patterns prevalent in these communities. Some have insisted that there is a "culture of poverty" to be found in America's ghettos.[1] The culture-of-poverty hypothesis holds that because the segregated black urban poor have lived for so long under such miserable conditions, many come to develop attitudes, practices, and self-concepts that inhibit their ability to improve their life prospects. Because of social distance or geographic isolation from mainstream institutions, these cultural traits are transmitted among peers and across generations, in an ongoing cycle with catastrophic consequences. Indeed, some of these cultural currents are thought to have become formidable obstacles to ghetto residents making good use of their available opportunities. In particular, some social bases of self-esteem that exist in ghettos would appear to have engendered dysfunctional social identities that lead to further impoverishment.

A number of social scientists studying urban poverty explicitly reject the culture-of-poverty hypothesis, at least in this crude form.[2] They do not believe there is a culture specific to poverty, for the cultural responses to poverty vary enormously across time and place and between immigrants and natives, even in ghetto neighborhoods.[3] Today many who offer scientific cultural analyses of the urban poor (call them the *new cultural analysts*) do not accept the idea that there is one totalizing or cohesive subculture in poor black communities.[4] While acknowledging the existence of salient and distinctive cultural patterns in ghetto neighborhoods, they emphasize that there is tremendous heterogeneity even within the same poor black neighborhood. Orlando Patterson, for instance, has recently argued that there are at least four distinct "cultural configurations" in ghetto neighborhoods, which he calls "the adapted mainstream," "the proletarian," "the street," and "the hip hop."[5] And the cultural configurations embraced among the ghetto poor are not generally straightjackets from which the poor cannot escape but more often frames or repertoires that the black poor draw on (sometimes implicitly) to navigate their social environment and to make sense of their lives.

Moreover, apart from these empirical and conceptual disagreements, the new cultural analysts reject the label "culture of poverty" because of its misleading associations and political baggage. They are particularly skeptical of those who use the idea of a culture of poverty to blame the black urban poor for their circumstances or to absolve government of any responsibility for alleviating the plight of the black poor. New cultural analysts often leave open the question of who is ultimately responsible for the disadvantages the ghetto poor face, and even when they do make claims about responsibility, their analyses are generally compatible with government having an obligation to improve the life prospects of the black urban poor. In addition, few believe that the cultural traits of the ghetto poor are the primary causal determinants of the persistence of ghettos or that these traits operate independently of structural factors. Lastly, new cultural analysts rarely invoke the older language of "pathology" or "dysfunction" when describing the cultural patterns of the black poor. Indeed, some think that the cultural traits prevalent among the ghetto poor enable them to survive in their challenging social environment.[6]

Still, some contemporary social scientists (and certainly many people in the broader public) believe that cultural factors help to explain ghetto poverty, even if they insist that structural factors have equal or greater explanatory significance. Among those who think there are cultural aspects to ghetto poverty, some believe there are cultural traits associated with ghettos that hurt poor ghetto residents' chances of improving their lives through mainstream institutions and conventional paths of upward mobility. The issue, then, is not cultural divergence from convention, as unconventional forms of social life are not in themselves troubling. Worries arise only when such divergence leads to significantly reduced life prospects given the patterns of social organization typical of contemporary liberal-capitalist societies. What those who take this position today, including some new cultural analysts, have in common with some older culture-of-poverty theorists is the following belief: that a significant segment of the ghetto poor diverge culturally from mainstream values and norms, and this divergence generally inhibits their upward mobility or escape from poverty. Call this the *suboptimal cultural divergence hypothesis* (or "cultural divergence thesis" for short).

I shall assume that the cultural divergence thesis is basically sound. I don't claim to know that the thesis is true. But I believe it is a plausible, widely held, and empirically grounded hypothesis worth taking seriously, and I evaluate some practical prescriptions premised on it. My principal concern is with what should, and what should not, be done *if* the thesis is true. Specifically, I draw out and reflect on the normative implications of one possible response to suboptimal cultural divergence among the ghetto poor, a response firmly rooted in the medical model of social reform. This response, which I call *cultural reform*, is to intervene in the lives of poor ghetto residents to shift their cultural orientation away from these suboptimal traits toward ones that will aid their exit from poverty. To many who care about the plight of the ghetto poor, the need for cultural reform may seem obvious. However, there are cultural reform efforts that, I show, cannot be adequately justified to the ghetto poor, particularly those forms that entail government involvement in the reform effort. The focus of this chapter is on the practical limits, moral permissibility, and overall wisdom of state-sponsored cultural reform. I'm particularly concerned to demonstrate its incompatibility with liberal-egalitarian values and to reframe the relevant issues within the systemic-injustice framework I've been defending. I begin by further clarifying what I take the cultural divergence thesis to entail and then turn to exploring what cultural reform might involve.

Suboptimal Cultural Divergence

It is imperative to keep in mind that the category "ghetto poor" is defined in terms of a structural location within U.S. society. Specifically, membership is constituted by a person's racial classification (black), class position (poor), and residential neighborhood (ghetto). The group is *not* defined in terms of shared cultural characteristics. The term "ghetto poor" is not meant as a (more palatable) synonym for "underclass," which is sometimes defined partly in terms of behavioral or cultural traits. And there is no suggestion that the ghetto poor are a cohesive cultural group or that all of the ghetto poor share a unique subculture.

Moreover, the version of the cultural divergence thesis I consider does not assert that it is a characteristic feature of poor black people in ghettos that they possess a set of debilitating cultural traits. It is now widely acknowledged among cultural analysts that there is considerable cultural diversity among the poor in these neighborhoods. It cannot be said that all or even most of the ghetto poor are in the grip of a self-defeating culture, because many can be characterized as having resisted its pull and many hold to mainstream beliefs and values.[7] Even those among the ghetto poor who do diverge from the cultural mainstream are not a culturally homogeneous group, as they often diverge in different ways and to different extents.[8]

However, one can agree that many (perhaps most) poor blacks in ghettos hold mainstream beliefs and values and yet maintain that an alarming number do not and that, moreover, this divergence from the mainstream negatively impacts their life prospects.[9] One might also worry that even though some among the ghetto poor have so far evaded the grasp of these suboptimal cultural configurations, they are especially vulnerable to succumbing to those negative influences; and perhaps all black youth residing in or near ghettos, whatever their class background, are vulnerable to being ensnared. Thus, even though, strictly speaking, not all poor black residents of ghettos are currently in need of cultural reform, they might be viewed as a "high-risk" group that cultural reformers may seek to target.

In the version of the cultural divergence thesis under consideration, some of the attitudes and practices among the ghetto poor are viewed as cultural adaptations to severely disadvantaged conditions and unjust treatment.[10] They are learned adjustments to socioeconomic hardship and social exclusion. Weak and strong versions of this claim have been defended. According to the weak version, some poor denizens of ghettos have developed ghetto-specific cultural traits but would give them up if they believed they had real opportunities to succeed in mainstream society. For such persons, these cultural traits are (more or less) consciously adopted strategic responses to a perceived lack of opportunity. For instance, William Julius Wilson notes that it might be rational to comply with ghetto norms to get by on the mean streets of urban America but that these norms are not conducive to success in the wider society.[11] He insists that if poor black men and women were provided the job training and employment options that would enable upward mobility, most would choose to abandon ghetto-specific cultural traits.

If the weak version of the cultural divergence thesis is correct, cultural reform might nonetheless seem apt. Because of mistaken but widely shared beliefs, some of the ghetto poor might not realize there are opportunities available that they aren't seizing, or they may not fully appreciate how their cultural characteristics inhibit their success. Some, while willing to abandon ghetto-specific cultural traits if provided adequate opportunities in mainstream society, may find it difficult to fully leave these traits behind without outside intervention. Cultural traits can become "second nature"—preconscious habits or implicit frames that are difficult for agents to detect in themselves or to break (speech patterns, worldviews, or bodily comportment). Even if they can shed their suboptimal cultural traits on their own, some may need help acquiring the needed mainstream traits—the relevant cultural competence—that would facilitate their upward mobility. Moreover, given current political realities, it may not be feasible to create a fairer opportunity structure or a more equitable distribution of income and wealth. Some might nevertheless be able to escape poverty if they successfully underwent cultural reform, which would enable them to take better advantage of existing opportunities.

According to the strong version, the relevant divergent cultural patterns may have started out as mere strategies for survival under hardship, but some of the ghetto poor have come to accept these traits as components of their *social identity*. Individuals have been socialized into these patterns and now maintain them, at least in part, because of their perceived intrinsic value or their association with valued communities. The cultural characteristics in question have become self-perpetuating, and in the absence of outside intervention they will likely remain even if educational and employment opportunities significantly improve, more progressive redistributive policies are enacted, and antidiscrimination laws are better enforced.

It is of course possible that, just as there are many among the ghetto poor who do not diverge significantly from the cultural mainstream, there are some from this group to whom the weak divergence thesis applies and some to whom the strong version does. If we treat the strong and weak versions of the cultural divergence thesis as claims about a significant *portion* of the ghetto poor rather than claims about the ghetto poor in general, then there is no need to view the two versions of the thesis as incompatible. Moreover, I make no claims about what percentage of the ghetto poor fall into the mainstream, weak divergence, or strong divergence categories, assuming only that a non-negligible number fall into each.

Which Cultural Traits?

There is much disagreement about which cultural configurations prevalent in ghettos are suboptimal from the standpoint of the ghetto poor's socioeconomic prospects. However, relying on the work of influential proponents of the cultural divergence thesis,[12] it is possible to draw up a list of candidates. There are cultural analysts who suggest that some among the ghetto poor have a value-orientation that is in opposition to or incompatible with many conventional measures of success or that disdains what is perceived as "white" paths to success. So, for example, some among the ghetto poor are said to lack conventional occupational ambition or to reject the American work ethic. Some cultural analysts insist that there are many among the ghetto poor who have hostility or skepticism toward formal education (though perhaps "street wisdom," autodidacticism, or folk knowledge is valued instead). There is said to be pessimism, even fatalism, about the prospects for upward mobility through mainstream channels. Some in ghetto communities are believed to devalue traditional co-parenting within a nuclear family and to eschew mainstream styles of childrearing (close monitoring of children, active school involvement, provision of nutritious meals, intolerance for misbehavior, and consistent enforcement of parental directives). Many of the ghetto poor are thought to distrust established authority, particularly officials of the criminal justice system but also clergy and educators; and this attitude is often accompanied by a belief that such authority is corrupt and thus unworthy of respect. The ghetto poor, particularly poor black youth, are sometimes portrayed as regarding the use of vulgar language (such as "nigger" and "bitch") and street vernacular as appropriate in contexts where such modes of expression are widely viewed as crude, uncivil, or offensive.

In terms of what is accepted and sometimes valued, many among the ghetto poor are said to have a hedonistic orientation toward intense and immediate pleasure—pursuing frequent casual sex, gambling, drinking, fighting, recreational drug use, and so on—joined with a refusal to delay such gratification and a high tolerance for risk. Some parents are said to rely on harsh and arbitrary punishments or to tolerate delinquency. Many, especially black boys and young men, are thought to regard promiscuity and sexual infidelity as morally acceptable, and they attach little or no stigma to teenage pregnancy, nonmarital childbearing, paternal desertion, or single-mother households. Some are believed to be highly invested in regularly experiencing long stretches of idleness with no planned or organized activities (chillin'). Many are said to be oriented toward crude materialism and a preoccupation with clothing style, often seeking personal prestige through the conspicuous consumption of luxury items and high-status brands. Street crime and interpersonal aggression are tolerated and sometimes embraced, including a readiness to use deception, manipulation, and even violence to achieve one's aims.

Not all of the values allegedly suboptimal for the ghetto poor contrast sharply with the mainstream. The relevant cultural divergence might be a matter not of the values themselves but the way they are held (tenaciously or weakly, for instance), the priority they are given in practice, the way they are interpreted, or the context within which they tend to be expressed and acted on. For example, patriarchal conceptions of masculinity, anti-intellectualism, and materialism are widespread in American society, cutting across lines of race, class, and place. But some among the ghetto poor are believed to enact these values and norms in extreme ways, to give these values and norms much greater precedence in their lives than the average American, to interpret them in nonstandard ways, or to invoke them in inappropriate contexts. In such cases, the divergence from the mainstream is a matter not of the content of the values and norms but of the manner in which they are adopted and understood and their role in practical deliberation.

Recall that according to the weak version of the cultural divergence thesis, these cultural traits are components of a repertoire or part of a conceptual frame that agents strategically deploy to advance specific purposes in particular contexts. On the strong version, the traits in question represent more fundamental commitments and may form part of the agent's social identity. Focusing on the latter, we can regard a person's ghetto-oriented and suboptimal beliefs, values, and practices as constituting a *ghetto identity* if (a) they figure prominently in the person's positive self-concept; (b) they are relatively stable across different social contexts (that is, there is little or no situational frame switching); and (c) the agent is resistant to changing them as a matter of principle. Thus, on the strong view, even given a chance to attend (or send their children to) a good school, to obtain a well-paid nonmenial job, or to move to a low-poverty neighborhood, many ghetto residents would still cling to their ghetto identities.

Some cultural practices prominent in American ghettos—for example, music, visual art, dance, humor, creative linguistic practices, and clothing and hairstyles—have symbolic and expressive dimensions that cannot be reduced to or explained by ghetto poverty.[13] These expressive and aesthetic traits draw on and extend black cultural traditions that can be traced back for generations prior to the formation of the modern ghetto, and blacks who have never lived in a ghetto or even been poor value and participate in them, along with many who are neither black nor poor. In addition, some dimensions of cultural life in ghettos, while perhaps in some sense being a collective response to ghetto conditions, have political meaning or intent and so are not simply a matter of coping with, adapting to, or surviving the conditions of poverty. Some hip hop music, for instance, offers social critiques of ghetto conditions and expresses a spirit of resistance to the structures and dynamics that reproduce these horrendous circumstances (see Chapter 9).[14] Those who advance the cultural divergence thesis need not deny that the cultural traits possessed by ghetto denizens include such expressive, aesthetic, or political elements, but some may regard these elements as suboptimal insofar as they inhibit upward mobility among the black poor or spatial mobility out of ghettos. Consequently, some cultural reformers may seek to limit their influence on the ghetto poor, particularly on black children.

Sophisticated proponents of the cultural divergence thesis are careful not to equate "ghetto identity" with "black identity." To be sure, it is said that poor urban blacks developed and value these cultural traits and that the relevant traits draw on, or have an affinity with, familiar black traditions and folkways. Nevertheless, it is sometimes claimed that those who have a ghetto identity define themselves, not only in opposition to mainstream American institutions and culture, but also often in opposition to self-concepts associated with blacks who are successful by conventional measures or who attained their success through mainstream avenues. Insofar as a ghetto identity is regarded as "black," it should be thought of as a mode of blackness that many who identify as black reject or distance themselves from. Within black vernacular, blacks readily distinguish between "ghetto blacks," "working-class blacks," and "bourgie blacks," and these designations (which are sometimes used as epithets) are meant to track race, class, place, *and* culture.[15] Moreover, many black Americans who think of themselves as having a strong black cultural identity accept the cultural divergence thesis. For instance, in a recent Pew Forum survey, in response to the question "Have the values of middle-class and poor blacks become more similar or more different?," 61 percent of blacks answered "more different."[16] Indeed, many middle-class blacks actively participate in cultural reform efforts as part of a program of racial uplift.[17]

Cultural Reform

Confronted with compelling evidence in support of the cultural divergence hypothesis, some might acknowledge that cultural change in ghetto neighborhoods is needed but recoil from the idea that *government* should play an active role in bringing about such changes—apart from making necessary changes to those aspects of the basic structure that negatively affect the lives of the urban poor. The approach I examine would be less hesitant to get the government involved in effecting cultural changes in the lives of the ghetto poor. Indeed, it might be thought that such state intervention is essential if ghetto poverty and its associated ills are to be adequately addressed.

Cultural reform should be distinguished from mere behavior modification. The state might try to change the behavior of the ghetto poor without attempting to change their cultural configurations, regarding any cultural changes that do occur as unintended by-products of intended behavioral changes. For instance, the state might use incentives or penalties to induce behavior thought to be more conducive to upward mobility. If nonmarital childbearing or refusing to work is believed to contribute to poverty, then the government might step in to penalize such behavior with the hope that poor people will choose to work and get married if they want to have children (see Part II for discussion of such policies). This would be behavior modification, not cultural reform. With behavior modification, there need not be a presumption that the undesirable behavior is part of a learned cultural pattern or social identity. The behavior may simply be, for instance, the result of individual (rational or irrational) decision making or habit. If there is a discernible pattern of such behavior in a group, this may simply reflect similar decision making or common errors in practical reasoning among those in the group.

By contrast, cultural reform is premised on the assumption that the relevant behavioral changes will only occur, or are more likely to occur, or will be more durable if some cultural patterns in poor black communities are modified. Here there is a presumption that the suboptimal behavior in question is shaped or influenced by a set of cultural configurations. Thus, the cultural reformer would harness the power and resources of the state (perhaps in conjunction with private firms and nonprofit organizations) to bring about the desired cultural changes.

There are at least three types of cultural changes that might be sought, and each type has different normative implications. The first and least radical would be *cultural augmentation*. Here the cultural reformer seeks to add to the cultural repertoire of the ghetto poor without attempting to remove or alter any of their existing cultural traits. The idea would be to equip poor blacks with some mainstream cultural tools (sometimes called "cultural capital"), which they could then choose when and whether to use and to what ends. Their prior cultural attachments, whatever they happen to be, would not then be threatened. The second and more radical change is *cultural removal*. This would involve eliminating or neutralizing any existing cultural traits believed to be suboptimal. This type of intervention would not, however, involve instilling new mainstream cultural traits. Cultural removal would work best if, as some cultural analysts insist, most among the ghetto poor already embrace mainstream cultural values and norms. Simply removing or defusing any suboptimal traits might then be sufficient to put them on a path out of poverty or the ghetto. The most radical approach to cultural reform would be *cultural rehabilitation*. It would combine cultural augmentation with cultural removal—getting rid of existing suboptimal traits and replacing them with mainstream cultural traits.

Which types of cultural traits are targets for cultural reform? The particular traits identified for augmentation or removal will affect how controversial and potentially problematic the mode of cultural reform would be. Attempts to change shared *beliefs* among the ghetto poor would be the least controversial, provided the beliefs in question pertain to matters of fact (rather than to what is desirable or valuable) and provided the beliefs are not religious convictions. For example, if some among the ghetto poor share the belief that formal education will not improve their life prospects or that there are no decent jobs available to them, and if this belief is factually incorrect, then a cultural reformer might try to change this erroneous perception or prevent its spread.

The cultural reformer might also attempt to change the *skill set* of those targeted for reform. Some cultural analysts maintain that the cultural repertoire of poor blacks includes social skills for operating in ghettos. But these ghetto-specific skills may not be helpful in the wider world and, deployed in a mainstream context, may hurt one's chances of success. Effectively navigating the mainstream social world so as to improve one's socioeconomic situation also involves the deft deployment of cultural skills. Insofar as the ghetto poor lack these skills, the cultural reformer might seek to impart them. This type of cultural augmentation is unobjectionable, at least in principle. Once these skills are acquired, the agents can decide whether to make use of this practical know-how and for what purposes, and they can continue to rely on their ghetto-specific know-how if they so choose.

Cultural deskilling would be another matter. A person can lose an acquired skill if he or she does not use it enough. Either the ability degrades over time or one forgets how to deploy it properly. So deskilling may be possible if the ghetto poor were deprived of opportunities to use their ghetto-specific skill set or were prevented from drawing on it. Unless the ghetto poor voluntarily went along with this, such a practice, given the constraints it would impose on them, would raise serious questions about the legitimacy of the state's interference with their liberty.

Some customs—shaking hands, saying "thank you," making eye contact, smiling, enunciating words—become *habits*. The cultural reformer may therefore seek to change some cultural habits, either by instilling new habits or breaking old ones. Many customs are preconscious or second nature and are performed almost involuntarily. Given how difficult it is to control or break a habit once it has formed, the cultural reform of habits could prove morally problematic.

Even more controversial would be attempts to change the *values* or *cultural identities* of the ghetto poor. Getting into this sensitive terrain might, however, seem unavoidable. Some of the relevant cultural traits that appear to be suboptimal (if not destructive)—again, from the standpoint of escaping poverty—do not concern factual beliefs, cultural skills, or customary practices. They have to do with ideals and values, with what *ends* are desirable and worthwhile. What constitutes a "good" job? What constitutes "success" in life? What does it mean to be a "responsible" parent or to maintain a "healthy" family? Is it wrong to smoke marijuana or take heroin? Do police officers and the laws they enforce "deserve" our respect? These and similar questions turn on matters of value. They are normative questions. It is difficult to see how cultural reform could be successful and yet avoid such questions entirely.

Once we know what kind of cultural change is sought and which types of cultural traits are targeted for change, we still need to know which age groups should be targeted. Preadolescent children are the most malleable, so they might seem like the best candidates. Even teenagers in early adolescence (ages ten to fifteen) may seem promising, if more challenging. Provided their parents are adequately informed about and consent to the programs, such initiatives are permissible, even if cultural reform takes the form of cultural rehabilitation. Though parental authority can be overridden where there is child abuse, endangerment, or neglect, within these parameters family autonomy should be respected. If a parent wants to enroll his or her child into a program or school that engages in cultural reform, this would not be any worse than when parents send their kids to a religious or boarding school.

Things get more complicated with late adolescents (ages sixteen to seventeen) and young adults (ages eighteen to twenty-five). Given their cognitive, emotional, and moral development and the imperative to teach them to run their own lives, late adolescents, though not adults, are properly allowed autonomy over significant domains of their lives.[18] They are also expected to take full responsibility for many outcomes of their choices, even when these choices could adversely affect their long-term life prospects. This is widely acknowledged, even by the U.S.

government, as late adolescents are permitted to drop out of school, to accept employment, and to operate motor vehicles, and are sometimes subject to criminal prosecution as adults. Young adults (assuming no serious mental illness or severe cognitive disabilities) are rightly treated as fully competent to govern their own lives, with all the rights and responsibilities this entails.[19] Thus, cultural reform directed at late adolescents and young adults is potentially more problematic than reform directed at young children. I leave aside older adults, as they are unlikely to be viewed as good candidates for cultural reform.

Before offering a more in-depth treatment of the practicality and moral permissibility of cultural reform, I outline the particular methods the state might use or sponsor to bring about the relevant changes. The cultural augmentation of factual beliefs through the provision of information or rational persuasion is the most benign. Few would object to this, provided it is based on sound scientific research and is devoid of deception and manipulation. Attempting to eliminate the false factual beliefs of the ghetto poor through information or reasoned argument isn't problematic either.

Things get more complicated with instruction and training programs. Teaching involves the provision of information and dissemination of knowledge but generally goes well beyond this. It can entail skills training, inculcating desirable habits (or breaking undesirable ones), instilling values, and shaping identities. The relevant skills, habits, and values can perhaps sometimes be imparted through lectures, discussion, and distributing information. But sometimes a more directive and supervisory approach, with monitoring for rule compliance and mechanisms of accountability, is the only effective method.

Counseling could also be used as a cultural reform technique. Such counseling might be no more than advice and encouragement, and so almost as benign as the provision of information or the intervention of a friend. But the counseling could take a more explicitly therapeutic form, in which the client is expected to submit to the direction of the counselor. The counseling could also be faith-based, in which nonrational means of persuasion (such as the exploitation of guilt or intimations of divine disapproval and sanctions) are sometimes used. Would therapeutic or spiritual counseling be problematic as a technique of cultural reform? Much will depend on the power relationship between the counselor and the client and, in particular, on whether the client has a choice in whether to seek the type of counseling in question and on whether the client has the option to break off the counseling relationship without repercussions. If poor blacks seek counseling because they believe they have suboptimal cultural traits and think counseling would help to change these, then there is little reason to object to the practice.

Of course, if information and reasoned argument, voluntary educational and training programs, and voluntary counseling services were all that were needed to bring about the relevant cultural changes, cultural reform would not raise such difficult moral questions. One might think that a more aggressive and intrusive approach may appear necessary, however. Those selected for cultural reform may not see the need for change even after having been informed of the relevant facts. The cultural traits targeted for change may be recalcitrant, and the individuals singled out for cultural change may not be disposed to participate in the relevant programs. Even those who do choose to participate may not continue with them long enough or may not fully cooperate with those running the programs. This naturally raises the issue of the permissibility of incentives and sanctions.

Incentives, particularly financial ones, may seem benign. However, when they are conditionally offered to the poor, especially to those severely disadvantaged, they can be morally troubling. When one is socioeconomically disadvantaged and in need of basic resources, it can be very difficult to turn down a financial offer, especially if one has dependents in need of things you cannot otherwise provide. Thus, many among the ghetto poor might participate in cultural reform programs (say, at the behest of their case workers), not because they see their value and just need a little encouragement, but because they desperately need socioeconomic resources. Depending on their alternatives, they may be effectively compelled to submit to cultural reform even if they regard it as degrading or insulting. So we must be careful when describing cultural reform programs as "voluntary," as some may constrain freedom in objectionable ways without being strictly coercive.

The imposition of penalties raises the most serious worries. Not only might the ghetto poor object that they are being forced to submit to a demeaning cultural reform process, but they might also object to any suffering, deprivation, indignities, or loss of liberty such penalties would involve. Pointing out that these punitive measures are imposed for their own good won't be an adequate response to these complaints. Some more compelling justification must be offered.

Moral Reform

Having outlined various types of cultural reform, let me focus on the normative and practical implications of one type, which I designate *moral reform*. Moral reform goes beyond correcting mistaken beliefs or expanding the cultural repertoire of the ghetto poor. It is a form of cultural rehabilitation that targets not only beliefs and skills but habits, values, and identities. The social policy goals of moral reform are to break or limit adherence to suboptimal cultural traits and to instill or strengthen attachment to mainstream cultural traits.

The relevant mainstream cultural traits include a commitment to hard work, thrift, economic self-sufficiency, delayed gratification, academic achievement, civility, respect for authority, moderation in drink and play, reverence for the institution of marriage and the nuclear family, and responsible reproduction and good parenting. Though moral reform is sometimes directed toward young children, I focus on moral reform directed at late adolescents and young adults (often designated as "youth"), as this raises the most difficult issues of political morality.

Moral reform might be carried out directly by government agencies or accomplished through publicly funded but privately operated and community-based organizations. The kinds of policies, programs, and techniques I have in mind include the following.[20] Moral reform could involve making work or job training a condition for receiving public aid with a view toward instilling an appropriate work ethic, labor-force attachment, and the value of economic self-sufficiency.[21] Such a program could include empowering social workers with the authority to regulate the lives of those who rely on public assistance. For example, social workers might threaten to withhold, reduce, or cancel benefits for those who refuse to adhere to work requirements. The government could criminalize "vices" (drug use, gambling, panhandling, loitering, and prostitution) associated with a suboptimal ghetto lifestyle or make the abandonment of such practices a condition for housing assistance or other aid. There could be programs that exhort and counsel the ghetto poor to make more responsible choices (about reproduction, marriage, parenting, and so on). Moral reform could involve, as some new integrationists advocate, moving poor black people out of ghettos to low-poverty (white) neighborhoods with the expectation that they will come to absorb values and norms of conduct prevalent in these more advantaged communities. The ghetto poor could be given middle-class mentors and role models so that they might come to assimilate mainstream norms and develop cultural capital. The state might enable greater involvement of faith-based institutions or clergy in the lives of the ghetto poor with the expectation that certain religious beliefs and values might take (stronger) root.[22]

One important thing to keep in mind about such programs and policies is that even when they take the form of incentives and sanctions, the point of moral reform is not simply to modify behavior but *to restructure the soul*—to change fundamentally the values, character, and identity of those in the grip of what are regarded as debilitating cultural patterns. To use an expression coined, in another context, by Kwame Anthony Appiah, moral reform would be a type of "soul making" that a state might engage in to help citizens lead more successful lives.[23] The idea behind moral reform is that once the reform is complete, after the programs are over and the incentives and sanctions are no longer being applied, those who have undergone the reform process will now *govern themselves* in accordance with mainstream norms without further special interventions. To use the language of the medical model: cultural reform is an antidote or treatment for the cultural ailments that afflict the ghetto poor.

"Liberal" Moral Reform?

Social conservatives who advocate moral reform tend to view it (sometimes along with private charity) as the *sole* remedy for ghetto poverty, because they generally regard the basic structure of U.S. society as just and thus not in need of fundamental reform (at least not in an egalitarian direction). Libertarians would presumably not accept moral reform as a legitimate aim of government, at least when dealing with adults. They do not regard the state as having the authority to interfere with the personal choices of adult citizens. Indeed, they generally believe it is impermissible for government to take paternalistic actions and that the state's authority is limited to protecting basic rights. On their view, citizens should be free to have a bad character and to embrace self-destructive cultural traits, provided in acting on these dispositions they do not violate the rights of others. Moreover, libertarians generally do not believe that the state should institute redistributive schemes to reduce inequality or social welfare measures to alleviate poverty, at least not using public funds extracted through taxation.

But can liberals consistently support moral reform? A liberal who supported moral reform would presumably view such measures as only *part* of the solution to ghetto poverty. State-sponsored moral reform would have to be joined with policy efforts to make the opportunity structure fairer and the distribution of resources more equitable. Liberals who accept the suboptimal cultural divergence thesis typically regard the relevant cultural traits as a *response* (perhaps not fully conscious or deliberate) to unjust structural conditions. These injustices include pervasive racial discrimination (for example, in employment, housing, lending, and law enforcement) perhaps rising to the level of institutional racism; diminished life prospects due to unfair economic and educational disadvantages; inadequate public services; and the fact that the social safety net is not large enough and has too many holes to catch all those who fall because of economic restructuring, recessions, and unexpected shifts in the labor market.

I won't discuss directly conservative or libertarian perspectives on moral reform in ghettos, though some of what I say has implications for these views. While liberals obviously disagree about the extent of its unfairness, they generally concur that the structure of U.S. society is unfair. Liberals also tend to think that government should do something proactive about poverty, instituting feasible antipoverty measures as necessary. Some might therefore be tempted to accept (or, indeed, may wholeheartedly endorse) moral reform as part of a liberal solution to the problem of ghetto poverty. And yet liberal moral reform is neither wise nor morally coherent, because it does not give proper weight to the importance of "self-respect."

Self-Respect and Injustice

Self-respect is a value open to a variety of interpretations. Rawls emphasizes the importance of ensuring that citizens have an opportunity to develop and maintain a sense of self-respect.[24] Instead of using the term "self-respect" to refer to what Rawls has in mind, I use "self-esteem" (a term Rawls uses as a synonym). Following others, I distinguish this value from a different though related one that we might also want to call "self-respect."[25]

Self-esteem has two aspects: (1) a secure conviction that one's fundamental purposes are worthwhile and (2) confidence in one's ability to realize these purposes. So, self-esteem is a kind of self-confidence—confidence in the value of one's basic ambitions and confidence in one's ability to realize these aims. Or put another way, self-esteem is a combination of self-worth and self-efficacy. We have a healthy sense of self-esteem when we regard our fundamental ends as valuable and consider ourselves competent to secure these ends. We have a diminished or damaged sense of self-esteem when we think our plans in life lack substantive value or we are plagued by self-doubt.

In any pluralist society, where by definition there is deep disagreement about fundamental values, citizens often adhere to conflicting conceptions of the good life. But a *primary good*, again following Rawls, is something that all rational persons can be expected to want regardless of their fundamental purposes, as such goods are generally useful (and often necessary) for achieving our various aims. Such goods include liberty, leisure, health, education, income, and wealth. Self-esteem is a primary good because in its absence none of our practical aims will seem worthwhile or we won't attempt to achieve those things we regard as valuable. Apathy, depression, and despair may take over. Moreover, one generally feels shame when one experiences an injury to one's self-esteem. This shame is a response to one's failure to exhibit the personal qualities and achievements one regards as most worthwhile.

Rawls views self-esteem as a *natural* primary good (rather than a social one), because society, and in particular the state, has no mechanism for distributing self-esteem directly.[26] There are, however, *social bases* of self-esteem that a basic structure can support (or undermine). One's sense of self-worth (the first component of self-esteem) is socially supported when those one admires appreciate and affirm one's values and achievements. We will usually develop and maintain a sense of self-worth provided we belong to at least one association or community within which our activities are publicly affirmed. These associative or communal ties also strengthen self-efficacy (the second component of self-esteem), for they reduce the likelihood of failure and provide collective defense against self-doubt when failure does occur.

Rawls is no doubt correct when he suggests that in a just democratic society, we should expect a diverse array of informal communities and formal associations, within which members will develop ideals that cohere with their aspirations and talents. In keeping with my focus on nonideal theory, the question I address is, What should we expect in an *unjust* society? In an unjust society, there may also be a variety of communities and associations with their own ideals, and these forms of group affiliation may also develop among those who are severely disadvantaged. Moreover, the cultural traits that characterize some of these communities and associations may have been cultivated in response to, or otherwise shaped by, the unjust institutional arrangements. These affiliations may nevertheless perform essentially the same social function—namely, sustaining and enhancing self-esteem—as their counterparts under just arrangements.

Let's distinguish *self-respect* from self-esteem. Self-respect can be an element of a person's sense of self-worth. But unlike self-esteem, the role it plays in constituting self-worth is not contingent on a person's particular ambitions or self-confidence. Self-respect is a matter of recognizing oneself as a rational agent and a moral equal and valuing oneself accordingly.[27] Self-respect is embodied and expressed in the way one conducts oneself. Those with self-respect live their lives in a way that conveys their conviction that they are proper objects of respect. For example, they resist the efforts of others to mistreat them and openly resent unfair treatment. Moreover, persons with self-respect do not believe that they must *earn* just treatment—through, say, some display of virtue or personal achievement. They know that their capacity for rational and moral agency alone is sufficient to justify their claim not to be treated unjustly.[28]

When a healthy sense of self-respect is widespread in a society, this helps to sustain just practices and to deter injustice. And where there is systemic injustice, the self-respect of society's members often moves them to reform their institutions. Those with a robust sense of justice should therefore be concerned to maintain and foster self-respect in themselves *and* others. However, self-respect has value quite apart from its contribution to maintaining or establishing a just society. Its value should not be reduced to how it promotes social welfare. Moral agents are permitted to preserve, affirm, and strengthen their self-respect even when doing so would not ameliorate unjust conditions, would not lighten their material burdens, or would be personally costly or risky. As the philosophers Thomas Hill and Bernard Boxill have argued, the person who lacks self-respect fails to have the right attitude about his or her moral status.[29] By putting up with injustice without complaint or protest, such persons do not give moral requirements the regard they merit.

This Kantian conception of self-respect focuses on the need to show respect for moral duties. But those most burdened by injustice have additional reasons to preserve and express their self-respect. Maintaining one's self-respect in the face of injustice is not simply about respecting the authority of morality. The sense of personal investment in such respect would be inexplicable if self-respect were merely about respecting moral principles. Self-respect has value from a *personal* point of view and not only from an impartial vantage point.[30] A life lived without a healthy sense of self-respect, particularly for one who is oppressed, is an impoverished life for the particular person whose life it is.

Oppression can erode a person's sense of self-respect, causing one to doubt one's claim to equal moral status. We can understand an *attack* on one's self-respect as an action, policy, or practice that threatens to make one feel that one is morally inferior, that one does not deserve the same treatment as others. To maintain a healthy sense of self-respect under conditions of injustice, the oppressed may therefore fight back against their oppressors, demanding the justice they know they deserve, even when the available evidence suggests that justice is not on the horizon. They thereby affirm their moral worth and equal status.

Agents who take action to affirm their moral standing often take pride in such actions, particularly when these acts entail some personal risks or costs. When one is subject to persistent injustice and yet successfully defends one's self-respect, this is a moral achievement. A robust disposition to resist attacks on one's self-respect can therefore be a source of self-esteem. Such self-valuing is what we might call *moral pride*. Conversely, willful submission to injustice can be a blameworthy failure that generates *moral shame* in the subject. We surrender or sacrifice our self-respect when we acquiesce to mistreatment or when we suffer such indignities in silence.

Persons with a strong sense of self-respect sometimes refuse to cooperate with the demands of an unjust society. They stand up for themselves, are defiant in the face of illegitimate authority, refuse to comply with unjust social requirements, protest maltreatment and humiliation, and so on, even when they know such actions will not bring about justice or reduce their suffering. Self-respect, then, can be a matter of living with a sense of moral pride *despite* unjust conditions.

Though self-respect has intrinsic value and great moral importance, it should not be regarded as a trump in moral deliberation. Moral agents need not and should not defend their self-respect at all cost. It is sometimes justifiable (or at least excusable) to sacrifice a bit of self-respect to protect others from harm, to avoid grave harm to oneself, or to achieve some worthy goal. Such sacrifices are sometimes necessary, all things considered. However, the agent with a healthy sense of self-respect experiences them *as sacrifices*—as the painful loss of an intrinsically valuable good. When you no longer care that others are wronging you, putting up no resistance, or when you routinely trade fair treatment for mere material gain or social status, you have lost all self-respect. The duty of self-respect, like the duty of justice, is thus a central element in the political ethics of the oppressed.

With these remarks as background, I can now state my principal objection to moral reform: even if the suboptimal cultural divergence hypothesis is basically sound, moral reform attacks the ghetto poor's social bases of self-esteem and fails to honor their need to preserve their self-respect. These two consequences create serious practical limitations and moral pitfalls, and they suggest that moral reform is afflicted with the downgraded-agency problem characteristic of the medical model of social reform. Moral reform is furthermore incompatible with respect for personal autonomy—that is, with respect for an agent's legitimate claim to govern his or her own life as that agent judges fit. In the remainder of this chapter, I elaborate these concerns and then suggest an alternative approach that I believe avoids these difficulties, is more in line with core liberal values, and is more likely to be effective in achieving the needed cultural and structural reforms.

Practical Limits of Moral Outreach

As outlined earlier, the methods of moral reform vary greatly. One class of methods, *moral outreach*, relies on dialogue, lectures, sermons, education, training, and counseling. The idea is to effect a change in cultural patterns through, for example, moral exhortation, role models, counseling services, education programs, or faith-based efforts. Many of these interventions are no more than attempts to convince some among the ghetto poor that their cultural ways are obstacles to their escape from poverty. Other interventions might seek to make some residents of ghettos ashamed of their suboptimal mores by, for example, subjecting them to public censure or withdrawing esteem. Or measures might be taken to encourage them to take pride in exemplifying mainstream values and identities, perhaps supplemented with attempts to get targets of moral reform to identify less with suboptimal ghetto cultural configurations and more with the successful habits and values of middle-class persons.

The main challenge for moral outreach is getting its targets to listen to appeals and to take advantage of relevant programs. Moral outreach would seem to have the best chance of success with those for whom the weak version of the cultural divergence thesis applies—those who strategically employ a ghetto-specific cultural repertoire only because of their belief that they lack adequate opportunities for socioeconomic advancement. Willing cooperation with moral reform programs might be forthcoming among those who became convinced that the existing opportunity structure is actually such that they could escape poverty were they to assimilate to more mainstream cultural ways. There might also be some willing cooperation if those targeted for moral outreach were looking for *any* chance at escape from poverty, even if, for example, they knew that the opportunity structure is seriously unjust and that most among the ghetto poor, no matter what reasonable efforts they made, would therefore remain in poverty. They would only have to be convinced that there are more exits from ghetto poverty than there are people actively trying to leave and that, with the appropriate cultural changes, they could be among the lucky few.

But what if there are many who have suboptimal ghetto identities (those for whom the strong version of the cultural divergence thesis applies) *and* the basic structure is unfairly stacked against them? Here it seems that moral outreach would have limited success. After all, our conception of the good determines what we feel ashamed of and take pride in. That is to say, shame and pride are relative to our fundamental goals and to the communities with which we identify. If targets for moral reform reject mainstream values and embrace ghetto identities, as the strong version of the cultural divergence thesis asserts, they will not be readily shamed into conforming to mainstream norms; nor should we expect them to take pride in embodying mainstream virtues. They will have developed alternative sources of self-worth that do not depend on mainstream institutions for validation.

A similar point can be made about self-efficacy. Some among the ghetto poor may be confident that they would succeed, even by mainstream standards, *if the basic structure they faced were fairer.* Because they believe their efforts to meet mainstream standards of success are likely to be thwarted by a deeply unjust social structure, these persons may develop alternative ambitions.[31] Where people blame the unfairness of the basic structure for their inability to achieve their aims, they need not experience low self-esteem. And we have even less reason to suspect diminished self-esteem in those cases where, in response to their belief that their society is unjust, people develop basic aims that they believe to be worthwhile and within reach.[32]

Indeed, the more that perceived "outsiders," official agents of the state in particular, attack ghetto identities, the more we should expect those who subscribe to these identities to hold firmly to them. By hypothesis, there are distinctive forms of affiliation in ghetto neighborhoods that are central bases for the positive sense of self-worth of many among the ghetto poor. Those with such ghetto identities will therefore demand a compelling reason to change their conception of the good. In the absence of a reasonably just opportunity structure, garnering the esteem of their more advantaged fellows is unlikely to be reason enough.

Recall that the focus of this chapter is on state-operated or state-supported moral reform. In response to the alleged debilitating effects of some ghetto cultural patterns, there are some who propose not government intervention but moral outreach by black elites, a kind of group uplift or self-help.[33] Though such moral appeals may not be inherently objectionable, the strong version of the cultural divergence thesis suggests that this outreach would be rather limited in its effectiveness. In many ways black elites are representatives of the mainstream. They exemplify its values and practices and, accordingly, have been rewarded with valuable social positions and public esteem. Insofar as the ghetto poor are alienated from mainstream values, they are likely to look upon black elites with similar suspicion. This is all the more likely if, as I have argued elsewhere, many among the ghetto poor believe that black elites' moral exhortations are motivated less by genuine empathy and group solidarity and more by elites' feeling embarrassed in the eyes of their white peers by the unruly behavior of poor urban blacks or by their fear that they might be mistaken for a person with a ghetto identity.[34]

Racism and Cultural Explanations of Black Poverty

There is a second practical limitation to moral outreach, namely, the persistence of ideological racism. Some of the cultural traits attributed to or associated with the ghetto poor (for example, attitudes toward authority, work, violence, parenting, sex and reproduction, school, and crime) closely resemble well-known and long-standing racist stereotypes about blacks (their supposed tendencies toward lawlessness, laziness, dishonesty, irresponsibility, ignorance, stupidity, and sexual promiscuity). These stereotypes have long been invoked to justify the subordination, exploitation, and civic exclusion of blacks. An implication of the cultural divergence thesis is that ghetto conditions have produced a subgroup of blacks who, because of their cultural patterns, exhibit characteristics that racists have long maintained are "natural" to "the black race" and that these cultural traits are at least part of the explanation for why they are poor. I suspect that this implication is part of the reason many people are suspicious of (and sometimes hostile to) cultural analyses of black urban poverty—they smell like rationalizations for the racial status quo. And the odor is not made better by the fact that these analyses are rooted in social-scientific research rather than biological studies, as the social sciences have been a rich source of antiblack ideology.[35] To make matters worse, moral reform suggests that the ghetto poor are effectively incapable of altering these suboptimal traits on their own, as it calls for state intervention to change them. Moral reform programs, even voluntary ones, implicitly endorse the idea that poor blacks have personal deficiencies that they alone cannot remedy. In an era when biological racism has been largely discredited and claims that blacks are biologically inferior are not publically acceptable, moral reform will inevitably strike many as the functional equivalent of classic racist doctrines.[36]

Perhaps such a response to moral reform wouldn't be entirely fair. After all, there may be truth in the cultural divergence thesis. And yet, many among the ghetto poor have reason to believe that some of their fellow citizens are attracted to cultural explanations of black poverty because of racial prejudice and bias. The types of claims made about the black poor, whatever their merit, are often perceived as emanating not from genuine empathy but from racial hostility, a sense of white superiority, or indifference to the plight of disadvantaged blacks. In light of this, some poor ghetto denizens may distrust efforts to change the cultural patterns in their neighborhoods. Their suspicion would be well grounded, for some who advocate moral reform no doubt do so because of race-based contempt or a desire to maintain the racial status quo.[37] On grounds of self-respect, then, the oppressed may refuse to avoid "confirming" the stereotypes that are often used to justify their subjugation. In the absence of serious structural reform, the suggestion that the ghetto poor do not value hard work and education or that they are criminals and irresponsible parents will strike some among the ghetto poor as yet another racist excuse for not improving social conditions in ghetto neighborhoods.

The point here is not philosophical but practical: namely, *if* some among the ghetto poor possess ghetto identities, as the strong version of the cultural divergence thesis supposes, then these persons are likely to dismiss outright or strongly resist attempts by representatives of the "mainstream" to undermine or alter those identities. Moral reform efforts targeted at those with ghetto identities, particularly when those efforts depend on voluntary cooperation, will therefore be self-defeating.

Moral Paternalism and Compromises with Injustice

Recognizing the practical limits of moral outreach, moral reformers may give up on this strategy or supplement it with more aggressive measures. They may advocate cultural rehabilitation through a system of rewards and sanctions. This strategy would not depend on the willing cooperation of the intended beneficiaries. The moral reformers would attempt to arrange society's incentive structure to produce a deep cultural transformation in their subjects. Their subjects, however, may not (fully) realize what their benefactors are attempting to accomplish, or may not willingly go along, or may not desire the change in themselves that the reformers want to effect. In this approach, moral reformers work *on*, not *with*, the ghetto poor. Their methods are intended to be effective despite resistance from the black urban poor. Call this mode of moral reform *moral paternalism*.

Many liberals find the idea of moral paternalism distasteful, and in a more just world they would eschew it. But faced with current political realities and in light of their abiding concern to help the poor and disadvantaged, some may be tempted to advocate moral paternalism. For example, sympathetic liberals could argue that they do not urge moral reform because they believe the criticisms typically leveled at the ghetto poor are entirely fair or generally spring from nonracist motives. They might simply insist that cultural traits that seem to confirm black stereotypes make it harder to generate among the general public the goodwill that is needed to change the structural conditions that create and perpetuate ghettos. These liberals may lament the fact that too many Americans regard the ghetto poor as "undeserving" and that, on this ground, these citizens are unwilling to invest the necessary public resources to eliminate urban poverty. However, without the support of at least some of these people, liberal structural reform is not feasible, and so the black poor would continue to suffer needlessly. In response to this political reality, some liberals may be prepared to attach stiff penalties to even minor legal infractions (littering, loitering, black market activity, and such), to impose work requirements on welfare recipients with young children, to aggressively monitor and supervise the behavior of ghetto denizens, and so on, because without successful moral reform of the black urban poor, structural reform efforts won't be efficacious.

I have serious doubts about the soundness of the social-theoretic assumptions behind any such strategy, in particular about whether reducing stereotypical behavior and attitudes will garner the desired public goodwill. But leaving this aside, this "liberal pragmatism" threatens the self-respect of the ghetto poor. If, as some cultural analysts maintain, the suboptimal cultural traits of the ghetto poor are a response to systemic injustice, then it is not reasonable to expect the urban poor to submit to moral reform to "prove" their worthiness for government interventions to improve structural conditions. Capitulating to the widely held and insulting view that they do not "deserve" better life chances is fundamentally at odds with the ghetto poor maintaining their self-respect. Fair treatment and a just basic structure are things they are entitled to in virtue of their status as moral equals and rational agents and cannot be justly withheld on account of their (alleged) suboptimal identities or values. The ghetto poor have legitimate justice claims against their government that are not negated by what they do in response to that government's historical and ongoing failure to honor these claims. As equal citizens taking part in a system of social cooperation, each acquires legitimate claims on fellow participants as defined by just rules of political association; and we should not regard what a citizen is entitled to by justice as proportional to, nor dependent upon, the quality of his or her moral character.[38]

I may seem to have left myself open to the following rejoinder: Sometimes advancing the broader cause of justice means compromising with particular injustices. Sacrifices of self-respect are unpleasant, even painful, for those who must make them, but they are sometimes necessary in the short term to make progress in the long run. Threatening the self-respect of the current generation of the ghetto poor may simply be the price of the social reform needed to ensure that future generations do not grow up in ghetto conditions.

I do not deny that sacrifices of self-respect can be justified. It may be perfectly reasonable for one to endure indignities to protect the vulnerable, to preserve one's life, or even to advance the cause of justice. What I'm opposing is the idea that others are permitted to decide when you should make such sacrifices. It is one thing to ask or even implore the ghetto poor to sacrifice some self-respect to achieve needed social reforms. It is quite another to demand that they make these sacrifices on pain of penalty or to take measures that effectively force them to accommodate themselves to injustice. Moral paternalism robs the ghetto poor of a choice that should be theirs alone—namely, whether the improved prospects for ending or ameliorating ghetto poverty are worth the loss of moral pride they would incur by conceding the offensive view that they have not shown themselves to be deserving of better treatment. Whether such sacrifices of self-respect are, all things considered, worth it should be left to those who bear the heaviest burdens of the unjust social system liberals seek to reform.

Using one generation of the ghetto poor as unwilling instruments to bring about justice for the next generation is also wrong. We should not treat the ghetto poor as if they did not have purposes, including moral aims, of their own, as if they were mere things to be turned to purposes, however noble, that we see as fit. As moral agents who should be regarded as equals, they ought to be sought out as willing participants in efforts to bring about just social conditions. In addition, their basic interests in equal liberty and public respect should not be treated as tradable for welfare gains for others, not even when the beneficiaries would be their descendants, as this would represent a fundamental compromise in their standing as equal citizens with autonomy.

Some liberal proponents of moral paternalism might advocate such measures in ghettos, not as a pragmatic political strategy in a conservative era, but based on a sincere belief that certain cultural traits prevalent in ghettos damage the well-being of the ghetto poor, making their already awful situation worse. It might be held, for example, that the ghetto poor do not (fully) appreciate the devastating effect of these cultural traits on their lives. Moral paternalism, then, could be viewed as a compassionate response to suboptimal cultural divergence, even if some among the ghetto poor fail to see how such an intervention is in their best interests.

The poor in ghettos nonetheless have reason to find this stance condescending and offensive. Such paternalistic attitudes are fundamentally incompatible with the liberal value of respect for persons. The ghetto poor are free persons and so rightly expect to be accorded the respect due all who have this status. Showing that respect means, among other things, regarding persons as capable of revising their fundamental aims in response to good reasons and as capable of taking responsibility for their basic ambitions in life.[39] Apart from their interests in meeting their material needs, persons have a fundamental interest in being treated with this kind of respect. Though the liberal aspiration to meet these other needs is laudable, this goal is not a sufficient reason to override their fellow citizens' claim to be treated as free and equal. In addition, paternalism, as is well known, is hard to justify under just background conditions. Paternalism toward a segment of society acknowledged to be victims of social injustice is all the more suspect. A high burden of proof must be met to even consider such problematic measures.

Dignity, Injustice, and the State

There is, however, a third conception of "self-respect," which we might call *dignity*. Like self-esteem and self-respect, dignity has two components: (1) the belief that, no matter one's circumstances, one should do whatever is within one's power to secure one's basic physical and psychological well-being (including one's future well-being) and (2) the will to act on this belief.[40] Why is maintaining our dignity a worthwhile end? We are by nature self-conscious rational animals, capable of assessing the reasons in favor of and against various courses of action and capable of acting for good reasons and not simply from impulse, habit, or appetite. In fact, our status as objects of moral concern and respect rests partly on our capacity for rational deliberation and free action (and not merely on our capacity to experience pleasure and pain). It is therefore imperative that we safeguard our rational nature, not permitting our capacity for rationality to drop below a reasonable level. We can do this only if our basic welfare—healthy and normal human functioning—is not severely compromised.

Persons with dignity, concerned to show respect for their rational agency, remain resilient in the face of adversity, not allowing hardships, even unjust ones, to make them feel so defeated that they effectively give up on life. Wallowing in a sense of helplessness, willfully engaging in self-destructive behavior, and no longer caring about whether or how one survives demonstrate that one does not value one's rational agency sufficiently. Consider, for example, the person who has succumbed to a life organized around substance abuse due to an overwhelming sense of hopelessness and worthlessness, brought on by living under oppressive conditions. When people sink to this level of degradation, as some living in ghettos arguably have, it is obvious that they need assistance from others whether they recognize this or not. Their capacity for rationality has been so damaged that they don't even recognize the loss of dignity they have undergone, or despite apprehending this terrible loss, may be incapable of regaining it on their own. Some liberals might argue that moral paternalism, while unjustified under ordinary circumstances (including some unjust conditions), is permissible in such extreme cases.

So let's suppose that some among the ghetto poor, unbeknownst to themselves, do need help freeing themselves from a culture of defeatism and debasement that endangers their dignity, and that information, rational persuasion, and voluntary programs would be insufficient to the task. It would still be morally problematic for a person or organization, *qua representative of the state*, to presume to be the appropriate agent to provide this unrequested help, at least when this assistance takes the form of moral paternalism. The freedom of the ghetto poor is already constrained by unjust conditions, which the state has failed to rectify. It would add insult to injury for the state to further constrain their freedom with a view to preventing them from making themselves worse off. In short, given its failure to secure a just basic structure, the state lacks the moral standing to act as an agent of moral reform. The state could perhaps earn this standing, but only after it had made substantive and sustained efforts to ensure a just social structure, thus establishing its legitimacy and goodwill in the eyes of those it seeks to help.[41] In the meantime, nongovernmental organizations and private individuals must fill the gap, perhaps using public funds but even then with limited government intrusion.

We should be alert, though, to the possibility that what appears to be a tragic loss of dignity might in fact be an affirmation of self-respect. Though their actions may suggest diminished dignity, those with suboptimal cultural characteristics might not have given up on life and might not be suffering from weakness of will. Rather, they have reasons to view their outlook as a realistic posture in light of their government's wrongful actions (from malign neglect to vicious assaults) and their fellow citizens' self-serving contempt. They can permissibly choose to accept the risks of their cultural attitudes and practices rather than attempt to live in accordance with mainstream values while lacking the resources and opportunities they are due. And they can do this with a justified sense of moral pride. Perhaps what they most need and desire, then, is not unsolicited state-sponsored help but simply justice. One way to respect this reasonable stance would be to honor the prerogative of the ghetto poor to decide when their defiant behavior and suboptimal cultural traits are worth the personal costs and risks.

Moral Reform and Duties to Others

The form of liberal egalitarianism defended here does not rely on the dubious idea that the oppressed must never be criticized for how they respond to injustice. Not all criticisms of the unjustly disadvantaged are problematic victim-blaming. Moral criticism of the ghetto poor is sometimes warranted despite the unjust conditions that circumscribe their lives (though not everyone has the standing to make such criticisms).[42] Those mired in ghetto poverty, just like many among the nonpoor, sometimes have ambitions that are not in fact worthwhile but morally base and wrong. They sometimes choose immoral means to achieve their legitimate goals. And they sometimes give undue weight in deliberation to some of their group affiliations. So, for example, it is morally objectionable that some use deadly violence to secure luxury goods and social status, that some sexually degrade and assault others, and that some allow gang loyalty to trump what should be overriding moral considerations like respecting the rights of others and assisting the weak and vulnerable. These bases of self-esteem are not worthy of respect. And sometimes they are appropriately condemned, at least by those who have not been complicit in creating or perpetuating these practices.

The ghetto poor, like the rest of us, have moral duties to others that are not voided because of unjust social conditions. We should refrain from violent aggression against others and should not abuse, endanger, abandon, or neglect the children in our care, for instance. There should be legal proscriptions against these wrongful actions, even when these acts are perpetrated by the unjustly disadvantaged. Accordingly, it will sometimes be permissible and even morally required for the state to use coercive means to ensure that these duties are fulfilled and their corresponding rights protected (see Chapter 8). Thus, one legitimate rationale for intervening in the lives of the ghetto poor is to protect innocent persons, including children, from legally proscribed harmful immoral conduct. It is a requirement of social justice that the state play this role in the lives of those within its territorial jurisdiction. A state that fails to do so treats those under its rule unjustly, just as it does when it fails to secure a fair distribution of the benefits and burdens of socioeconomic cooperation. When this protective function goes unfulfilled under unjust social conditions, like those that exist in ghetto neighborhoods, the state compounds the burdens on the oppressed and undermines its own legitimacy in their eyes.

This raises the difficult question of whether moral reform of criminal offenders can be justified on the grounds that it is needed to protect third parties from harmful wrongdoing. So, for example, the cultural rehabilitation of violent criminal offenders might be regarded as a crime-control measure, as an effort to reduce recidivism. More controversially, moral reform could be directed at parents who have abused or neglected their children. This abuse and neglect might be attributed to suboptimal parenting styles acquired through intergenerational or peer influence. Perhaps moral reform would be justified in these cases. This isn't obvious, though. When the criminal justice system or children's protective services do intervene to protect the rights of persons against the wrongful actions of others, moral reform may not be needed, advisable, or even permissible. Behavior modification without cultural rehabilitation—for example, through well-constructed and fair punitive measures—may be all that is called for and justifiable. I'll return to some of these questions in Chapters 7 and 8, where I discuss crime and punishment.

For now my concern is with how cultural patterns in ghettos may hold back the socioeconomic advance of some in their grip and whether moral reform is a legitimate antipoverty strategy. I am not addressing whether moral reform is an appropriate response to criminal deviance or parental malfeasance. State interventions aimed at ensuring that people fulfill their moral responsibilities to others have a different normative status from interventions aimed at ensuring that people do not harm their own interests. It is the latter rationale for moral reform that is the subject here. And my objection is to moral reform whose objective is helping the black urban poor escape poverty.

Three Egalitarian Responses

Many egalitarians adamantly oppose state-sponsored moral reform, especially in the context of societal injustice. They believe that government should not be in the business of structuring the intimate lives or moral consciousness of embattled citizens but should rather focus its efforts on protecting basic liberties, ensuring a fair distribution of resources, meeting vital needs, and maintaining a just opportunity structure. There are two important egalitarian responses to the cultural divergence thesis that deny the validity of the thesis itself. The first insists that the cultural lives of the ghetto poor do not actually diverge from the "mainstream," if by that one means the average American.[43] These egalitarians point out that the attitudes and practices associated with the ghetto poor—laziness, hedonism, devaluation of academic achievement, materialism, promiscuity, rudeness, substance abuse, lack of respect for authority, nonmarital reproduction, irresponsible parenting, and violence—are also pervasive among the affluent and the vaunted middle class. The cultural patterns found in the ghetto are not specific to it but are part of a much broader cultural current within the United States. The difference, they maintain, is that the poor have far fewer resources than their more advantaged fellow citizens. This means that they are much less able to bear the costs of this lifestyle. Thus some of the burdens of the ghetto poor's choices (higher taxes, urban blight, school disruption, and street crime) are shifted onto those with greater means. Many among the affluent resent this fact and therefore adopt punitive, authoritarian, or paternalistic responses to the disadvantaged living in the deteriorated urban core. But this resentment is unjustified, for the distribution of the benefits and burdens of social cooperation in the United States is profoundly unfair and so the responsibility for these "negative externalities" cannot be (solely) placed on the ghetto poor. Moreover, targeting the ghetto poor for moral reform is hypocritical, as many so-called mainstream Americans possess the same cultural traits they decry.

A second egalitarian response acknowledges that cultural patterns in ghettos do diverge from the mainstream but insists that this divergence is not suboptimal.[44] According to this view, group cultures are adaptive collective responses to the structural environment. The ghetto poor are simply responding rationally to the constraints of high ghetto walls—though perhaps they do not conceive of their values and practices in such terms—with the result being, not a suboptimal culture, but a culture that fits the external environment. This culture would change, perhaps swiftly, with improved material circumstances and greater protection of civil rights, as the formerly poor would rationally adapt to their better conditions. Thus, if we tear down these walls (that is, make the basic structure more just), we would thereby effect a positive change in the culture of ghettos without having to resort to moral reform.

These two positions are important rivals to liberal moral reform. Though I will not assess them here, I mention them for two reasons: because they are alternatives worthy of serious consideration and because I want to distinguish them from the one I defend. I close this chapter, then, by sketching a different kind of egalitarian response to the cultural configurations found in ghetto neighborhoods, a liberal-egalitarian response that does not depend on rejecting the suboptimal cultural divergence hypothesis.

Self-Esteem, Self-Respect, and Collective Resistance

Recall the relevant normative commitments of liberal egalitarianism. To be reasonably just, a society must: take effective measures to defeat racism in all its forms (ideological, institutional, and structural); ensure that wrongful discrimination does not diminish persons' life chances; establish and maintain the conditions for fair equality of opportunity (eliminating, as far as possible, the effects of class origins on individuals' relative life prospects and labor-market competitiveness); and provide a guaranteed minimum income and adequate social services so that no one is forced to live in degrading forms of poverty. I have also argued (and will provide further support in chapters to come) that, as a factual matter, these principles of justice are not currently realized in the United States. If these normative premises and the factual claim are correct, it almost certainly will take a social movement to realize liberal-egalitarian ideals, for there is currently strong resistance to such reform. If we want to build and sustain such a movement, it is not enough to act on behalf of the unjustly disadvantaged. We should also enlist and welcome their active involvement, including the participation of the ghetto poor.

The effort to garner and maintain the cooperation of the ghetto poor faces a number of challenges, however. One challenge is brought into focus by the cultural divergence thesis. The thesis holds that stigma, blight, segregation, fragile families, street crime, lack of opportunity, and material deprivation have shaped the ambitions, values, practices, and identities of many ghetto denizens. In particular, an attitude prevalent in ghettos (though not exclusive to them) is political cynicism, a belief that the social system is deeply corrupt and that therefore meaningful structural change cannot be achieved through mainstream channels.[45] Such a stance naturally leads to low levels of political participation in electoral politics and political organizations (such as political parties and labor organizations). This is hardly surprising, because a familiar response to long-term, second-class citizenship is an absence of civic engagement and an acceptance of unjust conditions as inevitable. If, as the cultural divergence thesis maintains, such attitudes encourage the development of corresponding social identities and forms of group-based self-esteem, then it may be necessary for some cultural configurations of the ghetto poor to change after all. Without this change, the politically alienated among the ghetto poor cannot be regarded as suitable allies in a collective effort to bring about just social conditions, at least not through ordinary democratic means.

The difficulty is how to effect this cultural change without undermining the self-esteem, attacking the self-respect, or calling into question the dignity of those who have been most burdened by the social injustices that call for rectification. Are there considerations in favor of a change in their cultural ways that it would be reasonable for the ghetto poor to accept? Considerations that threaten their self-respect, convey paternalistic sentiments, or question their dignity are not reasonably acceptable, for reasons already explained. Moreover, as a practical matter it might help the cause of social justice if alternative social bases of self-esteem were developed or made available without being coupled with a moralizing attack on ghetto cultural patterns. Even if their resistance to changing their cultural attachments is not entirely rational, many among the black urban poor will naturally reject any suggestion that their cultural ways are having a corrosive effect on their life chances, for some have found meaning, solace, and self-worth in these cultural traits. In addition, as I have argued, the state lacks the moral standing to demand that the ghetto poor change their perspective or practices, at least until it establishes a more just social scheme. So it falls to concerned private citizens and organizations to convince the politically alienated among the ghetto poor that active resistance to the current social arrangement is not pointless, that organizing, mobilizing, and putting pressure on government officials and private firms can yield positive results.

It is often said that the oppressed should resist the injustices perpetrated against them. This duty to resist has at least two distinct normative grounds. There is, as discussed in Chapter 2, the duty of justice, which entails an obligation to try to end or lessen injustice or, at a minimum, to show enough moral concern to publicly condemn serious societal injustices. The duty of justice can enjoin us to openly resist social injustice when such acts would, for example, embolden the oppressed to fight back against those who would dominate and exploit them; invite potential allies to join in the struggle for justice; or make those with the power and inclination to halt injustices aware that injustices are happening. Acts of resistance that are a response to the duty of justice are intended as contributions to effecting a more just society.

An important thing to note here, though, is that the duty of justice does *not* require active resistance if it is reasonable to believe that such efforts would be ineffective or counterproductive in achieving justice. Thus, an appeal to the duty of justice is unlikely to move the politically alienated among the ghetto poor.

In light of this, my suggestion is to make an appeal (perhaps indirectly) to the self-respect of the ghetto poor. Because political resistance to injustice expresses and potentially boosts self-respect, the black urban poor have reasons of self-respect to participate in a movement for social change, even when they have reason to doubt the ultimate success of the collective effort. These are reasons the ghetto poor can reasonably accept. And these reasons already move many, as is apparent in the resentment and rage they exhibit when confronted with the arbitrary and sometimes malicious exercise of police power. Because the injustices characteristic of ghettos are threats to the self-respect of the black poor—that is, these injustices can potentially weaken their confidence in their equal moral worth—engaging in a collective struggle for social justice with others similarly committed can restore or fortify the self-respect of the ghetto poor. In addition, maintaining a robust sense of self-respect in the face of injustice can enhance self-esteem. We can increase our moral pride by successfully protecting ourselves against threats to our self-respect. We can do this, not only through defiance of authority or transgressing mainstream norms, but also by protesting wrongs perpetrated against us, preventing others from violating our rights, or criticizing the beliefs and values that are used to justify our suffering and disadvantage.

Efforts to change the basic structure of U.S. society should include the ghetto poor, not just as potential beneficiaries of such efforts, but as potential allies. There are already grassroots organizations and activists working to empower the ghetto poor and to increase their political participation. These efforts should be supported, joined, extended, and emulated. Not only could this dramatically increase the numbers of those pushing for social reform, but it might also help to sustain or create alternative sources of self-esteem for those attracted to suboptimal cultural values and practices. Many could find self-worth (in the form of moral pride) in working together with others to bring about just social conditions or to thwart unjust actions and policies. But for this to occur on an effective scale, forms of political solidarity that foster a commitment to the values of justice and mutual respect would need to be strengthened. Consequently, each member of these political associations could have their activities affirmed by the other members, thereby buttressing individual and collective self-efficacy. Provided these alliances produced some concrete political victories and realistic hope for further gains, the result might well be the creation of more constructive social bases of self-esteem than those the ghetto poor sometimes embrace today. Those who want to act in solidarity with the ghetto poor can therefore legitimately encourage them to find self-esteem in the collective pursuit of corrective justice.

PART II

Of Love and Labor

FOUR

Reproduction

A common view about the ghetto poor is that they often remain in poverty and in disadvantaged black neighborhoods because they grow up in severely disadvantaged family environments and so have sharply diminished life prospects from the start. It is widely thought that such families are disadvantaged both because they are headed by young single mothers who lack the resources, maturity, or skills necessary to adequately care for their children and because the fathers of these children fail to fulfill their parental responsibilities. In other words, many believe that a main factor in explaining the persistence of ghetto poverty is that some blacks create children when they lack the means, competence, or commitment to ensure the proper care and development of these children. Procreation under these conditions is commonly held to be not only unwise but also *wrong*—plunging the already poor into deeper disadvantage, harming the offspring, and unfairly burdening fellow citizens. If more responsible procreating and parenting were to occur, so it is claimed, there would be a significant drop in poverty and perhaps ghettos would finally disappear. Specifically, some believe that if more blacks would delay childbearing until they are older and financially secure, would get married or form stable co-parenting unions if they are going to have children, and faithfully carry out their parental duties (including child support when unions aren't formed or dissolve), the cycle of poverty in ghettos could be broken. This is how the ethics of procreating and parenting intersect with questions of social justice and ghetto poverty.

Even setting aside neighborhood characteristics and the quality of available schools, there are compelling reasons to avoid the formation of poor families, particularly when the prospective parents are very young.[1] Growing up under persistent poverty negatively affects cognitive and verbal ability and thus academic achievement. Many children of poor mothers are born premature and have low birth weight, which increases the risks of various health-related and developmental problems. Poor mothers who are very young and have limited education provide their children with less cognitive stimulation than those reared by older and more educated parents. Mothers' youth and inexperience loom large here, because the impact of home environment from birth to age five has long-term effects. The households of poor children are often stressful, with frequent disruptions in routine, including abrupt changes in residence, sometimes caused by eviction.[2] The economic pressure on poor parents induces depression, irritability, and explosiveness, which can lead them to be inconsistent, arbitrary, or harsh with discipline. Young parents tend not be particularly good role models, for they often fail to exemplify the virtues needed to flourish in life—self-control, delayed gratification, determination in the face of adversity, independence, and so on. Poor children have greater emotional and behavioral problems, including low self-esteem, anxiety, impulsiveness, and aggression, which are often made worse if their poverty endures.

That so many children grow up in poverty is deeply troubling and urgently demands a public response. Few would disagree with this judgment. The controversial question is what type of response would be both effective and justifiable to everyone affected. Many liberal egalitarians insist that antipoverty programs that intervene at the family level (for example, by providing social services to children and their parents) won't be effective unless they are joined with measures that attack the structural and neighborhood causes of poverty. They would argue that most of the family-related problems are due to institutional racism, unjust discrimination, unsafe neighborhoods, and a lack of economic resources and opportunities, such as access to adequate education, affordable housing, and well-paying jobs. Still, some would allow that some antipoverty interventions into the lives of poor families are justifiable. Many liberals believe teen pregnancy, nonmarital procreation, family instability, father absence, and failures to pay child support contribute to the persistence of ghetto poverty. Even if the adults involved are not responsible for their initial disadvantage, they are responsible for how they choose to respond to that disadvantage, and some responses not only make their plight worse but also are blameworthy. Some liberals therefore think it is permissible to intervene to help the ghetto poor make better choices and even to penalize irresponsible choices in order to encourage better behavior.

Others take a less sympathetic stance. They regard the procreative choices and inadequate parenting of some among the ghetto poor as imposing unfair burdens on the public, not only in the form of higher taxes (to pay for social services and income subsidies) but also in the form of juvenile delinquency and crime. They believe that procreative and parental irresponsibility, even among the poor, wrongs both the children involved and the public. Such conduct, they insist, is a violation of civic reciprocity and warrants a punitive response. And they are not inclined to increase public expenditures to assist these disadvantaged families beyond meeting the basic material needs of poor children.

Drawing on elements of the Personal Responsibility and Work Opportunity Reconciliation Act (1996)—commonly referred to as "welfare reform"—I want to consider three types of family-targeted antipoverty policies that find support across the political spectrum, focusing explicitly on their underlying justification. These policies were conceived and implemented within the medical model framework, and I argue that they suffer from all three problems that often attend that model—status quo bias, downgraded agency, and unjust-advantage blind spots.

The first of these policies uses the structure of welfare benefits to deter nonmarital childbearing. This approach involves such tactics as placing strict limits on the lifetime receipt of welfare benefits (five years), keeping these benefits low, not increasing benefits for parents who have additional children (family cap), making the receipt of these benefits conditional on meeting work or job-training requirements, providing mainly in-kind benefits (food stamps, housing vouchers, educational benefits, and access to medical care) rather than cash assistance, and imposing stiff penalties for noncompliance with program expectations (including cutting off benefits). These are attempts to meet the basic material needs of poor families while discouraging poor people from engaging in nonmarital procreation.

A second type of antipoverty policy involves the promotion of marriage or stable unions and cohabitation between parents who share a child. Many among the public are concerned about the apparent negative effects of single-parent families on children, and so policymakers have proposed and instituted a range a social programs aimed at fostering healthy marriages, reuniting separated spouses or partners, encouraging cooperation between unmarried parents (whether never married or divorced), and preventing divorce.[3] Indeed, one of the explicit aims of the 1996 welfare reform legislation is the promotion of two-parent families and marriage.

The final type of antipoverty policy I consider is child support enforcement, which can occur through court orders, withholding from paychecks, and tax refund confiscation. Child support enforcement, in the view of some policymakers, has a triple function. It serves to encourage responsible contraceptive use and thus to reduce nonmarital births, as absent fathers with child support obligations will presumably be disinclined to take on greater financial liability; and others, knowing of these fathers' burdens, will be deterred from irresponsible sexual behavior. It could also encourage stable unions or marriage between those who share kids, as the threat of child support payments would discourage divorce or break ups and motivate absent fathers to reconcile with or marry their children's mothers. And it could ensure that absent fathers fulfill parental obligations, at least the financial ones. The underlying rationale for the first two functions is straightforward: If fathers must bear increased costs for nonmarital births and single motherhood, then, assuming most men are rational, this should reduce the incidence of both.[4]

The point of reflecting on these antipoverty measures is to evaluate interventions into family formation and family life with the aim of identifying the moral limits of such interventions and to think systematically about the ethics of procreating and parenting under conditions of injustice. In this chapter, I first define key terms to sharpen the questions at issue and then consider three plausible standards for determining when procreation is wrong and a violation of civic reciprocity. Next I identify some limits on state interference with the reproductive decisions of the poor. I continue the discussion in Chapter 5 by defending an account of the family's role in maintaining a just society and explaining how persons come to have parental responsibilities. In light of those remarks, I identify a serious problem with current policies of child support enforcement. Finally, I explain what kinds of public support disadvantaged single-parent families are owed under conditions of injustice and why this support is owed.

Families and Fragile Families

Let's fix terminology. I begin with the notion "parent," which has several meanings. I say a person is a *biological parent* if he or she is the physical source of a sperm or ovum from which another person was created.[5] A person is a *moral parent* if he or she has moral rights or responsibilities of parenthood with respect to another person. A person is a *social parent* if he or she is generally regarded by custom, tradition, or convention as having parental rights or responsibilities with respect to another person. A person is a *legal parent* if the law (by statute or judicial decision) assigns him or her parental rights or responsibilities with respect to another person.

In a parent–child relationship, the same person can be a biological, social, moral, and legal parent of the child. But this needn't be and often isn't the case. For instance, it is an open question whether a given social parent is actually a moral parent and vice versa. Although many adults (and even some children) will perform caretaking roles in the life of a child, moral parents have primary responsibility for the children in their charge and have considerable discretion over their care and upbringing, including the authority to decide who will supplement their caregiving. These rights and responsibilities may or may not be fully instantiated in law or legally recognized. Moreover, the law may construct parenthood in ways that are not morally justified or that are even unjust. So it's important not to conflate moral and legal parenthood.

The concept *family* is highly contested and fraught. No notion of what a family is can be normatively neutral, but to address the social-theoretic and practical-philosophical questions outlined above we need a working notion that doesn't beg the questions at issue. My purpose is not to define the "ideal" family, nor to settle by definitional fiat which family (or family-like) formations merit approbation and public support or warrant disapproval and state intervention. Rather, the relevant concept must aid us in understanding how certain families, given their structure and internal dynamics, could be viewed as perpetuating ghetto poverty and help us frame the corresponding normative questions.

I propose that, for purposes of our inquiry, we understand the family in terms of one of its fundamental social functions: a family is the primary sociospatial unit within which parents are expected to provide children with day-to-day, individualized care and to guide them into adulthood. Because "parent" has at least the four meanings just defined, "families" take at least four forms—biological, social, moral, and legal. I'm primarily concerned with the family in its moral sense and will use "parent" to mean moral parent unless otherwise indicated. With that and our other desiderata in mind, we might define a "family" as a cohabiting social group of at least one parent and his or her child (or children), where the group functions as a socioeconomic unit. On this definition, a single child can be a member of more than one family if the parents of the child share custody but live apart. Also, a family living on the street, in a car, or at a homeless shelter is of course still a family, in the sense that its members live together and, circumstances permitting, plan to live together in a stable residence. They are cohabiting, just not in a stable residence.

This definition has limitations. By tying family conceptually to household or living arrangements, there can be a parent who is not in the same family with his or her child simply because the two live apart. It would be odd to regard the nonresident parent as not a member of the same family with his or her kids (perhaps he or she is away performing military service or serving a prison sentence but expects to be a full member of the household upon return home). A child away at a boarding school isn't living with his or her parents either. We can modify the definition by saying that the nonresident parent or child is a part of the cohabiting unit if he or she is morally entitled to reside in the household (though, as a matter of fact, he or she may not do so on a regular basis). So there is a distinction between *visiting* and *cohabiting*: you are a mere visitor if you have no independent claim to reside at the residence but stay there only at the discretion of an adult who does have a claim to reside there.

What this kind of definition reveals is the need for the concept *householder*, which is not to be confused with the traditional idea of a "head of household." The householder is an adult who, because he or she owns or rents the residence, has a right to live at the residence and to decide (within the limits of the lease) who else can reside there. There can be co-householders, where more than one adult in the household is entitled to determine its occupants. A *single-parent family*, then, is a family in which only one parent is householder. This covers the case where a biological father occasionally resides in the home of his child's mother but only at the discretion of the mother (which is not an unusual scenario). A mother and her child living at the mother's *parent's* residence represent another kind of "single-parent family."[6] This way of conceiving of families also makes sense of the notion of "broken" families. It is not necessarily that an adult has ceased to be a parent. Instead, a parent is no longer a member of the household with his or her children.

The parents of a child need not be married or even romantic partners to constitute a co-parenting household unit and thus a family. Analysts writing about black urban life frequently speak of "out-of-wedlock births" or "nonmarital births" as a social problem. But the main concern (whatever the terminology) is not that the children are products of biological parents who aren't married and don't plan to marry. If the parental-household union is strong and expected to be enduring and the partners are committed to parenting their children together in the same household, then whether the partners are married is irrelevant. The issues are whether the union is stable and whether there is joint commitment to co-parenting and cohabiting. Dual parenthood is generally deemed important because, given the current labor market, it is difficult for one person to handle all the necessary childcare while maintaining a full-time job. Two people can divide the required labor, both workplace and domestic.

Many express concern about the sharp rise in the number or proportion of "female-headed households" or "single-mother families." Again, this can mislead. The problem is not the decline of patriarchal family units, which from a liberal-egalitarian point of view is a welcome development. Few liberals, given their commitment to gender equality, now think that men should have authority over the mothers of their children or that fathers have greater parental authority than mothers. And, assuming the same limited economic resources, few would regard the situation as better for these poor families if they were single-*father* families. An affluent single parent, of whatever gender, who can live comfortably without working much or who has dependable childcare assistance when at work is not generally in danger of becoming poor or neglecting his or her children. Even a single parent who lives with another responsible adult (say, her cohabiting lover or her mother) can often manage to stay out poverty, assuming the living arrangement is stable. Thus, neither marriage nor single-parent households as such are the central worry.

The real issue concerns the single parent (and it is almost always a mother) living as the sole adult in the household and who has limited earning power and no meaningful wealth. She will have difficulty avoiding or escaping poverty, and as a result her children will be deeply disadvantaged, often with long-term negative consequences for their lives. And if such single mothers do manage to earn enough to avoid poverty, it is unlikely that they will have sufficient time and energy to adequately care for, guide, and supervise their children. It is these socioeconomically disadvantaged, single-mother households that are taken to be prime examples of "fragile" families. Their fragility is a reason many believe it would be better if they were not formed at all. That is, many think single women who are poor and have limited earning power should avoid having children until they significantly enhance their marketable skills, find a suitable partner with whom they can co-parent in a stable household, or both.

If these disadvantaged single-mother families receive reliable financial and childcare assistance from noncustodial fathers, they are generally better off, which is one reason many advocate tough child support enforcement. But many of the fathers of these children are deeply disadvantaged themselves, with few resources and limited earning power, and thus are rarely able to contribute much while also covering their own household expenses.[7] However, two low-skilled parents in a stable union, sharing the same household and pooling resources (including domestic and workplace labor), can often manage to live above the poverty line, which would greatly benefit their children. And so some policymakers propose programs that help low-skilled parents stay together or get back together, not because they want to promote traditional marriage per se, but because two-parent families have a better chance of avoiding or escaping poverty.[8]

Wrongful Procreation

Much of the contemporary commonsense morality of reproduction has been deeply shaped by long-surpassed technology. There is now biomedical technology that substantially reduces the chances of creating unwanted children. As a result, women who have access to these effective means of contraception have considerable control over their sex lives and bodies. They can avoid pregnancy without abstaining from sex, without depending on unreliable contraceptive methods, and without relying solely on their male sexual partners to take care of contraception (say, through the use of condoms or the withdrawal method). Should they get pregnant (whether by accident or on purpose), they need not accept the role of parent, as safe and affordable abortion procedures are available (assuming the law does not prohibit their use).

But the sexual revolution, created in part by political struggle but also by technological innovation, has not abolished all moral questions about consensual procreative activity. Difficult questions remain about the ethics of procreation and reproductive freedom that bear directly on our inquiry. When poor single women create children, does it harm their offspring or otherwise constitute wrongdoing? Do poor single women treat their fellow citizens unfairly when they procreate despite not being economically self-sufficient? When, if ever, is it permissible for the state to interfere with the reproductive decisions of poor people? This section addresses the first two questions and the next section addresses the third.

Some among the ghetto poor are, arguably, *imprudent* when it comes to creating children, in the sense that their *own* interests are thereby set back. Generally speaking, it is not wise to create a child when one is single and poor with dim employment prospects, for one would likely be made even worse off as a result. But we should distinguish the wisdom of having a child from its moral permissibility. Some are inclined to view these issues as overlapping because they think imprudence is often a blameworthy vice. My concern, though, is with procreation that arguably wrongs offspring or the public, leaving aside for the moment whether it is also bad for the procreators or a sign of bad character. The relevant wrongs pertain to procreation as such (the simple fact of creating vulnerable persons who will need years of caretaking) and to procreating with intent to parent.

Choosing to become a teenage single mother is widely thought to be wrong. Unless a competent adult is prepared to take primary parental responsibility (at least initially), the newly created child would likely receive inadequate care and guidance, as the young mother would probably lack the necessary life experience and maturity to meet these obligations. If the would-be mother will wait, she can still have a child when she is older and thus more likely up to the task of parenting. So delaying childbirth would not prevent her from experiencing the welcome challenges and unique pleasures of motherhood. But is there a similar argument to be made to the poor single woman who wants to be a mother? Should she, though already a competent adult, delay childbearing until she has greater material security? And if so, what moral principle requires this?[9]

According to one argument, the relevant moral principle would likely concern how much foreseeable risk of harm it's permissible to impose on offspring through procreating. All procreation exposes progeny to some risk of harm. Some of these dangers aren't knowable in advance, and the degree of risk can be difficult to determine. The moral principle would have to direct our attention toward known risks, the kind any reasonable person can be expected to foresee and, accordingly, seek to avoid or reduce. Life has many perils, even for those born into the most advantageous circumstances. So unless all procreation is wrong, the issue has to be risk of serious harm.[10] And because misfortune can befall anyone, rich and poor alike, we also have to be talking about a serious risk—a morally unacceptable risk of serious harm. I do not know where to set the risk threshold. I will leave that vague and intuitive. But what constitutes "serious harm"?

We should surely avoid creating persons who we can foresee will live lives so miserable and filled with gratuitous suffering that, from an impartial point of view, it would have been better had they never lived at all. Given this moral fixed point, it might be thought that, because of the "nonidentity problem," those with seriously disadvantaged yet still worth-living lives do not have a valid complaint against their parents for creating them.[11] For if their parents had chosen not to have a child or even to delay procreation for as little as a month, the disadvantaged child would not have existed (assuming that a person's existence depends on having developed from a particular ovum fertilized by a particular sperm). There is no way for that *same* child to exist and yet not be disadvantaged by having been born to a poor single mother. The tempting thought "If only my mom had waited until she were married or more financially secure to have me, I would be much better off now" is understandable but incoherent.

In light of this, Peter Vallentyne defends the view that the sole special procreative duty one has to one's offspring is to refrain from producing children with *negative initial life prospects*, that is, children whose lives are highly unlikely to be worth living at all.[12] We could call this the *Life Worth Living Principle*. However, this principle would not make procreation impermissible for the average poor single mother in the United States, even one living in a ghetto. The average teenage mother could probably satisfy it. Although morally responsible procreation requires that we meet this standard, I suspect that the standard is too permissive. But even if it is not, for the sake of argument, let's consider more demanding principles.

Elizabeth Harman believes we can harm our offspring by creating them, but she does not think we harm them by making them worse off than they would have been had we not created them.[13] Future persons are harmed when we take an action that will cause them serious and chronic pain, early death, physical deformity, bodily damage, and so on, and they are harmed even if they would not have existed had the action not been taken. The harmful action can also *benefit* the newly created individual (by giving them a life well worth living). But these compensating benefits alone are insufficient to make imposing the harms permissible.[14] The principle Harman therefore proposes is this: We act wrongly if we fail to choose an alternative course of action that would allow us to offer parallel benefits without the parallel harms.[15] Call this the *Harm Principle*.

The Harm Principle would condemn the procreation decisions of only those poor single women who have the *option* to delay procreation while they acquire an adequate co-parent, increase their earning power, or both. If neither finding a partner nor escaping poverty is a realistic possibility during childbearing years, then procreating even when this would cause bodily harm to offspring would not be wrong (provided it doesn't violate the Life Worth Living Principle), for the parallel benefits of a worthwhile life could not be conferred without imposing the parallel harms. Moreover, the bodily harm done must be attributable to being poor and single, and not to some other (possibly related) cause, such as drinking heavily, chain smoking, or abusing drugs throughout pregnancy. Given these qualifications and the kinds of bodily harms Harman has in mind, I doubt that the Harm Principle would make procreation impermissible for the average poor single black woman.

To see this, let's distinguish three ways a female procreator could violate the Harm Principle.[16] First, she might violate it because of the harms *gestation* will impose on her offspring. For example, a poor single woman could violate it because, given the state of her resources and health during pregnancy, her offspring will likely be born unhealthy and suffer the long-term effects of this ill health. While there is some risk that poor single black women will create persons who fail to have or maintain a healthy bodily state (say, because of low birth weight or premature birth), the risk would not appear to be intolerably high. Most poor black women in the United States have access to the nutrition and medical care necessary to create babies without serious health problems or birth defects.

A poor single woman could also violate the Harm Principle because of the *family environment* the child will be born into. If the woman knows that her child's vital needs will go unmet or the child will be exposed to physical abuse in the household, then she should not reproduce until she can provide a better home. But unless she had good reason to believe that she would abuse or neglect her child or that she would be unable to prevent someone else in the household from doing so, it does not appear that responsibility for any bodily damage or shortened life span that occurred because of her familial circumstances could be attributed to the mother's choice to procreate. In fact, the single mother who is sole householder will often be able to prevent abusive adults from residing with her children. So unless she is prone to violence or negligence or knows she could not meet her child's material needs, the fact that she is poor and single would not be sufficient reason to refrain from procreating.

Third, the Harm Principle could be violated because of the *neighborhood* environment the newly created child would inhabit. Some ghettos are known to be highly dangerous—with, for instance, alarming violent crime rates (see Chapter 7). If poverty has forced one to live in a very violent neighborhood and one knows that moving to a safer community is highly unlikely in the near future (at least not before the fetus is viable), this might be a sufficient reason to delay childbearing until a less violent neighborhood can be formed or found. Exposing a child to a dangerous neighborhood when one cannot insulate the child sufficiently from its hazards could be wrong by Harman's standard (assuming moving to a safer neighborhood is a feasible option).[17] Yet not all poor black neighborhoods are hazardous to their inhabitants' health. And even the ones that do have a violent crime problem may not pose a serious threat to very young children. A young (prospective) mother might reasonably believe that she will be able to move away before her child was at risk.

Still, the Harm Principle, if sound, has some relevance for the ethics of procreating under ghetto conditions. Needlessly putting one's offspring in harm's way—whether because of factors having to do with gestation, family environment, or neighborhood context—is one mode of procreative wrongdoing. It is just that few poor single mothers engage in this kind of wrongdoing. Ironically, some disadvantaged single black women procreate permissibly precisely because their socioeconomic situation is so constrained, as they don't have the option to procreate outside of poverty. Thus, the Harm Principle does not justify a general policy aimed at deterring nonmarital births among the poor, as this would needlessly interfere with the procreative freedom of most disadvantaged women.

But I believe there is another, more relevant form of wrongful procreation. Instead of relying on a conception of "harm" to understand procreative wrongs, James Woodward offers this principle: You should not bring a child into existence when you know (or should know) that it is highly unlikely that you will be able to fulfill your obligations to the child.[18] Woodward understands such obligations in terms of the correlative rights of children, but this isn't crucial to the main point. Indeed, it isn't necessary that the obligation undertaken be an obligation to a particular child, which might seem impossible, given that the child doesn't exist and so can have no interests to protect at the point of the procreation decision. One could of course vow to care for any child created from one's gametes and thus be blamed for making a commitment that one should have known (and perhaps did know) one probably couldn't keep. And one can certainly undertake an obligation to the public, on whose behalf one will take primary responsibility for the care of the child. The general underlying moral idea is that in deciding whether to assume an obligation, one should take into account the likely effects on others should one fail to fulfill the obligation. In particular, one should keep in mind that others will be depending on you to follow through on your commitment. Better not to assume the obligation if there is a good chance that one will not be able to meet it.[19]

Some obligations are undertaken through voluntary procreation. For example, procreators should see to it that their offspring are properly cared for. If one procreates with the reasonable expectation that some third party will do the parenting (as in surrogacy, gamete donation, or prearranged adoption), then provided the child would be in good hands, no relevant procreative wrong has occurred. When procreation is undertaken with the understanding that the procreator will parent the offspring, this is to accept the obligations of parenthood. In both scenarios, the corresponding ethical principle is this: you should not bring a person into existence when you know (or should know) that it is highly unlikely that you will be able to fulfill the obligations thereby created. Let's call this the *Reproductive Responsibility Principle* (RRP). Given this principle, if a poor single woman wrongfully creates a child, the wrongfulness of her act is to be explained by the fact that she knew (or should have known) that, because of her limited resources or lack of childcare assistance, she would very likely be unable to fulfill responsibilities she would incur through procreating.

The Reproductive Responsibility Principle provides a more demanding standard for judging procreative choices than the Life Worth Living Principle, and it allows us to understand failures to live up to our procreative duties without supposing that such failures are always to a particular person (that is, it gets around the nonidentity problem). It rightly focuses on the permissibility of the procreative *choice* rather than solely on what happens to the child after it is born, which often is not within the control of the mother or could not have been anticipated. The emphasis on assumed obligations also allows us to include moral considerations other than the imposition of unnecessary bodily harm, such as failures to educate, instill self-discipline, and foster autonomy. And finally, it enables us to see how procreation could wrong the public, who may be forced to meet needs of children that should have been met by those who created them.

Unless we regard parental obligations as fairly minimal and easily fulfilled, it would seem that at least some disadvantaged women living in ghetto poverty procreate in violation of RRP. For instance, there are single mothers who create more children despite knowing that they are having great difficulty properly caring for their existing children. If such persons have no feasible plan for escaping poverty, there is a good chance that they will not be able to give their new offspring sufficient care and guidance. Just what percentage of poor single mothers are in this situation, I do not know. Maybe, from the standpoint of public policy, the number is negligible.

But to fully assess whether a welfare policy that deters nonmarital births is warranted, let's suppose that when the average poor single woman chooses to procreate, she violates RRP with respect to her offspring. Would it follow that she also thereby violates it with respect to her fellow citizens? After all, public funds may now have to be used to satisfy the needs of her children that she could not meet. By creating deeply disadvantaged children when she could have avoided doing so and knew (or should have known) that she would struggle to adequately care for them, has she displayed a lack of civic reciprocity?

The answer depends on whether the basic structure of U.S. society is reasonably just. If it is not, as I have argued and will further support in the chapters to come, then procreation by poor single women living in ghettos does not represent a failure of civic reciprocity. The public at large is (at least partly) responsible for the fact that these women lack the necessary means to provide adequate care for their young and so cannot justly complain of being wronged. If the reason I failed to meet you at our agreed-upon time is that you have wrongly withheld money you owe me and I need that money to pay for transportation, then you cannot reasonably claim to have been wronged if, despite my reasonable efforts, I don't show up at the appointed time. This would be true even if I could have made it there on time had I chosen to make an arduous and long trek on foot. And if I do manage to meet you at the appointed time by, say, taking a taxi, it hardly seems unfair to you if you are stuck paying the fare.

This normative conclusion does not entail that these single mothers do no wrong in procreating. But if the explanation for their inability to meet obligations to their children is that they have been denied resources they were due because of past or ongoing injustices, then their wrongs (if they are wrongs) are ones for which the public shares responsibility. Though these women perhaps should not have taken on primary caregiving responsibilities given their constricted material circumstances, the public is partly responsible for their failure to fulfill these obligations. And if the public has been complicit in this wrong, it cannot reasonably complain of the burdens imposed by this wrongful procreation. In particular, it cannot justly condemn these women for choosing to create children they could not adequately care for without further public support. Nor can it be just for the state to act to deter nonmarital births on the grounds that such childbearing unfairly burdens the public.

There is still the question of whether the state can permissibly act to prevent nonmarital births among the ghetto poor on the grounds that it is protecting *children*—those future persons whose interests are at stake. If poor single mothers engage in wrongful procreation, then it might seem that the state, even if it is in some ways complicit in this wrongdoing, can justifiably act to prevent such procreation.

Limits of Reproductive Freedom

Reproductive freedom is the liberty to create or to refrain from creating children, a basic moral right that any society must respect if it is to be just. My concern is less with the right *not* to procreate (for example, access to contraception and abortion) and more with the right *to* procreate (for instance, the right to have a child when one is young, single, or poor). I distinguish the ethics of procreating (whether, and under what conditions, it is permissible or blameworthy to procreate) from reproductive freedom (a right against state interference with reproductive decisions). As discussed, it can be wrong to create a child under some circumstances. However, reproductive freedom concerns the moral limits on state interference with individual reproductive decisions and thus the scope of procreative liberty. We must recognize that a procreative decision may be morally wrong and yet it might be unjust for the state to interfere with that decision.

There is a sex-based asymmetry in reproductive freedom. Both men and women have the liberty to choose whether, when, and with whom to have consensual sex. Both men and women have the right to use contraception. But only women, and not the men who impregnate them, have the liberty to decide whether they will carry a pregnancy to term. So although both men and women contribute to pregnancy and thus share responsibility for its consequences, only women have the right to decide whether they will gestate and bear children. I assume that this asymmetry, when backed by law, is not an illegitimate restriction on men's reproductive freedom but is, in fact, required by justice—given women's legitimate interest in controlling what happens to their bodies, including whether a child will develop within their wombs.[20]

Reproductive freedom would be *limitless* if it entailed the liberty to create as many children as one chooses to, regardless of one's personal circumstances (including the ability to care for and raise them) and no matter one's intentions in creating them (including one's intention to care for and raise them). If reproductive freedom isn't limitless, the question then is whether and under what conditions the state has the authority to interfere (through directives, incentives, sanctions, or physical force) with individuals' reproductive decisions and on what grounds.

I assume that, within a just society, the state has some legitimate regulatory powers with respect to reproduction, and so reproductive freedom has limits. The state may, for instance, regulate access to contraceptive methods, as some drugs or biomedical technology may be too dangerous for use. The state may prohibit reproduction between close biological relatives to prevent genetic disorders. It may also use legal regulations to ensure safe abortion. Though more controversial, the state may be justified in interfering with reproductive decisions when there are severe problems of overpopulation and, perhaps, underpopulation.[21] Overpopulation could threaten the welfare of existing people or future generations. Underpopulation could make it difficult to maintain a just social structure, for the ratio of old to young could make it difficult to meet the needs of the old.

In a just society, the state may legitimately restrict the procreative choices of adolescents. For example, in exercising its authority to determine the age of majority, the state can set the age at which individuals can give valid consent to sex, thus limiting the reproductive freedom of underage teenagers. Penalizing boys or men who have sex with underage girls can therefore prevent teenage pregnancy without violating anyone's reproductive rights. But what explains the legitimacy of such government action?

It might be thought that the reproductive freedom of teenage girls is not actually limited because they are not penalized for having sex or getting pregnant, only the boys or men who have sex with them are penalized; and the boys or men are free to have sex with adult women (and even with teenage girls if married to them). But this can't be correct. Few would think that women's reproductive freedom is not limited when physicians are prohibited from performing abortions or making contraception available. Teenagers would have more reproductive freedom if boys and men were not penalized for having sex with teenage girls.

In *Michael M. v. Superior Court* (1981), the U.S. Supreme Court held that the state of California could penalize for statutory rape on the ground that adolescent girls should be protected from the physical and psychological consequences of pregnancy. The statue is premised not on the idea that the male is a "culpable aggressor" but on the need to prevent teenage pregnancy. This is clearly a paternalistic law. It is not justified on the ground that future children need to be protected from unfit (because too young) mothers. It is an attempt to protect the young from the negative consequences of their own choices (analogous to prohibiting dropping out of school before age sixteen). Even apart from worries about parental competence, there is the concern that many pregnant teenagers drop out of school and have limited marketable skills and work experience. Without significant help from others, single teenage mothers will have difficulty staying out of poverty.

Paternalism toward teenagers can be justified. Such paternalistic reasoning cannot however be extended to the procreative choices of adult women or the men who have consensual sex with them. So the fact that the state may interfere with the procreative choices of teenagers is unlikely to be a good guide to whether the reproductive freedom of poor single women can be limited on the ground that their decision to procreate would be morally wrong.

Let's assume that the public has a legitimate stake in preventing violations of RRP—the principle that one should not bring a person into existence when one knows (or should know) that it is highly unlikely that one will be able to fulfill the obligations thereby created—because of the public's interest in protecting future children from unfit parents.[22] What kinds of measures could it justifiably use to deter people from violating it? The state may not permissibly use forced sterilization, the coercive implantation of IUDs, or involuntary abortions, for these measures would violate the right of individuals to control what happens to their bodies and their right to medical privacy. Apart from education and information, incentives and penalties would seem to be the only alternatives.

Punishment could seem ruled out from the start, as it might be thought objectionable to penalize someone for an action before anyone is actually harmed by it. Punishing poor single pregnant women would fall into this category. But no one thinks it is wrong to penalize a drunk driver before he injures someone. By driving he has undertaken an obligation (to drive safely and follow the rules of the road) that he is highly unlikely to be able to fulfill. This drunk driving is enough to make him blameworthy because he is exposing others to a morally unacceptable high risk of harm. However, perhaps penalizing wrongful procreation before the child is born is like penalizing an inebriated person before he has gotten behind the wheel. The fact that he intends to drive or has made plans to drive is not a sufficient reason to punish him, as he has not yet imposed an unjustified risk on others. After all, he may change his mind before actually driving. Similarly, a woman may have gotten pregnant intending all along to bear and raise the child but then (realizing she will not be able to meet her obligations to the child) terminating her pregnancy before the fetus is viable or putting the child up for adoption before actually harming it. The interests of future persons are then protected, and the requirements of RRP are satisfied.

Thus, if antiprocreation penalties are justified, these penalties would have to be applied only after the single mother has assumed parental obligations to the child. The trouble is, such penalties would likely make the children in poor single-mother families even worse off. Prison time or fines for these mothers would be self-defeating. Such penalties would make it that much harder for these mothers to fulfill their obligations to their children, thus undermining the point of preventing violations of RRP. Forcibly removing the children to foster care, even on a temporary basis, is a drastic and severe measure best reserved for serious neglect and abuse, as parent–child involuntary separation is usually traumatic for children. Removing at-risk infants from their mothers would also likely be considerably less cost-effective than simply supplementing the incomes of poor single mothers so they can effectively meet their parental obligations.

It's important not to confuse punishing wrongful procreation with punishing parental misconduct. Wrongful procreation has to do with carrying out immoral reproductive decisions—creating persons when one shouldn't have. The wrong lies in undertaking obligations one can't fulfill. Failing to fulfill the obligations—say, by not providing adequate care and supervision for an existing child—is an additional wrong. If wrongful procreation can be punished legitimately, then penalties can be applied prior to any actual parental misconduct. Punishing parental wrongs could deter wrongful procreation, as some prospective procreators might refrain from procreating if they think they are likely to perpetrate parental wrongs and to be punished for these violations. This suggests that punishing wrongful procreation is in reality unnecessary because punishing actual parental wrongs should be sufficient to deter wrongful procreation.

Welfare Provision and Reproductive Freedom

Yet punishment is not the only way that the state, through law, can constrain reproductive freedom. The state could use, and has used, law to distribute public benefits in a way that aims to discourage irresponsible procreation. For instance, the tax scheme could limit tax exemptions for certain kinds of families.[23] However, when dealing with the poor, structuring the provision of welfare benefits has seemed, to many, more effective and fairer. The state tries to discourage poor single mothers from further reproduction by making public support conditional on, for example, meeting work requirements and facilitating the establishment of paternity.[24] It also places lifetime limits on welfare receipt to discourage multiple births. The idea behind such rules is that poor single women who are tempted to procreate would then think twice, as the public support their prospective families would receive would be paltry, and these women would have to submit to conditions they might find onerous if they are to receive this support. On the assumption that no one has a *positive* right to procreate, it might be thought that the public has no obligation to equip prospective procreators with the means necessary for permissible reproduction. The state need only supply means of subsistence and health care to families who cannot afford them. Moreover, advocates of this aspect of welfare reform believe that these provisions can come with strings attached, as they do not believe that welfare recipients have an unconditional claim on public support.

The conditions these mothers would have to meet, although they might be unwelcome, do not constitute punishment, because these families, by receiving welfare provisions, are made better off, at least financially. According to defenders of welfare reform, the key difference between punishment and conditional welfare is that the state is not depriving these families of something they (if not for the violation) would otherwise be entitled to, as it would be in the case of a fine. It is giving them something that they lack and have no independent claim on, just not being terribly generous about it. So on this view, meager and conditional welfare support does not violate reproductive freedom and might be an effective and nonpunitive way to prevent wrongful procreation. Poor single women still have their full liberty to procreate, but given their limited means, they have less incentive to do so.

Dorothy Roberts has argued that these elements of welfare policy are racist and sexist.[25] She views welfare reform (at least the aspects that bear on reproductive freedom) as a tool of oppression whose use is motivated (at least in part) by prejudice and hostility toward blacks, particularly black women. She argues that such policies serve an ideological function—to justify an oppressive social structure by suggesting that racial inequality is caused by bad reproductive decisions rather than injustice. There is an old and persisting ideology that portrays black women as unfit to be mothers. This system of representations depicts black women as sexually promiscuous, as procreating with abandon but without providing proper parenting for their young, as "matriarchs" who demoralize black men and cause them to desert their families, as "welfare queens" who create more children to increase their welfare benefits, and as creating irreparably impaired children ("crack babies") by abusing drugs during pregnancy.[26] Black reproduction is viewed as degeneracy—as leading to the transmission of inferior genes, made worse by the bad habits of black mothers during pregnancy, and made worse still by the bad example of black parents' deviant lifestyles. These stereotypes, Roberts argues, are false and offensive, and they obscure the real causes of racial inequality.

Roberts's critique is compelling. I have no doubt that such an ideology is at work. However, her critique, as important as it is, does not settle the question of whether there is a valid justification for welfare policies that deter reproduction among poor single women. It is clear that advocates of such policies could have racist or sexist motives, and some people might endorse them because they accept racial or gender stereotypes or are infected with implicit bias. But others might endorse them because they want to encourage responsible procreation and reduce black poverty. One might also think that, even though these interventions into the reproductive lives of the black poor are frequently premised on a mistaken diagnosis of the fundamental causes of black poverty, these policies (perhaps combined with others) would nonetheless reduce such poverty and, more generally, improve the lives of disadvantaged black women. This position, I believe, merits a response and so, for the sake of argument, I assume that some disadvantaged blacks make reproductive choices that contribute to perpetuating ghetto conditions and that violate the Reproductive Responsibility Principle.

Using the structure of welfare benefits to prevent violations of RRP could (at least in principle) be effective, nonpunitive, nonracist, and nonsexist. Yet for reasons already discussed, it cannot be fully justified to poor single mothers, particularly those among the ghetto poor. The false background assumption here is that the public has provided the ghetto poor with all the resources and opportunities to which they are entitled as equal citizens.

We can see the mistake by highlighting a disanalogy between teenage mothers and adult poor single mothers in ghettos. The teenager is unfit to parent because she is too young and inexperienced. The disadvantaged woman is unable to parent adequately only because she lacks resources and opportunities.[27] If the public had fulfilled its obligations to these women by ensuring that they were not subject to pervasive racism and sexism, that their class background did not severely diminish their life prospects, that their neighborhoods were safe for raising children, and that they were not disadvantaged because of unrectified past injustices, then perhaps they could not rightly complain if their reproductive freedom is limited by the structure of welfare benefits. As it is, these welfare measures unfairly reduce the value of these women's reproductive liberty and compound the injustices they face. Notice that this argument does not rely on the premise that reproductive freedom is limitless or that no welfare benefits can be conditional on their recipients following certain rules. The argument rests on the claim that the basic structure of U.S. society is unjust and that principles of corrective justice do not permit using the provision and administration of welfare benefits to deter nonmarital births among unjustly disadvantaged women.

Perhaps some procreation among the ghetto poor is wrong. But this wrongful procreation, insofar as it results from limited financial means, does not wrong the public. Nor is a punitive response to this wrongful procreation justified. The state and the public at large are deeply complicit in these procreative wrongs. And there are other available ways for the public to address wrongful procreation among the ghetto poor—namely, working collectively to bring about a more just basic structure. Short of undertaking that immense but necessary task, the permissible means of discouraging poor single women from procreating (here assuming they would be in violation of RRP) are limited to such efforts as rational persuasion, educational programs, the provision of information, and voluntary counseling. And even here, as we've seen with cultural reform, the state may lack the standing to play this role in the lives of the oppressed, thus leaving such outreach efforts to those the ghetto poor have more reason to trust.

FIVE

Family

Because of the sex-based asymmetry in reproductive freedom, some might think that the state has more leeway to constrain or influence the procreative choices of boys and men—they do not get pregnant, so issues of bodily integrity and medical privacy do not arise regarding them. Perhaps if they can be discouraged from impregnating women they don't plan to co-parent with, the number of these fragile families can be reduced. Moreover, even when these single-mother families are formed, their vulnerability could be mitigated if the biological fathers of these children were to help with childcare and provide material support.

When considering single-mother families in ghettos, many strongly disapprove of biological fathers who are absent from their children's lives. Orlando Patterson, for example, has emphasized that most black children are now being raised without the consistent care and financial support of their fathers, which he attributes to the fact that "the great majority of Afro-American mothers have been seduced, deceived, betrayed, and abandoned by the men to whom they gave their love and trust."[1] Some fathers refuse to participate in raising their children or they are in prison and consequently have limited contact with their children. Some fathers who are involved in their children's lives abuse drugs, participate in street crime, or are violent toward their children or their children's mothers. They set a bad example for the children, encouraging them to develop problematic attitudes and habits. Even when they are neither absent nor a troubling presence, these fathers may elect not to provide much material support or, though willing to support their children, may lack adequate financial resources to do so.

There is evidence that the absence of a fit father (or father figure) has a negative effect on children's life chances.[2] This negative impact is said to be even greater when these children are raised in poor single-mother families. Some would insist that both poverty and father absence are due to the moral and prudential failings of the adults involved in creating these disadvantaged families. But as I have argued, their poverty is at least partially due to social injustices, and thus the state is complicit in the wrongful creation of these fragile families. Yet the biological fathers of these vulnerable children may share some of the blame for their vulnerability. Were these men to fulfill their parental duties, perhaps fewer black children would grow up poor.

Some argue that the frequent public condemnation of black fathers is largely unjustified, because most of these fathers are active in their children's lives and often provide informal financial support.[3] Perhaps most black fathers fully carry out their parental responsibilities. Still, we can consider that minority who are absent and provide little, if any, material support. Do they thereby wrong their children, the mothers of their children, or their fellow citizens?

As with the issue of procreation ethics and reproductive freedom, there is a pertinent philosophical question here: What facts and principles, when taken together, make it the case that a person comes to have parental obligations? The responsibility to pay child support will turn on the right answer to that question.

Parental Obligations and the State

The correct account of how a person comes to have parental *obligations* might diverge from the correct account of how a person comes to have parental *rights*. It is parental obligations that are at issue. Of course, for some parental responsibilities (such as the duty to aid the child in her or his development of rational capacities and a sense of justice), parents will need to be equipped with certain rights or prerogatives if they are to effectively carry out these responsibilities. But with some parental responsibilities (such as the responsibility to meet the material needs of one's children), parental rights will not always be necessary (the parent need only pay the required amount at the appropriate times).[4]

Simply identifying the basic needs of children (their need for physical care, love, material necessities, education, discipline, supervision, and so on) is not enough to ground parental responsibilities. Everyone has a general moral duty to see to it that such needs are met. We should come to the aid of the needy and vulnerable when we can do so at not too high a cost to ourselves. However, our concern is with children's *claim rights*—the rights that give rise to corresponding *special duties* for specific persons. We need to know who in particular has a duty to meet a given child's basic needs and for how long.

When it comes to philosophical theories of parenthood, the fundamental divide is between those who view the obligation to parent as an ordinance of nature that law merely codifies (for example, a preinstitutional private association of a heterosexual couple and their biological children) and those who see the obligation as ultimately rooted in moral concerns about the welfare of children that can be addressed through a variety of institutional practices. This latter view we might call *conventionalism*.

All children—given their vulnerability, limited abilities, and dependence—need to be cared for and raised until they are adults capable of participating in social life as equals to other citizens. We might regard this care work and upbringing as the sole responsibility of the state (a quasi-Platonist view), the sole responsibility of parents, or a responsibility divided between parents and the public. I will not consider quasi-Platonist views, which would abolish the family altogether.[5] (Plato would abolish it only for the ruling class of guardians.) But there is a plausible variant that I will briefly describe and that I shall call the *state-construct* account of parental responsibility.

On this view, the public at large, relying on the instrumentalities of the state, has ultimate responsibility for raising children into adult citizens. This responsibility can be provisionally delegated to private individuals and specific public institutions, who then carry out their assigned childcare duties with oversight by the state and in accordance with state regulations. Parents (like teachers) are effectively trustees carrying out fiduciary duties, called upon to look after the interests of specific children. The state would confer parental authority so that appointed parents have the discretion to effectively meet the needs of the children in their care. If prospective parents are deemed unfit to play this role, the state can justly deny them the right to parent even if they are the biological parents.[6] If they are selected but then do an inadequate job, the state can revoke (permanently or temporarily) their authority to make parental decisions. On the state-construct view, parenthood is entirely a creature of law, and biological parents have no extralegal claim to parent their biological children. Reproductive freedom is respected (that is, individuals are free to create children), but this liberty does not entail a right to parent one's offspring. Once children are born, they are citizens and their welfare rights are regarded as paramount, not something to be weighed against the rights of their parents. Consequently, individuals are not taken to have a basic interest in having an opportunity to play the role of parent, at least not one that the state must recognize if it is to be just.

Though it breaks sharply with common sense, the state-construct view has merit as an account of parenthood.[7] It also has deficiencies. I will bring out both its virtues and limitations by offering an alternative that captures what I think is right about the state-construct account but that denies that family relations are entirely a product of law. This account will also give weight to individuals' interests in becoming parents. I call this view the *institutional* account of parenthood. On this perspective, which I regard as a version of conventionalism, parental obligations are duties within the institution of the family, which is a component of the basic structure of society.

Families and the Basic Structure

A just society is structured to continue indefinitely and to maintain its just structure across generations. Every society, as an ongoing system of cooperation, has a vital stake in caring for and raising children so that they might eventually take their place in society as healthy, law-abiding, civic-minded, and contributing adults, taking care of the old and replacing them once they die. The family is part of the basic structure because it plays this *functional* role in society.[8] A society cannot be maintained from one generation to the next without families or some family-like institution. There must be procreation and childrearing, as new workers are needed to replace older ones. The family also plays a crucial role in the moral and educational development of children so that they can become full participants in a democratic society. Given these fundamental ends, families can take a variety of forms. They need not be traditional heterosexual, monogamous, two-parent domestic units with a male "head," and there is no presumption that the nuclear family is "natural" or that a just liberal state must privilege it over other formations.

Although there are moral limits to state intervention into family formation and family life, it is a mistake to view the family as a "private sphere" that should be free from government interference and regulation. The institutional account considers three sets of interests when determining the rights of families and the limits of state involvement in family affairs: children's interests, parents' interests (including interests of prospective parents), and the public's interests. It is these interests that give the public in a liberal-democratic polity a stake in the formation, structure, and internal dynamics of families.

For one thing, children, like the adult members of society, are citizens, and so the state has an obligation to protect their basic interests. Children's rights (including their welfare rights) must be secured, even against their parents. Thus, the state may intervene in family life to ensure that children are not mistreated. The home environment also has a significant and enduring effect on children, impacting their life prospects in various ways. Given the demands of fair equality of opportunity, the public must be concerned that children have a good start in life, and children's starting places will be deeply shaped by their familial experiences.

The adults in a family may seriously wrong one another. Women are particularly vulnerable to violence (including sexual assault) at the hands of their husbands or romantic partners. So the public has a stake in protecting the basic interests of adults within the context of family life. As Claudia Card has argued, it is cohabitation—a defining feature of the modern family—that makes women and children vulnerable to domestic violence.[9] The family as an institution, when structured unfairly or situated in an unjust society, can also reinforce or worsen gender inequality and women's disadvantage.

Moreover, if parents do not ensure their children's proper development (including their moral development), their children will likely grow up to become burdens on their fellow citizens—through delinquency, crime, economic dependency, physical and mental health problems, and such. So state regulation of family life is not paternalism toward the adults involved but a matter of protecting the legitimate interests of children and the public. In addition, the members of a just society support their social order because they share the knowledge that it is just; so the public has a stake in its citizens' developing a sense of justice, which occurs initially in the family.[10] So the family must be so structured and equipped to ensure this moral development.

For all these reasons and more, the public, through the instrumentality of the state, is justified in regulating the institution of the family. This does not mean that the state has unlimited authority to shape family life. The family is a part of the basic structure of society, but the principles of justice apply to the structure taken as a complete scheme of social cooperation, not to the internal structure of the family as such. The principles of justice do place normative constraints on the family—its internal structure and dynamics must be compatible with its members' rights as free and equal citizens. The family, though in some ways a private association, is not immune from the demands of justice.

The family in the United States is not only a social convention or an informal association but also a part of the coercive structure of society.[11] Parental authority over children (including the right not to have one's parenting decisions interfered with by others) is backed by law (for example, children are not allowed to permanently leave their homes) and revocable by judicial decision. Law defines the scope of parental prerogatives and discretion (for example, law requires that parents educate their children but gives them considerable freedom to choose where their children will receive instruction). Child custody is determined and enforced by law. Some parental obligations are legally enforceable (for instance, the obligation to feed, clothe, and house children and to not deny them essential medical care). Inheritance law and the tax scheme regulate intergenerational wealth transfers within families. And, of course, law governs marriage, including the disposition of marital property and the distribution of income after divorce.

Family law, like criminal law, is a part of the coercive apparatus of the state. This is another reason to regard the family as part of the basic structure of society. As noted, families are essential to material and social reproduction, and they have a deep and lasting influence on the persons raised in them, impacting every family member's relative life prospects. But the family is also a component of the basic structure because it enlists and is regulated by state power. Though there are noncoercive conventions associated with marriage and parenting and spouses and parents are free to make choices within the law about how they will relate to each other and their children, standing as a "legal parent" or "legal spouse" carries enforceable rights and responsibilities.[12]

Parental Obligations as Associative Duties

Parental responsibilities are *associative duties*—special duties one has to others in a social relationship in virtue of the intrinsic or extrinsic value of that relationship. As Samuel Scheffler has argued, not all associative duties are voluntarily assumed; some simply come with standing in a particular relationship to another.[13] Civic duties—one's obligations to one's fellow citizens—are best understood as involuntary associative duties, because individuals do not generally choose to become members of their societies (unless they immigrate) but instead are born into them.

Colin Macleod makes a useful distinction between *pragmatic* associative duties and *pure* associative duties.[14] Pragmatic associative duties are special duties persons have to particular others because assigning these duties to those occupying certain social roles is the most feasible and effective means to realizing an important moral objective (such as attending to the care and upbringing of children). Pure associative duties are binding in virtue of the intrinsic value of these relationships, not because of their instrumental value. Obligations between friends are prime examples of pure associative duties. One of the things that make parental obligations so complex and confusing is that they have pragmatic and pure dimensions, and thus parenthood is not simply a state construct.[15]

In *Political Liberalism* Rawls says that the "political domain" is nonvoluntary and not grounded in ties of affection.[16] He contrasts the political with the associational, which he regards as at least partially voluntary. He also contrasts the political with the familial, which he does regard as "affectional." This way of explaining the difference between the political, the associational, and the familial is not quite right, however. As Susan Moller Okin correctly points out, even if the family is in some ways a voluntary association, it is not like other associations (such as churches or clubs), because the family is a part of the basic structure.[17] Moreover, as with political society, one does not choose, at least not initially, to be a member of a family.[18] One is born into it, making the family, at least for children, a nonvoluntary association. Children's obligations to obey and accept the guidance of their parents is imposed rather than assumed. For prospective parents and spouses, the family is a voluntary association and parental and spousal obligations are assumed. From the standpoint of the members of a family, familial obligations are, at least often, pure associative duties.[19] People do, of course, sometimes marry or stay married solely for economic reasons or for the sake of their children's welfare. However, I regard these purely pragmatic arrangements as second-best scenarios (which is not to say they are uncommon). But as argued earlier, the public also has a legitimate interest in family relations, and from its standpoint familial obligations are simply pragmatic associative duties. Therefore some parental duties flow from the special relationship parents have with their children (a relationship primarily rooted in love and intimacy, though sometimes extrinsic considerations come into play) and some flow from civic responsibilities (which are rooted in principles of reciprocity and the social requirement to see to the care and upbringing of children).

It might be thought that parental responsibilities should be understood not as associative duties but as role obligations. For instance, Michael Hardimon regards associative duties as gaining their normative force through group membership, but he thinks that role obligations gain their normative force in virtue of the justified public rules that define an institution.[20] However, I think both normative notions apply in the case of families. Individual families are social groups (not institutions), and some obligations spring from the relationships between members of a family—sibling, spousal, parent–child, and so on. When I speak of "the institution of the family," I don't mean individual family units but the system of public rules that define the roles of parent and spouse and that give legal force to kinship relations (for example, inheritance rights and decision-making power over the affairs of dependent, ill, incapacitated, or deceased kin). In other words, role obligations can exist within forms of association (such as the roles of parent, citizen, party leader, and union boss).

Allowing biological and adoptive parents to take primary caretaking responsibility for children is an efficient and fair way for a society to meet the needs of newly created citizens (which is not to say it is the *only* efficient and fair way to handle childcare and childrearing).[21] It is efficient because individuals who choose to become parents, whether through direct procreation or adoption, are typically deeply invested in their children, have profound love for them, and are willing to make immense sacrifices (including the ultimate sacrifice) to ensure their children's welfare and development. They are often willing to play the role of parent regardless of the level of public support they receive in their parenting efforts (which is not to say that the public should exploit these natural feelings of affection and special concern). It would be inefficient to pay people not already personally invested to play this role. Children also need love, and publicly supporting individuals who already love a child is more cost-effective and realistic than paying professionals to care for the child and hoping that the paid caretaker comes to love the child. (I am assuming that we cannot love at will, and so we cannot literally pay someone to love a child.) These intimate bonds of affection must also be stable. Even if children can build loving relationships with professional childcare staff, these relationships are unlikely to be stable, as there are inevitably personnel changes in any workplace and each person has a basic liberty to choose and change occupations.

It is perfectly consistent with an institutional view that the state simply *assign* parental responsibilities to particular private individuals, even if these individuals do not want the role. On a view of this sort, parents effectively would be conscripted. However, on the institutional view I'm defending, individuals acquire parental responsibilities by explicitly or implicitly electing to play the role of parent. Giving prospective biological and adoptive parents the option to choose to take primary responsibility for childcare and childrearing is a fairer way to distribute the burdens of this responsibility. Rather than the duty being imposed, only those who voluntarily take up the role have this responsibility. Everyone would have a fair opportunity to avoid its burdens. Parental duties would then be, in part, civic duties that any citizen acquires if he or she assumes the role of parent. Failure to fulfill these duties would be a wrong committed not only against the children involved but also against the political community, a kind of lack of civic reciprocity.

Acquiring Parental Obligations

Taking a conventionalist approach to parenthood, Elizabeth Brake argues that parental rights and obligations have their source in institutional roles defined by variable social and legal conventions.[22] She also maintains that voluntary acceptance of parental obligations is necessary for such obligations to be morally binding. This acceptance need not be through explicit oral or written agreement. It can be implied, provided the bound person knows (or should know) the convention for undertaking the obligation and grasps the significance of the obligations thereby incurred.

I agree with these conclusions of Brake's insightful analysis. However, I do not share her reasons for thinking that voluntary acceptance is necessary for parenthood. She believes "special obligations only arise through voluntary undertaking or as compensation for some harm."[23] I do not accept this claim, as my discussion of associative duties indicates. We can have special obligations, even in the context of institutional roles, despite not having elected to undertake them and even when we have caused no harm. But in the context of parent–child relationships, the stakes are sufficiently high for those involved and the objectives are of a sort that we have good reasons for allowing each an adequate opportunity to accept or reject the role of parent before treating persons as having parental duties and holding them accountable if they fail to honor them.

Obviously, (potential) sexual partners don't always arrange explicit parental contingency plans prior to sex or even childbirth.[24] So under what conditions should we regard someone as having implied his or her willingness to parent? In other words, setting aside explicit agreement (which is clearly sufficient), what should count as voluntary acceptance of the role of parent? Joseph Millum treats *consensual sex* as implied consent to parent should the sex lead to childbirth.[25] (When I speak of "sex" from this point forward, I mean *coitus*.) He correctly takes the social convention to be well known and broadly endorsed. But we cannot justify holding biological parents responsible for child support by simply citing a widely recognized social convention. We must justify reliance on the convention given its costs to those who satisfy its conditions (in this case, many years of financial costs and other sacrifices). Millum does so by arguing that the convention is fair to those who participate in consensual sex, given that they can avoid parental responsibilities by agreeing in advance to (1) abort the fetus should an unwanted pregnancy occur, (2) put the child up for adoption, or (3) assign one of the child's biological parents full responsibility for rearing the child. But he acknowledges that this may be insufficient to fully justify the convention to all affected and that fairness may require that we alter the convention in some way. I want to suggest one way that the convention should be altered to better satisfy conditions of fairness.

The traditional convention, properly understood, is reasonably fair to women, provided that abortion is accessible, safe, and affordable and that making children available for adoption is a viable option. (And although this view is controversial among some, I take it that a just society would ensure that these conditions are met, given the importance of the interests that such measures would protect.) The convention affords women considerable control over their bodies and future and does not penalize them for having sex. However, there is a source of unfairness in the convention for men who engage in sex for pleasure but do not want to be fathers, which is revealed if we recall the sex-based asymmetry in reproductive freedom (see Chapter 4).

Claudia Mills frames the issue well.[26] When a woman becomes pregnant, regardless of whether she took responsible contraceptive measures, she retains the right to choose whether to become a parent; but the man who impregnates her, regardless of whether he took responsible contraceptive measures, has little choice about whether he will become a parent. And what choice he does have is conditional on her choice. If he wants to be a father but she chooses to terminate the pregnancy, then he won't be a father and has no valid claim against her. If he does not want to be a father but she nevertheless chooses to give birth and to keep the baby, he will be not only the biological father but also socially and legally regarded as the parent of the child, with the corresponding obligations. If one of the two wants to put the child up for adoption but the other wants to keep it, then their situation is symmetrical, but even then only *after* the pregnant woman has declined the option of abortion, which is her choice alone. In all cases, once she becomes pregnant, whether he becomes a parent is within her hands. Thus, in fact, women consent to parent, not by having consensual sex, but by bearing children that they don't put up for adoption. On the prevailing convention, only men implicitly accept parental responsibilities through consensual sex alone.

So, when should we regard a man as having implicitly undertaken the role of parent? Here I believe is a more reasonable convention than the "sex-equals-implied-acceptance of parenthood" norm: If neither sexual partner uses contraception and this fact is known to both, then (absent explicit communication to the contrary) the male partner has implied his acceptance of parental responsibilities should a child be created from his sperm. Under the proposed convention, the manifest use of contraception could be treated as an adequate sign that one does not want to be a parent (at least not yet or not with this particular sexual partner). There is not sufficient reason to treat consensual sexual intercourse, by either sex, as implied acceptance of parenthood, and there is good reason to allow men more control over whether they will become parents.

When a man uses contraception or otherwise makes it explicit that he does not want to father a child, his sexual partner has been given fair warning that if she bears his biological child, he might not assume the obligation to parent the child. (He could of course change his mind if she becomes pregnant or once the baby is born, but she has no assurance of that.) He has taken measures to avoid pregnancy, thereby making it clear that he does not seek to procreate.[27] With both the question of contraception and the man's attitude toward parenthood settled, the woman has the information necessary to decide whether to risk pregnancy by having sex with this particular individual. She therefore has an adequate opportunity to avoid single parenthood. The availability of effective contraception (including morning-after pills, which are 85 to 89 percent effective three to five days *after* sex) enables women to have sex without having to endure pregnancy, without being forced to become mothers, and without having to rely solely on abortion or adoption to avoid motherhood. The availability of effective contraception alone gives women considerable control over their reproductive lives, quite apart from what their male sexual partners do or say.

But in deciding whether to risk pregnancy by having sex, it is reasonable for a woman to expect (and prudent for her to seek) some reliable indication of whether her sexual partner is willing to parent should she bring a fetus to term. When this expressed will (which might be only implicit) is positive, this would commit the man to parenting or at least to child support until the child reaches adulthood. A woman may, understandably, also want assurance that, should pregnancy occur, the man who impregnated her will be forced to provide child support if she decides to bear his biological child. But this, I think, is too much to ask. Given the fair warning requirement and the availability of contraception, abortion, and adoption, she is already in a good position to control her fate (with respect to sex, procreation, and parenthood) without this further assurance, which would entail great and unwanted burdens for him.

Some might object that women who believe that abortion is wrong (on moral or religious grounds) do not have adequate control over their reproductive lives unless the men who impregnate them will be forced to provide child support should these men not do so willingly. In reply, I would first note that the fair warning requirement and the availability of contraception and adoption are probably jointly sufficient to afford women adequate control over their reproductive lives. But if this is regarded as insufficient empowerment in view of reasonable disagreement over whether abortion is wrong, these women can secure the requisite level of control by refraining from having sex with men who do not openly express their willingness to parent should a child be born. This is a fairer response to public disagreement over the permissibility of abortion than compelling men to accept parenting responsibilities when they have made it clear that they don't want them. It is also fairer than permitting women to have sex for pleasure without this committing them to parenting but not allowing the same freedom for men. It is fairer to all concerned to expect those who oppose abortion to accept this small cost (that is, precoital, explicit arrangement of parenting contingencies) of their moral or religious conviction than to expect the public to shift the burdens of this conviction onto those who don't share it.

It is important that children not be created unless procreators are reasonably sure that there are fit adults available and willing to care for and raise them.[28] Giving individuals the opportunity to choose this parental role while also expecting sexually active adults to use contraception if they do not want to undertake it is a good way to satisfy this condition. Moreover, when a person has chosen the role of parent and has not been forced to play it, the fulfillment of parental responsibility will mean more to the children involved. They are then able to view parental care and support as an expression of love and not merely an involuntary fulfillment of duty. The fact that a person has chosen the role is also a good indication that he or she will attempt to fulfill its responsibilities in a conscientious way.

But a man cannot reasonably complain when the woman he impregnates decides to hold him liable for parental care and child support if he had an adequate opportunity to decline the role of parent but failed to seize it. This is *not* because he has somehow forfeited his right to object by having sex with her. If he uses contraception or if it is mutually understood that his sexual partner uses it, then it wouldn't be reasonable to construe his sexual activity as acceptance of parenthood should his sperm be used to create a child. The use of contraception voids the inference that he seeks to be a parent or that he is indifferent to whether he becomes a parent. Of course, if she gets pregnant, she is free to terminate the pregnancy or to bear the child and he has no standing to overrule her decision. But her reproductive freedom does not entail a claim right on the biological father for childrearing help or child support. (If either deceives the other about contraceptive use, then it is not clear that consensual sex has occurred.)[29]

An attractive feature of this account of parental obligation is that it treats biological parents and adoptive parents, opposite-sex parents and same-sex parents, on a par. All parents acquire parental duties in the same way—by voluntarily assuming them. One can assume them at conception, during gestation, at birth, or at some time after birth. Some might even assume them conditionally *prior* to conception, effectively promising to parent *if* a child is born, an agreement not uncommon among married couples or committed partners. The only difference would be *when* the role is undertaken.

An aspect of this account that may trouble some, however, is its implication that biological fathers who made it explicit prior to conception that they did not want to be fathers or who used contraception do not have parental responsibilities.[30] They have not accepted the role through their words or deeds and so do not have parental duties, not even child support obligations. Thus if this account is correct, the state cannot justly require child support payments from these men. Because many single-mother families, particularly those among the ghetto poor, are formed because the relevant biological fathers have not assumed the obligation to parent, the institutional account of parenthood has far-reaching implications for justice and the ghetto.

Responsibility for Pregnancy

One way to resist this conclusion (without falling back on sex as implied willingness to parent) is to offer an alternative account of how individuals acquire parental obligations that does not make voluntary acceptance of parenthood a necessary condition. The most influential argument of this sort relies on a "torts model" of parental responsibility. The basic idea is this: The fact that one has *caused* a needy and vulnerable child to exist makes one liable for its defenseless state, creating long-term special duties of care beyond the general duty of mutual aid. For example, James Nelson argues that causal responsibility for the existence of a child is the basis of parental obligations.[31] He maintains that being causally responsible for harm or the threat of harm gives one moral responsibility for aiding the person harmed, protecting her from harm, or compensating her for harm done. He says, "In the absence of special considerations, such as force or fraud, those causally responsible for the child's existence—and hence, her existence as a morally considerable being at serious risk of death, suffering and other harms—have a particular obligation to attempt to preserve their children from such risks."[32]

We must be careful, though, not to confuse causal responsibility with moral responsibility or to assume that moral responsibility always follows from causal responsibility. When thinking about moral responsibility, we should also, following T. M. Scanlon, distinguish between *attribution* responsibility and *substantive* responsibility.[33] Responsibility as attribution concerns when it is appropriate to take an action or attitude as a basis for morally appraising the agent (particularly with respect to praise or blame), whereas substantive responsibility has to do with what individuals are morally required to do for one another. The biological father who used contraception is still causally responsible for impregnating the mother of his biological child, and it is undeniable that if not for his sperm, the child would not have been created. It is much less clear that he can be blamed for not accepting parental obligations. Even if he can be fairly criticized for not offering child support (say, on grounds that he is being selfish or callous toward the plight of the single mother and her child), this does not mean that he has an enforceable obligation (substantive responsibility) to provide this support.

Attribution responsibility for the newly created child would appear to be properly attached to the mother who gave birth to it. The biological father, in the case under consideration, has not set out to create a child, has made it clear prior to sex that he does not seek to be a father, and has taken contraceptive measures to avoid this outcome. The child's existence is either an accident (which reasonable measures were taken to prevent) or the result of the mother's choice to bear the child despite her knowledge that the father did not wish to be a parent. Pregnant women, and pregnant women alone, have the liberty to decide if the embryo will be gestated and a child birthed. Brake argues persuasively that the biological father, provided he has not accepted the role of moral father, has no parental liability when the mother can freely and safely choose abortion.[34] And even if a pregnant woman forgoes abortion, she may still have the option of making the baby available for adoption (assuming the biological father chooses not to assume parental responsibility). If a pregnant woman rejects both abortion and adoption despite having been warned prior to conception about the biological father's intentions, why should parental responsibilities be imposed on the biological father? The mere fact that he had sex with the mother is insufficient reason to impose this burdensome and unwanted duty.

Against this conclusion, Mills insists that the biological father's parental obligation rests on the fact that he created a helpless person who exists *only because of* the father's voluntary actions.[35] However, in addition to the problem just explained—namely, that the child exists only because the mother allowed it to gestate and gave birth to it—the "if-not-but-for" condition (counterfactual dependency) is overly inclusive, as the child might die in utero or during childbirth if not for various medical professionals (or even if not for the taxi driver who gets the mother to the hospital just in time). Indeed, the child would not exist if not for the voluntary acts of its many ancestors. Talk of "creation" here is also misleading. The father has contributed to the creation of a *zygote* whose ultimate fate lies with the mother. He played no role in bringing the embryo to term, whereas numerous other persons may have (friends, the mother's family members, a midwife, medical professionals, and so on). Lots of people may contribute to bringing a child into the world, but this fact alone does not give them parental obligations.

Mills's argument seems plausible, but only because it rests on a suppressed premise—that gamete providers are not just causes but *the morally relevant* causes of the child's existence. But by what principle do we single out gamete provision from other causes that involve agents?

One might argue that the biological father, by having sex with the biological mother, *set into motion* a series of events (some of which were, admittedly, consequences of others' decisions) that he *knew* could result in a child and that this initial voluntary act and foreknowledge are sufficient to give him parental responsibilities should his biological child be born. Yet the friend or dating service that sets up a woman and man on a date also satisfies these conditions. It is more plausible to say that this foreknowledge gives the man a strong reason to take precautions to prevent an unintended pregnancy if neither seeks parental obligations. No one thinks that automobile manufacturers are morally responsible for compensating victims of car accidents (assuming the cars are built safe), despite the fact that they set into motion automobile use and that accidents are known to happen. Biological fathers who use reliable contraception are similarly situated.

But let us suppose that biological fathers, no matter what birth control measures they may have taken, always share blame and thus some responsibility for the vulnerable condition of their biological children. Still, as Brake points out, *parental* obligations are not best understood as compensatory justice.[36] Or to put it in the terms developed earlier, associative duties are not the same as reparative duties. To conceive of parental obligations on the model of torts would give us an impoverished and peculiar conception of parenthood. It would treat parental duties as a matter of our compensating for the fact that, by creating children, we have put them in a helpless state. It might even suggest that we have *wronged* them by creating them, and that parenting is simply our attempt to rectify the injury caused by our immoral reproductive actions.

Being a cause of a helpless human being certainly gives one moral reasons to which one should respond. As David Archard argues, having caused the existence of a human being in this vulnerable state, one should make sure the child is not left to die or suffer.[37] If, however, the procreator has ensured that the child is in the hands of someone willing and able to care for the child, he or she has fulfilled the obligation. The key distinction here is between having an obligation to ensure that *someone* parents the child one caused to exist and having an obligation *oneself* to parent the child. If the mother is willing and able to care for the child, then the father has discharged his procreation liability. He has effectively ensured that the child has an adequate primary caregiver. All biological fathers owe their children at least this, but parental responsibilities rest on facts other than (or at least in addition to) being their cause.

This conclusion may strike some as morally obtuse. However, two qualifications should make it seem less so. First, strict liability penalties for biological fathers could be justified on the ground that they create incentives to take precautions to avoid unwanted pregnancies. This seems wise. Without such penalties, some men might be tempted to be careless or reckless when having sex with fertile women, potentially contributing to the creation of unwanted children. Strict liability penalties would reduce this moral hazard. They would also promote the sharing of responsibility for birth control between men and women, and so can also be justified on gender equity grounds.[38]

Because women with unwanted pregnancies face the bad alternatives of abortion, putting a child they birthed up for adoption, or being a parent when they do not want this role, they don't need the additional incentive structure of strict liability penalties to deter them from irresponsible sex. Still, the financial obligations typical of child support payments are disproportionate to the outcomes and inequities we want to prevent. Lighter penalties (perhaps three to five years of payments rather than eighteen years) would be fairer to those involved and probably just as effective in deterring procreative irresponsibility and inequity in the sharing of contraceptive responsibility. Moreover, given that strict liability does not imply wrongdoing, we cannot justify increasing the penalties to current child support levels.[39]

Treating child support as *punishment* might make sense as a penalty for someone who has assumed the role of parent but failed to carry out its duties. The parent who deserts his or her family wrongs the child by refusing to meet the child's emotional and material needs and wrongs the other parent by failing to live up to obligations they have jointly undertaken. When a couple decides together to co-parent, this arrangement imposes long-term obligations. If one partner in the arrangement abandons the family or refuses to parent, he or she is properly held liable for child support and blameworthy for failing to provide it. If the parents break up, neither is absolved of parental responsibilities, even if neither is at fault for the failed romantic relationship.

When I speak of penalties for accidental pregnancies, however, I am mainly concerned with cases where the biological father has not assumed parental responsibilities. On the strict liability account, the fine may be imposed without the presumption of fault and without condemning the father for not assuming parental obligations (for example, without labeling him a "deadbeat dad"). This is not because those who accidentally father children are never at fault. They may, as a matter of fact, have acted recklessly, negligently, even maliciously, and thus would merit blame and censure. But because of the difficulties in determining fault in accidental pregnancies, it may be best in some cases to impose penalty without assessing responsibility. The point would be to encourage responsible sexual activity. Importantly, the proceeds from these penalties would not be construed as compensating the state for providing the support a father should have provided as part of his parental obligations. The money may be used to support the child of the biological father, may be pooled to help children in need of greater support, or may be used for some unrelated purpose.

This leads to the second reason we should not reject out of hand the counterintuitive conclusions reached above about paternal liability. Distinct from the question of whether biological fathers have parental duties to their biological children is the question of what (if any) obligations they have to the mothers of their biological offspring. Though only women have the right to terminate a pregnancy, both biological parents made a joint decision to have sex knowing that pregnancy was a possible outcome. If the woman becomes pregnant without intending to, it would not be fair if she had to carry all the burdens of their joint decision. She now faces a difficult choice with no cost-free options, and given his role in placing her in this situation, it is reasonable to expect him to share in these burdens. For instance, it seems only fair that he should cover her medical costs for an abortion or for prenatal and postnatal care (assuming, for the sake of argument, that the public needn't cover it). Perhaps he should pay a flat fee to defray unanticipated nonmedical costs associated with pregnancy. Despite her having the options of abortion and adoption, it might also be reasonable to expect the biological father to offer some financial and emotional support from the late stages of pregnancy until the postpartum period when the mother is physically (and perhaps psychologically) able to work again. To be clear, this would be a matter of duties, not to the child, but to the mother. She may need support while she is pregnant and while she recovers from pregnancy, and the father should contribute to this. We can call this assistance *pregnancy support* to distinguish it from child support, and such support needn't be limited to money.

Mother Support

But what about "mother support," the assistance a mother often needs in caring for her children? As Mills says, "It is worth noting . . . that it is prima facie suboptimal to have one person assuming obligations of both father and mother, for this is bound to produce some subsequent strain as one individual (the mother) attempts to carry out the obligations of two."[40] However, this assumes either that all biological parents are moral parents (which I think is false and, in any case, question begging) or that the child has a valid claim on the parental services of two specific adults rather than on however many adults are needed to provide adequate care. The claim that every child *needs* two parents is highly contentious, even if most would agree that, other things being equal, two parents are better able to ensure a child's welfare than a single parent.

Moreover, even if the mother finds her parental role difficult to shoulder alone, this does not mean that the biological father is to blame for her burdens. If my argument is correct, then provided he has used contraception or otherwise indicated in advance that he does not intend to undertake a parental role and that abortion and adoption are viable alternatives, he has not treated the mother unfairly—because his actions have not placed her in a situation where she lacks an adequate opportunity to avoid single motherhood.

Because the ghetto poor are deeply disadvantaged by an unjust social structure, poor black single mothers and the children they care for are often in a difficult, and sometimes desperate, situation. The disadvantaged biological fathers of these children should be concerned about the fate of children in ghettos, even if, strictly speaking, they lack parental obligations to any of these children. They, *like the rest of us*, have a general duty to help meet the needs of the weak and vulnerable when possible. But they may also have special duties rooted in bonds of solidarity among those similarly oppressed. If they avow a commitment to, say, black solidarity and yet are indifferent to the many unfair obstacles that black single mothers and poor black children face, their black comrades may appropriately criticize them for failing to live up to their political commitment. The mutual concern and loyalty required by solidarity suggest that these men should do their part to support group self-help practices, including participating in formal and informal efforts on the part of black communities to protect the vital interests of disadvantaged black children. Choosing to be a single mother, and thus the *primary* caregiver, should not mean taking on all childcare work that occurs outside of schools. And in the absence of appropriate public support (such as childcare subsidies and public childcare centers), black men—whether they are biological fathers or not—can play important roles in the lives of disadvantaged black children, including assisting their mothers, extended family, and community in rearing them. This commitment, generally much less demanding than assuming parental responsibility, can be viewed as a component of a larger community-based endeavor that bell hooks refers to as *revolutionary parenting*.[41] As such, it is an element in the political ethics of the oppressed.

Many disadvantaged black men share households with a single mother and her children in a ghetto community. Sometimes these women are these men's romantic partners or occasional lovers, though not always. Sometimes these children are these men's biological offspring, sometimes not. The employment prospects of the men and the women are often grim (see Chapter 6). But because of recent shifts in the U.S. labor market and discriminatory practices (including a strong bias against hiring former felons), there is often more work available for low-skilled black women (usually in the service sector) than for their male counterparts. It might therefore make practical sense for those men who have found it difficult to find employment to take on the larger share of childcare and other household responsibilities, thereby freeing the women up to earn more income for the household. This reversal of the traditional domestic division of labor could also be considered revolutionary parenting. It would serve not only to give these disadvantaged mothers the support that they need but also to break down oppressive gender stereotypes and to resist patriarchal ideals. In addition to making it easier to survive under difficult circumstances, such a stance would represent a bold and admirable act of solidarity with black mothers and with women more generally.

Of course, those outside of black communities who seek to act in solidarity with the ghetto poor should also assist these vulnerable families. The mothers and their disadvantaged communities should not be left to carry these unjust burdens alone. And here the fact that some biological fathers have exacerbated these vulnerable families' disadvantaged condition is a reason for them to supply some level of support to ease these burdens. In arguing that some disadvantaged black biological fathers lack parental obligations and thus should not be forced to pay child support, I am not thereby suggesting that they have no duties at all toward their biological children. But the fact that they played a role in creating these children is not the source of these duties.

In the absence of broader structural reform, if men had the freedom to decide whether to accept the role of parent and paternity alone was insufficient to establish parental obligations, this would obviously impose enormous burdens on mothers and would worsen gender inequality. It is incredibly difficult to be a single mother in American society today (all the more so when one is poor, black, or both), and so it is tempting to ameliorate the situation of such women by simply conscripting biological fathers into the role of parent, garnishing their wages and punishing them with jail time if necessary. Yet, were we to look at the problem from within a systemic-injustice framework, we might come to see that the problem of gender-based disadvantage within the family could and should be addressed by making changes elsewhere in the institutional arrangement of the basic structure. Universal preschool, generous maternity leave, professional childcare services, free birth control, and other such measures would go a long way. But at the heart of the problem are questions of *economic justice*—the way we share the benefits and burdens of material production and how the labor market is regulated (see Chapter 6). If we focus narrowly on altering family structure in ghetto communities, we fall into status quo bias and end up leaving a lot of injustices unaddressed.

Children as Public Goods

In order to determine which burdens of single parenthood are unfair to single mothers, we cannot look solely at the obligations of biological fathers. We must also consider the level of *public* support for single-mother families that justice requires, which the institutional conception of parental duties encourages us to do. Even if we assume that paternity imposes prima facie parental duties on biological fathers, a single woman who wants to raise her child without the biological father's involvement may waive her right to child support. If the father also waives his parental rights, the state has no ground to require child support. However, with poor single-mother families who receive welfare, the state imposes child support duties on biological fathers not only to enforce a duty thought to be owed to the child or mother (which I have argued is often a mistake) but also to recoup public costs of welfare support.[42] The normative assumption behind this practice is that because neither the state nor the broader public played a role in creating these children, the public does not owe these families welfare support.

If we focus solely on the liberty to procreate and the benefits to parents of having children, then we can be led to think that parents should bear all the costs of childrearing. Children are sometimes thought of as mere "consumption goods" for which parents should pay. Or parenting is seen as a "private project" for which parents should internalize the costs.[43] The care and guidance of children is sometimes viewed as a personal matter that does not concern the public, apart from ensuring that children are not neglected or abused.

But in light of the *public* benefits that children generate, public expenditures on childrearing are justifiable to those who choose not to have children of their own. Rolf George, for example, has argued persuasively that children, once they become adults, benefit everyone in society, and thus the costs of creating and raising them should be equitably shared between parents and the public.[44] On his view, fair-play principles apply because nonparents cannot be entirely excluded from these benefits (at least not without prohibitive costs) and cannot avoid enjoying the benefits: nonparents would be free-riding on the labor and other costs of having and raising children were they not to contribute to covering these costs.[45]

Children are the future workforce and thus are key elements in the material reproduction of society. The work of the young benefits the old, just as the work of adults benefits children. The childless therefore benefit from the work of parents and their children. The elderly also benefit from the care work of the young. Children properly raised and cared for are more likely to become law-abiding citizens. They are more likely to support the political order (assuming it is just) and to respect the civil rights of others. The work of raising them up to be good, productive citizens should thus be shared.

Serena Olsaretti strengthens the public goods argument by showing that when public consumption of external benefits makes producing them more costly, the public has an obligation to share the costs.[46] Her example is that the public's demand for a highly educated workforce increases the labor and financial costs of parenting. The costs of parenting are, in part, socially imposed—they are created by social expectations and by what is necessary, given existing socioeconomic circumstances, to provide one's children with a decent start in life. If not for the way the society is structured, the costs of raising children would be less. Olsaretti also emphasizes that children are "socialized goods"— socioeconomic institutions are purposefully structured in such a way that the public benefits from parents' labor. The social scheme distributes the benefits of childrearing to everyone. She also makes the overlooked point that because we all benefit from the public funds to which taxpayers contribute, we all benefit from the parenting labor of others, for every taxpayer was once someone's child.

Taking the public goods argument to be sound, I want to situate and develop it within the conception of justice and the family I've been defending. We should think of the natural duty of justice and the fair-play principle as applying to the social scheme as a whole and not (or at least not only) to separate institutions within the scheme. The system of cooperation that constitutes society is an ongoing enterprise, which requires material, biological, and social reproduction. All members of society must do their part to maintain the scheme over time, from one generation to the next. The key institutional practices within the basic structure of society are families, the economy (including property relations and market mechanisms), educational institutions, the health care system, and state apparatuses (with their lawmaking, adjudicative, and enforcement mechanisms). These social institutions serve essential social functions in any modern society.[47] We cannot do without them.[48] There is a complex social division of labor here, and the work that parents do is fundamental. We need a fair way to distribute the burdens of maintaining this complex system, as we all enjoy numerous benefits from it.

We all benefit from the developed talents and ambitions of others when they choose socially beneficial occupations. By offering good compensation and social esteem, we should actively encourage individuals to develop their talents into socially useful skills and to pursue socially valuable occupations. Part of the reason we should share the costs of education is that we all benefit from a skilled workforce and an educated citizenry. Parents also play a crucial role in developing the talents of their children and in instilling a sense of moral and civic responsibility. This parental role, while intrinsically rewarding, is also challenging, time-consuming, labor-intensive, financially costly, and sometimes painful. When children become healthy, law-abiding, civic-minded, and productive adults, they are public goods produced in part through the hard work and sacrifice of parents. The public therefore has strong reasons to facilitate, support, and promote good parenting.[49] Given the responsibilities involved and what is at stake, it would be unfair—and unwise—to leave parents to internalize all the costs of rearing the next generation.[50]

This vision of political morality is one in which the public must certainly ensure educational opportunity and health care for all. But the public might also, as it does in the United States, allow mortgage-interest deductions and other home-buying assistance to enable families to provide stable residences for rearing children. It might give child tax credits or childcare deductions for professional childcare services to offset some of the costs of raising a family. And it could also subsidize the incomes of disadvantaged families to ensure their access to material necessities and to enable a nurturing home environment. Parents provide the personalized care, love, discipline, guidance, and household stability necessary for proper child development. State institutions and families, as essential components of the basic structure of society, must both fulfill their substantive responsibilities if the liberties and opportunities of all members are to be secure. Reasonable people can disagree over what constitutes a fair distribution of costs and labor burdens between parents and the public. But justice requires some such division.

To be clear, it is not a thesis of the institutional conception of the family that children should be created so that we might have fresh workers, a larger tax base, or people to care for us when we are old or infirm. Nor is there any implication that we have children for the sake of the children we create, because we cannot benefit beings that do not yet exist. Prospective procreators have reproductive freedom that should not be infringed to advance the public good. Individuals have children for their own idiosyncratic reasons and probably rarely because their offspring will contribute to social and material reproduction. Individuals should not set out to create children unless they are confident that they or others are prepared to help with care and upbringing. Those who assume the role of parents should prepare their children to face the challenges that life will throw at them.[51] They should also guide them so that they might take their place in society as equal citizens. But because childrearing confers essential public benefits, the public should share in its costs.

Limits of Child Support Enforcement

Today in the United States when the fathers of kids who receive welfare make child support payments, they pay the state, not the mothers of their children. Mothers receiving welfare sign over their legal right to child support from biological or adoptive fathers in exchange for public support. States may give a small portion of the child support revenue to mothers (though federal law does not require this), but they keep most of it to defray the costs of supporting poor families. The underlying rationale would appear to be that these fragile families are an unfair burden on taxpayers and so owe the public for this support.

The tactics used to ensure child support payments give the state considerable power over poor parents. Noncustodial parents can rack up penalties for being late with or not paying child support. Some states will suspend the professional, business, or driver's licenses of individuals with outstanding child support debts. Bank accounts and other financial assets can be seized and liens placed on property. In some cases, jail time can be imposed (for contempt of court) when there is a pattern of nonpayment. Courts can order these individuals to participate in programs aimed at finding them work so that the state can extract child support payments. This aggressive enforcement scheme can lead some men to avoid the licit economy so that the state cannot garnish their wages. It can lead them to disappear or remain hidden from mainstream society so that the state cannot locate them, which also has the consequence that the children will have even less contact with their fathers.

If I am right that not all biological fathers have parental obligations toward their biological children, then it is unfair to require child support of biological fathers who have not undertaken the role of parent. Perhaps they owe pregnancy support to the mothers of their children. Maybe they should be penalized in accordance with strict liability principles as part of a general policy to encourage responsible sexual conduct. But they should not be penalized or condemned for failing to live up to their parental obligations to their biological children, as they do not have such obligations. In fact, if they refuse to make child support payments, not only is this not a failure of parental responsibility, but it should be regarded as justified resistance to unjust demands.

Many who have been raised by single mothers feel that there is a void in their lives where a father's love should have been. They feel that they have been robbed of something they had a natural right to—a loving relationship with the men who created them. To suggest that these feelings are irrational would be unduly harsh and may appear a failure to acknowledge deep human needs (for example, to develop an identity rooted in one's ancestry).[52] While I endorse a conception of parent–child relationships that gives less weight to biological relatedness, my argument does not depend on denying any value to bare biological descent.[53] But I doubt that the loving relationships some seek to have with their biological fathers is best fostered by an aggressive child support regime. Love can be given only willingly and certainly not under duress. And perhaps a move away from a paternity conception of moral fatherhood would do a lot to dissipate the sense of void that some children of single mothers feel when they contemplate the absence of their biological fathers.

Indeed, some children of single mothers might be able to build meaningful relationships with their biological fathers if these fathers were viewed as some birth parents are in open adoptions (adoptions where birth parents maintain some kind of relationship with the adoptive family).[54] Though the biological father may have decided against undertaking parental responsibilities, he may be willing to make himself available for regular (or at least occasional) contact with his offspring. He is more likely to do this if the state isn't pursuing him for child support, which he may feel that he does not owe. He is also more likely to cultivate a relationship with his biological child if the mother does not condemn or resent him for not undertaking the role of parent, as he may believe that these attitudes are unjustified. The mother, as parent and thus primary caretaker, should have the discretion to limit or preclude contact between her child and the child's biological father (as she would with her child and any other adult), at least until the child is old enough to decide the matter. But allowing some form of contact might satisfy a child's felt emotional needs, and so should be seriously considered.

There are, of course, biological fathers (along with some adoptive ones) who have undertaken parental duties but are unable to fulfill them for lack of resources. Some in this situation have engaged in wrongful procreation: they have undertaken obligations they knew (or should have known) they were unlikely to be able to fulfill. Still, child support enforcement against them is not always legitimate. As with many poor single women, these disadvantaged men have often been unjustly denied rights, opportunities, and resources to which they were entitled. Any failure to pay child support due to this unjust disadvantage reflects a public failure to maintain a just basic structure.

Public Support for Single-Mother Families

Since the 1960s there has been a dramatic rise in the number of single-mother families, and these families are generally worse off economically than their dual-parent counterparts.[55] Some single-mother families are vulnerable because a parent has died. Others are vulnerable because they are *broken* families—households that previously contained two adults in a partnership jointly committed to parenting and to dividing household and earning labor but where one of these adults no longer resides in the household. If the noncustodial parent, though able, does not provide financial and other means of support to the family he or she has left, this sometimes constitutes a wrong to the children, to the custodial parent, and to the public. The parent, having assumed these obligations, is in default of civic and other duties and is rightly held accountable. But not every disadvantaged single-mother family has had a parent die or leave the household.

Disadvantaged heterosexual black women (in particular those with little education and income) have a limited pool of men from which to find a partner, largely because the men they might be able to partner with are generally disadvantaged themselves. William Julius Wilson has argued, for example, that the dramatic rise in black single-mother families is due in large part to the weak marriageable pool of black men.[56] This pool is weak, he insists, because so many of these men do not have access to regular employment and thus have limited earnings (see Chapter 6). Sara McClanahan and Christine Percheski recently reviewed the evidence and concluded that black male unemployment and underemployment have a "large" negative effect on union formation and stability.[57] The women simply do not want to marry many of these men because they are unlikely to improve (and may even worsen) the economic situation of these already disadvantaged women.[58] So, many poor black women delay marriage (or never marry). However, they tend not to delay childbearing, and single parenting worsens their economic disadvantage. On average, women make less than men, mothers make less than women who aren't mothers, and single mothers lose out on the income a dual-parent family can earn.

Though every child has two biological parents, not every child has two moral parents—that is, two parents on whom the child has claim rights to parenting. It cannot therefore be legitimate for the public to view single-mother families that were never dual-parent families ("unbroken single-parent families") as substandard or in violation of civic obligations. If families merit public support in part because of the public benefits they bestow, then single-parent families have an equal claim to such support. This level of public support should not treat the dual-parent family as the normative default, thus penalizing unbroken single-parent families. That is, the support level should not be set on the assumption that two parents will contribute to the workplace and domestic labor necessary to sustain a household. While I agree with those feminists who insist that treating the dual-parent family as the normative standard is unfair to black women and stigmatizes single-mother families, my central thesis here is that a dual-parent normative model is unjustified on a liberal-egalitarian conception of the family's role in a just social order.[59]

One reply might be to insist that these disadvantaged women should delay childbearing until they can find an adequate partner to co-parent with, not because they would otherwise be in violation of the Reproductive Responsibility Principle, but because their children's life prospects will be brighter as a result. It could be maintained, for instance, that even though not all biological parents should be made liable for child support, it is permissible for the public to strongly encourage co-parenting because this is in children's best interests. To that end, the state could set family-support levels on the assumption that there will be two parents in the household to share responsibilities for earning and childcare. This would be an effort to encourage prospective parents to find partners to share these tasks on the grounds that children do better if they have two parents.

What could justify such a policy? It should be clear that the public does not have an obligation to ensure that children have *optimal* familial circumstances. Nor do parents owe their children the best family environment they can possibly provide. Even if co-parented children fare better on average, that is not a sufficient reason to discourage single parenting if these parents are able to carry out their parental responsibilities. From the standpoint of the public and children, single parenting is a problem only if it compromises children's basic interests, including their interest in being able to take their place as free and equal citizens once they are adults.

One might argue that discouraging single-parent families can be justified on grounds of fair equality of opportunity. The life prospects of children raised in dual-parent homes are, on average, better than those of children raised in single-parent homes. So one might conclude that the family, as an institution of the basic structure, should be organized to avoid creating this inequity. Yet, even setting aside differences in natural endowment due to genetic inheritance, families can advantage and disadvantage children in all sorts of ways, and quite apart from their available economic assets.[60] The choice between co-parenting and single parenting is not the only way. It is not plausible that justice requires the state to regulate family life with the aim of evening out any advantages caused by different parenting patterns or practices. Should no one have a nanny, uncle, older sibling, grandmother, or community that assists with childcare if everyone doesn't have one?

Whatever fair equality of opportunity entails practically, it cannot mean that the state must balance out all the advantages and disadvantages of different family formations and family dynamics so that all children with the same natural endowment and resources have the same prospects for success in the competition for valued social positions. A more plausible interpretation of the practical implications of fair equality of opportunity is that the state should (a) ensure that everyone has a real opportunity to develop their talents through education, (b) maintain effective antidiscrimination measures so that all can compete for positions on fair terms, and (c) distribute income and wealth (between families and across generations) in such a way that all can share equitably in the advantages of economic cooperation and that class background is no barrier to achievement.

Thus the fact (if it is a fact) that the children of single mothers do not fare as well in life as children of married parents does not, in itself, constitute an injustice that demands remedy. It is not a problem that needs fixing. From the standpoint of justice, the worry can't be about relative life prospects. It has to be that single-parented children tend to have bad life outcomes in absolute terms—for example, that they tend to have mental health problems, to drop out of high school, to abuse drugs, to be delinquent, and to get pregnant as teens. Even here, though, it can't be that single-parent families are simply *more likely* to have these problems. Children in stable, dual-parent homes sometimes exhibit these problems, too. The concern would have to be that single parenting poses an unreasonably high risk of these problems such that the state is justified in intervening to discourage the formation of single-parent families.

I doubt that treating dual-parent families as the normative default can be justified in a just social order. But even if it could be justified in just conditions, it would be appropriate to depart from such a default in a society that suffers from serious and longstanding racial, gender, and economic injustices. Given the concentrated disadvantage characteristic of American ghettos, it may be better to provide greater public support for single-mother families rather than encourage unions between biological parents. Insofar as marriage programs seek to reconcile or unify poor mothers with the biological fathers of their children, it makes these women vulnerable to exploitation and domestic abuse.[61] Some of these fathers, in light of their various disadvantages and troubles, would not make fit husbands or parents. Their plight, too, is often due to injustice, and consequently they have legitimate claims to redress. However, until their situation is remedied or at least improved, it is unreasonable to demand that single mothers partner or co-parent with them. As the disadvantaged respond to and navigate the injustices they face, families will take different shapes, and the broader public should accommodate this variety as we work collectively toward a more just basic structure.

The position of "parent" is a valued role in society. One has a just grievance if one is unfairly encumbered in the pursuit of this social role. The role is not, of course, distributed by fair competition; nor should it be. We do not have to demonstrate that we are the best person available for the job. Nor are we entitled to the position simply because we are willing and able to fulfill it. But there should not be unfair social obstacles in the way of our attempt to play the role. Unjust social disadvantage, like ghetto poverty, is such an unfair obstacle. It can frustrate persons' legitimate expectations that they will be able to assume and effectively carry out the role of parent. And given the situation of many disadvantaged black women, the social role of parent should not be open only to those who are able to find an adequate partner with whom to co-parent.

When background conditions in society are unjust and some are poor because of this injustice, it is unreasonable to expect the unjustly disadvantaged to forgo procreation altogether. Raising a child is a valuable pursuit that can bring meaning and fulfillment to a life.[62] Being hindered in this pursuit because one is unjustly disadvantaged adds to the oppression of impoverishment and naturally causes resentment and sometimes elicits defiance among those with a strong sense of self-respect. Each should have a fair opportunity to lead a satisfying life, and for many (though of course not all), the experience of raising a child and enjoying the loving relationship that parenting can bring is central to their idea of a full and meaningful life.

When acquiring satisfying paid work is not realistic, as is true for many of the ghetto poor, being a parent can become all the more essential for a satisfying life. When individuals are not able to secure enjoyable work, to find an adequate life partner, or to be a parent, this can make for a bleak existence. Adventure, status seeking, bodily pleasure (sex, food, drugs, and so forth), material consumption, and money can become the central aims in life. While many no doubt want meaningful work, to be a parent, and to have a partner with whom to share their lives, some will prioritize work and parenting over partnership and will prioritize parenting over unfulfilling or underpaid work. This should not surprise us. Nor should we be so quick to condemn the formation of single-mother families in ghettos, given the limited options ghetto denizens face.

If they refrain from childbearing to avoid irresponsible reproduction, disadvantaged black single women are being wrongly deprived of an important and intrinsically valuable form of life because they have been unfairly denied the resources needed to properly care for a child. To deprive them of the opportunity to parent on the ground that they are financially ill-equipped to be a parent would add insult to injury. In fact, principles of rectification may require that we enable some who are oppressed by ghetto conditions to become effective parents, empowering them to take up the task. One way to make amends for burdens the unjustly disadvantaged endure is to give them the support they need to be competent parents and thus to find fulfillment in this important social role.

SIX

Work

Joblessness is an influential explanation for why ghettos persist: It is the fact that so many among the ghetto poor do not work regularly, proponents of the explanation argue, that accounts for why people in these communities often remain poor. Some advocates of this view maintain that joblessness not only keeps the ghetto poor in poverty but also has negative ramifications beyond mere income disadvantage. For instance, joblessness is said to increase crime and juvenile delinquency, to encourage welfare dependency and single-mother households, to undermine self-esteem, to foster a self-defeating ghetto subculture, and to weaken vital institutions of civil society (for instance, religious institutions, political organizations, and neighborhood social networks).

In view of the significance of joblessness, some social scientists, policymakers, and commentators have advocated strong measures to ensure that the ghetto poor work, including mandating work as a condition of receiving welfare benefits. Indeed, among both conservatives and liberals, work is often seen as a moral or civic duty and as an indispensable basis for personal dignity. This normative stance is also now instantiated in federal and state laws, ranging from the tax scheme to welfare benefits.[1]

This chapter reflects critically on this new regime of work. Do the normative principles to which its advocates typically (though sometimes only tacitly) appeal actually justify the regime? Is there a general duty to work? And if so, what type of duty might it reasonably be thought to be, and what kinds of activities could plausibly count toward fulfilling it? I conclude that the case for an enforceable moral or civic duty to work is not as strong as many believe and that there are reasonable responses to joblessness that do not involve instituting a work regime. But even if we were to grant that, under *just* conditions, there is a general duty to work (as I suspect there is), I maintain that the ghetto poor would not be wronging their fellow citizens were they to choose not to work and to rely on public funds for material support. In fact, I aim to show that many of the black urban poor have sufficient reason to *refuse* to work.

Work and Dissent

Who are the "jobless"? The category *jobless* is not the same as the category *unemployed*, at least not as the latter is traditionally understood. The jobless include those who are unemployed but looking for work and those who are unemployed but who, for reasons other than retirement or disability, have dropped out of the workforce.

Why are the jobless not working? Answers vary. Some common explanations emphasize *involuntary* joblessness. For instance, some among the ghetto poor do not work because jobs for which they qualify are simply unavailable. The labor market is slack and the ghetto poor, given their lack of relevant job-related skills, are surplus labor. Because of economic restructuring and globalization, there is a mismatch between skills and jobs. Many available jobs in the United States are open only to skilled or educated workers, and many poor urban blacks lack the necessary competence or credentials. Where there are jobs for low-skilled workers, there is sometimes a mismatch between the location of these jobs (suburbs) and the residences of the black poor (inner city). This spatial mismatch is exacerbated by an inefficient and underdeveloped mass transit system and by housing discrimination and high rents in suburban neighborhoods, which effectively keep the ghetto poor from commuting to or residing in communities where decent jobs for the low-skilled are more plentiful. There is also continuing employment discrimination in the low-wage labor market, particularly racial and gender discrimination (which can work in combination). Sometimes poor single mothers are unable to find adequate or affordable childcare, which forces them to stay at home to care for their children. There are also ghetto denizens who are addicted to drugs, suffer from mental illness, possess severe disabilities, or have criminal records—characteristics that make it difficult to acquire or keep a steady job, at least without substantial support. These explanations are not mutually exclusive. What they all have in common is that they account for joblessness by highlighting factors largely outside the control of the ghetto poor.[2]

However, when it comes to explaining why so many among the ghetto poor are not working, some emphasize *voluntary* joblessness. In other words, some ghetto denizens choose not to work even though there are jobs they could get and retain if they sought out these opportunities and, once hired, complied with workplace rules. It is this case of voluntary nonwork that angers many U.S. citizens and that advocates of the work regime hope to remedy.

Some claim that the jobless ghetto poor choose not to work because it is not in their material interests to do so. On this view, a rational cost–benefit analysis demonstrates that, say, welfare or the underground economy would be a better option, all things considered. Some advocates of the new work regime have responded by ending welfare as an entitlement, replacing it with strict time limits and work requirements for benefit eligibility, and cracking down on urban crime, and especially on the drug trade, pushing for long prison terms and aggressive enforcement measures. The idea is to change the incentive structure to encourage work in the licit economy.

Others go further, claiming that the jobless ghetto poor choose not to work, not simply out of economic interests, but because of character flaws or other moral failings. These advocates of the work regime believe that when the black urban poor elect not to work, this is morally blameworthy and irresponsible. Their recommended policy response is to craft laws and design institutions that effectively compel the ghetto poor to work, or penalize them if they continue to refuse.

Implicit in this policy response is the assumption that the reasons the jobless black urban poor have for refusing to work are not, or could not be, sufficient to justify this refusal. This assumption is widely held, quite old, and sometimes accepted by respected black leaders. For instance, at the turn of the twentieth century, Booker T. Washington and W. E. B. Du Bois, despite their other well-known political differences, agreed that many blacks remained economically disadvantaged because they willfully avoided gainful employment.[3] This tendency to avoid work, which they attributed to socialization under slavery, is said to make black families economically vulnerable and dependent and to slow the advancement of the race. Neither black leader asked whether some blacks might be justified in refusing to accept the jobs available to them.

I would not deny that high jobless rates in ghettos are worrisome and have far-reaching consequences. It does not follow from this social analysis, however, that inducing or mandating work is the right solution to the problem of ghetto poverty. The new work regime is premised on the assumption that there is a duty to work (at least as an obligation of the poor) and that it is morally permissible for the state to mandate work (or at least that the poor may be made to work). Neither assumption is obvious. And a variety of alternative responses to voluntary nonwork on the part of the ghetto poor are possible and plausible.

Let me suggest another factor—a *moral* factor—in the explanation for why some among the ghetto poor choose not to work. Perhaps some do not accept the jobs available because they believe that *the basic structure of U.S. society is deeply unfair and thus, on grounds of justice and self-respect, refuse to accommodate themselves to their low position in this stratified social order.* This position is different from the one defended by Howard McGary, who argues that because the ghetto poor regard the basic structure of U.S. society as unjust, many, sensing that the deck is stacked against them, lack the *motivation* to overcome all the obstacles they face in order to succeed. In particular, on McGary's account, they are not motivated to work hard or perhaps to work at all.[4] I agree that some may not be motivated to work because of the unfairness of the social scheme. Persistent and pervasive injustice can erode effort and ambition. But I want to go further to claim that some may *consciously refuse* to work because of this unfairness.

Refusing to work can be a manifestation of dissatisfaction with the current social arrangement, the expression of an unwillingness to cooperate with an unjust system. Though the oppressed may be keenly aware of their impoverished circumstances, instead of complying with what they take to be unreasonable societal expectations, they sometimes decline to acquiesce to the status quo even when their material prospects might be made worse as a result. Based on compelling interpretations of the vernacular and expressive culture that emanates from and appeals to many in ghettos (see Chapters 3 and 9), I am confident that some among the ghetto poor take exactly this stance of dissent, or something similar.[5] Others, were the question put to them in a suitable form, would, I suspect, sincerely affirm this position, though they may not have previously considered the question in this explicit form. I concede that I do not know how large either group is. Nor can I prove that their numbers are large or growing. However, regardless of its magnitude, there is, I believe, emancipatory potential in the stated moral stance, which under the right circumstances could advance the aims of corrective justice. My goal is to show, not that this stance is widespread, but that it is justified.

As I have emphasized, social scientists and political commentators who write about ghetto poverty rarely take seriously the moral reasons of the black urban poor, particularly when these reasons sharply diverge from mainstream opinion.[6] Some do acknowledge that the poor's refusal to work can sometimes represent a "protest" against low-paying and demeaning jobs.[7] But they rarely suggest that, rather than being against a particular job opportunity, this protest is against an institutional framework that affords them only such miserable employment options.[8] Others accept that some in the ghetto choose nonwork as a form of protest against "the system," but they think these claims of injustice have little, if any, merit and serve mainly to rationalize (or to provide psychological compensation for) nonworkers' individual failures.[9] Mostly, though, commentators simply assume that the U.S. liberal-capitalist order is basically just and that labor-market outcomes are fair provided employers do not intentionally discriminate.

What Is Work?

In debates about work and welfare, there is much ambiguity about the meaning of "work." Articulating and defending a general account of what constitutes work would take us too far afield. But as we assess the new work regime, it will help to see that what should count as "work" depends on the point of demanding the relevant activity from the ghetto poor. If, for example, the point is to ensure that the ghetto poor are not a financial burden ("parasites" or freeloaders) on their fellow citizens, then "work" might be defined as any activity that the market remunerates. If the point is to bring discipline and order to the lives of the ghetto poor (a type of character rehabilitation), then "work" might include almost any structured and supervised activity, regardless of whether it is paid, including volunteer work or community service. If the point is to discourage the supposed vice of "welfare dependency" and to foster economic self-reliance, then any compensated activity, whether paid by private firms or by government funds, could count as "work."

Many complain that the nonworking poor are failing to make useful contributions to society while simultaneously benefiting from the productive contributions of others. But many with this complaint regard as "work" only (legal) activities for which a person gets paid. This misleadingly conflates earning income through market-remunerated activity with making a positive contribution to society. It would leave out lots of socially beneficial activities for which people are often not paid. Feminists have argued persuasively that *care work*—care for children, the sick, the disabled, and the elderly—is typically performed by women, generally devalued by society, and mostly unpaid.[10] Given how socially important, even necessary, such work is, this is profoundly unfair and insulting, especially if these women are also expected to do paid work and men are expected to do little, if any, care work. If the point of demanding work is that the ghetto poor should engage in activities that contribute to the public good, then care work—particularly raising children—should definitely count (see Chapter 5).

In addition, due to environmental dangers, technological advances, and an abundance of low-skilled labor in other parts of the world, it may be more efficient or otherwise beneficial to *discourage* some people from participating in the U.S. labor market, at least as it is currently structured. They could still do socially useful work that the market will not reward without public expenditures, such as building infrastructure, protecting the environment, maintaining public parks, and staffing public recreational facilities.

Insofar as work should involve making a positive contribution to society, one might also object to regarding as "work" certain paid activities that, though lawful, arguably have a negative impact on society, such as the production and sale of pornography or the running of gambling establishments. The fact that there is a market for such goods and services does not mean that, overall, they contribute to social welfare.

Another ambiguity in debates over work and welfare concerns *time*. Any duty to work must include a time dimension. Advocates of the new work regime often seem to assume that "workers" should always be working—occupying a full-time job (forty or more hours a week), forty-eight to fifty weeks a year (excluding leaves for illness, injury, or maternity), every year of their adult lives (excluding periods of full-time education), until retirement age. But why are these the only kind of "workers" who have fulfilled their moral or civic duties with respect to work? Arguably, we should consider someone a worker in good moral or civic standing even if he or she takes periods off from work—say, to do care work (if this is not considered "work"), to augment or develop new skills, to participate in activities that, though not considered "work," promote social welfare, or to just take a break to do something more personally satisfying. And even during the periods when one is working, how much work is adequate—ten, eight, or six hours a day? Forty, thirty, or twenty hours a week? In a society that places a high value on individual liberty and choice, one could imagine a work regime in which each citizen is expected to work a certain number of hours over a lifetime but where each has considerable discretion over how these hours are distributed over the course of his or her life. Setting aside the details, the point is that even in a society that regards work as a duty, there can be a variety of work regimes and we should consider whether a less onerous regime, with more opportunity for leisure, would be both desirable and feasible.

Full Citizenship without a Duty to Work

Could a modern liberal-democratic society be just in the absence of a general expectation that all will work? Before discussing defenses of a duty to work, let's briefly consider three alternative social arrangements—libertarian self-sufficiency, guaranteed basic income, and welfare rights conditional on need—that don't require work as a condition of full civic standing.

Libertarians (at least those who lack sympathy for egalitarianism) emphasize, not work per se, but economic self-reliance. They hold that individuals or family units have an obligation to be economically self-sufficient. No one should rely on their fellow citizens for assistance unless they are incapable of supporting themselves through the opportunities the market affords. On this view, each citizen has a duty to make material provision for himself or herself and for his or her dependents. Citizens should not (willingly) burden one another by calling on the resources or labor of other citizens as a means of support. Most important, no citizen has a civic duty, enforceable by the state, to meet the material needs of others (though a citizen may have an unenforceable moral duty to give to the needy).[11] There is no general civic requirement that everyone work, because citizens may support themselves through investments if they are wealthy or through the goodwill of family, friends, or charities if they are poor. The key point is that citizens, regardless of whether they have adequate resources, have no justice-based claim against their government or fellow citizens for material support.

Though a general work regime, applicable to all citizens, cannot be justified on libertarian principles, a society that made welfare benefits *conditional* on work might be acceptable to some libertarians. It could be argued that although there is no general civic obligation to work or to cultivate a strong work ethic, *if* welfare benefits are publicly provided, then those who accept these benefits should have to work as a condition of receiving them. Because self-supporting citizens have no civic duty to support the poor, it is perfectly just for would-be benefactors to demand work from their beneficiaries. One rationale for this demand is that welfare benefits conditional on work encourage self-sufficiency, whereas unconditional welfare benefits encourage dependency. Through such work, welfare beneficiaries would learn to become self-supporting and will be better off for it. A more self-interested rationale is that self-supporting citizens should get something in return for supporting citizens who are not economically self-sufficient. There is, as it were, "no free lunch," so the poor should perform socially useful work in exchange for the public material provisions they receive.

While I won't argue against it here, I don't believe that the libertarian conception of justice is adequate.[12] But even were we to adopt libertarian principles, the case for the fairness of welfare benefits conditional on work, *at least as it applies to the ghetto poor*, would be weak. In addition to advocating limited government and free markets, libertarian accounts of justice all emphasize justice in economic appropriation and transfer, including intergenerational wealth transfers through inheritance, as fundamental to a legitimate polity.[13] They also emphasize the importance of having a dynamic conception of societal justice, where material progress over time is regarded as the appropriate standpoint for judging the justice of social arrangements, rather than taking a static or end-result view of citizens' holdings and material welfare, which might seem to justify redistributive measures.[14] Yet given the history of slavery and Jim Crow—three and a half centuries of gross and far-reaching injustices on almost anyone's principles—no one can plausibly argue that the current, racially skewed distribution of resources is entirely the result of just appropriations and transfers.[15] Nothing approaching adequate reparations for slavery or Jim Crow have been offered to the descendants of slaves or the victims of the segregation regime.[16] Given that contemporary ghetto poverty is plausibly explained, at least in part, by historical injustices in appropriation and transfer (what some term *structural racism*), it is far from clear that welfare conditional on work, which assumes just background conditions, is justifiable to the black urban poor.

If blacks were no longer burdened by the injustices of the past or had been fully compensated for the disadvantages they have inherited, I suspect that there would be far fewer blacks who were not self-supporting, thus satisfying the libertarian demand that each family be economically self-sufficient. I won't rest my case against the new work regime on the validity of black reparations claims. Nor do I believe justice requires families to be economically self-sufficient (see Chapter 5). However, any libertarian defense of making welfare benefits conditional on work owes us a satisfactory response to damage done to the ghetto poor due to historical injustices. Erecting a work regime in response to the needs of impoverished ghetto denizens hardly seems like an appropriate way to make amends for or bring closure to the unspeakable injustices of the past.

An alternative conception of full citizenship that also doesn't regard work as a civic requirement holds that citizens are entitled to a guaranteed, unconditional basic income or initial capital stake.[17] On this view, each individual has a right to his or her fair share of society's assets, which have been built up over many generations; and each should be free to use this fair share as he or she sees fit. Those who want to work, either for greater income or intrinsic satisfaction, are free and perhaps encouraged to do so. But those who choose not to work and instead live off their basic income or capital stake (at least for a time) are not acting unfairly toward their fellow citizens who choose to work. The goods and services that we all take advantage of are the product of, not only contributions from contemporary workers, but also work from past generations and, just as important, technological advance and nature's bounty. One's fellow citizens have no right to complain if one takes one's per capita share of these assets without agreeing to work. On this view, there should be an all-volunteer workforce, where no one is compelled to work under threat of penalty or out of economic need. Compulsory service would be required only under special circumstances (shortages in basic material necessities, for example). Fiscal policy would focus on growing the economy and spurring technological advance, while tax policy would distribute the gains of increased productivity equitably to all citizens and not just to those who work or own capital.

A similar but less radical view holds that citizens have an unconditional right to basic welfare benefits *if they are in need*.[18] Those who have adequate means of support, either through voluntary work or personal wealth, are not entitled to the benefit. The welfare entitlement could perhaps be means-tested but need not depend on demonstrating a willingness to work. The idea would be that welfare benefits should be extended, as a social right, to those unable to find work, those incapable of working, *and* those who do not want to work (for whatever reasons). Both this regime and the one described in the previous paragraph assume an economy in which enough people will freely choose to work, either for intrinsic satisfaction or monetary gain, such that all citizens could live a decent life without there being any general societal demand that all citizens work. It is of course an empirical question whether such regimes could be realized or would be stable over time. And I take no position on this complex factual matter.

Work and Human Flourishing

Americans are known for their work ethic. On one interpretation of this ethic, work—and perhaps *hard* work (whether measured in time, sacrifice, or exertion)—is a central element of a broad conception of human flourishing, or what Rawls would call a "comprehensive conception of the good."[19] Living in accordance with the work ethic involves more than choosing work over idleness. For instance, one is to work diligently, conscientiously, and responsibly; one is to be on time for work, to not complain (too much) about the demands of work, and to put in extra time and effort if doing the job well requires it. But I will leave aside these other dimensions of the work ethic, for my argument does not turn on them.

Political liberalism (as opposed to comprehensive liberalism) denies that a liberal-democratic state can legitimately enforce any particular conception of the good. On this view, the state should be tolerant of different conceptions of human flourishing (provided these are compatible with the maintenance of a just social structure), rather than attempt to mold individuals in accordance with some contested conception. Individuals should be free to develop and live according to their own vision of the good life, which may include a contested view about which kinds of activities or lives are meaningful and worthwhile, so long as they live up to their civic obligations.

There are, however, people who believe that the state not only may encourage (through incentives, say) a particular conception of the good that includes an ethic of work but also may legitimately enforce it through penalties. These political perfectionists are similar to (and sometimes include) those who believe that a Christian life is the only worthwhile life and that government may use its power to promote Christianity and to discourage non-Christian forms of life. Like some Christians, these advocates of the new work regime view laziness as a serious moral vice or character flaw and thus think voluntary non-workers warrant the contempt of their fellow citizens. Many hold that being a working person is necessary for having a positive sense of self-worth or dignity and thus that the idle have reason to feel shame or guilt.[20]

Of course, social conservatives are not the only ones who view work as necessary for human flourishing and personal dignity. Karl Marx, a perfectionist of a rather different sort, also believed that work is a key component of human self-realization.[21] On his conception of the good, freely engaging in socially useful and intrinsically meaningful work in a joint cooperative effort is the essence of human fulfillment. Unlike social conservatives, Marx did not think *wage labor* qualified as the relevant kind of work. He had several reasons for thinking this, but I will focus on two. First, people who perform wage labor typically do so, not because it contributes to fulfilling the needs of others or because they find it intrinsically satisfying, but only because it satisfies their own narrow, material needs—because it pays the bills. Second, and more relevant, Marx did not think work could be truly fulfilling unless it is freely chosen. In other words, truly fulfilling work cannot be compelled, by either the state or market imperatives.

The contrast between these two conceptions of work as a source of the human good is instructive. The particular lesson I want to highlight is the tension between valuing work as a component of human flourishing and advocating a political regime that forces people to work. If it is to be a valid source of self-esteem or an expression of virtue, work must be engaged in *for the right reasons.* If a person works only because he or she would otherwise live in a perpetual state of material deprivation or because he or she seeks to avoid the disdain of fellow citizens, it is hard to see the moral worth of such work. Pride and self-approbation do not seem to be the appropriate response. Shouldn't one work because this is what being a good person (or good citizen) demands and not simply because the state will come down on you if you refuse? The question I am asking is not so much whether it would be legitimate to enforce a work ethic but whether such an ethic could be enforced yet still play the role in human fulfillment that perfectionists have in mind. I doubt it. In registering this doubt, I do not mean to deny that a person forced to work might nevertheless find some satisfaction or meaning in the work he or she is compelled to do. Rather, insofar as human flourishing requires working for the right reasons (for example, because Christian virtue or our "species being" requires it) and not simply due to duress, a work regime founded on this conception of the good would be self-defeating.

Advocates of the American work ethic might concede that forced work cannot function as a valid source of pride or an expression of virtue. They may nonetheless insist that the state should strongly discourage and perhaps punish idleness. It should do so either because such sanctions may, in time, effect a positive change in the moral motivation of the lazy (and thus serve an educative function) or because such sanctions will help to preserve a general societal ethos of work (presumably necessary to sustain a prosperous nation and virtuous citizenry) even if they do not change (all) those to whom the sanctions are applied. These variants are worthy of further consideration. My primary interest, however, is in those defenses of the new work regime that might be compatible with the liberal idea that the state should not enforce particular views of what a good life consists in, and work-ethic justifications do not qualify, despite their obvious appeal to many.

Work and Reciprocity

The most compelling defense of a civic duty to work that does not rely on perfectionist values is based on the idea of *reciprocity*. There are different conceptions of "reciprocity" and thus different ways of justifying a civic duty to work on this normative ground. At least three approaches are worth considering.

One approach uses a benefactor/debtor model and treats civic duties as obligations of gratitude.[22] On this model, "society" or "the state" (understood as a collective agent composed of citizens) is said to provide each citizen with many indispensable goods and services. Therefore each citizen owes a debt of gratitude to society, which is to be paid, at least in part, through socially useful work. This reciprocity argument suggests that the noncontributing person's moral fault is *ingratitude*. A polite "thanks" is insufficient; each must *show* his or her sincere appreciation and goodwill toward the public by contributing socially beneficial labor. The benefits each citizen receives by living in society come from the goodwill of the public. These benefits are not something that each citizen is owed simply in virtue of his or her membership in the society.

A different approach to thinking about reciprocity is to model it on market exchanges for mutual advantage. One version of this view asserts that the public (through governmental institutions) provides many benefits to citizens—physical safety, social services, secure possessions, a regulated market, the rule of law, and so on. In exchange for these benefits, the public reasonably expects not only obedience to law but also socially beneficial work. This puts individual citizens in a semicontractual relation with the public at large. The benefits of governance are not provided unconditionally (as an entitlement or right) but are offered in exchange for work (perhaps among other things). In a sense the benefits are merely advanced, like a loan, with the expectation that they will be paid back, not in kind, but with socially useful work. The citizen who receives the benefits of governance but fails to perform work in exchange has therefore *defaulted on a loan or violated a contract*. Voluntary nonwork is, in effect, a breach of the civic contract.

Perhaps the most persuasive version of the reciprocity argument (and the one most at home in the normative framework I have been advancing) appeals to considerations of fairness.[23] On this view each citizen

should make some labor contribution to the public good in light of the
benefits of social cooperation he or she enjoys. Those who cooperate
make sacrifices and take risks to produce the goods and services from
which all in society benefit. It would be wrong, a form of parasitism or
free riding, to take advantage of the cooperative labor of others without
making a labor contribution of one's own (unless one has a good excuse).
The noncontributor's moral error, then, is that he or she acts *unfairly*
in refusing to work.[24]

All three versions of the reciprocity argument have some plausibility.
But before examining the implications of this argument for the question of voluntary nonwork among the ghetto poor, several preliminary
questions should be asked. First, the basic form of the argument is to
claim that all citizens *benefit* from what government or others in society
have done and thereby *owe* something in return. Even if it is conceded
that, because of benefits received, *something* is owed, why is *work* the
only way to pay the debt? Conforming to the dictates of law and respecting private property, both of which entail restricting one's liberty
to do as one pleases, arguably are payment enough. The loss of liberty
and the burden of self-restraint are real costs, after all; and each member
of society benefits from the fact that others comply with the law and
honor property claims. Respecting the law and complying with the
norms of a market-based society could be an expression of gratitude for
the benefits of social life, something of value offered in exchange for material support, or a contribution to the maintenance of a polity defined
by the rule of law.[25]

Second, why should we think that a duty to work exists even in those
societies in which a labor contribution from everyone is not needed
to supply essential goods and services? The reciprocity argument is
most powerful when the benefits provided are not just valued by the
beneficiary but in some sense are *needed* by the beneficiary.[26] To use old-
school Marxist terminology, there is *socially necessary labor* and then there
is *surplus labor*. It may be that in the United States today, socially necessary labor does not require all adults to work and a voluntary work
regime would be sufficient to supply the goods and services needed for
all to live a satisfying life. This situation is already true of military service: citizens of the United States are afforded adequate security from
external threats without mandating that all able-bodied citizens serve
in the military. An all-volunteer military is sufficient. Why restrict the

liberty of, or impose costs on, citizens when this is not necessary to maintain a just polity?

Third, even if there is a reciprocity-based civic obligation to work, it is not clear that the state has the authority to enforce it.[27] Should the failure to fulfill the duty to work result in downgraded civic standing, such that material support may permissively be withheld or withdrawn? Perhaps the voluntary nonworker, like the person who chooses not to vote, should be regarded as a bad citizen or as unpatriotic. Perhaps he or she should not garner the esteem or respect of fellow citizens, and may even merit their contempt. But just as many consider it wrong to enforce a civic duty to vote, we might also consider it wrong to enforce a civic duty to work. Moreover, as others have noted, it may be difficult to define "socially useful work" in the precise way needed for a law to be impartially administered and consistent with liberal neutrality.[28] And gathering the information about who is shirking work responsibility or incapable of contributing may be demeaning, intrusive, or insulting.[29] Furthermore, on the benefactor/debtor conception of civic duties, it would be morally perverse, and perhaps self-defeating, to force the ingrate to demonstrate gratitude.[30] If the ingrate has to be forced, then he or she is probably not really grateful and thus the public cannot properly receive the work performed as gratitude.

Fourth and finally, assuming there is a civic obligation to work and that the state legitimately enforces this duty, does government have an obligation to ensure that there is work for all who are able and willing to work? That is, is there a *positive* right to work such that the government should provide employment if the private sector fails to? (A *negative* right to work—a right not to be prevented from accepting the job of one's choice—is generally recognized as a basic human right. For example, a regime that prohibited women from accepting work outside the home or that allowed husbands to prevent their wives from accepting employment would be in violation of this right. This right is secure only if everyone has an opportunity to freely accept a job and no unfair barriers are erected to inhibit a person's acceptance of employment. But this negative right does *not* entail that anyone, whether government or private citizens, has a duty to ensure that there are jobs for all who seek them.) To require work as a condition of full civic standing when not every citizen has the option of employment would be unfair. Those who could not find work would be stigmatized as civic inferiors, as effectively useless to the rest of his or her fellow citizens and as parasites on the productive. A civic duty to work should therefore be paired with the state's obligation to maintain a full-employment economy.[31] A government could make the positive right to work effective if, for example, it enacted economic policies that spur job growth, supplied jobs in the public sector for those unable to find employment in the private sector, and offered subsidies or tax breaks to private firms that hire hard-to-employ workers. And insofar as guaranteeing a right means actively facilitating the exercise of that right, the right to work might also require government to provide the appropriate training and educational programs to meet the labor demands of a dynamic economy and to make services available to support the unemployed in their search for suitable jobs. In the United States, no such positive right to work is generally recognized.

Refusing to Work as a Form of Dissent

Despite these reservations and unanswered questions, the idea of a civic obligation to work has much to be said for it. From the standpoint of fairness, there is something undeniably compelling about the precept "All who eat should work," even if the precise content of this idea is difficult to articulate and defend. (Notice that the principle "All who eat should work" does not imply "Those who do not work shall not eat." The former states a duty while the latter states a penalty for nonperformance. As suggested earlier, one might believe there is a nonenforceable duty to work.) And it is hard to see how a societal system of cooperation could be sustained in a fair way if able citizens don't have a duty to contribute to maintaining the material conditions of social life. Thus, I will assume that there is a civic duty to work, rooted in the idea of reciprocity.[32] The burden of the remainder of this chapter is to show that, despite this general duty, the ghetto poor often have overriding reasons to refuse to work.

Some of the legitimate reasons the ghetto poor have for refusing to work could perhaps be accommodated without altering the basic structure of U.S. society. That is, these objections could be answered by instituting relatively moderate reforms, some of which have already been initiated. To enact all the necessary reforms, however, the tax scheme would have to be made considerably more progressive, and perhaps almost everyone's taxes would have to increase, which many U.S. citizens would resist, some vehemently. Still, no fundamental rethinking of distributive justice would have to occur, just garnering the necessary political will—no small task, to be sure.

For example, the ghetto poor may reasonably refuse to work if the jobs available pay too little. In an affluent society, those who work full-time should not have to live in poverty, a principle widely endorsed even in the United States. One approach to this problem is to raise the minimum wage so that a full-time worker at that wage could support a moderate size family (say, two children). Another, perhaps complementary, approach would be to offer income supplements (through tax credits, employer subsidies, or cost of living subsidies).[33] In effect, the government could "top up" full-time workers' wages so that they are above the poverty line (here assuming, for the sake of argument, that the federal poverty line is an adequate measure of impoverishment). The Earned Income Tax Credit, though not entirely adequate to the task, is a step in this direction. Given the wide geographic variance in cost of living (a fact to which the federal poverty standard does not give sufficient weight), a complementary strategy would be for public sector employers to pay their workers a decent wage by local standards and for government to require private firms that receive public funds to do the same, which would mean paying some low-skilled workers above the federal minimum wage. Such measures would be especially important to the ghetto poor, because they live in large metropolitan areas where the cost of living is often high. A number of cities have passed living-wage ordinances in response to grassroots activism by, and on behalf of, low-income workers.

Given their difficulty securing jobs that pay a living wage, some among the ghetto poor might reject work requirements on the grounds that low-skilled workers in the new economy lack an effective right to organize and to join and maintain labor unions. Many employers of low-skilled workers have erected barriers to unionization, sought to intimidate or mislead workers who express an interest in forming unions, and exploited racial and ethnic antagonism to weaken worker solidarity.[34] This means that workers have little leverage to bargain for fair compensation, benefits, and reasonable working conditions. The government could respond to this concern by cracking down on union-busting tactics and making it easier for workers within and across firms to form and maintain unions. Domestic workers and other low-skilled service workers (which includes many low-income black women) could also be aided insofar as they seek to form or join labor organizations.

Some of the ghetto poor might refuse work because the jobs available are physically arduous, highly unpleasant or "dirty," or extremely dangerous, where these costs and risks are not adequately compensated.[35] However, if these were the only jobs available, better jobs in the public sector could be created, thus putting pressure on private firms to increase compensation. And through labor regulations, the government could ensure that decent and safe working conditions prevail in all businesses, large and small, that operate in the country.

A person might also refuse to work if the jobs available require an unreasonable amount of time or exertion, leaving workers with little opportunity or energy for non-work-related activities. In an affluent society where work is required of all, it would be unfair for some to have so much more leisure than others and unjust for some to have essentially no leisure time at all. In response to this concern, the government could demand fewer hours per day (or days per week) to remain in good civic standing. And employers could be required to give longer paid vacations to full-time workers.

One would also be justified in refusing to work if working would prevent one from adequately caring for one's children.[36] Because parents have a duty not only to provide materially for their children but to *nurture* them—to ensure their proper emotional, physical, moral, and cognitive development—parents may legitimately refuse to work if this would interfere with the fulfillment of these essential parental duties. To deal with this concern, childcare subsidies could be provided or publicly financed childcare centers could be formed. Alternatively, single parents of young children could be exempted from work requirements altogether. Some measures of this sort have already been implemented, though they would have to be expanded to be fully adequate.

Again, the objections to a reciprocity-based work regime so far mentioned could be met with relatively moderate social reforms; although perhaps these would not be sufficient to establish a just basic structure, they would constitute meaningful progress. However, some of the reasons a citizen might have for refusing to work cannot be accommodated without changing the structure of U.S. society in fundamental ways.

Here I focus on three such reasons that, considering the situation of the ghetto poor, are particularly pertinent.

The Injustice Objection

All three reciprocity arguments are vulnerable to the objection that the basic structure of U.S. society is grossly unjust.[37] In a society that is manifestly unjust, it can be reasonable to refuse to work, even if there would be a civic obligation to work under more just conditions. Such refusal to cooperate can be a form of political protest. Even if we set aside disadvantages caused by past injustices (such as slavery and Jim Crow), which continue to affect black life chances, there are ongoing social injustices that heavily burden the ghetto poor. For instance, the structure of economic opportunity that they face is deeply unfair. Public schools are still unequal and racially segregated, and many urban schools are substandard.[38] Consequently, the ghetto poor are severely disadvantaged when it comes to opportunities to develop marketable skills. There are great inequalities in wealth, which shape life chances in countless ways and which poor families in the ghetto are also on the losing end of. Even putting aside these general egalitarian concerns, racial discrimination in employment, housing, and lending are still a problem, and there are persistent racial disparities—in income, wealth, employment, infant mortality, health outcomes, and life expectancy—that go back to the antebellum era.[39] Moreover, the overall work burden is unfairly distributed in society—that is, others are not doing their fair share of the work—and, to make matters worse, this unfair distribution is racially marked, with blacks (and Latinos) doing a disproportionate share of menial labor, hard work, and dirty jobs.[40]

If these injustice-based criticisms of U.S. society are sound, and I think they are, this undermines the force of the reciprocity argument for the new work regime. Taking these criticisms seriously, let's first consider the benefactor/debtor model. It is hard to see why the ghetto poor should be grateful to be citizens of the United States. In light of the burdens of injustice that they are forced to carry, resentment or indignation, not gratitude, is the apt response to their situation. To expect otherwise would be like expecting a child who has been subject to consistent parental abuse and neglect to be grateful to be a part of his or her family. One frequently raised response to this objection is to point out that the ghetto poor of America could have been born into much worse circumstances—such as the slums of São Paulo, Bombay, or Jakarta. But again, emphasizing this comparative advantage would be like attempting to exonerate abusive and negligent parents on the grounds that they feed their children well.

Even if the ghetto poor do have some things to be grateful for (say, the rule of law or national defense) and should express this gratitude in some concrete way, I fail to see why full-time employment is the best or only way for them to show their appreciation. They could, for instance, choose to show their gratitude and fidelity to the nation by fighting to make their society more just. And if they believe that, under current circumstances, work requirements for the poor are unjust, they may carry out this fight by refusing to cooperate with the new work regime, engaging in a form of resistance. However, instead of objecting to a particular unjust law, as with traditional civil disobedience, they would be objecting to the social scheme as a whole.

What about the market exchange model? As is well known, attempting to derive political duties from the idea of a contract has numerous difficulties. The biggest problem is that contracts must be freely entered into if they are to be binding, and most citizens of existing polities cannot be said to have made a voluntary agreement to live under the political regime into which they were born. The vast majority of the ghetto poor, having been born in the United States and possessing meager, if any, means of support, certainly cannot be said to have chosen or consented to live under the dominion of the U.S. government. Tacit consent arguments are sometimes thought to be better than explicit consent arguments. But these arguments depend on there being a suitable alternative to living under the political regime in question, and the ghetto poor, like most citizens of the United States, cannot just leave for another country. Hypothetical consent arguments, to the extent they are able to do any justificatory work, turn on it being rational to have agreed to the terms to which one finds oneself being held. But in a hypothetical agreement *among equals*, what rational person would consent to a basic structure in which he or she could turn out to be a poor black denizen of a ghetto who is required to work to maintain full civic standing?

Even if we allow that a civic duty to work can be grounded in the idea of a market exchange, the injustice objection stands. The ghetto

poor have not received many of the benefits they have been "promised"—
including equality of opportunity and the equal protection of the law.
We can therefore view their refusal to work in an unjust social scheme
as the moral equivalent of a rent strike against a slumlord: they refuse to
pay their civic debt until the government makes good on its promise to
treat all citizens fairly. The ghetto poor have not breached a civic contract; instead the government has so fundamentally failed to fulfill
its responsibilities that the aggrieved citizens, the ghetto poor, can
rightfully refuse to comply with their "agreement" to work. At a minimum, the government's failures constitute a material breach of contract, and thus the ghetto poor have a just claim to damages.

The fair-play argument suffers from difficulties similar to those of
the market exchange argument. Most fair-play arguments depend on the
idea that the benefits of social cooperation are freely accepted, not imposed.[41] But as Jeremy Moss rightly points out, because welfare recipients,
who are typically poor single mothers, are among the most vulnerable
in society, they cannot correctly be said to have freely accepted welfare
benefits.[42] What real choice do they have?

But let's set aside these concerns about how voluntary the acceptance
of these benefits is. Still, it would be unfair to accept the benefits of a
cooperative scheme *only if the scheme itself is just.* Or, to put it differently,
the moral requirement that all participants in a social practice play by
its rules is valid only if the rules are fair to each participant. No fair-
minded person would seriously suggest that, because slaves receive the
benefits of food and shelter, they thereby owe a labor debt to the slave
regime that makes these benefits possible. The situation of ghetto denizens is analogous, if less dire. They undoubtedly receive some benefits
as citizens of the United States (food stamps, some basic social services,
defense against external threats, and so on), but because they are so burdened by the structural injustices of the social system, they should not
be considered free riders if they refuse to comply with a civic work
requirement.

The Exploitation Objection

A different though related reason the ghetto poor might have for refusing to work is that, under current circumstances, work requirements,
or the specific terms of work, are exploitative.[43] One way of developing

this objection uses the injustice objection as a premise. Though one may rightly be regarded as an *exploiter* if one refuses to work within a just basic structure, one may be among the *exploited* if one is forced to work under unjust conditions. Here's a paradigm case of economic exploitation: To garner benefits by extracting labor from persons who are powerless to resist because unjust circumstances have been imposed on them. The systems of slavery, serfdom, colonial subjugation, and apartheid are examples of such an arrangement. Insofar as the ghetto poor are forced to work because of a correctable, unjust basic structure, they too are rightly regarded as among the economically exploited. The legacy of slavery and Jim Crow, along with continuing employment discrimination and unequal educational opportunity, have created (or helped to create) a large class of blacks who are poor and unskilled. The result is that the black urban poor have been fashioned into a source of cheap, expendable, and exploitable labor, from which the affluent benefit.

But the exploitation objection would still have force even if the basic structure of U.S. society had not exceeded the threshold for tolerable injustice. Many Americans maintain that the ghetto poor remain in poverty because they failed to take advantage of opportunities and engaged in blameworthy behavior. Had they worked harder, avoided risky behavior, delayed childbearing until marriage, developed useful skills, and so on, they would not be in such a dire situation. Because of this irresponsible conduct, it is argued, they deserve their vulnerable economic position—or at least they should bear the economic costs of their unwise behavior—and it is therefore not exploitative for their fellow citizens to require them to work as a condition of material support. However, even if we allow that such charges are aptly applied to adults whose bad choices have left them confined to ghettos, what of those persons who grow up under ghetto conditions? After all, a shockingly high percentage of the black poor were *born* into ghetto conditions.[44] Their disadvantage is the result of bad brute luck, not bad option luck. In view of their undeserved economic disadvantage and insecurity, even if economic reciprocity is, in general, a requirement of justice and the basic structure of U.S. society is reasonably just, forcing the indigenous black urban poor to work is exploitative.[45] It is a case of profiting from the labor of people who are compelled to work because of weaknesses and vulnerabilities that are not of their making.

In fact, the situation is even worse than this. Under the new work regime, the indigenous ghetto poor are in a *self-reproducing exploitative relationship* with affluent citizens. The structure of a self-reproducing exploitative relationship is as follows:

X and Y are in a self-reproducing exploitative social relationship if:
(i) Y is regularly forced to make sacrifices that result in benefits for X; (ii) X obtains these benefits by means of a power advantage that X has over Y; and (iii) as a result of conditions (i) and (ii) X's power advantage over Y is maintained (or is increased) and Y remains in the condition of being forced to make sacrifices for X's benefit.[46]

This account helps us see why some exploitative relationships tend to persist: the very structure of these relationships tends to secure their continuance.

Because of the new work regime, this self-reproducing exploitative relationship exists between the indigenous ghetto poor and their more affluent fellow citizens. The basic problem is this: many of the ghetto poor who have submitted to the requirements of the new work regime nevertheless remain poor.[47] They simply become part of the working poor, often serving the private needs of the well-off—performing the roles of maids, nannies, dishwashers, maintenance workers, and so on. Others fall back into poverty because of recessions, periods of economic restructuring, or mass layoffs. Many of the schools available to the ghetto poor are so substandard that they do not enable upward mobility. Thus, when work requirements do not allow for skills enhancement or promotion to better-paid positions, these requirements are reasonably interpreted as attempts by the affluent to profit by extracting burdensome and unrewarding labor from the weak and vulnerable. Work enforcement, under these circumstances, is disempowering—it ensures that the ghetto poor are a permanently exploitable class.

The Expressive Harm Objection

In addition to the injustice and exploitation objections, the ghetto poor may refuse to cooperate with the new work regime because they believe that work mandates demean and stigmatize them. I offer four versions of this objection, all of which I believe to be valid.

The social identity of most black Americans is defined, in part, by being the descendants of slaves.[48] As Alexis de Tocqueville argued, once the status of "slave" was something only a black person could have, the stigma of forced servitude became attached to "blackness" itself. This stigma is so powerful that it stained blacks that were never slaves and has persisted for generations after slavery was abolished. To be black has come to mean, in the minds of many, being a member of a people who, because of cowardice and servility, and to its everlasting shame, submitted to slavery. And this stigma is one of the reasons African Americans have insisted that black slaves actively *resisted* slavery, from armed rebellion to shirking work. The ghetto poor may thus justifiably fear that were they to accommodate themselves to the new regime of work, with its state-sanctioned work mandates, this would reinforce or resurrect this stigma.

It may be objected that this account, however applicable in the past, no longer applies to the black condition. Many would argue that the stigma of slavery has faded and will never return. I doubt that this is true.[49] Nevertheless, this historical stigma tells us something important about what forced work means to a people who are descendants of slaves. As members of a historically oppressed yet proud social group, many blacks feel a duty to remember the horrendous moral crimes perpetrated against their ancestors. Some demand reparations for these wrongs even now. Almost all embrace the imperative, as part of their heritage, to resist race-based oppression, particularly those forms that are similar or related to past racial injustices. Blacks are therefore suspicious of and often bristle at any social arrangement that has the look or feel of race-based servitude. And quite apart from the conscious intent of those who support the new work regime, the symbolic meaning of such an arrangement when targeted at the most vulnerable and powerless segment of the black population is, I think, a sufficient reason to be defiant in the face of its demands.

The second version of the expressive harm objection focuses not just on race and class but also on place. Recall that ghettos are defined as poor black metropolitan *neighborhoods*. "The hood," as ghettos are sometimes called, is a place most people do not want to pass through, let alone reside in.[50] It is that dangerous place where the "underclass" dwells, a place that elicits fear, contempt, and pity. It is a place of dishonor set apart to contain the undeserving dark masses.[51] The stigma attached to the ghetto is not just a racial stigma or a poverty stigma but a stigma that marks residential neighborhoods and thereby their inhabitants. Thus, unless the new work regime enables people to exit the ghetto or transforms poor black neighborhoods into mixed-income ones, ghetto denizens may reasonably refuse to comply. For in the absence of realistic exits or concerted efforts to establish the conditions of egalitarian pluralism, forcing the ghetto poor to work would be the functional equivalent of state-sponsored labor camps or workhouses for the black poor, as the workers would still be effectively confined to the dark ghetto. The black urban poor may legitimately refuse to accept jobs under these circumstances on the grounds that to willingly comply would be humiliating and demeaning.

A third version of the objection centers not only on race and class but also on gender. Most of those being forced to accept employment by the new work regime are poor black mothers. Often the work that is available to them is domestic service in the homes of affluent white families. Refusing this kind of work can be resistance to the ideological image of the "mammy"—the self-sacrificing, deferential, faithful, and obedient house servant—and its associated social roles.[52] This ideological representation of the "good" black woman was used to justify the exploitation and subordination of black women under slavery. Black urbanization during the Jim Crow era forced most black women into domestic work, as employment discrimination prevented black men from earning a family wage and black women from securing industrial or clerical jobs. In light of this history, poor black women, who are often criticized for being bad mothers, have reason to resent being made to look after the children and clean the homes of the unjustly advantaged, particularly when these affluent families are white. The symbolism of the role is too often humiliating, and accepting it can feel like submitting to one's subordination. Indeed, this expressive harm objection might be extended to a range of jobs in the service sector. As Patricia Hill Collins has argued, a lot of the work in the contemporary service industry—fast food, hotel room cleaning, and childcare centers—is reminiscent of traditional domestic service but in a routinized and impersonal setting.[53]

Fourth and finally, many Americans have racial animus toward or unconscious biases against black citizens. In particular, there is considerable evidence that some Americans, under the influence of ideological racism, oppose welfare entitlement programs because they are hostile to or prejudiced against blacks, with whom such programs are generally associated.[54] A long-standing and deeply offensive stereotype about blacks is that they are lazy. The ghetto poor would have grounds to refuse work if they have a justified belief that their fellow citizens have erected a work regime out of racial prejudice, whether as a means to punish shiftlessness or as a paternalistic effort to correct habits of indolence. A work regime, despite its ostensible race-neutrality, would then be justly considered a veiled expression of contempt for black citizens and a sign of the society's lack of respect for its black members. It would be a form of intrinsic institutional racism.

All four of these expressive harm objections are that much more forceful if the injustice and exploitation objections are sound. Submitting to subordinate status within an unjust and exploitative regime is abhorrent to anyone with a healthy sense of justice. But for blacks to accommodate themselves to an unjust and exploitative regime that stigmatizes and conveys contempt for poor black people is, for some at least, a fate worse than ghetto poverty. The ghetto poor, apprehending the symbolic meaning of a work regime, may therefore reject it as insulting and choose nonwork to affirm their self-respect.[55]

PART III

Rejecting the Claims of Law

SEVEN

Crime

It is commonly believed that ghettos persist because they have severe crime problems and are inhabited by many previously incarcerated individuals. Crime rates in and around ghettos are high.[1] The prevalence of street crime, particularly violent crime and property offenses, makes ghetto inhabitants feel insecure in their neighborhoods, further adding to their already heavy burdens. The illegal drug market, so common in black urban neighborhoods, engenders drug-related violence and invites organized crime. Drug dealers form gangs, and they arm themselves to protect their drug supply and cash and to enforce contracts and defend or expand their market share. Supplying these illicit drugs also encourages and exacerbates drug habits, which have well-known negative externalities, including violent crimes committed under drug influence and property crimes committed to feed drug habits. Because the ghetto poor are so often the victims of property crimes (theft, robbery, burglary, vandalism, and fraud), their economic vulnerability is worsened. Parents in or near these neighborhoods worry that their children will be attracted to street life, encouraged to experiment with habit-forming drugs, or tempted by gang affiliation.[2] The stigma and problems associated with high-crime neighborhoods deter businesses from opening or remaining and affluent families from residing in them. If these communities are to flourish, crime levels in these neighborhoods must be reduced.

Many who reside in ghetto neighborhoods have been incarcerated.[3] Their felony records make it difficult for them to find work or housing, as it is not illegal to deny a person a job or an apartment because they have been convicted of a felony.[4] Most convicted felons were already disadvantaged by their limited job-related skills, low educational achievement, and lack of work experience, and they are not eligible for many forms of public assistance. The formerly incarcerated, who are mainly (though not only) boys and men, are thus among the worst off in ghetto neighborhoods. Families who depend on them for financial and other forms of support are also made worse off by high incarceration rates and the treatment of ex-convicts.

Some who write about the ghetto-crime-incarceration nexus focus primarily on crime and its negative consequences. They believe this criminal activity wrongs individuals and the public and makes these communities worse off. Consequently, they tend to emphasize punitive measures that might deter this conduct. Others who take up the subject focus mainly on high incarceration rates and their negative consequences. They tend to emphasize the need to reduce the power of the criminal justice system over these vulnerable communities. But generally, both of these responses fail to address a fundamental normative question: Do the ghetto poor have an obligation to respect and abide by the law?

Crime as a Response to the Ghetto Plight

Many among the ghetto poor do respect the law, accept conventional morality, and make an effort to conform to mainstream standards of public and private conduct. Some accept dead-end, menial, and low-wage jobs as they struggle to maintain a decent life for themselves and their families.[5] Most value work and desire to be economically self-sufficient.[6] Some graduate from high school or pass the GED; some get postsecondary education or job training; and a few even go on to graduate from college. In short, a substantial segment of the ghetto poor are not alienated from the wider society, its major institutions, or its basic social norms.[7] However, many *are* alienated, some deeply so.[8]

High-poverty neighborhoods with few good employment options lead some residents, especially those unemployed for long periods, to consider securing income through unlawful means.[9] Ghetto poverty creates desperation and feelings of shame, and some, seeking to escape the weight of their social conditions, or at least to make it more bearable, resort to crime. Of course, crime does not just occur in ghettos.

People from all races, classes, and types of neighborhood engage in criminal activity for money, status, power, or amusement. When poor persons from ghettos choose crime, however, they do so under conditions of material deprivation and institutional racism. Thus their criminal activity sometimes expresses something more, or something other, than a character flaw or a disregard for the authority of morality.

Some rely on crime to supplement income derived from work, welfare benefits, or private assistance. Others, such as those who have dropped out of the legitimate labor market altogether, who do not qualify for welfare benefits, or who cannot rely on kin support, use crime as their primary source of income. Although the line is fine and easy to cross, some persons commit crimes without allowing "the streets" to define their social identity or corrupt their souls.[10] Nevertheless, to engage profitably in street crime one must develop the appropriate skills, strategies, and dispositions. This repertoire is simply *street capital,* assets one can use to secure income in the underground urban economy. Just as one may use financial capital without being, strictly speaking, a "capitalist," one can draw on street capital without being a "criminal."[11] For some, though, crime is a vocation, and as such it has its own set of disciplines or what I will call "ethics." There are two broad criminal ethics that I want briefly to describe. These descriptions are to be understood as *ideal types,* constructed to highlight the core features of a particular action orientation by abstracting away from characteristics that are extraneous. Real people will rarely embody these ethics consistently or fully, though some may aspire to do so.

"Gangsters" use violence, threats, and intimidation to forcibly extract money, goods, and services from others. They are fearless and use force to get what they want. They are skilled fighters and adept at the use of weapons. They can strike terror in their victims with little effort. To achieve their aims, they maim and even kill, sometimes without mercy or remorse. The criminal domain they operate in includes robbery, gambling rackets, loan sharking, and extortion. "Hustlers," by contrast, use deception, manipulation, and treachery to achieve their objectives. They are skillful liars. They are cunning and proficient at subtly exploiting their victims' personal weaknesses. As amateur psychologists, they have a gift for understanding human nature, a talent they use to garner their victims' trust, only to betray them. Their domain includes theft, fraud, prostitution, and swindling. Both gangsters and hustlers flout the law and have little, if any, respect for the authority of mainstream institutions. These attitudes are appropriate to their trade; it is rational (in the narrow means–ends sense) to cultivate them once one has chosen street crime as a way of life.[12] These two ethics are not mutually exclusive; one need only consider the modus operandi of many pimps.[13] Nowhere is this more obvious, though, than in the selling of illegal drugs in and around ghettos.

Although few accumulate significant wealth from it, the selling of illegal drugs is a way to make money fast, as there is regular demand. This feature of the trade provides a strong incentive to turn to it when in pressing financial need. But given the nature of this organized crime, it is also a dangerous business, and in an era of law-and-order politics—with its accelerated growth in the penal system, highly punitive attitudes, aggressive policing, limitations on judicial discretion in sentencing, and increased prosecutorial authority—it can lead to long prison terms.[14] Those who practice the trade successfully and are willing to accept these risks and costs sometimes come to wholeheartedly identify with the gangster-hustler ethic. Many gang members embrace this ethic and develop forms of group solidarity in order to defend their financial interests against rival gangs. Those who join these gangs are generally expected and encouraged to show loyalty to other members but not to outsiders.[15] And when a member of one's gang is killed or attacked, violent retaliation is generally expected.

Many who engage in street crime are eventually caught and spend time in federal penitentiaries, state prisons, county jails, or juvenile detention centers. Under state confinement, the street repertoire is often augmented, the gangster and hustler ethics are reinforced, and hostility toward the institutions and officials of the criminal justice system hardens.[16] Once released, many ex-convicts have an increased incentive to return to crime, because their job prospects and earning potential are even dimmer with a criminal record.[17] The cycling of people from ghetto to prison and back again spreads a criminal ethos, an outlaw subculture, throughout many poor urban areas.

The norms that govern the world of street crime also have an enormous impact on ghetto residents who want to avoid participating in and being the victims of crime.[18] For example, the widespread use of guns by drug dealers and muggers creates a demand for these weapons in ghetto neighborhoods. Many residents, including children, arm themselves for protection, believing that the police cannot be relied upon to provide adequate security.[19] A looming sense of danger and a high propensity for violent interpersonal conflict sow seeds of distrust, making it difficult for a broad sense of community to form or thrive. Residents, always on guard, view strangers with suspicion, for one can never be sure that others are not looking to take advantage of you. In adapting to these conditions, many residents who are not directly involved in crime develop survival strategies that are similar to or mimic the strategies of gangsters and hustlers. To avoid being victimized one must appear shrewd and capable of defending oneself, with deadly violence if necessary. Here the familiar male adolescent desire to appear "tough" can take on lethal dimensions, with frightening consequences for those who live in urban communities; and many adolescent girls, though under somewhat less pressure to display a readiness to resort to violence, are also drawn into some of these antisocial roles. Under these conditions a ghetto "street" culture has emerged, where the traits of the gangster and hustler, usually condemned in mainstream society, are sometimes viewed as virtues.[20]

So far I have not mentioned the racial significance of crime in ghetto communities. Yet this dimension is crucial to understanding the choices many poor urban blacks make. As discussed in previous chapters, racism continues to have a negative impact on the life chances of racial minorities in the United States.[21] The impact of ideological, institutional, and structural racism is deepest in dark ghettos, because racism and neighborhood disadvantage combine to create a uniquely stigmatized subgroup of the black population. The peculiar consequences of this dynamic, especially when joined with the ghetto subculture just described, play out in many arenas. Two of these (employment and neighborhood dynamics) have been discussed at length already and so I will be brief. A third (the criminal justice system) merits extended discussion.

Many working-age ghetto residents have limited education, are low skilled, and have gone long periods without legitimate jobs. In metropolitan labor markets there are often more applicants for low-skilled jobs than there are jobs available, so employers can be selective, engaging in so-called statistical discrimination. These employers are aware that a street subculture affects social life in ghettos and that many poor people do not work regularly. This leads some employers to expect blacks from ghettos to be generally violent, dishonest, and unreliable.[22] This racialized stigma affects the job prospects of all black ghetto residents, even those who reject the outlaw ethic and seek to conform to mainstream norms. The frustration of dealing with racial discrimination by employers probably leads more blacks into the criminal underground than would otherwise end up there.

Some who want to find work might be able to if they could move to low-poverty neighborhoods. Some have suggested that there are more job opportunities for low-skilled workers in these areas than in or near ghettos.[23] However, rents and related housing costs are higher in these other communities, often making these neighborhoods out of reach. Most middle-class people, including many middle-class blacks, do not want to live among the ghetto poor and do not want their children to be forced to attend the same schools with them. So they are willing to pay a high premium to reside in better neighborhoods, driving up already high housing costs. Low-skilled inner-city workers could also get to jobs in the suburbs if they had cars, which most cannot afford. Public transportation systems in most metropolitan areas are woefully inefficient, creating long commuting times, and are often too expensive for the working poor to use daily.

Yet, as discussed in Chapters 1 and 2, it would be a mistake to think that the black poor find it so difficult to exit ghettos solely because of the uncoordinated decisions of individuals or impersonal market forces (and even if these factors were the complete explanation, it would not follow that justice permits us to tolerate these unintended consequences). Racial discrimination in housing and efforts by neighborhood organizations to segregate poor blacks in the inner city (including opposition to busing and advocacy of neighborhood schools) also play a part.[24] Therefore it is enormously difficult for the black poor to leave ghettos, because either they cannot afford to move out or residents of nonghetto areas— whether because of racial prejudice, class bias, or narrow self-interest— inhibit the urban poor from joining these more advantaged communities. Many among the black poor are effectively confined to ghetto neighborhoods.[25] They must, therefore, confront the miserable job prospects, failing schools, and crime that exist in these communities. Faced with these obstacles, some choose to drop out of the legitimate labor market (sometimes, as I have argued, as a form of resistance). But because they still need income, some turn to illegal means to generate it.

Racialized Mass Incarceration

A large and strikingly disproportionate number of black people, especially young black men but also many women, are or have been under the supervision of the criminal justice system. According to the U.S. Department of Justice, in 2013, of the more than 1.5 million persons in U.S. federal or state prisons, 37 percent were black males (despite black men comprising only 13 percent of the male population), 32 percent were white males (63 percent of the male population), and 22 percent were Hispanic (17 percent of the male population).[26] Almost 3 percent of American black men were in prison in 2013, compared to 0.5 percent of white men and 1 percent Hispanic men. Among males ages 25 to 39, black men were imprisoned at six times the rate of white men. Among males ages eighteen to nineteen, black males were imprisoned at nine times the rate of white males. Of the 744,600 inmates held in county or city jails at midyear 2014, blacks comprised 35 percent, whites 47 percent, and Hispanics 15 percent.[27] An estimated 1 in 51 U.S. residents (4,751,400 adults) were on probation or parole at year-end 2013.[28] Of those on probation, 30 percent were black, compared to 54 percent white and 14 percent Hispanic. Of those on parole, 38 percent were black, compared to 43 percent white and 17 percent Hispanic.

There is a growing scholarly literature (in legal studies, history, and the social sciences) that attempts to explain the causes and consequences of these and similar disturbing social facts, phenomena that I will call *racialized mass incarceration*.[29] Once they are made aware of it, many people are deeply disturbed, some outraged, by racialized mass incarceration. In recent years there has been sustained activism against and frequent condemnation of racialized mass incarceration. What do critics object to? A range of things, it turns out.

Some commentators insist that the creation of draconian criminal laws and enforcement mechanisms were motivated, at least in part, by racial hostility and prejudice.[30] Covert *racism* is, on this view, the principal reason state officials became more punitive and targeted poor black communities. On this account, mass incarceration is a form of intrinsic institutional racism. Of those who take this position, some maintain that racialized mass incarceration was prompted by a backlash against the triumph of liberalism in the sixties and a strategy to exploit white fear and racial stereotypes for political gain. Or, in an interesting twist, some argue that mass incarceration was actually a *frontlash* strategy on the part of conservative elites to roll back the gains of the civil rights movement by moving to a seemingly colorblind concern with crime.[31]

Others, without asserting that the U.S. criminal justice system is racist, regard the racial *disparity* in incarceration rates as morally problematic.[32] Like disparities in income, employment, and wealth, racial disparities in rates of incarceration trouble many as yet another form of *racial inequality*, which many regard as a reflection of continuing discrimination in U.S. society and a legacy of past racial injustice. Or, relatedly, some object to the *disparate impact* of mass incarceration on poor black communities.[33] The idea is that mass incarceration perpetuates racial subordination, worsens blacks' disadvantage, and stigmatizes African Americans as criminal deviants. On this view we should be concerned about mass incarceration because it reinforces the already low social standing black people have in American society. Because of racial disparities in the numbers of persons under the supervision and control of the criminal justice system, the general stigma attached to criminal conviction taints all blacks, especially young black men and boys from ghettos. Black urban youth are sometimes seen as having a propensity to criminal behavior, which greatly disadvantages them when they seek employment, decent housing, and good schools.[34] Such claims are bases for charges of extrinsic institutional racism.

Some point out that mainly *poor* people are incarcerated while the affluent, when charged with similar crimes, typically go free or face only minor penalties.[35] According to this view, mass incarceration is an outgrowth of rising economic inequality and an instrument for disciplining the poor in an era when the welfare state has been effectively dismantled.[36] Or, emphasizing global capitalism and neoliberal efforts to privatize prisons (funneling public funds to private firms), racialized mass incarceration is sometimes viewed as, in part, the outcome of the emergence of a prison industrial complex, whose function is not to control crime but to maximize profits for corporations and to create employment for rural (mostly white) workers.[37] The raw materials (and sometimes the exploited labor) for this public–private enterprise are said to be mainly the (mostly black and Latino) urban poor, whose labor has become useless in a market economy in an era of deindustrialization.

Some object to the *types of crimes* for which people are incarcerated. In 2012, of the persons incarcerated in state prisons, 54 percent had been convicted of a violent offense (such as murder, robbery, rape, or aggravated assault), and just under half for a drug, property, or public order offense.[38] Drug offenders comprised 16 percent of the state prison population in 2012 and 51 percent of the federal prison population in 2013. Some believe that prison time should be reserved for violent offenders who need to be neutralized to prevent further serious rights violations. Restitution, fines, community service, probation, anklet monitoring, home confinement, and drug-addiction treatment should be used to deal with these lesser crimes.[39] There is also the question of the *severity* of the punishment, given the criminal offense. Here the objection is that the punishments meted out fail to fit the crime—they are disproportionate and excessively punitive, particularly for those convicted for drug possession.

Some critics of racialized mass incarceration point to wrongs that occur prior to the imprisonment of offenders (or even prior to sentencing).[40] There is racial profiling and other illicit race targeting by police. Some activities are criminalized that arguably shouldn't be (for example, the use and possession of certain drugs). Some who are charged with crimes may lack the resources to mount an effective defense and may not be provided with adequate legal counsel. The police may use intimidation, threats, or violence to get suspects to waive their basic liberties (rights to be silent, to an attorney, or to be free from unjustified search and seizure). Prosecutors may be unfair or arbitrary when deciding whom to prosecute and what charges to file. The threat of long sentences for more serious crimes is often used to pressure defendants into accepting unfavorable plea bargains.

Then there are wrongs perpetrated against inmates while they are incarcerated. Correctional facilities are often extremely violent places. Inmates themselves commit some of this violence (including sexual assault), from which the vulnerable are inadequately protected. But correctional officers also commit verbal and physical abuse (sometimes rising to the level of torture), and they are rarely disciplined or fired for these violations.[41] Inmates have little access to mental health care, despite the fact that many suffer from diagnosed mental illnesses. Rehabilitation has been all but abandoned. Prison overcrowding is a serious problem in some states. Solitary confinement for prison infractions is overused and can cause lasting and irreparable psychological harm.[42] While certainly not unusual, the practice of incarceration in the United States is arguably needlessly cruel and inhumane, raising serious questions about its constitutionality and compatibility with human rights requirements.

Some critics point to wrongs that occur after a prison sentence has been served. The ex-offender may no longer be eligible for education grants, welfare benefits, or public housing. In some states the ex-offender is no longer permitted to vote in elections and thus is treated as a permanent outsider to the political community.[43] Those listed as felons in criminal justice databases have a difficult time finding work or a place to live, as employment and housing discrimination against ex-offenders is neither illegal nor generally thought to be wrong.

I accept many of these criticisms of the U.S. criminal justice system and of Americans' attitudes toward crime and criminal offenders. They must be attended to in any attempt to come to terms with the injustices faced by blacks in ghettos. However, these criticisms do not answer the objections that many have to the problem of crime in ghettos. Even if the public response to such crime has been racist, class biased, draconian, exploitative, inefficient, or otherwise cruel and unfair, there is still the question of whether when poor blacks perpetrate crimes they thereby violate their civic responsibilities, thus meriting public condemnation and state-imposed penalty. The public response to crime in ghettos over the last four or five decades has been deeply troubling, and criminal justice reform—from policing and prosecuting to prisons and release conditions—is urgently needed. But there remains a pressing question: How should we think about and respond to the crime itself?

Is Crime Unreasonable?

Imprudence is rightly regarded as a vice, and some of the lawbreaking the ghetto poor engage in is no doubt unwise, given its risks, costs, and negative long-term consequences for the actors themselves. The ghetto poor are sometimes criticized on the ground that their attitudes and conduct make their situation worse (see Chapter 3), but this issue lies outside the concern of the present chapter. The concern here is this: When the ghetto poor refuse to respect the law and engage in criminal activity, are they being *unreasonable*?[44] That is, do these forms of transgression express an unwillingness to honor the fair terms of social cooperation that others accept and abide by? If the ghetto poor accept the benefits of the social scheme but violate the norms that make the scheme possible whenever doing so would advance their self-interests, then their nonconformity is opportunistic and may therefore appear unjustified to those complying with these norms. But as I have emphasized, whether their deviance is unreasonable depends on the justness of the overall social scheme. And as we have seen, there are strong reasons to conclude that the scheme is deeply unjust.

Let's distinguish three possible assessments of the basic structure of U.S. society. On the first, we judge the United States to be a fully just society. This assessment is untenable. On the second, we judge that there are some injustices that should be addressed but that the United States is not fundamentally unjust. On the third, we judge that the society is fundamentally unjust and requires radical reform to bring it in line with what basic justice demands. The question, then, is what obligations the ghetto poor would have if the second or third assessment were correct.

To sharpen the question further, let's distinguish between civic obligations and natural duties.[45] Civic obligations are owed to those with whom one is cooperating in order to maintain a fair basic structure. They are the obligations that exist between citizens of a democratic polity as defined by the principles of justice that underpin their association. Civic obligations have binding normative force because of the contingent associational ties between citizens, that is, because of the formal or informal bonds that define a set of persons as a distinct people or nation. By contrast, natural duties are unconditionally binding, in that they hold between all persons regardless of whether they are fellow citizens or are bound by other institutional ties. Both civic obligations and natural duties are moral requirements. The key difference is that one has civic obligations qua citizen and natural duties qua moral person.

Within the liberal-egalitarian framework I have been defending, civic obligations are rooted in the political value of reciprocity. As a beneficiary of the basic goods and services afforded by the scheme of cooperation, each citizen has an obligation to fulfill the requirements of the main institutions of his or her society when these institutions are just. Such reciprocity forbids the exploitation of fellow members of the society. Rawls, for example, rightly insists that one should not attempt to gain from the labor contributions of others without doing one's fair share to uphold the social arrangement. Just as important, he also correctly maintains that we do not have obligations to submit to *unjust* institutions, *or at least not to institutions that exceed the limits of tolerable injustice.* As we human beings are imperfect, no social arrangement can ensure that citizens will face no injustices. Yet no citizen can be expected to tolerate serious, burdensome, and repeated injustices over the course of their lives. One difficulty we must face, then, is ascertaining just where to draw the line beyond which injustices become intolerable.

Rawls does not provide such a standard. One standard we might use, though, is to live with unjust socioeconomic inequalities if the *constitutional essentials* are secure. For Rawls these essentials are the familiar basic rights of a liberal-democratic regime—such as freedom of speech, conscience, assembly, and association; the right to vote and run for office; the right to due process and judicial fairness—and the political procedures that ensure democratic rule.[46] The constitutional essentials also include freedom of movement, free choice of occupation, and formal justice (the impartial and consistent administration of institutional rules). And crucially, they include a social minimum that secures the basic material needs of all citizens.[47] The constitutional essentials do not, however, include fair equality of opportunity (Rawls's egalitarian interpretation of the equal opportunity principle). Nor do they include the difference principle (his requirement that socioeconomic inequalities always work to the benefit of the least advantaged).

A plausible rationale for using this standard for tolerable injustice is that it is most urgent to secure the constitutional essentials, given their indispensable role in creating social stability, and that reasonable people can disagree over how much socioeconomic inequality can be justified and over when existing institutional arrangements satisfy agreed-upon principles of economic justice. The constitutional essentials establish the political legitimacy of a social order by publicly affirming the equal status of all citizens under the rule of law. If an otherwise unjust society met this standard, this would not mean that citizens should not agitate for more socioeconomic equality or use democratic processes and other socially accepted political channels to fight for policies that would achieve a more egalitarian basic structure. It would simply mean that their civic obligations were still fully binding and so they should fulfill these obligations as they work for a more just social arrangement.

Assume for the moment that this proposed standard for tolerable injustice is currently met in the United States. Would it be reasonable to expect the ghetto poor to fulfill their civic obligations, even as they justifiably resent and protest continuing socioeconomic inequalities? Many U.S. citizens, regarding their society as imperfect but reasonably just, believe that the attitudes, conduct, and values of many of the black urban poor (particularly the so-called street element) are in conflict with legitimate expectations for civic responsibility. Each citizen reasonably expects other citizens to fulfill their basic obligations as a citizen, to do their fair share in sustaining an institutional arrangement that works to everyone's advantage. In particular, most U.S. citizens think that everyone, including the poor, should obey the law. Thus, when the ghetto poor engage in criminal activity or show contempt for legal requirements and law enforcement officials, this is widely regarded as a blameworthy failure of reciprocity on their part.

I doubt that this widely held view is correct, however. If the constitutional essentials are currently met, then they allow too much inequality for the social order to claim political legitimacy. A social order that relegates a segment of its citizenry to humiliating forms of exploitation cannot reasonably expect allegiance from that oppressed group. To be sure, reasonable people can disagree over how much socioeconomic inequality can be justified to the least well off. But when the disadvantaged are regularly subjected to such stigmatizing and demeaning forms of servitude as the ghetto poor have been, a bright line has been crossed.

One might reply that if the ghetto poor feel that they cannot accept the jobs available and still retain their dignity, then they should simply get by on whatever public welfare provisions are available or on private aid but without resorting to crime. Leaving aside for the moment the questionable adequacy of current welfare benefits, we can appreciate the limits of this response if we keep in mind that the basic structure of any society will, in predictable and alterable ways, encourage certain desires and ambitions in its citizens; and lawmakers generally take into account how the overall incentive structure in society will be affected by the policies they enact. Any affluent, mass-consumer, capitalist society will encourage—indeed actively cultivate—the ambition to live comfortably (if not get rich). This is, after all, how such economies reproduce themselves: by creating continual mass desire for a wide range of consumer goods and services. If such a society guarantees only the constitutional essentials, without providing every citizen with a real opportunity to reach the goal of material comfort, then it is far from obvious that those who are inhibited in this pursuit, because they lack resources, are being unreasonable when they choose crime as an alternative to subsistence living on welfare or through charity.

This point is different from Jeffrie Murphy's claim that because capitalist societies encourage greed, envy, and selfishness, it would be unfair to punish poor citizens who, in acting on these socially sanctioned motives, commit crimes. As he says, "There is something perverse in applying principles that presuppose a sense of community in a society which is structured to destroy genuine community."[48] My point is rather that affluent capitalist societies encourage the expectation that, with a reasonable degree of effort, any able-bodied person has a fair chance to live a life of material comfort. So if one develops a life plan based on this expectation yet the expectation is frustrated, not because of one's lack of effort or ability, but because of inequities in the prevailing opportunity structure, one is not necessarily being unreasonable when one chooses unlawful means to attain the expected standard of living.

As noted, the core value underlying civic obligations is reciprocity. The problem with using the constitutional essentials as the threshold for tolerable injustice is that it does not ensure genuine conditions of reciprocity for the most disadvantaged in the scheme. Each citizen should be secure in the thought that he or she has equal standing within the scheme of cooperation. This means that the scheme should be organized so that it publicly conveys to each participant that his or her interests are just as important as any other participant's. Given how difficult it is to determine whether fair equality of opportunity is fully satisfied, perhaps that egalitarian principle sets the bar too high for tolerable injustice.[49] Still, in a society that allows wealth to be concentrated in the hands of a small elite and that relies primarily on the stock and labor markets to distribute income, the standard for tolerable injustice should include an adequate opportunity to avoid demeaning forms of labor. Those who are denied this opportunity can rightly object that they are not being treated as equally valued members of a scheme of cooperation that is supposed to be mutually advantageous. Wealth could be more widely distributed and income supplements made more generous to the economically disadvantaged so that they don't have strong reasons to think that their fellow citizens are taking unfair advantage of their economic vulnerability.

It might be objected that the ghetto poor, despite their disadvantages, do have *some* chance (albeit not the same chance as other citizens) to find good jobs. After all, some poor ghetto residents do manage to do this. Why is this not a sufficient sign that the system accords them equal concern? In any case, because the ghetto poor are not taking full advantage of the employment opportunities that are available, how can their complaints about the intolerable injustice of the system be taken seriously? In reply, I would say that if poverty-level income were an unavoidable by-product of economic cooperation under the material conditions that prevail in the United States, the first objection would have merit. With adjustments to the tax scheme, however, public schools could be dramatically improved and low-wage earners could be brought up to a decent standard of living. The public and their elected representatives simply lack the commitment to justice to make the relevant adjustments.

To the second objection I would note that one way to register one's principled opposition to an unjust social system is to forgo chances to benefit from its unfair opportunity structure. G. A. Cohen makes this important point when responding to the anti-Marxist claim that members of the working class are not forced to sell their labor power to capitalists, because any one of them, or almost any, could start their own small business and thus exit the proletarian class.[50] He raises the important possibility that some workers, out of solidarity with the others, may object to taking an individual escape that is not part of a general liberation for all. Some members of the ghetto poor could reasonably take a similar position.

Not only does the constitutional-essentials standard for tolerable injustice allow too much inequality, but there is reason to believe that not even this standard is currently met in the United States. Institutional racism (both intrinsic and extrinsic) still exists across a number of major social institutions. There has, in addition, been a sharp reduction in welfare benefits and other social entitlements for the poor and unemployed (provisions that, arguably, were not adequate to begin with), and many are now forced to work for poverty wages to receive even these meager benefits (such as workfare programs and the earned-income tax credit). These circumstances suggest that the constitutional essentials are not secure. Having the constitutional essentials codified in law, even with judicial review, is not sufficient to regard them as secure, as even a cursory knowledge of the history of the black struggle for equal citizenship should make clear. Civil rights laws must also be impartially, consistently, and effectively enforced (formal justice), so that all citizens, regardless of race, gender, or class background, can be confident that those with institutional power over them will respect their rights. The existence of the dark ghetto—with its combination of racial stigma, neighborhood disadvantage, inadequate schools, fragile families, forced servitude, and shocking incarceration rates—is simply incompatible with any meaningful form of reciprocity among free and equal citizens.

Many among the ghetto poor justifiably feel that by demanding that they work in miserable low-paying jobs to secure their basic needs, more-advantaged citizens are simply trying to keep their taxes low or, worse, attempting to exploit the labor of poor people. And when the poor refuse this unfair arrangement, they are stigmatized as lazy, ungrateful, and criminal. From the standpoint of many poor ghetto residents, the social order lacks legitimacy.[51] There appears to be a conspiracy to contain, exploit, and underdevelop the black urban poor, to deny them equal civic standing and punish them when they decline to accommodate themselves to injustice. This appearance of conspiracy is, I believe, a reflection of the underlying failure of the basic structure to embody the value of reciprocity. If we are to take equal citizenship seriously, then not only should we refrain from attempting to gain from others' labor without carrying our fair share of the burdens of maintaining the system of cooperation, but we should not demand labor from those being deprived of their fair share of the benefits from the system. I would conjecture that in an affluent society with a recent history of overt racial domination and civic exclusion, no reasonable standard for tolerable injustice is compatible with persistent ghetto conditions. If this conjecture is correct, then when the ghetto poor in the United States refuse to respect the authority of the law qua law, they do not thereby violate the principle of reciprocity or shirk valid civic obligations.

It is perhaps worth noting that Rawls insists that even within a reasonably just society (say, where the constitutional essentials are secure), there is a limit to how much injustice people should have to endure. In particular, he thinks that, as a society seeks to reform itself, the burdens of injustice should, over time, be distributed more or less evenly across different sectors and groups in society, so that the weight of oppression does not fall mostly on any one social group. Thus he says, "The duty to comply [with reasonably just institutions] is problematic for permanent minorities that have suffered from injustice for many years."[52] Even if the United States is reasonably just (according to some defensible standard for tolerable injustice), the heavy burdens that the black urban poor are forced to carry, and the length of time they have had to carry them, may justify their refusal to comply with public demands until their load is significantly lightened. Many of them are also, of course, members of a cohesive social group—a *people*—whose recent ancestors suffered under slavery and Jim Crow and whose disadvantages are, in part, a legacy of more than three centuries of white supremacy. These long-standing grievances only strengthen the reasons the ghetto poor have to refuse to accept the authority of law.

Crime and the Duty of Justice

However, even if their society is fundamentally unjust—that is, exceeds the limits of tolerable injustice—this does not mean that the ghetto poor have no moral duties to one another or to others. Only someone who holds a purely instrumental or utility-maximizing conception of reason could think that an unjust social order rationally justifies a war of all against all, in which the only valid value systems are those of the gangster and hustler. The ghetto poor do have duties, natural duties, that are not defined by civic reciprocity and thus are not negated by the existence of even a grossly unjust social order.[53]

Among these is the duty not to be cruel. There is a duty to not cause unnecessary suffering. There is a duty of mutual respect: to show due respect for the moral personhood of others. There are also many other basic duties. Such duties are not suspended or void because one is oppressed. And the affluent do not forfeit their right against violent attack simply because they have profited from an unjust social system. The existence of these natural duties makes some of the attitudes and actions among the ghetto poor impermissible, not because they are forbidden by law but because they cannot be morally justified. This means, at a minimum, that the reckless and gratuitous violence, the selfish indifference to others' suffering, and the disregard for the humanity of one's fellow human beings that are all too common in some poor urban neighborhoods should not be tolerated. Neither can we allow gender-based violence and sexual harassment, which are menacing features of ghetto life for many women and girls.[54] There should also be special mindfulness of how impressionable youth are and, in particular, of how observing the behavior of adults shapes a child's moral development.

Yet fulfilling one's natural duties to others may nevertheless be compatible with a number of unlawful actions. Taking the lives of others, except in self-defense or in defense of others, is almost never justified. However, taking the possessions of others, especially when these others are reasonably well off, may be permissible. Mugging someone at gunpoint does not show sufficient respect for the victim's claim to be free from threats against their person. But shoplifting and other forms of theft might be permissible. In light of the hazards of participating in gang culture, recruiting children into gangs shows insufficient concern for the weak and vulnerable. Yet given the advantages of concerted group action, participating in gangs may be a defensible and effective means to secure needed income. Something similar can be said in favor of prostitution, welfare fraud, tax evasion, selling stolen goods, and other off-the-books transactions in the underground economy.[55] There are, of course, many complex questions here about when coercion, threats, or deception may legitimately be used; and there is the salient question of which drugs may be sold to consenting adults without wronging them or others.[56] I will not pursue these issues. My goal is not to mark the precise line between permissible crimes and impermissible ones but only to offer reasons for thinking that not all crimes perpetrated by the ghetto poor are wrong and that condemning criminal transgressions as a violation of civic responsibility is misplaced.

I do, however, want to draw out the practical implications of a natural duty that I have been relying on throughout—the duty of justice. This duty, recall, requires each individual to support and comply with just institutions and, where just institutions do not exist, to help to bring them about. Exactly what it would mean to fulfill this duty under conditions of injustice naturally depends on a given agent's concrete circumstances. Depending on the conditions that prevail, the duty of justice, as a component of the political ethics of the oppressed, gives rise to two types of imperatives. On the one hand, there are choices one should make when it appears possible to overcome, mitigate, or evade the injustices one faces. Then there are choices one should make when freedom or perhaps even relief seems unattainable. So, then, there is an ethic of resistance aimed at liberation and an ethic of resistance aimed at living with self-respect despite insurmountable injustice.

Acting on the duty of *mutual aid*—that is, the duty to help the needy, vulnerable, and weak when you are able—can be a way of expressing solidarity or forging bonds with the oppressed. Such in-group mutual assistance is perfectly permissible, sometimes praiseworthy, and often vital. It, too, has implications for the ethics of the oppressed. The duty of mutual aid should not, however, be confused with the duty of justice, for what a person does to fulfill the one duty may not always fulfill the other. In fact, widespread mutual aid among the oppressed is compatible with their active or passive acceptance of unjust conditions. The members of an oppressed group can work together for their mutual survival without aiming to remove or alter the forces that subjugate them.

The duty of self-respect, which is fulfilled by recognizing and affirming one's equal moral worth as a person, also provides a reason to resist injustice. But it differs from the duty of justice. One expresses self-respect by, for example, standing up for oneself when one has been treated unjustly, rather than meekly acquiescing. The duty of self-respect is a matter of defending one's equal standing in the face of injustice; the duty of justice is a matter of taking proactive steps to end or mitigate injustice. The duty of self-respect is a self-regarding duty; the duty of justice is one owed to others. The duty of self-respect demands action from those who have been wronged; the duty of justice demands action regardless of whether one has been wronged.

Of course, it would be unreasonable to expect individuals to work or sacrifice to bring about a just society when doing so would be very dangerous or extremely costly. Given the conditions in most ghettos, perhaps it is too much to ask of ghetto denizens that they make significant contributions to the cause of social justice. After all, many have more than they can handle just trying to meet their basic needs and hold their heads up. Yet it is reasonable to expect disadvantaged residents of ghettos, in addition to fulfilling their other natural duties, to refrain from taking actions that would clearly exacerbate the injustices of the system or increase the burdens on others in these communities, at least when these negative consequences could be avoided with little sacrifice. Nor should they do things that would clearly make a just society more difficult to achieve, provided that in refraining from such actions they can maintain their self-respect and meet their other basic needs.

Expecting the ghetto poor to honor their natural duties, including the duty of justice, is not a problematic form of victim-blaming. The ghetto poor should not be held responsible for the appalling social conditions that have been imposed on them because of the workings of an unjust basic structure and the wrongful actions of their fellow citizens. But they should be held accountable, particularly by those in their own communities, for how they choose to respond to these conditions. Demanding this basic level of moral responsibility treats them as full moral persons and as political agents in their own right.

As I have emphasized, too often ghettos are viewed as "sick" communities, burdened with myriad pathologies, that the state-as-physician (or some suitable social service organization, such as a charity or church) must "heal." Not only is the medical model approach too often an offensive expression of paternalistic sentiments (which have well-known black elite noblesse oblige variants), but also it is the wrong paradigm when we are dealing with a social problem whose origin lies in systemic injustice. We all, whether we belong to dominant or subjugated groups, have a duty to help establish just social arrangements. Given that the injustices at issue are features of a system of social cooperation that we all, winners and losers, participate in, we should view the project to correct these injustices as a joint one, or at least it should be so viewed by those who want to live in a just society rather than to profit from an unjust one.

Unfortunately, in light of the ill will, selfishness, and callous indifference some of the ghetto poor's fellow citizens exhibit, social justice might not be achievable unless the black urban poor take on a good deal of the burden in reforming their society. As has so often been true in human history, the oppressed must play a large role—sometimes they have to be the principal agents—in ending the unjust practices they are subjected to. For example, black citizens had to play significant roles in abolishing slavery and Jim Crow, despite having suffered most because of these systems of domination. The fact that this is, in some sense, "unfair" is irrelevant. The duty of justice is not based on the principle of civic reciprocity. It is a duty each has qua moral person, not qua citizen. So one cannot opt out of this duty because one's fellow citizens fail to fulfill it. Nor should one stop short of doing more than others in the struggle for justice on the ground that were these others to do their part, one would not have to do as much (though the criticism of these others is no doubt warranted).

Exactly how one should go about fulfilling the duty of justice, that is, which specific courses of action would satisfy it, will depend on the particular social circumstances one faces. As an imperfect duty, the duty of justice also allows each some discretion in how he or she will carry it out. In light of these circumstances, one must make an assessment of how best to contribute to improving things. This assessment will necessarily involve determining just how much assistance one can realistically expect from others and how best to enlist this aid. When viewed from this vantage point, ghetto residents should think carefully about how they respond to the injustices of the social order and consider whether the forms of crime they sometimes engage in are ultimately obstacles to effecting positive social change.

From Spontaneous Defiance to Conscious Resistance

One of the ways in which the ghetto poor have sometimes responded to their plight is to engage in spontaneous rebellion. This may take the form of openly transgressing conventional norms, expressing contempt for authority, desecrating revered symbols, pilfering from employers, evading taxes, vandalizing public property, or disrupting public events.[57] Spontaneous rebellion reaches its apotheosis in the urban riot, where looting, mass destruction of property, and brutal violence are on public display. When legitimate avenues for political action fail to produce results or are closed off, such public unrest can seem to be the only power the ghetto poor can wield collectively that has a chance of garnering concessions from the state.[58]

Many of these acts of defiance, though perhaps yielding limited political payoff, may be necessary for the ghetto poor to maintain their self-respect. If nothing else, such actions can be cathartic and can help prevent the oppressed from turning on each other as they seek an outlet for their justified anger. Yet not all expressions of rebellion are aimed at protesting or changing the social order. Some ostensible defiance, on closer scrutiny, reveals itself to be no more than a desire to exploit the system opportunistically, as when demagogues take advantage of the anger of the poor to gain personal power or when gangsters and hustlers take advantage of others' desperation merely for their own gain—capitalism by other means, as it were. What may have begun as principled resistance can become, because of encroaching cynicism, "life-is-unfair" resignation. Some juvenile deviance is little more than adolescent rebellion unchecked by proper adult supervision. The key practical question is how, if at all, this general impulse toward rebellion in U.S. ghettos can be transformed into enduring and effective forms of political resistance. I will not pretend to have the answer to this difficult question. I would, however, like to briefly outline what kinds of moral criticism of the ghetto poor might be appropriate in light of the aim of cultivating constructive forms of resistance, thereby giving some concrete content to the abstract duty of justice.

There are two different ways a society might be unjust.[59] The first way is when the publicly recognized standards for judging the justice of the basic structure are sound but the institutional arrangement of the society fails to satisfy these standards. In this case the society fails to live up to its own professed ideals, ideals that are *worthy* of public recognition. Alternatively, social arrangements may fit the prevailing conception of justice in the society or the political views of the ruling elite but nevertheless be unjust. In this case the dominant conception of justice is an *ideology*, a set of widely held beliefs and implicit assumptions that legitimates and thereby helps to sustain an oppressive regime.

In the first situation, the political opposition may be able to appeal to their fellow citizens' sense of justice or moral conscience, highlighting the gap between ideals and practice. Here, nonviolent civil disobedience, public demonstrations, or other forms of mass protest that attempt to arouse the public's sense of moral outrage may be productive. Since the era of New World slavery, the dominant tradition in African American activism has taken this approach. However, if the society is stabilized by a deeply flawed conception of justice, such as one that serves the narrow interests of corporate elites, politicians, and affluent citizens, then more drastic or unconventional measures may be warranted. Given a dominant ideology that advances a distorted view of what justice demands and that is widely endorsed because of narrow self-interest or illegitimate group interest, it might not be sufficient to appeal to the majority's sense of justice. Moral suasion and electoral politics may simply not be enough. Black radicals and left-wing feminists (by no means mutually exclusive groups) have taken exactly this position with respect to the United States, regarding this society as a deeply racist, patriarchal, and plutocratic social order. Those who oppose such a regime would have to develop a militant social movement that pushes the society in a more progressive direction, not "by any means necessary," but perhaps through means widely, though mistakenly, regarded as unjustified or unwise. The black urban poor have often been attracted to such doctrines.[60]

This contrast between the two ways a regime can be unjust, though analytically useful, is probably too stark for practical purposes. Some aspects of the basic structure (its educational, law enforcement, and economic institutions, for instance) may be regulated by a corrupt ideology, while other parts (say, its constitution or basic political organization) may be just or diverge moderately from reasonable and widely recognized standards of justice. Indeed, contrary to the view of some on the political left, this mixed assessment is, I suspect, the one most applicable to post-civil-rights America, as the Civil Rights movement did help to make blacks' constitutional rights considerably more meaningful. Thus, the political resistance, even if it takes a militant form, must take into account the reasonableness of existing aspects of the social scheme, including shared ideas of justice, and choose measures of opposition accordingly.[61]

To be sure, militant leaders must be willing to take political measures that some might find unacceptable, should overcoming serious injustices require these tactics. And political insurgency aimed at overthrowing an oppressive regime is sometimes justified. Yet given the proven difficulty of establishing and maintaining just institutions in the modern world, preserving the reasonably just components of an overall unjust system while pushing insistently for broader reforms may ultimately be a better strategy than abrupt radical reconstruction. Moreover, grassroots organizing and populist collective action would still require some measure of public order to be effective, and so the political institutions currently in place—with their provisions protecting freedom of speech, association, and assembly—could prove useful.

These are difficult and complex questions of political practice that philosophical theory can only do so much to illuminate. But no matter what form such opposition should take, the ghetto poor should be included in the resistance effort. In fulfilling the duty of justice, ghetto residents will need to build bonds of political solidarity with each other and cultivate appropriate allies. Such solidarity requires not only shared political values and the common goal of ending ghetto conditions but also a sense of compassion for those similarly oppressed. It calls for special concern, a willingness to help the most disadvantaged among you when you can. Solidarity demands loyalty to those you are working together with to change things for the better. Perhaps most important, it requires a sense of mutual trust, without which collective action cannot occur.

If such solidarity is to form and be sustained, however, an outlaw subculture cannot reign in the ghetto. A climate of fear and suspicion erodes any chance of developing mutual trust. It undermines empathy and compassion because those who appear to be in need might in fact be trying to exploit you, or worse. If loyalty to one's gang trumps all other loyalties or leads one to disregard the legitimate interests of those outside the gang, then no broader form of loyalty in ghetto communities can take shape, let alone stable forms of political organization. This means that the gangster and hustler ethics, as value systems, must be repudiated.

I am not suggesting that the ghetto poor are never justified in engaging in street crime. On the contrary, lacking acceptable alternatives, unlawful actions may be necessary to meet one's needs or the needs of others. Nor am I saying that one should never make use of the repertoire of gangsters and hustlers—street capital—to secure needed income. The political economy of the underground may require these tactics. What I do maintain is that the techniques of the gangster and hustler should not be used merely to gain power, status, or riches. No one should allow these practices to constitute their enduring social identity. And one should be careful not to let the streets take one's soul. Gangsterism and hustling must not be regarded as vocations, but (at best) as survival tactics, means of self-defense, or expressions of justified rebellion. Also, if street capital is to be converted into political empowerment in a resistance movement, then ghetto rebellion should not be merely opportunistic or remain cathartic but, whenever possible, should publicly register dissent. It is crucial, given the duty of justice and on grounds of self-respect, that the ghetto poor make *manifest* their principled dissatisfaction with the existing social order.

227

EIGHT

Punishment

When, if ever, is state punishment justified in a context where the state has failed to secure a reasonably just basic structure? To put it in the terms explained in the previous chapter, how should a criminal justice system operate in a society that exceeds the limits of tolerable injustice? I am not here thinking primarily about an unjust criminal justice system. That is, the problem I'm concerned with is not the fact that some societies routinely mistreat innocent persons, criminal suspects, those with outstanding warrants, defendants, and convicts, for example, through unjustified searches, racial profiling, police brutality, arbitrary and uneven enforcement, wrongful convictions, unfair sentences, and inhumane prison conditions. Imagine, if you will, a criminal justice system that is itself impartial and fair, given the content of its public rules and the way those rules are applied and enforced. But the system operates in a broader social context shaped by deep structural injustices—for example, unjustified economic inequality, widespread patterns of discrimination, and inadequate protection of basic liberties.

I maintain that serious injustices in the basic structure of a society compromise both the state's *authority to punish* criminal offenders and its *moral standing to condemn* crimes within its claimed jurisdiction. But I also think that a state in an unjust society, if that state fulfills certain requirements of fairness, may permissibly punish at least some legal violations, even some crimes perpetrated by the oppressed. On one plausible, even compelling, theory of punishment—what I'll call *penal expressivism*—these two theses would appear to be incompatible. So in addition to defending these two normative claims, I cast doubt on the truth of penal expressivism while retaining its key insights.

Legitimacy, Authority, and Enforcement

A set of legal institutions constitutes a *state* when it effectively rules, and claims the right to rule, over the inhabitants of a territory. We speak of the existence of a state (as opposed to a failed state or the "state of nature") only when inhabits of a given territory sufficiently conform their conduct to legal requirements such that social order and cooperation are maintained. States claim both the moral power to demand obedience to their laws from those within their territorial jurisdiction and immunity from outside interference with their internal affairs.

When we assess the *legitimacy* of a state, we may evaluate it from the standpoint of international relations or from the standpoint of those subject to its laws. The international community may assess a state for its human rights compliance to determine whether, for example, its claim of sovereignty should be respected or it should be subject to intervention. Those under the rule of a state's laws may evaluate the state on grounds of social justice to determine whether they have an obligation to obey. When I speak of "legitimacy" I am concerned with the normative status of the relationship between a state and the individuals (citizens, legal residents, and undocumented immigrants) it claims a right to govern. I won't address the relations between states or the limits of sovereignty.

It's useful to make a distinction between two types of legitimacy—justifiable-enforcement legitimacy and right-to-be-obeyed legitimacy.[1] The right to use coercion to enforce a rule is different from the claim right to have the rules one lays down obeyed. A state may have the right to enforce laws against, say, murder and rape simply because these are serious wrongs that violate basic moral rights. The duty to comply with these laws arises from one's natural duty to refrain from such reprehensible acts and from the contingent fact that the existing state is best positioned to maintain order and safety. The right to be obeyed, which we might call *legitimate authority*, includes the right to impose obligations outside the domain of natural duties (for example, duties to respect various property claims, to follow state regulations, and to pay taxes). In addition to enforcement rights, legitimate authority includes rights to command and entitlements to obedience, and the commands in question needn't prohibit things that are intrinsically wrong to be authoritative. It is the commands themselves—that is, when they come from the right source and under the right conditions—that make non-compliance wrong.

To have legitimate authority is to have a special kind of prerogative: a right to demand that others comply with a command or rule one has issued. It is the right to create obligations for others, obligations they wouldn't have if not for the command or rule. Within the limits of political authority, authoritative rules override reasons for acting contrary to the rule, and they do so, not because of the content of the rules, but because of who issued them or because of the procedures through which they have come about. The subject must obey because of the *source* of the rules, not because of their *substance*.

That a rule is authoritative in this way does not mean that the subject has a duty to obey the *person* issuing the command or rule. The person is to be obeyed (if they are) only because they occupy an authoritative role or office. The person with the moral power to issue commands or to make rules may not be the party to whom, ultimately, obedience is owed. And the person with this moral power may not be the source of this power. In a liberal democracy, obedience to the law is something members of a just society owe to each other on grounds of reciprocity. We fulfill this obligation by submitting to the demands of the legitimate state within whose jurisdiction we live, even when we happen to disagree with the content of these laws.

To make these ideas concrete, let's consider legal prohibitions or regulations of the sale and use of certain narcotics and stimulants— cocaine, marijuana, heroin, and methamphetamine—that have high potential for abuse or addiction. Many people think such laws are unwise and wrongly interfere with individual freedom. Others believe these laws are prudent and necessary to protect individuals from harm (including self-harm) and to ensure public health. Let's assume that reasonable people can disagree over whether such drug laws should be instituted, over whether violations of these laws should be classed as misdemeanors or felonies, and over what the penalty should be for violating these laws. Further assume that selling these drugs to competent adults who intend to consume them (even for nonmedical purposes) does not wrong these persons. (After all, they have the liberty to undertake dangerous activities provided they don't harm others; and it doesn't appear to be a violation of our natural duties to offer others habit-forming narcotics and stimulants even when we know these drugs are often abused, provided these dangerous properties are known to those who would use these drugs.) Were a state with legitimate authority, through democratic procedures, to proscribe the sale and use of such drugs, those within its jurisdiction would have a duty to refrain from selling and consuming these drugs, simply because the law demands this. Defiance of the drug laws would be wrong even if the sale and use of the drugs would not violate a natural duty. Yet if the state in question operates against the background of a seriously unjust basic structure, it is less clear that it would have a right to enforce such drug prohibitions or that citizens would have a duty to respect drug laws.

As discussed in Chapter 7, if a state fails to meet at least the minimum standard of justice, it does not have the authority to demand compliance with its laws as such, and those within the relevant territory have no obligation to recognize the state's claim to authority. In such cases the state lacks legitimate authority over those it claims to rule. Legitimate authority is, however, a matter of degree rather than all or nothing. As legitimacy goes down, the obligation to obey dries up before it evaporates. If the extent or type of injustice is serious enough, though, the duty to obey can be void or nonexistent.

Reciprocity and Protection

The legitimacy of a political order is to be judged by how well it maintains a fair system of social cooperation. We rightly submit to a state that claims legitimate authority over us when it protects our basic liberties (including those that enable democratic participation) and ensures an equitable distribution of the benefits and burdens of socioeconomic cooperation. It would violate fair-play principles to take advantage of the freedom and social benefits made possible by a just legal order without accepting the constraints of the law and contributing our share to maintaining the material conditions of social life.

The authority of law is not a matter of threats and brute force. Legitimate legal authority is part of the *normative order*, just as are our basic moral rights and obligations. When a state has legitimate authority, we should think of its laws as the official promulgation of rules that should govern the conduct of those within the state's territorial jurisdiction. Law lays down public rules that make explicit what conduct is expected and what conduct will not be tolerated. When a state maintains a just social order, those in the society should *willingly* submit to its legal demands. As members of a political community, each expects all others to comply with these rules out of a sense of reciprocity, not out of fear of sanctions.

State imposed penalties for violations of the law are part of the *coercive order* of society. These penalties back up the legal order. We need this backup enforcement mechanism because without it some would succumb to temptations to accept the benefits of law without doing their share to uphold the law. An effective system of legal penalties provides reasonable assurance to law-abiding members of society that free riding won't be allowed.[2] In the absence of this assurance, those who respect legal authority would likely lose their resolve to comply, as their willingness to do their share in upholding the legal order is contingent on the willingness of others to do theirs. This assurance is thus required for the stability of the legal order.

Our duty to uphold and support the legal order is valid only if the state does a reasonably good job of maintaining a fair system of social cooperation. If it fails to meet this standard, as I have suggested is true of the United States, we no longer have a duty to respect its claim to authority.[3] A person's *civic obligation* to comply with legal demands is contingent on the existence of a reasonably just social order. It is the duty of justice and simple reciprocity that ground the obligation to obey.[4]

If the authority of law and the duty to obey the law depend on a state's satisfying certain minimum standards of social justice, then we can say that a state that fails to meet these standards *lacks the legitimate authority to punish disobedience to its laws*. But the absence of legitimate authority does not entirely settle the question of whether the state could permissibly impose penalties for lawbreaking. Those who are most burdened by the injustices of a society may lack an obligation to obey the law (on reciprocity grounds); however, the state that claims jurisdiction over the territory within which the oppressed live may still have the right to impose penalties for certain crimes. That is, it may have enforcement legitimacy.

In particular, a state in an unjust society could still retain the right to penalize actions that are seriously wrong in themselves. There is a widely recognized moral right to repress actions that seriously threaten our lives, freedom of movement, bodily integrity, or material well-being. Indeed, there is a right to intervene, using threats and physical force if necessary, to protect *others* from unjust attack.[5] And this right, I believe, extends to the state. Or, put more precisely, the same principle that justifies natural persons using force to prevent harmful wrongdoing can (with suitable qualifications) justify a formal system of punishment.

Because we know that not everyone will respect the right of others to be free from unjust attack, the state has to be prepared to take action before would-be offenders can do serious harm. Restitution and reparation, while sometimes appropriate and welcome, come on the scene too late, after the harm has already been done. Extensive police presence and public surveillance could help control crime, but on the scale necessary would come at a high cost to liberty and privacy, and it's not clear what good it would do to curtail domestic violence and sexual assault, which generally occur out of public view. Incapacitation of those who have repeatedly engaged in harmful wrongdoing, while sometimes necessary, still allows a lot of unjust aggression to go unaddressed. *Threatened* penalties are therefore necessary to deter would-be aggressors before they have a chance to victimize others.

Under what conditions would it be permissible for a state that lacks legitimate authority to threaten, penalize, and neutralize persons who engage in immoral aggressive acts? I won't try to offer a comprehensive list of conditions, but certain requirements of *fairness* stand out.[6] First, the state would have to publicly announce that it was going to impose penalties for serious crimes and make clear what these penalties would be. A public warning is required, not only because realistic threats are often sufficient to deter and thus do less harm than imposing unannounced penalties, but also because such warning gives all subject to this immense state power an opportunity to stay away from the line of prohibition and therefore to reduce the risk of suffering unjustified penalties. Second, alleged offenders should have an adequate opportunity to publicly defend themselves against accusations that they have wronged others and to justify or offer excuses for their actions. Third, officials of the criminal justice system must apply the system's rules in a reasonably impartial and evenhanded way. Otherwise there is no semblance of justice, just the arbitrary and capricious threats of a dictator or rogue regime, which no one is bound to respect or comply with. And finally, the penalties should be humane and no more severe than is justified by the need to deter the type of unjust conduct in question.

Though a state in an unjust society may lack legitimate authority over those it seeks to coerce into compliance with its laws, it may nonetheless have a legitimate enforcement right to compel their compliance with legal requirements that forbid certain harmful wrongdoing. A state in an unjust society may, at a minimum, permissibly penalize prohibited violent acts that are wrongs in themselves *(mala in se)*. Such penalties would be justified by the need to protect innocent persons from harm due to wrongful aggression. This enforcement right may not, therefore, extend to penalizing the sale or use of mind-altering drugs among consenting adults. However, it would extend to penalizing those who use violence in the drug trade or who commit violent acts under the influence of drugs.[7]

For clarification, let's compare the view of the state's right to punish just described with an influential alternative: a retributive theory of punishment sometimes called the *benefits-and-burdens* account.[8] According to this theory, the criminal law should be conceived as a system of rules that prohibit the interference with basic individual freedoms. We all benefit from such a system and we each should therefore refrain from violating the rules that make these benefits possible. In accepting the benefits without assuming the burden of self-restraint, the criminal offender takes unfair advantage of those who comply with the rules. The institution of punishment assures those who voluntarily comply with the law that others will not be allowed to receive the benefits of the system without assuming the burdens. Punishment is conceived as an institutional mechanism of redistribution—it reallocates the benefits and burdens of social cooperation when they are upset by criminal noncompliance. The criminal offender has more freedom than fairness permits and therefore owes a debt for the extra freedom he has effectively stolen. Punishment reestablishes equity (puts the scales back in balance, as it were) by taking away the offender's excess freedom, freedom to which he is not entitled. Punishment is thus framed on the model of *restitution*—in effect, the offender has to "give back" what he has wrongfully taken (or at least its equivalent).[9]

I agree that, under *just* social conditions, crime violates requirements of reciprocity and that punishment can be a justified response to such violations. I also agree that punishment can be a practical and fair solution to the assurance problem. But I do not believe that punishment is plausibly viewed as a way to redistribute burdens so as to reestablish equity. Nor do I believe that the general justifying aim of punishment is retribution—that is, to ensure that criminal wrongdoers endure the suffering or deprivation they deserve. We can justify punishment because of its essential role in crime prevention, which is also necessary to stabilize the cooperative scheme as a whole. Also, on the benefits-and-burdens theory the moral idea of reciprocity is often used to explain *proportionality* in sentencing. I think reciprocity is an important value for understanding the *right* to punish, but not for understanding *how much* to punish.

The benefits-and-burdens theory also has implications for thinking about punishment in a context of social injustice. Jeffrie Murphy, for instance, claims that the right to punish is void when a society is marred by serious distributive injustice, because the permissibility of the practice of punishment depends on there being just background conditions. Within unjust societies, most criminal offenders (many of whom come from disadvantaged backgrounds) have not received their fair share of society's benefits and thus do not owe a moral debt for their crimes. Criminal deviance, Murphy argues, therefore cannot be justifiably punished until the structural injustices in society have been adequately remedied. While I agree that a state in a seriously unjust society lacks the authority to impose duties to obey the law, such a state, as suggested earlier, might have the right to enforce laws against dangerous wrongdoing to protect the vulnerable from unjustified harm.[10]

Jeffrey Reiman argues (and I agree) that the victims of social injustice, having been denied their fair share of the benefits of social cooperation, have a *reduced* obligation to obey the law. He also claims that some of the crimes (particularly property crimes) that the unjustly disadvantaged commit are justified on the grounds that they are merely reclaiming what rightfully belongs to them. I don't, however, think of property crimes among the unjustly disadvantaged as restitution for distributive injustice. The poor do sometimes appropriate the possessions of those with unjust riches. But they often rob, defraud, and steal from those who are unjustly disadvantaged. It's not plausible that any of these latter property crimes reestablishes equity. Some property crimes that burden the oppressed may nevertheless sometimes be justified as (perhaps symbolic) *resistance* to illegitimate authority. It is not that crime reestablishes a fair (or fairer) system of social cooperation but that such lawbreaking is a permissible way to express one's refusal to submit to unjust demands for compliance with the law. This defiance of law needn't set things right or make things better (though the fact that such defiance would make things worse is a *pro tanto* reason to refrain from it). The oppressed do not have an overriding or preemptive reason to respect the law. The legal order has no authority over them.

Reiman also maintains that though the poor are unjustly treated and their moral culpability for their crimes is therefore reduced, they are often morally guilty and responsible for *upsetting the peace* (that is, creating a social climate of fear and distrust), which reduces individual freedom. Because one justification for state authority is, he claims, to secure the peace (the other is to secure background justice), even a state in an unjust society may impose penalties for upsetting the peace. By contrast, I see social justice as the sole justification for legitimate state authority, and justice includes protecting people from unjustified violence and illegitimate restrictions on their liberty. I say instead that, given the natural duty of justice, the poor should do what they can to help establish just conditions. Undermining trust among those committed to working for a more just society is incompatible with the duty of justice because it makes solidarity unworkable. I do not think the burdens (including restrictions on liberty of movement) imposed on the affluent by the criminal deviance of the poor are sufficient to override the right of the poor to disobey the law. The poor should not be forced to carry all the burdens of an unjust social structure, and if some of their crimes limit the freedom of the more affluent, this is not unfair. Moreover, many violations of the peace can help to produce more just circumstances by forcing those in power to address the injustices that prompt the disturbances of the peace.

A state that lacks legitimate authority but possesses enforcement legitimacy is similar to the *dominant protective association* that Robert Nozick famously describes.[11] So again, for clarification purposes, a brief comparison is in order. As will come as no surprise, I don't agree that the "minimal state" is the most extensive state that can be justified. In fact, a state with mere enforcement legitimacy is, in my view, *unjust*. It should be striving to become fully just by ensuring equal political liberties and democratic accountability, a fair opportunity for all to secure valued positions in society, and an equitable apportionment of material advantages and work responsibilities. The state with mere enforcement legitimacy departs enough from what social justice requires that it lacks a claim to authoritative rule. But it sufficiently approximates justice in key respects that it retains the right to prevent and punish unjust aggression within a given territory.

I also wouldn't justify even this minimal state in the way that Nozick does. I do not assume (and seriously doubt) that there is a natural or private right to punish wrongdoing. Nozick, following John Locke, takes it that the state enforces moral prohibitions against injustice and that it inherits this enforcement right from the moral right of individuals to punish and to forcibly extract compensation for serious wrongdoing. I'm suggesting that the state enforces its *laws* that forbid criminal acts and that this exercise of power is justified when the overall legal structure, including its criminal justice system, is reasonably just. These laws will prohibit certain moral wrongdoing of course, and the state's right to criminalize these acts may extend only to serious and harmful wrongdoing. But this does not presume a preinstitutional individual right to punish those who do wrong. (This is not to deny that the right of a state to punish might rest on a more fundamental moral principle, like the permissibility of threatening aggressors to protect oneself and others from harmful wrongdoing.) The right to punish, on the view I'm defending, presupposes the existence of positive law and a functioning and fair judicial system. Thus, one difference between enforcement legitimacy and the mere right to protect those not liable to harm is that the state with enforcement legitimacy is part of a legal order.

Moreover, I am not assuming that there is a natural or preinstitutional right to accumulate property. Nor do I think of taxes as simply payment to the state for protective services. Property laws and tax policies are part of the basic structure and must be judged together (along with other fundamental aspects of the social scheme) on grounds of fairness and justifiable to all who are subject to them.[12] The right to punish and rights to property are to be justified as a system of public rules that constitute part of the basic structure of society.

I should make clear, however, that a state with mere enforcement legitimacy can and must penalize some economic crimes, and not just violent property crimes like robbery. The state cannot provide protection from unjust attack without revenue to fund the effort (personnel have to be paid and equipment and facilities must be secured and maintained), and it can't acquire this revenue without a tax base to draw on. This means that some among those being protected must have a way to make income within a functioning economy, which requires stable property relations and secure market transactions. Theft and fraud cannot be too prevalent, then, as this would make even a minimal legal order unworkable. The state with enforcement legitimacy can't allow all property claims to go undefended even when the distribution of income and wealth in society is unjust. Still, some nonviolent and low-level property violations can be tolerated (particularly those perpetrated by the most disadvantaged), as these crimes won't undermine the state or the social order. And, after all, the oppressed have no duty to respect the existing property/tax regime (given how unjust it is) apart from its instrumental role in supporting a stable and safe social order.

Condemning Crime

Within a *just* society, a criminal justice system would have more than one social function. Yes, it would be relied upon to keep lawbreaking within tolerable levels. But preventing crime would not be its sole legitimate purpose. It would also provide a political community with fair procedures for determining when its laws have been violated, including a fair way for those accused of lawbreaking to defend themselves against charges that they have violated the law. The criminal justice system is also an institutional mechanism for holding persons accountable for violating laws: it is used to call people to explain, justify, or accept responsibility for their criminal acts. In addition to crime prevention, due process, and holding people accountable, a criminal justice system in a just society may publicly *condemn* acts that have been duly demonstrated to violate the political community's laws against harmful wrongdoing. I want to focus on this *condemnatory* role of a criminal justice system and distinguish it from the system's *punitive* role.

Condemnation is the public expression, explicit or implied, of strong moral disapproval. Practices and speech acts that communicate condemnation are properly reserved for particularly serious wrongs, such as unjustified violent acts and criminal wrongdoing. Private individuals condemn crime but so do institutions like the state.

There are legitimate reasons for a state to publicly condemn criminal wrongdoing. The state might, for example, seek to reaffirm the political community's prohibition of the act in light of the transgression. Doing so makes it explicit that it would be a mistake to infer that the state doesn't take such violations seriously. The state might also want to indicate concern and respect for the victims of crime. By condemning a crime, the state communicates to victims that it takes their interests seriously and that their resentment toward those who wronged them is justified. And the state might also want to convey to offenders that it regards their conduct as unacceptable. Communicating condemnation to a criminal offender is one way to signify that any subsequent penalty is imposed because the person has committed some grave wrong. The wrongness of the act is why we seek to prevent acts of that type from occurring. Condemning the act is part of our explanation to the offender for why we are taking such drastic measures to repress such acts.

However, one purpose of state expressions of condemnation is to publicly disapprove of acts that *defy the state's legitimate authority*. In this case the condemnation is for disobedience to the law. A state might also condemn a criminal act for its inherent wrongfulness or the actor for his or her blameworthy ill will. But these further expressive acts of condemnation should be distinguished from condemning culpable failures to obey the law as such. If condemnation of disobedience is to be apt, then the state must have legitimate authority—it must have a right to demand obedience to its directives from those within its claimed territorial jurisdiction. A state with enforcement rights but that lacks legitimate authority might rightly condemn violent crimes for their wrongfulness. It could not rightly condemn offenders for their simple disobedience to its laws, though, as it is not entitled to obedience of this kind.

This way of thinking about the condemnatory functions of criminal justice shares some features with "penal expressivism," according to which an essential part of the justification for punishment is that penal sanctions *express* or *communicate* public condemnation of criminal acts.[13] I want to distinguish the view I'm defending from penal expressivism and, in the process, to raise some doubts about this influential view.

The central problem for penal expressivism is to explain why condemning crime requires hard treatment of offenders (for example, stiff fines, work penalties, imprisonment, deportation, and perhaps death). It would seem that we should be able to communicate our moral message of condemnation without imposing suffering or deprivation on those who do wrong. Yet Joel Feinberg insists that punishment has *symbolic significance:* it expresses attitudes of resentment, indignation, and disapproval. He also claims that condemnatory symbolism and hard treatment, while distinguishable for analytical purposes, are never separated in reality. Indeed, he maintains that legal punishment, *by definition*, involves both hard treatment and condemnation.

I don't believe that condemnation and punishment are inextricably linked—either conceptually or practically—in the way Feinberg maintains. A just state should certainly condemn violations of criminal law. It should not abide defiance of legal authority or egregious wrongs. But *at what stage* in criminal proceedings does (or should) condemnation occur and *what* exactly should be condemned? One might think that the state has already condemned the act when it prohibits it through law. The state effectively says, "This act is wrong and forbidden." But perhaps we can condemn only wrongful acts that are ongoing or have already occurred. If this is so, then the laws themselves don't condemn acts but only prohibit and perhaps deter them. Maybe the most we could say is that the state condemns *act types* through criminal legislation. It has not thereby condemned the particular concrete act of that type—the wrongful act performed by the offender. We might think, though, that the relevant condemnation properly occurs at the time of *conviction*— once the offender's admission of guilt has been formally accepted or when the judge or jury renders a guilty verdict after a trial—rather than at sentencing or when the sentence is being carried out. As conviction is the final public judgment of guilt, it would be natural to view it as also expressing condemnation of the legal violation and of the person for committing the prohibited act.[14]

Feinberg insists that not only is penal hard treatment (imprisonment in particular) inseparable from condemnation but hard treatment *itself* expresses condemnation. As he famously says, "the very walls of his cell condemn [the criminal] and his [prison] record becomes a stigma."[15] This doesn't appear to be strictly true, however. What of those being merely detained in jails prior to trial? They are being incarcerated only after being *accused* or *suspected* of committing a crime; they have not been convicted. A final judgment of guilt has not been rendered (though, once guilt has been settled, such jail time can be retroactively treated as "time served"). Imprisonment itself therefore can't express condemnation. It is more plausible to think that the public judgment of guilt (say, at the end of a trial) expresses condemnation. Of course if we take this approach, we need to explain what is occurring at the sentencing phase and during the period when the sentence is being carried out. But this poses no difficulty. A sentence is a matter of containing dangerous individuals or providing potential lawbreakers with an incentive to refrain from violating the law. The sentence just needs to be fair and a reasonably good deterrent or crime-control device. We needn't attach any *symbolic* significance to the sentence itself.

Feinberg is led to regard punishment as having symbolic significance because he believes that this expressive function is needed to distinguish punishments (for example, imprisonment or large fines) from mere penalties (such as minor fines). His mistake is thinking that the relevant distinction must be found in features of the *penalties* rather than in what type of *violation* the penalties are for. Some penalties are for minor legal failings (misdemeanors) and some for serious ones (felonies). While a state with legitimate authority will penalize and disapprove of all law-breaking (including parking violations), it will penalize and *condemn* crimes like murder and rape, as these are serious wrongs and bigger challenges to its authority. Criminal justice proceedings are reserved for wrongs that merit both penalties and condemnation. However, I see no reason that the condemnation must be encoded in the penalties.

I suspect that penal expressivism gains some of its plausibility from ambiguous uses of the word "condemnation." It is sometimes said that the state has *condemned* an offender to prison or to death. This goes beyond saying that the state, acting on behalf of the public, strongly disapproves of the criminal act to saying that the state has expressed an intention to deprive the offender of liberty or life or that the state has actually taken his or her liberty or life. There is nothing wrong with speaking this way. It is perfectly fine English. But we should keep the two senses of "condemnation" separate when attempting to explain and justify punishment. For clarity, we might distinguish condemnation (the public expression of strong moral disapproval) from *damnation* (imposing suffering or deprivation on wrongdoers). It would thus be true to say that a state can condemn an offender without damning the offender to prison; and that it can damn an offender to prison without condemning the offender.

R. A. Duff argues that punishment has not just an expressive purpose but a *communicative* one. That is, punishment involves reciprocal and rational engagement with the offender. Its point and justification is not mere condemnation but moral persuasion. As with other penal expressivist theories, though, Duff does tie this communicative purpose to hard treatment of criminal offenders, claiming that penal sanctions communicate condemnation. But he insists that these sanctions must also have a forward-looking (but non-deterrence-based) dimension if they are to be fully justified. Accordingly, for Duff punishment has three moral goals apart from condemning past wrongdoing: repentance, reform, and reconciliation. Repentance, he claims, requires that the offender take a period of time to reflect on his or her wrongdoing. Part of what a penal sentence accomplishes is providing a criminal offender with the necessary structure for moral reflection and an opportunity to come around to appreciating the moral reasons against such wrongdoing. This forced seclusion also functions as a formal apology to the community for breaking its laws, and once completed, the offender should be forgiven and allowed to join the community as a member in good standing.

By contrast, I believe the public condemnation of crime can be justified by its symbolic value alone. It establishes its value through what it communicates (warranted moral criticism and disapproval). Its worth does not rest on any beneficial practical consequences that may result from it, either for the offender or for the society (though these positive effects may be welcome). Such condemnation needn't be justified in terms of how it contributes to moral reform of offenders or to reconciliation of offenders with their fellow citizens. And the condemnation is not expressed through punishment but through formal conviction. Of course the guilty person's criminal act *merits* condemnation—that is, it merits strong public disapproval. Such a response is not only apt and permissible—in some contexts it would be a moral failure on our part if we didn't condemn such serious wrongdoing. But this is different from saying that the person who commits such wrongs deserves *prison*, and so, unlike Duff, the position I'm defending is not a form of retributivism.

No doubt the state's public condemnation of crime wouldn't and shouldn't be taken seriously if the state could do something to prevent such wrongdoing but didn't. We would then be justified in accusing the state of merely paying lip service to the wrongfulness of these acts, tolerating them, even tacitly approving of them. But the state could and should show its sincerity and good faith in condemning crime by doing what it can to prevent criminal wrongdoing.

Of prominent penal expressivists, Andrew von Hirsch and Uma Narayan hold a view most similar to the one I've been defending. I agree with the penal expressivists that the criminal justice system within a just legal order will have expressive dimensions—in particular, that it will condemn acts of criminal deviance. But I do not think the practice of punishment (imposition of penal sanctions for lawbreaking) can be justified, even in part, by appeal to the expressive (or communicative) functions of a criminal justice system. Von Hirsch and Narayan side with Feinberg and Duff in thinking that punishment expresses condemnation (or what they call "censure"). But they recognize that the need to express condemnation of crime is insufficient to justify the hard treatment that offenders typically receive. On their view, punishment is justified as public condemnation *plus* incentives to encourage compliance with the law.

For example, one can imagine the parties in Rawls's original position, after noting that those they represent might be morally weak, agreeing to establish a set of nonmoral incentives (penalties) to encourage themselves to comply with the principles of justice as articulated through law. If the political community should accept the practice of hard treatment as a prudential supplement to moral reasons for compliance, this avoids the problem of treating lawbreakers as enemies of the state, as outside the community, or as "mere means" to promote the common good. It also avoids the concern that on the view that the criminal law is an institution that issues general threats, citizens are treated as nonrational animals that need to be manipulated or frightened into obedience. The state isn't threatening us, on von Hirsch and Narayan's view. We, through the penal instruments of the state, are simply giving ourselves an incentive to comply with laws we make.

I deny that the condemnation of crime must be or should be expressed through penal sanctions. Yet I don't reject the idea of punishment as prudential incentive to obey the law. When it comes to the forward-looking dimensions of punishment, I wouldn't stop there, though. I think it can be permissible to threaten would-be offenders with penal sanctions as a way of deterring them from wrongdoing.

Standing to Punish and Condemn in Unjust Circumstances

A state that punishes crime under seriously unjust social conditions is vulnerable to various types of moral criticism, resistance, and defiance. I want to conclude this chapter by explaining how the moral deficiencies of such a state can make it illegitimate for the state to publicly condemn crime while the state nonetheless retains the right to punish at least some crime.

When a society falls below the threshold for tolerable injustice and its governing institutions are responsible for the injustices (for either perpetrating them or not preventing them), the state's *right to punish crime* is compromised. And if its criminal justice institutions are insufficiently fair, effective, or humane, the state's right to punish can be completely undermined.[16] Moreover, lacking the authority to create obligations through law, it has no moral basis for condemning *disobedience* to its laws as such, particularly the disobedience of those unjustly disadvantaged in society. Its laws serve to coordinate action and (when penalties are attached) to warn of impending sanctions. But the state's laws lack the moral power to impose duties of compliance. Such a state, if it is not too unjust, *may* have a right to punish serious and harmful wrongdoing as a defense of those whom it would be wrong to harm. However, it would lack the right to criminalize wrongful acts beyond these most serious ones, and it would lack altogether the moral standing to condemn defiance to legal authority.

Such a state might retain the moral standing to condemn wrongful acts, even the wrongful acts of the oppressed (more on that in a moment). But the state would not be justified in condemning the wrongful acts of the unjustly disadvantaged *on grounds of unfairness*. That is, given that the state has not secured basic liberties and has not maintained an equitable distribution of benefits and burdens in the cooperative scheme, when the oppressed violate the law, they do not take unfair advantage of the compliance of others. Their acts may be condemned on other grounds, but not for lack of civic reciprocity.

Loss of legitimate authority is not the only way that a state's moral standing to condemn crime can be compromised. Such standing can be vitiated or erased if the state is *complicit* in the crimes it would condemn. Victor Tadros explains the complicity criticism.[17] Such criticism, he argues, depends on the idea that the state participates in or contributes to the wrongdoing it condemns. The key premises in the complicity charge are that the state can foresee the violent consequences of unjust disadvantage and that it has the power and substantive responsibility to prevent these unjust social conditions from forming and persisting. For instance, it is well known that poverty engenders crime and that the state may unjustly contribute to impoverished conditions by failing to maintain a just basic structure. Insofar as violence in ghettos results from resentment toward unjust inequalities or exposure to severely disadvantaged neighborhoods, the state shares blame for the harmful consequences of this violence.[18] Therefore it is not in a moral position to point fingers.[19] And this loss of standing might extend beyond condemning legal defiance to condemning the wrongs themselves.

A state might also lose its standing to condemn a crime because it engages in the same kinds of wrong that it would condemn. This argument is advanced by Duff, who regards a state as lacking the moral standing to condemn an act if the state fails to sufficiently abide by the values it invokes to condemn the act. So if the political community (as represented by the state) is not adequately abiding by a moral rule it is ostensibly committed to (for example, rules against deceit, theft, and unjustified violence), then its standing to condemn those who violate the rule is compromised.

When a state is complicit in the wrongs it punishes or hypocritically punishes wrongs that it engages in, it lacks the moral standing to condemn these wrongs and is therefore rightly criticized for these unjustified expressive acts of condemnation. But does the state also lack the *enforcement right* to punish these wrongs? Tadros and Duff think so, because they believe that if the state lacks the moral standing to *condemn* a crime, then it also lacks the right to hold the criminal offender *accountable* for it (that is, he or she isn't answerable to the state, can't be tried by it, and so on). Tadros, for example, argues that the state cannot act as judge in cases where it bears some responsibility for the crime. Its complicity in these crimes makes it unsuitable to judge those accused of them. Thus, if the state cannot hold offenders accountable for their crimes, it can't permissibly punish them either.[20] Similarly, Duff argues that when the state fails to treat persons in accord with its professed fundamental values, it doesn't have the right to hold them accountable for their alleged failure to abide by those values. And if the state can't hold them accountable, then it can't permissibly punish them. Indeed, Duff thinks that if the state lacks legitimate authority, making it the case that citizens have no obligation to obey the law as such, then the state cannot permissibly punish *any* crimes, not even those that are *mala in se*.

These powerful arguments merit an answer. The Tadros/Duff rejoinder assumes that (1) an agent's right to hold others accountable for wrongs depends on that agent having the moral standing to condemn these wrongs and (2) the moral standing to condemn these wrongs depends on not having been complicit in them and not being guilty of similar wrongs oneself. I think (2) is probably true. But I'm skeptical of (1). Holding someone accountable for a wrong depends, not on having the standing to condemn the wrong, but *on having the standing to be an impartial judge of whether the accused committed the prohibited act.* If, given their complicity or hypocrisy, it is reasonable to regard state officials as biased against the accused or as incompetent to render a fair judgment, then they shouldn't be the ones to determine his or her guilt.

But the criminal justice system in an otherwise unjust society may be reasonably fair, and criminal justice officials may not be the source of the injustices the oppressed face. In that case, I believe the oppressed can be rightly tried and punished if (1) plausible accusations have been made against them that they have unjustly attacked another, (2) adequate efforts have been taken to make them aware that such acts would be penalized, (3) they have an adequate opportunity to publicly defend themselves against charges that they have violated the rights of others against violent attack, and (4) penalties are generally proportionate to offenses. In short, much will depend on whether the criminal justice system operates in a reasonably impartial and fair way, *not on whether the state has the standing to condemn crime.* In particular, enforcement legitimacy will depend on whether there is an independent judiciary with the power to adjudicate disputes between the state and defendants and with no stake in the outcome of these disputes.[21]

In many instances, of course, a society that is deeply unjust in other respects will also fail to maintain a fair criminal justice system. Many states that lack legitimate authority will therefore also lack legitimate enforcement rights. For example, there is compelling evidence that the criminal justice system in the United States does not treat disadvantaged blacks fairly. These persons currently are subjected to racial profiling and unjustified searches, exposed to gratuitous police violence and harassment, face racially biased juries, receive overly severe sentences, are subject to the arbitrary and excessive power of prosecutors, are not provided adequate legal counsel, and are not allowed to fully reintegrate into the political community after their sentences are served.[22]

Even if the criminal justice system does, as a matter of fact, operate in a reasonably fair and impartial way, the oppressed may have good reasons to doubt that it will treat them fairly. Suppose the accused is a poor black person with the justified but (let us assume) false belief that the system is corrupted by racial bias. He would be justified in refusing to submit to the state's efforts to hold him accountable for alleged lawbreaking. In this case the state might nevertheless retain its right of enforcement, but the accused has a right to resist being held accountable. He has no duty to submit to the state's mechanisms of accountability, so we can't blame him if he attempts to evade capture or won't cooperate with law-enforcement officials. But neither can we blame the state if it pursues him and brings him to trial. The coherence of this somewhat paradoxical conclusion can be seen if we view the enforcement right as a liberty right (rather than a claim right). The state has the liberty to hold people accountable for crimes they are justly accused of, in the sense that it has no duty *not* to enforce the criminal law. Yet this is not a claim right, so those who are accused have no duty to cooperate in the state's attempts to hold them accountable. And those who stand in solidarity with the accused have no duty to help law enforcement officials capture and punish the accused.

Let me now turn to a problem faced by Tadros's and Duff's positions but not by the view of punishment under unjust conditions that I've been defending. Both recognize that oppressed persons often commit violent acts against others who are also unjustly disadvantaged. In addition, they note that if the state does not punish those who perpetrate these acts, it would be failing to protect some of the most vulnerable in society against violent wrongdoing, thereby compounding the injustices they confront. Given their premises, the state in an unjust society faces a dilemma. Either it can punish those it has no right to punish or it can fail to protect those it has treated unjustly. So, on Tadros's and Duff's accounts, no matter which direction the state goes, it will perpetrate *additional* injustices, further weakening its claim to legitimacy.[23]

We can avoid this dilemma if we follow my approach, which distinguishes legitimate authority from enforcement rights and separates the ends of punishment from the function of public condemnation. Under conditions of serious injustice, a state's authority to rule and moral standing to condemn crime are indeed compromised, if not undermined. But enforcement legitimacy, and thus the right to punish at least some crimes, may remain intact. Though a state in an unjust society may lack the moral standing to condemn violent crime (due to complicity, hypocrisy, or lack of authority), it may have an enforcement right to penalize such crime in order to deter and contain it. The justification for this is the need to protect the vulnerable from unjustified harm. A state can sometimes be in a position to provide this protection in a way that is justifiable to those who wrongly threaten others.

Though lacking the moral standing to condemn, a state operating under unjust social conditions should punish only those who have done condemnable acts—acts that *merit* strong moral disapproval. These penal sanctions don't express condemnation, and may be applied simply as a crime control measure. If condemnation and punishment were inseparable (or if punishment is merely the vehicle through which we express condemnation for lawbreaking), then punishment under conditions of injustice can't be (fully) justified. Because punishment would just *be* condemnation, then not only would the state lack the moral standing to condemn violent wrongdoing, it would lack the standing to punish and thus prevent it, contrary to the duty to prevent unjustified attacks on others when you can. But if we separate *condemnation* of lawbreaking from *penalties* for lawbreaking (as I have been arguing we should), then we can explain how punishment can be justified even when authority to punish disobedience to law and moral standing to condemn crime have both been lost.

Crime Control and Social Reform

Some might worry that by permitting the state in an unjust society to punish crime, we would be only reinforcing its power to stigmatize the unjustly disadvantaged. This is especially worrisome for the ghetto poor, because there are well-known and long-standing stereotypes about black criminality and violence, and the state (including the criminal justice system itself) has played a large role in creating and perpetuating these stereotypes.[24] But responding to this concern is part of the reason that decoupling condemnation from penalties is so important. We should not assume that those who commit crimes under unjust conditions merit the political community's condemnation, as the state may have no authority to punish disobedience to law as such and may be complicit in their wrongdoing. The state should make it clear that it penalizes, perhaps reluctantly, only to prevent unjust and harmful aggression, recognizing that it may be partly at fault for these wrongs.

Given the risks and costs to disadvantaged communities of permitting a state that lacks legitimate authority to enforce the criminal law (for example, increased exposure to police harassment and brutality), some might insist that we opt for community-based solutions to unjustified aggression under nonideal conditions. Such solutions might be preferable if they are effective in controlling crime, they are fair to the accused, and victims are satisfied with these extra-state means of redress. The state shouldn't interfere with the development of these community-based measures when they meet these requirements, and perhaps it should facilitate them.

But it would be difficult to meet the necessary standards of fairness without the administrative apparatus of the state, particularly its judicial mechanisms. Without police, it would be challenging to identify criminal suspects, effectively search for them, or force them to answer for their alleged wrongful acts. Curbing sexual assault and domestic violence would be difficult without the investigative powers of law enforcement agencies. Moreover, ghettos with serious crime problems typically lack the necessary collective efficacy to reduce crime to tolerable levels.[25] So in the absence of effective and fair community-based solutions to violent crime, it would be permissible for the state to intervene to protect the vulnerable from unjustified harm, though this should be done, whenever possible, with community involvement and perhaps community oversight.[26]

A state with only enforcement rights should also seek to gain full legitimate authority by remedying the injustices in the basic structure of society. If it is to preserve its enforcement legitimacy, it should be making a good-faith effort to warrant and acquire the trust of the oppressed. Thus, it should not deprive ex-offenders of the public benefits of citizenship (such as income subsidies, housing assistance, grants and loans for education, and unemployment insurance). Given that the terms of political association are not remotely fair to these persons, it would be unreasonable to revoke privileges of citizenship as a form of punishment.

In particular, the unjustly disadvantaged should never be denied the right to vote, not even when they have violated criminal laws. Perhaps under just conditions those who commit violent crimes or repeatedly violate laws against criminal wrongdoing could justifiably have their voting privileges (temporarily) revoked on the grounds that they have committed a grave (and perhaps unforgivable) breach of trust with their fellow citizens and are now relegated to the status of a noncitizen legal resident. However, under seriously unjust conditions, the oppressed cannot be said to be in violation of their civic obligations when they commit crimes and thus cannot be justifiably punished for their failures to respect the law. In addition, many criminal offenders are from or (once released from prison) will return to ghetto neighborhoods, so to deny them the right to vote would (at least potentially) diminish the voting power of these already deeply disadvantaged communities. The members of these communities cannot garner civic engagement and political participation from residents who are prone to political alienation if the state condemns them to civic death. Such civically exiled residents would likely find it enormously difficult to muster the resolve to fight for a more just society when they lack basic civic standing. In the interest of politically empowering the oppressed, and given legitimate concerns about disparate racial impact, felon disenfranchisement as punishment should be abandoned.[27]

In addition to working to establish a just basic structure, a state with mere enforcement rights should be making efforts to reconcile with, and make amends to, those it has wronged. It should aim to regain legitimacy in their eyes and acknowledge its role in creating the conditions under which the disadvantaged are tempted to turn to crime. To achieve these ends, it not only should enfranchise the imprisoned and ex-offenders but also should institute educational and voluntary rehabilitative programs for those it punishes and should aid former prisoners with reintegration into society (for instance, providing skills training, counseling, employment, and housing assistance). And in the ghettos of America, it is absolutely essential that police officers be trained to

treat residents respectfully, even when they are suspects, and to cultivate relations of mutual trust with members of these communities.

We know that inequality, poverty, ghetto conditions, and low educational attainment are all strongly correlated with (if not causes of)
violent crime. So the state needn't—and shouldn't—rely exclusively on
punitive responses to crime. Criminal acts among the unjustly disadvantaged could be controlled through the establishment and maintenance of a more just basic structure. The losses this would involve (in
taxes and opportunities, for instance) would not be unfair to the affluent, because some of their advantages are ill-gotten gains—they are
derived from exploiting a manifestly unfair opportunity structure and
taking advantage of liberties that others are unjustly denied. Moreover,
the unjustly disadvantaged, as equal citizens, are *due* a fairer opportunity structure and secure constitutional liberties, so they wouldn't be
getting anything they aren't already entitled to.

NINE

Impure Dissent

If asked to give a prominent historical example of black American political dissent, many would proffer the Montgomery bus boycott (1955–
1956).[1] This extraordinary mass protest against racial segregation on
public transportation followed years of patient and diplomatic attempts
to persuade local authorities to end the grossly unjust practice. Though
facilitated by Rosa Parks's famous act of civil disobedience, the movement refrained from lawbreaking, used only nonviolent tactics, and was
grounded in Christian ethics. The protest was highly organized and disciplined, with clear demands, excellent leadership, and a well-considered
plan for action. Its participants demonstrated through their remark-
able personal sacrifice, courage, and determination that they believed
they were fighting for a winnable and righteous cause. No one could
reasonably call into question the participants' moral commitment or
sincerity. The movement's leaders, such as Edgar D. Nixon and Jo
Ann Gibson Robinson, were respected in the community as people of
tremendous moral integrity. The protest was also extremely effective in bringing about desirable social change—it ultimately led to the
U.S. Supreme Court deciding that segregation on public buses is
unconstitutional.

Effective mass mobilizations among blacks, particularly among black
youth, have been infrequent since the Black Power movement. (The recent Black Lives Matter campaign is inspiring and promising. But as of
this writing, the jury is still out on its effectiveness and lasting influence within the realm of law and public policy.) However, some black
youth, sometimes inspired by the recorded speeches of Malcolm X, re-

gard their engagement with hip hop music as itself a vital form of political dissent and resistance.[2] Though not all hip hop music has political ramifications or political intent, there is what is commonly called "politically conscious rap." Marginalized urban black youth (among others) produce, consume, and share this music.

But if you take an example like N.W.A.'s "Fuck Tha Police" (1988), a protest rap song against police brutality and harassment, it doesn't appear to have much in common with the Montgomery protest. "Fuck Tha Police," while rightly condemning the outrageous misconduct of the Los Angeles Police Department, is filled with profanity and racial epithets. It celebrates retaliatory violence against cops and valorizes gunplay and street crime. The song exhibits misogyny and homophobia. It proposes no constructive solutions to the problems it identifies. It was neither a component of nor an inspiration for a social movement for change. Eazy-E, the founder of N.W.A. (aka "Niggaz With Attitude"), was a former drug dealer, and most of the group's other recordings evinced a hedonistic and mostly amoral and apolitical stance. "Fuck Tha Police" could almost be viewed as the anthem for the 1992 L.A. riots.[3]

Indeed, there are striking similarities between some rap music and ghetto riots. Much hip hop expressive culture is the musical/video equivalent of an urban disturbance—a riot of sound and images, the throwing of lyrical Molotov cocktails. The language and imagery of some hip hop expresses and depicts rage. However, this rage is, at least ostensibly, a response to perceived injustices. The sense that serious injustices are ongoing is the putative source of the anger, hostility, and desire to strike back. Many hip hop songs, like urban riots, are politically ambiguous and morally dissonant, and thus often give rise to sharply opposed reactions.[4] Some observers see riots as senseless crime, violence, and mayhem on a mass scale, while others see them as spontaneous rebellions against injustice.[5] Similarly, many people view hip hop as nihilistic and devoid of serious political content, while others defend it as the political voice of marginalized urban youth.[6] And this divide manifests itself in intergenerational cleavages among blacks—the civil rights generation often viewing rap as symptomatic of the decay of meaningful black politics, the hip hop generation often heralding it as the expression of a new and improved black resistance.[7]

Politically conscious but normatively transgressive hip hop is easily ignored, dismissed, even condemned. In its defense I offer some reasons for regarding political rap as valuable political expression even when it fails to reach the level of rectitude associated with the Civil Rights movement.[8] To be sure, some political rap (like much of popular culture) is deeply problematic, from both a moral and a political point of view. There is much to be said against it. The question I want to address, though, is this: What, if anything, can be said in favor of today's marginalized black urban youth's engagement with political hip hop?

One kind of sympathetic response is to insist that pure political dissent can't be reasonably expected from youth, even those (perhaps especially those) who live in America's ghettos. The narcissism, impulsiveness, imprudence, rebellion, ignorance, and hedonism typical of young people are to be expected in their initial attempts at political participation. Tolerance, understanding, and patient mentoring might seem the only appropriate responses. With some encouragement and guidance, political maturity will likely set in.[9] After all, young people do grow up eventually.

Whatever its merit, that is not the response I defend. While some see political rap as a youth training ground for, or gateway to, political engagement, my interest is not just rap's potential or promise. There is, I maintain, value in some political hip hop even if it won't ultimately result in more traditional political participation. My main purpose in this chapter is to explain the *intrinsic* value of political hip hop, that is, its value apart from any beneficial social consequences that may flow from its production, circulation, or consumption. I develop a noninstrumental argument in favor of what I call *impure dissent*, showing that much political rap is best understood within a nonconsequentialist political ethics of the oppressed.

Political Expression and the Public Sphere

Although it has now become a commercial juggernaut and global phenomenon, hip hop at first was a youth culture that emerged from America's ghettos (in New York City in particular), and it often embodies sentiments and communication styles prevalent among young ghetto denizens.[10] This form of musical expression is not only, or even mostly, about politics. Moving listeners to bob their heads to a slick beat and to smile at a clever rhyme or vivid metaphor is the bread-and-butter of the genre. And perhaps only a small percentage of hip hop expression can be meaningfully described as "political." Nevertheless, this politically conscious rap, however much there is of it, is *political speech*. It constitutes an assorted set of communicative acts in the public sphere about central civic questions.

To be sure, this public sphere is not one cohesive forum with agreed-upon ground rules in which all of society's members are free to participate as equals in a rational dialogue about matters of public concern. Rather, in a highly stratified and diverse society like the United States, the public sphere should be understood as a decentralized network of forums that differ in internal discursive norms and constituencies.[11] In addition to mainstream publics (formal and informal), there are *subaltern counterpublics*—public arenas where members of subordinate or marginalized groups gather to discuss their common concerns, forge solidarity, and formulate strategies of resistance, free from the interference, constraining norms, and scrutiny of dominant groups.[12] And there are also *parallel publics*, which are alternative arenas for discursive exchange between members of marginalized groups but which largely operate according to mainstream norms.[13] So there is not a unified public sphere but multiple publics of different types, and many individuals participate in more than one public.[14] And while these arenas are sites of discursive exchange and expression, conflict and dissonance are just as important as consensus and mutual understanding.

Young people, black Americans, and the poor have often been excluded from the mainstream public sphere and large media outlets. Members of such groups therefore often seek discursive spaces of their own, where they can give voice to their distinctive concerns in their own style and idiom without having to conform to mainstream expectations. It is thus tempting to view political rap as a practice within the subaltern counterpublics of marginalized black urban youth—say, the functional equivalent of traditional oratory practices in many black churches during Jim Crow. Accordingly, the perceived impurities of political hip hop can be chalked up to outsiders' inability to understand or appreciate this esoteric or coded practice of ghetto youth. Criticism of the practice could then be rejected as a condescending and illegitimate interference with a subordinate group's internal norms of communication. There is probably truth in this response, but it is not the type of defense I want to offer.

Political rap is now communicated to multiple audiences within many different public arenas and is not confined (nor can it be confined) to subaltern counterpublics. New media infrastructure has enabled the rapid transmission of political messages across multiple "networked publics."[15] New information and communication technologies now facilitate and structure a multilayered public sphere. Young people, including disadvantaged black youth, are heavy users of web-based information and communication technology. They use this technology to create and share content and to form and maintain online peer communities.[16] Hip hop music, videos, and commentary are often the content created and shared, and these online communities are sometimes organized around a shared interest in hip hop culture.[17] Hip hop, which has always been intertwined with and kept fresh by technological innovation, has naturally adapted to the new technological environment.[18] In the digital/network age, its sounds and images are created with digital technology, circulated through various Internet platforms, and consumed using various digital devices. This includes politically conscious rap.

Varieties of Impurity

When the ghetto poor use hip hop to express political dissent, chief among their concerns is the criminal justice system—police violence and harassment, racial profiling, draconian sentences for nonviolent crimes, and harsh prison conditions.[19] They also focus on the low quality of public education available to black youth, including the content of the curriculum and the way teachers interact with black students. There is disquiet about the unavailability of decent jobs that pay a living wage and about discrimination in employment. Complaints are frequently voiced about the inability of the urban poor to influence government policy. They object to widespread poverty, economic inequality, and the low quality or unaffordability of housing. There are grievances expressed about the inadequacy of public services to poor communities. And there are critiques of mass media depictions of black youth and ghetto life.

Much of this dissent, however, can be described as *impure*: it contains valid political content, but it also incorporates other elements that diverge sharply from conventional or widely held normative standards. These deviant elements may seem to undermine its political aims. Impure dissent is meaningful political dissent that is mixed with such elements as messages urging the oppressed to embrace hedonistic consumption and vulgar materialism; relentless use of profanity, epithets, and other offensive language; enactment of negative group stereotypes; violent and pornographic images; romantic narratives about outlaw figures and street crime; approval of alcohol abuse and illicit drug use; xenophobia and homophobia; misogyny and affirmation of patriarchal norms; devaluation of education and other conventional paths to upward mobility; and celebration of base ambitions like power and celebrity. In labeling such expressions of dissent "impure," I am not passing judgment on them. The label is meant to be purely descriptive, and by using it, my aim is to identify a familiar phenomenon—normatively transgressive political dissent.

There are at least four types of impurity that a given instance of political dissent might contain. *Moral* impurities are those elements in the expression of dissent that are widely viewed as morally objectionable. *Political* impurities are the elements that are generally taken to conflict with or undermine desirable political aims. *Cognitive* impurities are those features that fail to satisfy widely recognized standards of rationality. And *aesthetic* impurities are components that most find unattractive, unpleasant, or repulsive. Political rap is often criticized on all four grounds, but I focus on moral and political impurities.

Some of what people object to in politically conscious but impure hip hop are its (alleged) negative social consequences—for example, that it causes people to view blacks in a negative light, incites violence, or corrupts the youth. These objections are premised on the idea that impure dissent has these negative consequences *in virtue of its impurities*. That is, the criticisms are not based solely on *how* people react to these messages (people might also react in counterproductive or irrational ways to "pure" dissent); they are also based on *what* people are reacting to— namely, the apparent morally abhorrent, politically problematic, irrational, and ugly aspects of this genre of expressive culture.

Dimensions of Dissent

Political dissent, broadly construed, has several dimensions within which one might find impurities. The *content* is the particular message (the specific propositions) communicated through the activity of dissent. This content can be true or false, right or wrong. Sometimes the content of hip hop dissent is relatively transparent and thus easy to discern. But often it isn't. Considerable interpretive skill and background knowledge may be required to extract the content. The main message might in some ways be morally or politically problematic, or there may be secondary messages that transgress conventional moral and political norms.

Inflection concerns the tone of the message. It has to do with whether the content includes elements that are, say, conciliatory, polite, respectful, and diplomatic or vulgar, abusive, offensive, and irreverent. The content, taken in the abstract, may be unproblematic, but the language or images used to express that message might have impure elements. Much of political rap is criticized for its inflection rather than its substantive content.

The *grounds* have to do with the agent's justification for the message of dissent. These grounds may be stated in the content of the message or may be implicit therein but need not be. Political opposition is sometimes publicly registered without a justification being offered for it. This is not unusual with dissent that takes the form of artistic expression. Reasonable dissent doesn't require that the grounds be made fully explicit in the content. But given the right conditions, dissenters should be prepared to defend the grounds of their dissent.

The *medium* has to do with the instruments (including one's own body) or technology through which a message of dissent is produced or disseminated. Using web-based information and communication technology to create and convey political messages is now entirely commonplace. It is no longer (if it ever was) transgressive to express political dissent through new media technologies. There are some who argue that the content of some dissent should not, or cannot, be communicated using new media; or that if such dissent is communicated, it will inevitably be coopted to serve the ends of political and economic elites. I won't pursue this issue.[20]

The *mode* is the type of activity (a political speech, petition drive, terrorist act, documentary film, or graffiti art) used to express the content of dissent. The activity itself might be immoral even if the content conveyed through the activity is not. I assume that *rapping* (rhythmically rhyming over musical beats), even when accompanied by video, does not fall into this category. But commercial hip hop (as opposed to underground hip hop) might be thought to be politically dubious. Political dissent joined with ambition for wealth and fame is widely thought to be an unholy alliance. And political messages can be blunted by the need to prioritize commercial profit over political content.[21]

The *mood* of dissent is defined by the mindset that animates the act. For instance, mood is about the attitude with which the dissident engages in dissent (with ambivalence, fanatical zeal, or cynicism) or the motive that prompts it (personal gain, amusement, or a sense of justice) or the intention of the act (to raise consciousness, provoke, frighten, or attract publicity).[22] Attitudes, motives, and intentions are all subject to moral appraisal.

It is also important to distinguish the act of dissent from its *messenger*. The perceived moral impurities of the dissidents themselves can taint their acts of dissent in the eyes of their interpreters. If the messenger is known to have committed serious moral wrongs or to have engaged in politically reactionary activities, then his or her acts of dissent might be regarded as impure even if the acts themselves are devoid of impurities. Ad hominem attacks on dissenters are a common way of dismissing the content of their dissent.

What Impure Hip Hop Dissent Is Not

Some seem to think that meaningful political dissent must be entirely earnest and devoid of play or enjoyment or else its message will be weakened. Perhaps because of the example of the Civil Rights movement (or certain representations of it), many feel that dissent must be delivered with the utmost moral seriousness, even piety. Self-restraint is expected. Humor must be eschewed. Fun is out of place. As a number of theorists have argued, however, when thinking about the scope of the "political," it is important to recognize that there are no sharp boundaries between politics, play, and pleasure.[23] So although some may regard politically conscious hip hop as inauthentic if it is mixed with entertainment, this is not the kind of "impurity" under consideration.

Nor is the kind of impure hip hop dissent I have in mind a form of "infrapolitics."[24] Its content is not generally covert, disguised, or veiled. The impure hip hop dissent that interests me is "in-your-face" political expression. It is openly transgressive. There is nothing subtle or cryptic about "Fuck Tha Police." The content of hip hop dissent may be esoteric and therefore widely misunderstood, but dissidents are not trying to hide the content of their message from the powers that be. The dissent is public and often highly visible (on the web and elsewhere). It is not a tactic to avoid notice or evade repercussions.

In his discussion of "black nihilism," Cornel West focuses not just on the loss of hope among black youth but on a loss of *meaning*.[25] He is concerned with what he regards as an *existential* crisis in black America. Marginalized black people, he claims, are looking for identity and a sense of self-worth in an unjust world. Although this search for meaning is no doubt to be found in impure hip hop dissent, my focus is on its self-conscious opposition to injustice, not on the ways in which it serves (perhaps without its participants' conscious awareness) as a psychological coping mechanism within oppressive conditions.

Although some impure hip hop dissent is arguably analogous to civil disobedience, much of it should not be so understood. Though it is attention grabbing, impure hip hop dissent need not be an attempt to garner the notice of the state or sympathetic citizens with the aim of moral suasion. Some impure hip hop dissent is also unlike civil disobedience in that the impure dissidents do not seek to demonstrate the moral purity of their motives or character. On the contrary, they make no pretense of being "respectable." With civil disobedience, dissenters typically accept the penalty for breaking the law to show that they act from moral conscience rather than ignoble motives. They are concerned to show that they are morally upright and break the law only to force the complacent to listen. Some impure dissidents have rather different aims and are not enacting a political strategy.

The point of impure dissent also need not be to foment revolution. The dissidents may not be trying to fundamentally change the social order. They may not be attempting to effect social change at all and may embrace some of the more decadent aspects of the society they regard as unjust. This attitude can be puzzling, but I hope to make it less so.

I should also say that I am not concerned with the *right* of dissent. I take it for granted that people have a moral right (though sometimes not a legal one) to dissent from social practices they regard as unfair, oppressive, or unjust. Nor is my concern the *limits* of dissent—when dissent goes too far to be legitimate (for example, acts of terrorism or violent revolution). My main interest is in hip hop dissent that is permissible as a communicative act in the public sphere but whose content, inflection, ground, medium, mode, mood, or messenger is widely perceived as morally or politically objectionable. These impurities are often thought to justify ignoring, dismissing, or condemning hip hop dissent.

An Example: Nas and the "Nigger" Album

Born September 14, 1973, a black youth named Nasir (which means "helper and protector") grows up in the notorious Queensbridge Housing Projects in Queens, New York. He is raised largely by his hardworking mother, Ann Jones, who provides a loving and stable household despite the ghetto's oppressive social environment. Nasir becomes disillusioned with school, dropping out after only eight years of formal education. Surrounded by poverty, crime, and alienation, and in possession of few job skills, he hears the call of the streets—drug dealing, theft, robbery, gambling—and, to some extent, heeds it. But he comes from a long line of musicians, including his father Olu Dara (a jazz artist), and is exposed early to the venerable African American musical tradition. Hip hop is thriving as a commercial enterprise at the time, and the young man has a distinctive voice and exceptional talent for rap. So the call of the street is not the only voice he hears. In April 1994, Nas, as he comes to be known, released to critical acclaim *Illmatic*, a recording that is universally recognized as a hip hop classic. On the album Nas raps about life in the ghetto with an uncanny mix of politically conscious lyrics and gangsta sensibility. The rapper is now internationally famous and has gone on to make several well-received albums exploring similar themes. He has a strong online presence (for example, on Facebook, Twitter, and YouTube) and is beloved and revered by the black, young, and urban.

But when Nas announced in 2007 that his next album would be titled *Nigger*, civil rights activists including Jesse Jackson, Al Sharpton, and representatives of the NAACP spoke out publicly and pressured the label to change the name. Sharpton, for example, argued that the album was undermining efforts to make using the epithet a hate crime and that it gave comfort to racists who want to demean black people. Jackson condemned the title as "morally offensive" and urged media outlets and fans to boycott the album.[26] And it should be noted that Nas's public announcement of the inflammatory title occurred just a few months after the NAACP had conducted a widely publicized symbolic funeral for the notorious "N-Word" at its annual national convention in Detroit.

Ultimately, after an acrimonious exchange in the press between Nas and his critics, Nas and his label Def Jam relented and released the album as *Untitled* (which was later nominated for a Grammy). On May 19, 2008, through the online magazine AllHipHop.com, Nas released the following statement about the name change:

> It's important to me that this album gets to the fans. It's been a long time coming. I want my fans to know that creatively and lyrically, they can expect the same content and the same messages. It's that important. The streets have been waiting for this for a long time. The people will always know what the real title of this album is and what to call it.

Nas, now forty-two years old, can't be regarded as young anymore. However, he does make music for youth, self-consciously so, and he strongly identifies with black urban youth in particular. Moreover, hip hop is almost universally viewed as youth music—though plenty of people over age twenty-five are fans or regular listeners. In the liner notes to *Untitled*, Nas says:

> May hip hop continue to scare the hell out of all the people who planned genocide against black people everywhere . . . may it crush those who constantly try to criticize it and stop it, and silence the youth just because they don't understand them. Ya plan backfired and now we run sh*t. If you would only listen to the youth more you would be in tune with what lies ahead in the future.

Also in 2008 Nas released a free mixtape produced by DJ Green Lantern called *The Nigger Tape*, which includes a few songs from *Untitled* and several others. It was an underground hit and remains widely available online.[27] A music video for the single "Be a Nigger Too," which appears on *The Nigger Tape* but not *Untitled*, is available on YouTube.[28] In it Nas begins his rap with: "This is my opening scripture/ I been preparing this album my whole life/ Might be uncomfortable for most of you listeners." The main theme of the album, mixtape, and video is black people's creative and reflective responses to American racism, including, of course, their response to the most hateful racial epithet in the English language. These hip hop/new media pieces articulate—through text, sound, and images—a political ethics of the oppressed for black youth in ghetto communities.

The songs that appear on *Untitled* and *The Nigger Tape* protest substandard public schools, police brutality and an unfair criminal justice system, segregation and poverty in the ghetto, and the low quality of public housing. There is a spirit of resistance, an unwillingness to accept defeat, and an undying will not only to survive but also to find pleasure and beauty in a life of undeserved hardships. There is some expression of hope for changes in the future, including some qualified support for Barack Obama and his message of interracial unity. But there is also a celebration of materialism, drug dealing and illicit drug use, street crime and pimping, gunplay and retaliatory violence. There is strong skepticism toward traditional modes of political engagement (such as organized protests and electoral politics). There is profanity, vulgar language, and a liberal use of the words "bitch" and "nigger." And the title cut from *Untitled* is a tribute to the notorious Louis Farrakhan.

The album, mixtape, and video all represent impure dissent. The relevant impurities have not gone unnoticed by critics and reviewers of the album.[29] One way the *Untitled* album represents impure dissent is that it includes pop singles with crossover appeal (for example, "Hero" and "Make the World Go Round"). This can give the impression, perhaps mistaken, that all the controversy over the title was just an attempt at publicity to increase sales or at least a capitulation to the demands of capitalism. Critics also complained that the album has no coherent message or new political ideas and that it offers no solutions to the well-known problems it dramatizes. Also, there is the fact that Nas gave in to the pressure to change the title. The rapper's apparent desire for fame and fortune led critics to mock Nas for insincerity and hypocrisy.

What Makes Impure Dissent "Political"?

Adolph Reed claims that black youth culture, and rap music in particular, celebrates cynicism and alienation.[30] It is, he claims, posturing posing as politics. It is not "resistance," as is often claimed, but submission and resignation. He maintains that hip hop culture rejects direct political action that challenges the state and dismisses conventional political action. He characterizes it as a disregard for civic engagement and the embodiment of defeatism. "There is," he says, "no politics worthy of the name that does not work to shape the official institutions of public authority that govern and channel people's lives. Anything else is playacting."[31]

There is a reply to this type of critique familiar from the Black Arts movement (widely regarded as the aesthetic arm of the Black Power movement), whose art has much in common with impure hip hop dissent. Consider, for instance, Amiri Baraka's poem "It's Nation Time," which uses the word "nigger" more than thirty times. The reply claims that impure dissent is, in fact, politically efficacious in bringing about social change, even revolutionary change, at least potentially or in the long run. For example, the kinds of defenses of impure dissent that Baraka provides are *instrumental* justifications—that it shakes people out of their petty bourgeois complacency, helps the oppressed to overcome their self-hatred and alienation, instills a sense of empowerment and unity among the dispossessed, raises consciousness about vital but suppressed ideals, educates and mobilizes the masses, and so on.[32] There is no doubt that those who produce and consume impure hip hop dissent sometimes regard it as having this kind of instrumental value. That is, they believe its ultimate objective is to change society, perhaps by mentally equipping or inspiring the oppressed to fight for justice.

Consistent with both Baraka's and Reed's perspectives, many people regard political dissent as having at least two essential elements: (1) a consciously chosen action that publicly expresses the conviction that a wrong has occurred or is ongoing, thereby condemning the wrong; and (2) an act of condemnation intended to garner ameliorative steps by some targeted group (such as the state or grassroots actors). Although the expression of condemnation is important, it might appear to be only cathartic or mere posturing (a way for the dissenter to appear as if he or she cares) if not also aimed at correcting the problem. Accepting this conception, some might regard hip hop dissent as *politically* impure if it fails to satisfy condition (2). However, I want to question the assumption that all valuable political dissent must be aimed at correcting a wrong or injustice.

To sharpen the issue, it may be helpful to reflect for a moment on Albert Hirschman's influential model of political engagement.[33] *Voice*, on his account, is any attempt to change an objectionable state of affairs by publicly expressing one's disapproval or dissatisfaction. With *exit*, those dissatisfied with a political organization or polity simply leave it, refuse to support it, and perhaps join another more to their liking, which can sometimes pressure the former organization or polity to change its ways. Voice and exit, in Hirschman's view, are both political tactics, sometimes used in combination, to bring about change. When exit is not an option (for example, when there is no place to go or one cannot leave), voice is what remains (leaving aside revolution).

Notice that on this account "voice" is deemed valuable because of its potential to influence those with decision-making power. However, I think we need a broader conception of voice in political affairs. We might contrast *voice as influence*, which is aimed at altering the status quo, with *voice as symbolic expression*, which is not primarily concerned with its impact on those in power. I'm seeking to understand the morality of dissent without relying on consequentialist reasoning, and this means, at a minimum, not reducing voice to influence. Many people think that the only point there could be to dissent is to effect social change and that its only justification is the moral right to influence government policy.[34] Dissent is not, however, always a means to some extrinsic end; it is not only a political tactic. Its value cannot be measured solely in terms of the good social consequences it brings about. Its "effectiveness" is sometimes properly measured by how well it gets its message across to its intended audience and not by whether that audience responds with political activism or policy initiatives.

Not all impure dissent should be understood as a kind of political activism or a substitute for activism. Impure dissent, in all its forms is, however, political speech, a form of communicative action in a complex and multilayered public sphere. Dissent is a public act. Messages of dissent call out to be agreed with, rebutted, and sometimes acted upon. The public sphere is widely viewed as a forum for reasoned communicative exchange about matters of public concern. So what are we to make of dissent, like much political rap, that does not appear to be offered in the spirit of rational exchange, when the call does not seem to be looking for a response? When dissent is one-sided in this way, it may be regarded as *morally* impure, for the dissenters are in effect refusing to listen to criticisms or replies to their claims. The dissenters may appear arrogant, thinking themselves infallible oracles; or they may seem to be lacking in an appropriate civic spirit of reciprocity.

There's another possibility, though. Perhaps the dissenters regard some of their critics as arguing in bad faith. These listeners' callous indifference to the plight of the oppressed, the dissidents may have concluded, is a sign that meaningful reciprocal exchange is not possible. Of course, those offering impure dissent may have open and fruitful exchanges with *some* members of the public (say, within various counterpublics or parallel publics), those they regard as having the *moral standing* to disagree (for instance, those among the oppressed or those who participate in and respect hip hop cultural expression).[35] But they may refuse to engage in dialogue with the public at large or with those in power.

So, when it takes the form of symbolic expression, impure hip hop dissent is often an unconventional act in the public sphere. But when political voice does not aim to effect social change or to advance public debate, what might be its point or value?

The Ethics of Symbolic Dissent

There is a *complicity* argument for symbolic dissent. Thomas Hill explains its main premise this way: One should avoid being a willing contributor to wrongdoing even if this won't prevent or stop the wrong.[36] Thus, impure dissent could have value as an avenue to avoid complicity with injustice. This kind of argument works well for those who could be mistaken for collaborators in the wrong or perhaps for third-party bystanders who are in some way associated with the perpetrators. Wealthy rappers like Nas can thus offer this kind of defense of their impure dissent. But the complicity argument does not work so well for the severely disadvantaged, like poor black kids still stuck in the ghetto. The oppressed are the ones being victimized by harmful wrongdoing. No one suitably informed could reasonably take them to be (culpably) complicit in their own degradation (which is not to deny that they might sometimes make choices that make their plight worse).

Hill argues that one justification for symbolic dissent is to "disassociate oneself from evil." This can be accomplished through publicly denouncing the wrongful actions and standing with the victims in solidarity. However, the need for disassociation presupposes that one has (perhaps implicitly) associated oneself with the offending group— that one is a member or could be reasonably regarded as a member. If one cannot just quit the group or if quitting would entail high costs that it would be unreasonable to expect one to bear, then one should at least make one's opposition to the group's action explicit. Again, the disassociation argument, when offered by rich and famous hip hop artists, may have merit. But it is hard to see how this works for marginalized black urban youth, many of whom participate in symbolic hip hop dissent. It is not plausible to conclude that they condone, say, the state's failure to ensure a just opportunity structure, to provide adequate public schools, or to maintain a fair criminal justice system. So they do not seem to have a compelling reason to disassociate themselves from the agents of injustice, as their silence cannot be interpreted as a sign of consent or approval. But Hill points us in the right direction with the idea that symbolic dissent is a way of expressing solidarity with the victims of an injustice.

Hill does not develop this idea, but to see how we might advance it, let's return briefly to Hirschman's framework.[37] In addition to voice and exit, Hirschman emphasizes the workings of *loyalty* within the dynamics of political engagement. Loyalty is the special attachment to an organization or polity that keeps one from exiting even when one is deeply dissatisfied with it. Loyalty leads one to stick it out despite one's discontent. Hirschman argues that loyalty can lead one to resort to voice (understood as influence) even though one could just leave. He also insists that, when one is dissatisfied, loyalty is rational only if there is a reasonable expectation that things will improve. It is this belief that reform is feasible that leads one to voice discontent, with the expectation that one will be listened to and positive changes will occur as a result.

Many organized protests during the Civil Rights movement—from the Montgomery boycott to the Selma campaign for voting rights—can be understood within Hirschman's schema. One can readily find in, say, King's famous "I Have a Dream" speech that familiar mix of militant dissent, loyalty to an imperfect nation, and hope for a brighter future. Many in the Civil Rights movement firmly believed that reform from within could be achieved. The framework also makes sense of the actions of ex-patriates like Richard Wright, W. E. B. Du Bois, and Stokely

Carmichael, figures who for years loudly protested against U.S. injustices, only to conclude that reform from within could not be achieved and therefore chose exit.

However, understanding the impure dissent of young ghetto denizens requires a revised framework of political engagement. Black ghetto youth often do not believe that they have the power to change their society. They often feel that their voices are completely ignored in public deliberation. Moreover, they generally lack the option of exit, from the ghetto or the society at large. So it is natural to wonder: Why are they still engaging in dissent, and what do they hope to achieve by it? I think the answers do have something to do with loyalty, but these loyalty-based answers don't fit Hirschman's treatment.

I want to suggest that impure hip hop dissent, in addition to publicly condemning an injustice, has at least three further expressive functions: (1) to openly affirm self-respect, (2) to publicly pledge loyalty to the oppressed, and (3) to explicitly withhold loyalty from the state. I have already discussed the intrinsic value of affirming one's moral worth in the face of injustice (see Chapter 3), and I take it that it's clear how impure dissent might serve this vital function. Symbolic dissent is also often a public declaration of loyalty to an unjustly disadvantaged group. This dissent is the expression of solidarity with the oppressed against perceived injustice, not so much because those in power may change course as a result, but because the dissenters want to make manifest whose side they are on. This expression of solidarity need not be an attempt to mobilize an oppressed group to engage in some political action. But it does go beyond attempting to express moral pride, avoid complicity with injustice, or disassociate oneself from evil. It is not simply about keeping one's head up or one's hands clean. Instead it is a positive expression of association with those most burdened by the injustices one condemns. Such dissent is a way of pledging allegiance to the downtrodden (or perhaps the affirmation of a vow already made), a way of signaling that one is prepared to come to their defense and can be trusted as an ally. Often the oppressed are eager to have their grievances acknowledged, to know that others recognize and empathize with their undeserved plight. Impure dissent is sometimes a response to this (implicit) call. In other words, rap songs like Nas's "N.I.G.G.E.R. (The Slave and The Master)" not only denounce the structural injustices that reproduce ghetto conditions, but they also say to the ghetto poor, "I'm with you in solidarity," or, in the black urban vernacular, "I'm a 'nigger,' too."

However, the audience for impure dissent is not limited to the oppressed. It often also includes the perpetrators of injustice, those otherwise complicit, and even third-party bystanders. This "speaking truth to power" need not be aimed at getting the powerful to change course, though. Where there is the conviction that no realistic hope exists for social justice, those engaged in political dissent may not be aiming at garnering assent from the powerful or the broader public. But while the dissenters may not be trying to convince others of the validity of their claims of injustice, they still seem to want the general public to know that they dissent, that they stand in opposition to some social practice, even when they know the public is highly unlikely to agree with, or even take seriously, their stance. The *content* of the dissent is what is being communicated, not the grounds of the dissent. So, what is the point of this act of communication with the wider public?

One possibility is this: By engaging in this symbolic expression, they are signaling publicly that they are withholding their allegiance from the state and other mainstream institutions. They are registering that they do not recognize the state's authority over them and are voicing their lack of respect for society's unfair rules. In its most radical form, this type of dissent is a way of publicly declaring one's unwillingness to submit to society's unfair expectations. And where the dissenters do yield to the power of conventional authority, they are putting everyone on notice that their compliance is not given out of loyalty or a sense of civic duty.

Where loyalty to a nation is expected of all its citizens, the traditional way to signal that one is withholding loyalty is to exit the society and join a different one—"love it or leave it." Yet one can withhold loyalty without literally exiting, and it is possible to voice dissent without doing so as a member of the loyal opposition. This *symbolic exit* is one of the things that impure dissent, as a performative act, can accomplish. Though the possibilities for achieving social justice are judged to be dim and emigration is not a viable option, instead of simply capitulating and standing by in silence or sighing and passively hoping that things get better, one may choose symbolic dissent.

This interpretation can shed light on one of the most notorious features of impure political rap—its tendency to celebrate lawlessness and outlaw figures. When civic loyalty is publicly withheld or disavowed, the reason may be that the dissidents regard the social order as so unjust and irredeemable that it has no legitimacy in their eyes. The society no longer has (if it ever did have) the power to summon spontaneous allegiance from many who are subject to its laws. In view of the long-standing and gross injustices that ghettos represent, legal demands in particular are sometimes treated as nonbinding.[38] As Nas raps in "Breathe" (2008), "In America, you'll never be free/ Middle fingers up, fuck the police/ Damn, can a nigga just breathe?"

The themes of lawlessness frequently found in hip hop dissent may not, then, be an expression of "nihilism," at least not if that term implies a rejection of all values—moral, political, and religious. Rather, they may be a public declaration that positive law (the rules that comprise a legal order) has no normative force, at least not for the ghetto poor. This is not the same as saying that morality has no normative authority, because the opposition to the status quo is generally premised on its injustice. Moreover, another expressive function of impure dissent—to communicate solidarity with the oppressed—is also motivated by a moral concern, namely, the undeserved suffering of the victims of injustice. This is, I believe, a defensible political morality rooted in the everyday experience of the dispossessed in America's ghettos. And therefore at least *some* of the moral and political impurities found in conscious rap are part of the point.

Impurity of the Dissenter

Even if we can accept (or at least tolerate) the moral and political impurities of the content and inflection of hip hop dissent, we might still object to the impurities of its messengers. If the dissenter is widely believed to be seriously deficient in virtue (perhaps he's an unrepentant former drug dealer or pimp), those who observe his acts of symbolic dissent may be inclined not to take him seriously as a political agent and therefore not to engage with the content of his message. There is the belief, perhaps mostly implicit rather than openly defended, that dissenters must be morally upright if their grievances are to be given an honest hearing. (Consider, again, the Montgomery bus boycott.) If the virtue condition is accepted, though, dismissal of impure hip hop dissent will almost always seem justified, for many who practice impure dissent are far from paragons of moral virtue. But the virtue condition is unfounded. It is an elementary fallacy to reject the content or ground of a claim simply because the person who puts it forward exhibits major vices.

Now, one might reasonably be reluctant to express agreement or solidarity with an impure dissenter if the dissent's impurity is evidence that the dissenter is insincere or an opportunist. So perhaps there is a *sincerity* condition (though not a virtue condition).[39] Here the dissent's mode (the type of activity used to express it) and mood (the state of mind that animates it) are relevant. For instance, all things being equal, underground hip hop artists have more political credibility than successful commercial rappers. This is fair. Impure dissent that gains artists immense fame or wealth makes it reasonable for observers to wonder whether the performance of dissent is simply a posture taken for private advantage, a cynical exploitation of the plight of the oppressed to fill the artists' pockets with cash. Similarly, we have reason to doubt the sincerity of impure dissenters when they regularly violate the moral principles on which their protest rests or culpably contribute to the reproduction of the unjust structures to which they are ostensibly opposed. Such hypocrisy and complicity can be evidence that the impure dissenter is not a trustworthy or loyal ally in the fight against injustice, notwithstanding the fact that his or her message of dissent has merit.

Sometimes, however, attacks on the sincerity of a rap artist are really misplaced criticisms of a fictional *character* the rapper plays within the context of a hip hop narrative or performance. Rap is a popular art form in which the MC often assumes a persona in accordance with the conventions of a subgenre. For instance, gangsta rap (like gangster films) follows certain familiar stylistic norms and narrative conventions. A rapper may deploy the voice of the gangster figure, rely on over-the-top violent lyrics, construct menacing crime stories, or use other conventions of gangsta rap to convey his or her message of dissent. It is therefore easy to confuse the norms of the subgenre with the content of the political message or to mistake the persona for the artist who adopts it.[40]

Some regard the lack of a consistent message (within a given song or album or across a body of work) as a sign of insincerity. For instance, Nas is notorious for one minute rapping about the greatness of the black militant Huey Newton and the next boasting about the size of the rims on his Lamborghini. And yet a hip hop song or album is not the musical equivalent of a treatise in political philosophy or even an op-ed. It cannot be held to the same standards of coherence. An album like *Untitled* may have multiple objectives, some of which may be in tension. Inconsistency and lack of cohesiveness may be markers of subpar art, but they are not necessarily signs of moral insincerity or a disregard for the truth.

Hip Hop and the Political Ethics of the Oppressed

Following conventional wisdom, we might conclude that there are basically three options for oppressed groups: (1) stand and fight for justice, (2) try to escape injustice by leaving the oppressive environment; or (3) quietly submit to injustice and attempt to eke out a tolerable existence within its constraints. These options are not mutually exclusive, as they can be combined or taken up sequentially. Fighting for change and escaping unjust circumstances can also be joined with impure dissent. That is, the oppressed can engage in normatively transgressive political speech as a tactic to effect change or as a last salvo as they exit the scene.

But there is a fourth option—open and principled dissent without fleeing and without expecting or fighting for change. When this symbolic protest takes the form of impure dissent, it is not a tactic to effect reform, because its messengers have lost hope for meaningful social progress. It is not a good-bye message either, because these impure dissenters are generally not seeking to exit, nor are they able to in most cases. But it is not mere submission or even accommodation, for impure dissenters are, despite the consequences, publicly and honestly voicing their dissatisfaction with the status quo and announcing their refusal to willingly go along with their society's unreasonable demands and expectations. They are effectively choosing symbolic exit, explicitly disavowing any loyalty to the polity and its norms. Yet they are, in a sense, proudly standing their ground, remaining firmly opposed to the prevailing social order and to the malicious, selfish, and complacent attitudes of their fellow citizens.

Viewed in this way, symbolic impure dissent can be a valuable public act of protest, a meaningful mode of resistance to injustice, an affirmation of self-respect. But its value is easily missed if we fail to recognize that the political morality of dissent includes noninstrumental elements that are purely expressive. This type of symbolic expression is not always aimed at shaping debate within the broader public sphere. Nor is its objective always to pressure the state into enacting reforms. But neither should it be viewed as merely cathartic, escapist, or some other way of "coping" with oppression. In publicly communicating condemnation of injustice, a healthy sense of self-respect, solidarity with the oppressed, and defiance in the face of illegitimate authority, impure dissent is a vital element of the political ethics of the oppressed, and hip hop is sometimes the vehicle for its expression.

Epilogue

Renewing Ghetto Abolitionism

The ghetto should be abolished. Like American slavery and Jim Crow segregation, the ghetto should never have come into existence. In calling for its abolition, I'm not suggesting that black neighborhoods should be proscribed or that their poor black inhabitants should be dispersed. There is nothing wrong with the existence of predominantly black urban communities and, in light of the long-standing predicament of black people in the United States, there is much to be said in favor of such neighborhoods. The problem is that too many black neighborhoods lack needed resources, are offered only inadequate public services and substandard schools, are beset with violent street crime, and are home to many stigmatized and unjustly disadvantaged people with little spatial or economic mobility.

Abolishing the ghetto should not be seen simply as a matter of overcoming racial prejudice or reviving the War on Poverty. It should instead be viewed as an aggressive attempt at fundamental reform of the basic structure of our society. We, as residents of the United States, are all implicated in the perpetuation of ghettos. The ghetto is not "their" problem but *ours*, privileged and disadvantaged alike. The ghetto is a sign that our social order is profoundly unjust. It is a sign obscured by a host of legitimating ideologies—racist, sexist, economic, moral, religious, and nationalist. Insofar as we uphold that order, we are complicit in the oppression of our fellow citizens and, for some at least, contributing to our own oppression. Our duty of justice calls for response.

In recent reform efforts, disadvantaged ghetto denizens are too often viewed more as unruly chess pieces than as moral agents and allies. Yet the myriad ways in which they register dissent—sometimes subtle, sometimes overt—suggest that many act defiantly out of a sense of justice. Their noncompliance with societal expectations—refusing to delay childbearing, to marry, to accept low-paying and demeaning jobs, to respect the law, and to submit to other "mainstream" norms—can be a healthy expression of self-respect and a morally rooted opposition to the status quo, not mere nihilism or despair. Even though some of their defiant acts of transgression may add to their burdens (and annoy, anger, and frighten the affluent), they are not unjustified and certainly don't warrant condemnation. Instead this rebellion should draw our attention to the failures of reciprocity embedded in the social institutions and informal practices that constitute the structure of our society. Of course not everything the ghetto poor do and say merits approbation, and some of their conduct is, frankly, harmful wrongdoing and should therefore be discouraged and sometimes punished. But there is much to be learned from the impure dissent that emanates from American ghettos, whether this dissent takes the form of hip hop expression or more implicit modes of communication. These valuable elements should be seen as part of a political ethic that we might label *ghetto abolitionism*.

Calls for the abolition of ghettos date back to the Civil Rights movement. The movement to end Jim Crow was based primarily in the South, where blacks were not fully urbanized, explicit segregation laws were enforced, and blacks lacked an effective right to vote or run for public office. It took years of organized protest, skillful political maneuvering, and the Civil Rights Act (1964) and the Voting Rights Act (1965) to abolish the Jim Crow regime (though its negative effects are still felt today). Meanwhile, in cities like Los Angeles, New York City, Philadelphia, Detroit, Chicago, Newark, and Baltimore, blacks had been locked in the ghetto for decades, despite the absence of explicit segregation laws and notwithstanding the freedom to participate in electoral politics. It was in these cities (and others) that early calls for the abolition of the ghetto rang out—in the fiery speeches of black militants; in the verse, essays, plays, and books by intellectuals and artists;

in the boycotts and union organizing of working-class people, and in destructive urban riots. These campaigns for social justice highlighted the plight of the oppressed in poor black urban communities, and demanded not only civil rights and an end to institutional racism, but also economic justice and a fair criminal justice system.

Consider the Black Panther Party's "Ten Point Program."[1] It called for the political empowerment of black communities, a full-employment economy and guaranteed income for the involuntarily jobless, reparations for years of labor exploitation, decent and affordable housing, quality education for all, universal health care, and fundamental criminal justice reform. The group recruited in ghettos, capturing the attention and raising the consciousness of poor black youth. Indeed, Huey Newton, cofounder of the Party, argued that the "lumpenproletariat"—the unemployable element of the working class with no assets or marketable skills who therefore often turn to the underground economy for income—had revolutionary potential.[2] Whatever one thinks of the ideology, tactics, or leadership of the Black Panthers, it cannot be denied that they mobilized to abolish ghettos on grounds of systemic injustice. Ghetto abolitionism, for these black radicals, was a collective effort, one that included the ghetto poor as allies, to (in my terms) fundamentally change the basic structure of U.S. society.

After the demise of the Black Power movement, the emergence of a relatively large black middle class (most of whom no longer live in ghetto neighborhoods), and the substantial increase of black elected officials (including many mayors of large U.S. cities), demands for the abolition of the ghetto have been less insistent and more muted. The call must be renewed. Perhaps that's what we're seeing in the recent Black Lives Matter movement to end unjustified police violence and racial profiling and in the youth-led uprisings in Ferguson and Baltimore. These welcome developments echo the fifty-year-old Black Panther Party demand for "an immediate end to POLICE BRUTALITY and MURDER of Black people."[3] Such defiant protest is an essential element of ghetto abolitionism, though it must move beyond a focus on racism and the police to a broader campaign focused on economic justice.

I join the call for ghetto abolition, and this book—which is insufficient as a solution to all of the complex problems of the ghetto—is meant as an answer to the call. It is a contribution to the intellectual arm of a collective effort that reaches back at least to Du Bois's *The Philadelphia Negro* (1899).[4] I offer no new political strategies or policy proposals. Others are better equipped for those tasks. What I have offered is a defense of a set of values and principles that should inform the next ghetto abolition movement (a nonideal theory of corrective justice with its accompanying political ethics). I've offered a way of conceptualizing the problem (as one of basic justice rather than black poverty). And I've defended a philosophical framework for responding to the problem (a systemic-injustice model rather than the medical model that now reigns in policy circles and among black elites). Let me close by briefly commenting on each of these ideas.

Ghetto abolitionism, when viewed within the systemic-injustice framework and in accordance with liberal-egalitarian principles, would aid more than just the ghetto poor. It would help all who are unjustly disadvantaged. It not only attacks racism in all its forms, but calls for more robust enforcement of antidiscrimination law. It opposes class-based stratification, demanding a more equitable sharing of the benefits of social cooperation, technological advance, and economic growth. It insists on equal and extensive liberty for all, from freedom of expression and association to the right to an unconditional social minimum and to participate as equals in collective self-governance.

Ghetto abolitionism must be a grassroots effort, at least initially. It aims to change minds, to extend the bonds of solidarity, to mobilize and organize, and ultimately to influence public policy, from local ordinances to federal law. Liberal-egalitarian policy, when in corrective justice mode, is not limited to antipoverty initiatives but seeks more comprehensive social reform. When it embraces ghetto abolitionism, as it should, such policy eschews the medical model of social problem solving and fully embraces the systemic-injustice paradigm. Fundamental questions about the basic structure of society are not avoided and considerations of civic reciprocity are kept clearly and constantly in view.

Given the duty to ease the burdens of the oppressed, policy efforts must lighten the load on the ghetto poor while we work diligently to bring about a fully just society. These efforts must respect the moral and political agency of ghetto denizens, however. This means, for instance, not treating residential integration as a policy goal. The ghetto poor should be economically empowered and protected from housing discrimination so that they have real freedom to choose their neighborhood communities. Reproductive freedom should be respected. And while some wrongful procreation among the ghetto poor may exist, a stingy welfare regime should not be used to deter it, as this would only compound the economic injustices faced by many black women. No doubt poor families would be better off if they had two adult co-parents to share the workload. But the public lacks legitimate tools to do any more than recommend this familial arrangement. As there is nothing wrong with single-mother families (provided they receive the public support they are due), the state isn't justified in maintaining a highly punitive child-support regime on the basis of paternity alone. Nor is the state a suitable matchmaker for the oppressed, and many who share a biological child would do better—for themselves and their children— by not sharing a household.

Policymakers should certainly expand employment opportunities for the jobless. But the employment options and wages for low-skilled workers would need to be significantly improved and workfare requirements dropped altogether if the state is to avoid pushing the black poor into exploitative and demeaning forms of servitude. While voluntary job training and skills enhancement programs are welcome, a state that has created and allowed the ghetto to persist lacks the moral standing to act as an aggressive agent of cultural reform in the lives of its most embattled citizens.

In view of the serious injustices that disfigure the basic structure of society, sinking it below any reasonable standard for tolerable injustice, the ghetto poor owe neither loyalty nor obedience to the state. Even the state's enforcement rights are in jeopardy in light of racialized mass incarceration and unnecessary (and often malicious) violence in law enforcement practice. Criminal justice reform has to be a priority. Due process is a constitutional essential that underwrites the state's moral right to punish criminal offenders, and some who commit violent acts in ghettos must be contained to protect the weak and vulnerable in those communities.

As my title indicates, this book is partly inspired by and a tribute to Kenneth B. Clark's important but neglected work *Dark Ghetto: Dilemmas of Social Power* (1965).[5] Clark is best known for his role in convincing the U.S. Supreme Court that school segregation negatively affects black youth, which led to "separate but equal" public policy being declared unconstitutional. He also conducted the noted series of televised interviews "The Negro and the American Promise," which featured Martin Luther King Jr., Malcolm X, and James Baldwin. The interviews were later transcribed and collected in the book *The Negro Protest*, wherein Clark, reflecting on the political ethics of blacks in America, concludes: "The Negro has no more or less virtues or frailties than those found in other human beings. He is an individual who varies as much in courage and cowardice or ambivalence as do other human beings. He reacts to injustices and cruelties with the same patterns of accommodation, intimidation, rebellion, or philosophy as do others."[6]

Although Clark's *Dark Ghetto* is rooted in psychology and my book is a work of philosophy, I am entering the long-overdue conversation his book initiated but that was never fully taken up. The post-civil-rights scholarly and public discussion of ghetto communities was shaped more by another work, made public the same year: Daniel Patrick Moynihan's "The Negro Family: The Case for National Action."[7]

I prefer Clark's treatise, not because Moynihan uses the inflammatory word "pathology" to describe features of black life in ghetto communities. Clark uses the word even more frequently and to refer to precisely the same phenomena (welfare dependency, single-mother families, nonmarital births, broken homes, disorder, delinquency, addiction, violence, and crime). I don't prefer *Dark Ghetto* because Moynihan "blames the victim" and Clark does not. Clark is actually much more critical of the conduct of ghetto denizens. I don't side with Clark because he is black and Moynihan white, or because Clark spent many years living in a ghetto and Moynihan did not. No doubt Clark's racial identity and past residence in a ghetto community give him greater standing (among blacks and whites alike) to be bold when assessing the actions and attitudes of the ghetto poor—a privilege that, arguably, I am exercising myself. But my claims rest on no presumption of epistemic privilege in virtue of my race or class background. Finally, my fondness for Clark over Moynihan is not because one is a "liberal" and the other a "radical," as both were avowed liberals.[8] Rather, I'm drawn to Clark's study because it seems to me to better exhibit the systemic-injustice model than Moynihan's infamous but influential report.

I do not endorse *all* of Clark's particular theoretical conclusions. I don't agree that dependence on public support is pathological or an unfair burden on the public, for instance.[9] Nor do I think reliance on public support is a threat to personal dignity. I do not accept his patriarchal conception of the family or of male gender identity. And I'm not inclined to see integration as a solution to black disadvantage. Yet I believe that Clark's book falls into fewer pits than Moynihan's report, rooted as Moynihan's was in the medical model approach to social problems.

Moynihan does insist that U.S. society has not provided substantive equal opportunity for all blacks and should seek racial parity in socioeconomic well-being. But he conceptualizes the problem of the ghetto as primarily one of "family instability," which, he claims, perpetuates the cycle of poverty and its associated dysfunctional conduct. He takes the linchpin of this problem to be high rates of male unemployment, which calls for an antipoverty strategy of enhancing job opportunities and increasing labor force participation. While he acknowledges the significance of past racial injustice in creating unstable black families, he says, "At this point, the present tangle of pathology is capable of perpetuating itself without assistance from the white world."[10] Drawing attention to his implicit reliance on the medical model of reform isn't to indict Moynihan. After all, as assistant secretary of labor at the time, he was attempting to persuade the Johnson administration to take proactive measures to address racial inequality. He wasn't addressing the general public or trying to spur or support a social movement for wide-ranging egalitarian reform. Nevertheless, the differences between his approach and Clark's are striking and important.

Clark consistently structures his explanatory claims around questions of social justice. He does not avoid making judgments of value or tackling controversial moral questions. He insists that objectivity in social inquiry is not equivalent to value neutrality.[11] And he speaks freely about empirical facts and social justice without attempting to reduce matters of value to matters of fact, without treating values as merely subjective, and without regarding disagreements about justice as intractable or irresolvable. He recognizes, and this is key, that the only way forward is to give both scientific research and ethical reflection their due.

Grasping the importance of listening to the voices of the ghetto poor, Clark's prologue, titled "The Cry of the Ghetto," consists of thirty-two quotes from ghetto denizens, male and female and of all ages, who reflect on their plight and register their strong dissent from the status quo, condemning racism and discrimination, economic inequality and exploitation, lack of access to decent education, police brutality and harassment, inadequate protection from violence, political marginalization, media representations of black life, and American imperialism. In Clark's text, the ghetto poor are treated as agents of social change, as playing a central role in rebuilding their communities, and as taking the lead in reform efforts.[12]

However, Clark does not romanticize the ghetto poor. He suggests, for example, that the ghetto outlaw persona is often mere pretense. He claims that self-esteem is sometimes acquired, perversely, through violent conduct. He notes the rampant political cynicism in ghetto communities. He believes that some ostensible dissent is nothing more than catharsis and posturing. Clark highlights the challenge of maintaining self-esteem and self-respect under ghetto conditions and the challenge of maintaining black solidarity in the face of internal class division. Yet he holds that the preservation of self-respect despite pervasive injustice is a prerequisite for any successful campaign for justice. In some acts of delinquency, he sees rebellion against oppression. For instance, he argues that dropping out of school is sometimes a defiant affirmation of self-respect in response to the condescension, low expectations, and racism of teachers. And he believes it would be productive to enlist delinquents and criminal offenders in the collective project of solving community problems.[13]

Clark regards unemployment and underemployment as problems, but he emphasizes the fact that poor blacks are often restricted to menial service jobs that pay poverty-level wages. Joblessness as such is not therefore the linchpin. It is the quality of the jobs available and the low wages that call out for remedy. To prevent urban riots, Clark suggests creating decent jobs and reducing socioeconomic inequality. This would require fundamental change, a dramatic movement toward a more just society, rather than mere work programs and social services for the poor. Indeed, Clark appreciates how the single-minded focus on "helping" disadvantaged blacks obscures and evades the fact that the ghetto poor are in "need" because they live under a social structure that is unjust and that has shaped their personalities, conduct, and ambitions. This benefactor stance also conceals the fact that there are people with a vested interest in leaving the basic structure more or less as it is. Social work and philanthropy are inadequate and insulting responses to the problems of the ghetto, because they are rooted in benevolence rather than justice and opt to leave black communities dependent upon the goodwill of others rather than empowering them.[14]

Clark invokes with approval the *internal colonization thesis*—the Black Power claim that the "white power structure" functions as a mother country over its black ghetto colonies. The analogy is not perfect, but it has the virtue of making vivid social relationships of domination and exploitation. Clark also focuses on the privileges of affluent whites, their tendency to rationalize their complicity in injustice, and their role in perpetuating ghetto conditions. And he even notes how some black leaders in the ghetto—clergy, informal spokespersons, and elected representatives—exploit the status quo for personal gain.[15]

Finally, one of the things that Clark appreciates is that the modern American ghetto is not only appropriate for social-scientific study but also ripe for philosophical reflection:

> To understand Harlem, one must seek the truth and one must dare to accept and understand the truths one does find. One must understand its inconsistencies, its contradictions, its paradoxes, its ironies, its comic and its tragic face, its cruel and its self-destructive forces, and its desperate surge for life. And above all one must understand its humanity. The truth of the dark ghetto is not merely a truth about Negroes; it reflects the deeper torment and anguish of the total human predicament.[16]

My book is "political" in the way some academic books are and political philosophy must be. While it is not a social-scientific study, it is informed, indeed deeply shaped, by such studies and offers an interpretation of their moral significance. But this book is also a philosophical meditation on life in America's ghettos. I was searching, and continue to search, for those deeper, elusive, and more general "truths" behind the familiar facts about poor black neighborhoods. I hope my empathy for the plight of disadvantaged ghetto denizens is evident. But though moved by a sense of identification and solidarity with them, I have tried to remain objective and self-critical throughout.

A philosophical treatise on the ghetto might seem foolhardy, arrogant, and quixotic. The issues are tremendously complex. The topic is so big that no lone individual can be expected to say anything about it that is at once true, significant, and comprehensive. The relevant empirical and philosophical literature is vast, more than one can master in a lifetime of study. And the subject is highly controversial, where emotions run hot and enemies (and strange bedfellows) are easily made. So it might seem wiser (or safer) for a philosopher to dip his or her toe in these dark waters rather than dive right in. Yet here I am, soaked from head to foot.

Though I have been developing its arguments for more than ten years, this book is not, as Kenneth Clark claimed his *Dark Ghetto* to be, a "study of the total phenomenon of the ghetto."[17] There are relevant issues—concerning education, democracy, and health, for example—that I have not addressed. I feel compelled, however, to make my current thinking public, trusting that readers will understand that all interdisciplinary work (particularly across the humanities–social science divide) has limitations of scope and depth. My hope is that other scholars, seeing merit in my approach, will be moved to supplement, build on, and correct these initial efforts. I don't expect mine to be the last word.

Notes

Introduction

1. For an informative history of the concept *ghetto* in social science and policy, see Mitchell Duneier, *Ghetto: The Invention of a Place, the History of an Idea* (New York: Farrar, Straus and Giroux, 2016).

2. For an insightful discussion of the downgraded-agency problem in the context of social-scientific studies of black urban poverty, see Cathy J. Cohen, "Deviance as Resistance: A New Research Agenda for the Study of Black Politics," *Du Bois Review* 1 (2004): 27–45. Also see Robin D. G. Kelley, *Race Rebels: Culture, Politics, and the Black Working Class* (New York: Free Press, 1994); and Robert Gooding-Williams, *In the Shadow of Du Bois: Afro-Modern Political Thought in America* (Cambridge, MA: Harvard University Press, 2010), chap. 6.

3. See, for example, John Rawls, *A Theory of Justice*, rev. ed. (Cambridge, MA: Belknap Press of Harvard University Press, 1999); Ronald Dworkin, *Sovereign Virtue: The Theory and Practice of Equality* (Cambridge, MA: Harvard University Press, 2000); and Brian Barry, *Why Social Justice Matters* (Cambridge: Polity, 2005).

4. Important exceptions include Michael Walzer, *Obligations: Essays on Disobedience, War, and Citizenship* (Cambridge, MA: Harvard University Press, 1970), pt. 1; Roger S. Gottlieb, "The Concept of Resistance: Jewish Resistance during the Holocaust," *Social Theory and Practice* 9 (1983): 31–49; Thomas Hill Jr., *Autonomy and Self-Respect* (Cambridge: Cambridge University Press, 1991), chap. 1; Howard McGary, "Resistance and Slavery," in *Between Slavery and Freedom: Philosophy and American Slavery*, ed. Howard McGary and Bill E. Lawson (Bloomington: Indiana University Press, 1992), 35–54; Lisa Tessman, *Burdened Virtues: Virtue Ethics for Liberatory Struggles* (Oxford: Oxford University Press, 2005), chap. 5; Ann E. Cudd, *Analyzing Oppression* (Oxford: Oxford University Press, 2006), chap. 7; Bernard R. Boxill, "The Responsibility of the Oppressed to Resist Their Own Oppression," *Journal of Social Philosophy* 41 (2010): 1–12; Carol Hay, "The Obligation to Resist Oppression," *Journal of Social Philosophy* 42 (2011): 21–45.

5. See, for example, G. A. Cohen, *If You're an Egalitarian, How Come You're So Rich?* (Cambridge, MA: Harvard University Press, 2000); and Liam B. Murphy, *Moral Demands in Nonideal Theory* (New York: Oxford University Press, 2000).

6. David Walker, *Appeal to the Coloured Citizens of the World*, ed. Peter P. Hinks (University Park: Pennsylvania State University Press, 2000), 14–15.

7. The exceptions include Bill E. Lawson, ed., *The Underclass Question* (Philadelphia: Temple University Press, 1992); Christopher Jencks, *Rethinking Social Policy: Race, Poverty, and the Underclass* (Cambridge, MA: Harvard University Press, 1992); Lawrence Mead and Christopher Beem, eds., *Welfare Reform and Political Theory* (New York: Russell Sage, 2005); and Clarissa Haywood and Todd Swanstrom, eds., *Justice and the American Metropolis* (Minneapolis: University of Minnesota Press, 2011).

8. For a brief but particularly helpful discussion of the place of liberal political morality in American and British political history, see Ronald Dworkin, *A Matter of Principle* (Oxford: Clarendon Press, 1985), 181–204.

9. Though less central to the arguments to follow, I also defend *political* liberalism (as opposed to comprehensive liberalism). While the state must protect and respect our autonomy (our capacity for rational self-governance), we should be free to choose our own ultimate ends, and it is not within the state's authority to dictate to its citizens just how they should value their freedom or lives. This is a liberalism that is neutral on conceptions of the good. See John Rawls, *Political Liberalism* (New York: Columbia University Press, 1996).

10. Michael C. Dawson, *Black Visions: The Roots of Contemporary African-American Political Ideologies* (Chicago: University of Chicago Press, 2001), 258–273; and Charles W. Mills, "Black Radical Liberalism (and Why It Isn't an Oxymoron)," delivered at the American Philosophical Association (Eastern Division) on December 27, 2014, in Philadelphia. Representative contemporary academic work in this philosophical tradition include Bernard R. Boxill, *Blacks and Social Justice*, rev. ed. (Lanham, MD: Rowman and Littlefield, 1992); Charles W. Mills, *The Racial Contract* (Ithaca, NY: Cornell University Press, 1997); Howard McGary, *Race and Social Justice* (Malden, MA: Blackwell, 1999); Tommie Shelby, *We Who Are Dark: The Philosophical Foundations of Black Solidarity* (Cambridge, MA: Belknap Press of Harvard University Press, 2005); Ronald R. Sundstrom, *The Browning of America and the Evasion of Social Justice* (Albany: SUNY, 2008); Derrick Darby, *Rights, Race, and Recognition* (Cambridge: Cambridge University Press, 2009); Lionel McPherson, *The Afterlife of Race* (forthcoming).

11. See, for example, Rawls, *A Theory of Justice*; Rawls, *Political Liberalism*; Dworkin, *Sovereign Virtue*; Susan Moller Okin, *Justice, Gender, and the Family* (New York: Basic Books, 1989); Marth C. Nussbaum, *Sex and Social Justice* (New York: Oxford University Press, 1999); Samuel Scheffler, *Boundaries and Allegiances: Problems of Justice and Responsibility in Liberal Thought* (Oxford: Oxford University Press, 2001); Liam Murphy and Thomas Nagel, *The Myth of Ownership: Taxes and Justice* (Oxford: Oxford University Press, 2002); T. M. Scanlon, *The Difficulty of Tolerance* (Cambridge: Cambridge University Press, 2003); and Joshua Cohen, *Philosophy, Politics, Democracy: Selected Essays* (Cambridge, MA: Harvard University Press, 2009).

12. Rawls, *A Theory of Justice*, 215–216.

CHAPTER ONE Injustice

1. John Rawls, *Political Liberalism* (New York: Columbia University Press, 1996), 15–18.

2. In his formidable attempt to show that Rawls's theory of justice is insufficiently egalitarian, G. A. Cohen has argued against Rawls's claim that the princi-

ples of justice apply only to the basic structure, insisting instead that they also apply to the choices of individuals and that the distinction between individual choice and institutional arrangement is arbitrary from the standpoint of justice. See G. A. Cohen, *Rescuing Justice and Equality* (Cambridge, MA: Harvard University Press, 2008), chap. 3. There is, I think, something to Cohen's argument (though perhaps not as much as he maintains). I provide a brief partial response in Chapter 5, but I won't take up the argument in detail. What I will try to prove, however, is that by focusing on the basic structure within nonideal theory, we can learn important truths about the political morality of resistance and reform. For helpful responses to Cohen's argument, see A. J. Julius, "Basic Structure and the Value of Equality," *Philosophy and Public Affairs* 31 (2003): 321–355; and Samuel Scheffler, "Is the Basic Structure Basic?," in *The Egalitarian Conscience: Essays in Honor of G. A. Cohen* (Oxford: Oxford University Press, 2006), 102–129.

3. Rawls, *A Theory of Justice*, 82; and Rawls, *Justice as Fairness: A Restatement*, ed. Erin Kelly (Cambridge, MA: Harvard University Press, 2001), 55.

4. See R. Richard Banks, Jennifer L. Eberhardt, and Less Ross, "Discrimination and Implicit Bias in a Racially Unequal Society," *California Law Review* 94 (2006): 1169–1190.

5. The discussion of racism in the main text is an abbreviated and somewhat simplified account of my views. For elaboration and detailed defense, see Tommie Shelby, "Is Racism in the 'Heart'?," *Journal of Social Philosophy* 33 (Fall 2002): 411–420; Shelby, "Ideology, Racism, and Critical Social Theory," *Philosophical Forum* 34 (Summer 2003): 153–188; Shelby, "Race and Social Justice: Rawlsian Considerations," *Fordham Law Review* 72 (2004): 1697–1714; Shelby, "Racism, Identity, and Latinos: Comment on Linda Martín Alcoff," *Southern Journal of Philosophy* 47 (2009): 129–136; and Shelby, "Racism, Moralism, and Social Criticism," *Du Bois Review* 11, no. 1 (2014): 57–74.

6. For helpful attempts to understand racism as an ideology, see William Julius Wilson, *Power, Racism, and Privilege: Race Relations in Theoretical and Sociohistorical Perspectives* (New York: Free Press, 1973); Robert Miles, *Racism* (London: Routledge, 1989); Colette Guillaumin, *Racism, Sexism, Power and Ideology* (London: Routledge, 1995); Lawrence Bobo, James R. Klugel, and Ryan A. Smith, "Laissez-Faire Racism: The Crystallization of a Kinder, Gentler, Antiblack Ideology," in *Racial Attitudes in the 1990s*, ed. Steven A. Tuch and Jack K. Martin (Westport, CT: Praeger, 1997), 15–41; Barbara J. Fields, "Slavery, Race and Ideology in the United States of America," *New Left Review* (1990): 95–118; Jim Sidanius and Felicia Pratt, *Social Dominance: An Intergroup Theory of Social Hierarchy and Oppression* (Cambridge: Cambridge University Press, 1999), chap. 4; and George Fredrickson, *Racism: A Short History* (Princeton: Princeton University Press, 2002).

7. Lawrence D. Bobo, "Somewhere between Jim Crow and Post-Racialism: Reflections on the Racial Divide in America Today," *Daedalus* 140 (2011): 11–36.

8. See Anthony G. Greenwald and Mahzarin R. Banaji, "Implicit Social Cognition: Attitudes, Self-Esteem, and Stereotypes," *Psychological Review* 102, no. 1 (1995): 4–27; and John F. Dovidio and Samuel L. Gaertner, "Aversive Racism," *Advances in Experimental Social Psychology* 36 (2004): 1–52.

9. The intrinsic/extrinsic institutional racism distinction does not correspond to the intrinsic/extrinsic personal racism distinction as developed in

K. Anthony Appiah, "Racisms," in *Anatomy of Racism*, ed. David Theo Goldberg (Minneapolis: University of Minnesota Press, 1990), 3–17.

10. Here I build on some ideas defended in Gertrude Ezorsky, *Racism and Justice: The Case for Affirmative Action* (Ithaca, NY: Cornell University Press, 1991).

11. For a defense of racial profiling along these lines, see Mathias Risse and Richard Zeckhauser, "Racial Profiling," *Philosophy and Public Affairs* 32 (2004): 131–170.

12. John A. Powell, "Structural Racism: Building upon the Insights of John Calmore," *North Carolina Law Review* 86 (2008): 791–816.

13. Manning Marable, "An Idea Whose Time Has Come," *Newsweek*, August 27, 2001.

14. Bobo et al., "Laissez-Faire Racism."

15. See Terry Eastland, *Ending Affirmative Action: The Case for Colorblind Justice* (New York: Basic Books, 1996). For an insightful critical discussion of this principle, see Bernard R. Boxill, *Blacks and Social Justice*, rev. ed. (Lanham, MD: Rowman and Littlefield, 1992), chap. 1. Also see K. Anthony Appiah and Amy Gutmann, *Color Conscious: The Political Morality of Race* (Princeton: Princeton University Press, 1996), 108–138; Glenn C. Loury, *The Anatomy of Racial Inequality* (Cambridge, MA: Harvard University Press, 2002), chap. 4; and Ronald Sundstrom, *The Browning of America and the Evasion of Social Justice* (Albany: SUNY Press, 2008), chap. 2.

16. See Owen M. Fiss, "Groups and the Equal Protection Clause," *Philosophy and Public Affairs* 5 (1976): 107–177; and Cass R. Sunstein, "The Anticaste Principle," *Michigan Law Review* 92 (1994): 2410–2455.

17. Boxill, *Blacks and Social Justice*, 12–18.

18. See ibid., 17; Larry Alexander, "What Makes Wrongful Discrimination Wrong? Biases, Preferences, Stereotypes, and Proxies," *University of Pennsylvania Law Review* 141 (1992): 149–219; Adrian M. S. Piper, "Two Kinds of Discrimination," *Yale Journal of Criticism* 6 (1993): 25–74; and Deborah Hellman, *When Is Discrimination Wrong?* (Cambridge, MA: Harvard University Press, 2008), 34–58.

19. Bernard Williams, "The Idea of Equality," in *Philosophy, Politics, and Society*, ed. P. Laslett and W. G. Runciman (Oxford: Basil Blackwell, 1962), 110–131.

20. Kurt Baier, "Merit and Race," *Philosophia* 8 (1978): 121–151.

21. See Alexander, "What Makes Wrongful Discrimination Wrong?"; and Lawrence A. Blum, *"I'm Not a Racist, But . . .": The Moral Quandary of Race* (Ithaca, NY: Cornell University Press, 2002), 78–90.

22. Paul Woodruff, "What's Wrong with Discrimination?," *Analysis* 36 (1976): 158–160; and Blum, *"I'm Not a Racist, But . . . ,"* 84–85.

23. John Arthur, *Race, Equality, and the Burdens of History* (Cambridge: Cambridge University Press, 2007), 30–33; and Hellman, *When Is Discrimination Wrong?*, 59–85.

24. For discussion of the practical importance of fair equality of opportunity in education, see Elizabeth Anderson, "Fair Opportunity in Education: A Democratic Equality Perspective," *Ethics* 117 (2007): 559–622; and Debra Satz, "Equality, Adequacy, and Education for Citizenship," *Ethics* 117 (2007): 623–648.

25. Here I draw on G. A. Cohen, *Why Not Socialism?* (Princeton: Princeton University Press, 2009), 17–34.

26. I am not suggesting that what I say here is an adequate reply to G. A. Cohen's critique of Rawls on the permissibility of economic incentives. See Cohen's *Rescuing Justice and Equality* (Cambridge, MA: Harvard University Press, 2008), 27–86. For replies, see Andrew Williams, "Incentives, Inequality, and Publicity," *Philosophy and Public Affairs* 27 (1998): 225–247; Joshua Cohen, "Taking People as They Are?," *Philosophy and Public Affairs* 30 (2002): 363–386.

27. For example, Anderson speaks of segregation as a process and a condition. See Anderson, *The Imperative of Integration*.

28. Mary Pattillo-McCoy, *Black Picket Fences: Privilege and Peril among the Black Middle Class* (Chicago: University of Chicago Press, 1999).

29. Sundstrom argues that a value-neutral definition of segregation is impossible. See Ronald R. Sundstrom, "Racial Politics in Residential Segregation Studies," *Philosophy and Geography* 7 (2004): 61–78. I agree that value commitments are generally reflected in social-scientific definitions of segregation; that is, the researcher's values will typically motivate him or her to define it in a particular way (e.g., to highlight what is thought to be normatively significant about the phenomenon) and he or she may have selected the definition to advance a moral or political viewpoint (e.g., that segregation causes or is caused by injustice). But the definition itself need not express, or presuppose, approval or disapproval of segregation and may be compatible with a range of normative stances on the phenomenon. The definition I offer is meant to be neutral on whether segregation patterns are good or bad, though it is motivated by normative concerns.

30. For discussion of this point and related issues, see Ronald R. Sundstrom, "Race and Place: Social Space in the Production of Human Kinds," *Philosophy and Geography* 6 (2003): 83–95. Also see Clarissa Rile Hayward, *How Americans Make Race: Stories, Institutions, Spaces* (Cambridge: Cambridge University Press, 2013), chap. 2.

31. For comparison purposes, in 2013 the overall poverty rate for the twenty-five largest U.S. metropolitan areas ranged from 8.5 percent (Washington–Arlington–Alexandria, DC-VA-MD-WV metro area) to 18.2 percent (Riverside–San Bernardino–Ontario, CA metro area). The overall poverty rate in the United States is 15.9 percent. See Alemayehu Bishaw and Kayla Fontenot, "Poverty: 2012 and 2013," U.S. Census Bureau (ACSBR/13-01).

32. For important discussions of concentrated neighborhood disadvantage, see William Julius Wilson, *The Truly Disadvantaged* (Chicago: University of Chicago Press, 1987); Paul A. Jargowsky, *Poverty and Place: Ghettos, Barrios, and the American City* (New York: Russell Sage, 1997); Robert J. Sampson, *Great American City: Chicago and the Enduring Neighborhood Effect* (Chicago: University of Chicago Press, 2012); and Patrick Sharkey, *Stuck in Place: Urban Neighborhoods and the End of Progress toward Racial Equality* (Chicago: University of Chicago Press, 2013).

33. The normative significance of the "clustering of disadvantage" is helpfully discussed in Jonathan Wolff and Avner de-Shalit, *Disadvantage* (Oxford: Oxford University Press, 2007), chap. 7.

34. Sampson, *Great American City*, 100–102.

35. See Douglass S. Massey and Mary J. Fischer, "How Segregation Concentrates Poverty," *Ethnic and Racial Studies* 23 (2000): 670–691. Also see Sampson, *Great American City*; and Sharkey, *Stuck in Place*.

36. Douglass S. Massey and Nancy A. Denton, *American Apartheid: Segregation and the Making of the Underclass* (Cambridge, MA: Harvard University Press, 1993); William Julius Wilson, *When Work Disappears: The World of the New Urban Poor* (New York: Knopf, 1996); and Mary J. Fischer, "The Relative Importance of Income and Race in Determining Residential Outcomes in U.S. Urban Areas, 1970–2000," *Urban Affairs Review* 38 (2003): 669–696.

37. See Mary Pattillo, "Extending the Boundaries and Definition of the Ghetto," *Ethnic and Racial Studies* 26 (2003): 1046–1057.

38. Some distinguish poor black neighborhoods that are densely populated (e.g., those in New York City) from those that are low density (e.g., some in Detroit), as there would appear to be cultural and institutional differences between them. See Mario L. Small, "No Two Ghettos Are Alike," *Chronicle of Higher Education*, March, 17, 2014. However, I will not rely on this distinction.

39. Loïc Wacquant, "Ghetto," in *International Encyclopedia of the Social and Behavioral Sciences*, ed. Neil J. Smelser and Paul B. Baltes (London: Pergamon Press, 2004).

40. See Boxill, *Blacks and Social Justice*, 79–85.

41. See Massey and Denton, *American Apartheid*; and Sheryll Cashin, *The Failures of Integration: How Race and Class Are Undermining the American Dream* (New York: Public Affairs, 2004).

42. U.S. Department of Housing and Urban Development, *Discrimination in Metropolitan Housing Markets: National Results from Phase I HDS 2000* (2002).

43. Melvin L. Oliver and Thomas M. Shapiro, *Black Wealth, White Wealth: A New Perspective on Racial Inequality* (New York: Taylor and Francis, 2006); and Dalton Conley, *Being Black, Living in the Red: Race, Wealth, and Social Policy in America* (Berkeley: University of California Press, 1999).

44. Cashin, *The Failures of Integration*, 83–85.

45. Stephen Macedo has argued, for example, that these local government arrangements are unjust because they violate fair equality of opportunity. See Stephen Macedo, "Property-Owning Plutocracy: Inequality and American Localism," in *Justice and the American Metropolis*, ed. Clarissa Rile Hayward and Todd Swanstrom (Minneapolis: University of Minnesota Press, 2011), 33–58.

46. See Sundstrom, "Race and Place"; and Hayward, *How Americans Make Race*, chap. 2.

CHAPTER TWO Community

1. See, for example, Orlando Patterson, *The Ordeal of Integration* (New York: Basic Books, 1997); Sheryll Cashin, *The Failures of Integration: How Race and Class Are Undermining the American Dream* (New York: Public Affairs, 2004); Michelle Adams, "Radical Integration," *California Law Review* 94 (2006): 261–311; and Elizabeth Anderson, *The Imperative of Integration* (Princeton: Princeton University Press, 2010).

2. Both are advanced in Stephan Thernstrom and Abigail Thernstrom, *America in Black and White: One Nation, Indivisible* (New York: Touchstone, 1999), 219–231.

3. See David R. Harris, "Why Are Whites and Blacks Averse to Black Neighbors?," *Social Science Research* 30 (2001): 100–116.

4. Mary Pattillo-McCoy, *Black Picket Fences: Privilege and Peril among the Black Middle Class* (Chicago: University of Chicago Press, 1999).

5. However, there is evidence that whites and blacks overestimate the poverty rate among blacks, just as they overestimate the number of blacks in the U.S. population (see Patterson, *The Ordeal of Integration,* 56). This factual mistake, which may also be regarded as a stereotype, would naturally lead people to think the correlation between blackness and poverty is much stronger than it is, and so proxy discrimination can seem more rational than it is.

6. Ibid., 44.

7. Donald R. Kinder and Lynn M. Sanders, *Divided by Color: Racial Politics and Democratic Ideals* (Chicago: University of Chicago Press, 1996).

8. John Rawls, *A Theory of Justice,* rev. ed. (Cambridge, MA: Harvard University Press, 1999), 99–100. Also see Jeremy Waldron, "Special Ties and Natural Duties," *Philosophy and Public Affairs* 22 (1993): 3–30.

9. Wilson has famously argued that, after the fall of Jim Crow, many middle-class blacks migrated out of the ghetto into more advantaged, white suburban neighborhoods, leaving behind greater concentrations of the black poor in the central cities. See William Julius Wilson, *The Truly Disadvantaged* (Chicago: University of Chicago Press, 1987). Also see Richard D. Alba, John R. Logan, and Brian J. Stults, "How Segregated Are Middle-Class African Americans?," *Social Problems* 47 (2000): 543–558; William A. V. Clark, "Race, Class, and Place: Evaluating Mobility Outcomes for African Americans," *Urban Affairs Review* 42 (2007): 295–314; and Patrick Sharkey, "Spatial Segmentation and the Black Middle Class," *American Journal of Sociology* 119 (2014): 903–954.

10. Lawrence Bobo and Camille L. Zubrinsky, "Attitudes on Residential Integration: Perceived Status Differences, Mere In-Group Preference, or Racial Prejudice?," *Social Forces* 74 (1996): 883–909.

11. Tommie Shelby, *We Who Are Dark: The Philosophical Foundations of Black Solidarity* (Cambridge, MA: Belknap Press of Harvard University Press, 2005).

12. See Bernard R. Boxill, *Blacks and Social Justice* (Lanham, MD: Rowman and Littlefield, 1992), chap. 8.

13. For a brief overview of black separatist arguments, see Howard McGary, *Race and Social Justice* (Malden: Blackwell, 1999), chap. 3. Also see Andrew Valls, "A Liberal Defense of Black Nationalism," *American Political Science Review* 104 (2010): 467–481; and Shelby, *We Who Are Dark,* chap. 3.

14. See Kyle Crowder, "The Racial Context of White Mobility: An Individual-Level Assessment of the White Flight Hypothesis," *Social Science Research* 29 (2000): 223–257; Michael O. Emerson, Karen J. Chai, and George Yancey, "Does Race Matter in Residential Segregation? Exploring the Preferences of White Americans," *American Sociological Review* 66 (2001): 922–935; and Lincoln Quillian, "Why Is Black–White Residential Segregation So Persistent? Evidence on Three Theories from Migration Data," *Social Science Research* 31 (2002): 197–229.

15. Maria Krysan and Reynolds Farley, "The Residential Preferences of Blacks: Do They Explain Persistent Segregation?," *Social Forces* 80 (2002): 937–980.

16. See Iris Marion Young, *Inclusion and Democracy* (Oxford: Oxford University Press, 2000), chap. 6.

17. For more on this point, see Lawrence Blum, "Three Kinds of Race-Related Solidarity," *Journal of Social Philosophy* 38 (2007): 53–72.

18. Anderson, *The Imperative of Integration*.

19. Ibid., 33–38. This position is also advanced in Patterson, *The Ordeal of Integration;* and Glenn C. Loury, *The Anatomy of Racial Inequality* (Cambridge, MA: Harvard University Press, 2002).

20. Anderson, *The Imperative of Integration*, 33.

21. Owen Fiss, *A Way Out: America's Ghettos and the Legacy of Racism*, ed. Joshua Cohen, Jefferson Decker, and Joel Rogers (Princeton: Princeton University Press, 2003).

22. Ibid., 37.

23. Because of widespread discriminatory practices and a U.S. Supreme Court mandate *(Hills vs. Gautreaux)*, the Chicago Housing Authority ran a mobility program from 1976–1998 whereby poor segregated blacks who met eligibility requirements (e.g., small families, moderate debt, and acceptable housekeeping practices) could move to predominantly white or integrated metropolitan neighborhoods using housing certificates.

24. Inspired by the results of *Gautreaux*, in 1992 the U.S. Congress authorized the Moving to Opportunity (MTO) housing voucher program and social experiment in five cities—Baltimore, Boston, Chicago, Los Angeles, and New York. An experimental subgroup of eligible participants had to leave subsidized project-based housing in high-poverty neighborhoods (more than 40 percent poor) and move to neighborhoods with less than 10 percent poverty for at least one year. Though MTO did not have racial integration as its explicit aim (its focus was reducing concentrated poverty), it was a de facto integration program, because few black neighborhoods have low-poverty rates, which meant that black participants almost always had to move, at least initially, to a white or integrated neighborhood to meet program requirements.

25. Anderson is completely dismissive of black nationalists, who generally reject integration as a solution to black disadvantage. Anderson justifies this dismissal on the grounds that black nationalists are preoccupied with identity recognition rather than emphasizing resource redistribution, and so have no practical solution to black disadvantage. However, this tendency to overemphasize recognition is not characteristic of left-wing black nationalism, which has always been concerned with racial domination, class subordination, and imperialism. Many black nationalists liken U.S. white supremacy with European colonialism. This is a way of highlighting labor exploitation and other economic injustices in America, not simply racism. Moreover, most black nationalists during the Black Power era demanded reparations for past racial injustices and some even demanded land and sought secession. These were demands to redress racial inequality, not simply calls for the recognition of marginalized identities and cultures. See, for example, Rod Bush, *We Are Not What We Seem: Black Nationalism and Class Struggle in the American Century* (New York: NYU Press, 2000); Nikhil Pal Singh, *Black Is a Country: Race and the Unfinished Struggle for Democracy*, (Cambridge, MA: Harvard University Press, 2004); Peniel E. Joseph, *Waiting 'til the Midnight Hour: A Narrative History of Black Power in America* (New York: Henry Holt, 2007); Michael C. Dawson, *Blacks In and Out of the Left* (Cambridge, MA: Harvard University Press, 2013).

26. See W. E. B. Du Bois, *Dusk of Dawn: An Essay toward an Autobiography of a Race Concept* (New Brunswick: Transaction, 1984); Harold Cruse, *Plural but Equal: A Critical Study of Blacks and Minorities and America's Plural Society* (New York: William Morrow, 1987); and Derrick Bell, *And We Are Not Saved: The Elusive Quest for Racial Justice* (New York: Basic Books, 1987). For a recent comprehensive statement of this position, see Roy L. Brooks, *Integration or Separation? A Strategy for Racial Equality* (Cambridge, MA: Harvard University Press, 1996).

27. Mary Pattillo, "Investing in Poor Black Neighborhoods 'As Is,'" in *Public Housing and the Legacy of Segregation*, ed. Margery Austin Turner, Susan J. Popkin, and Lynette Rawlings (Washington, DC: Urban Institute Press, 2009), 31–46.

28. Sometimes the focus is on having "contacts" and sometimes it's on the *information* learned through people you know. Social ties can be useful because the people in our social networks can do us favors and vouch for us when it counts (e.g., by providing job references). But if it is the *information* about employment opportunities that matters, then one can often get information (sometimes more reliable information) through other channels—such as advertisements, employment websites, job centers, co-workers, classmates, teachers, and school guidance counselors. One needn't rely on one's neighbors.

29. There is evidence that such bridging bonds do not form. See Susan Clampet-Lundquist, "Moving Over or Moving Up? Short-Term Gains and Losses for Relocated HOPE VI Families," *Journal of Policy Development and Research* 7 (2004): 57–80; and Robert J. Chaskin and Mark L. Joseph, *Integrating the Inner City: The Promise and Perils of Mixed-Income Public Housing Transformation* (Chicago: University of Chicago Press, 2015), chap. 6. For an overview of the evidence, see Edward G. Goetz and Karen Chapple, "You Gotta Move: Advancing the Debate on the Record of Dispersal," *Housing Policy Debate* 20 (2010): 209–236.

30. Anderson, *The Imperative of Integration*, 123–127.

31. For a thorough review of the empirical support for the contact hypothesis, with a particular focus on the conditions that facilitate and inhibit prejudice reduction through contact, see Thomas F. Pettigrew and Linda R. Tropp, "A Meta-Analytic Test of Intergroup Contact Theory," *Journal of Personality and Social Psychology* 90 (2006): 751–783.

32. Of course, if eligibility to attend a public school depends on residence in the surrounding neighborhood and neighborhoods are segregated, then public schools will not be locales for interracial interaction, at least not between students.

33. See, for example, the essays in *The Integration Debate: Competing Futures for American Cities*, ed. Chester Hartman and Gregory D. Squires (New York: Routledge, 2010). Also see the U.S. Department of Housing and Urban Development's final impacts assessment of the Moving to Opportunity experiment (2011): http://www.huduser.org/portal/publications/pubasst/mtofhd.html. The investigators report: "Families in the experimental group did not experience better employment or income outcomes than the other families. The children in the section 8 and experimental groups did not have better educational achievements than those in the control group and were not significantly less likely to engage in most forms of risky or criminal behavior."

34. Rawls's remarks about the "burdens of judgment" are relevant here. John Rawls, *Political Liberalism* (New York: Columbia University Press, 1996), 54–58.

35. Anderson, *The Imperative of Integration*, 186–187.

36. For some empirical support for this speculation, see Jacob S. Rugh and Douglas S. Massey, "Segregation in Post-Civil Rights America: Stalled Integration or End of the Segregated Century," *Du Bois Review/FirstView* (2013): 1–28.

37. Anderson, *The Imperative of Integration*, 189.

38. Ibid.

39. Of course, one cannot literally choose the racial demographics of one's neighborhood. The racial composition of a neighborhood depends on the choices of others to join or exit it. One can choose to live in or leave a neighborhood because of its current or projected racial demographics. But others have a right to join or exit it too, thus perhaps upsetting one's preferred racial composition.

40. See, for example, V. Denise James, "The Burdens of Integration," *Symposium on Gender, Race and Philosophy* 9 (2013).

41. Jennifer Hochschild, "Creating Options," in Fiss, *A Way Out*, 68–73. Also see Valls, "Liberal Defense of Black Nationalism."

42. Martin Luther King Jr., "The Ethical Demands for Integration," in *A Testament of Hope: The Essential Writings and Speeches of Martin Luther King Jr.*, ed. James M. Washington (New York: HarperCollins, 1991), 117–125. I discuss King's vision of racial justice (and criticize Barack Obama's) in my "Justice and Racial Conciliation: Two Visions," *Daedalus* 140 (Winter 2011): 95–107.

43. While I embrace King's vision of interracial unity, the position I've been defending is, in some ways, at odds with his idea of redemptive suffering—the Christian-inspired notion that the suffering of righteous agents of social change can transform the moral consciousness of those on the wrong side of justice. But the resolution of that dispute will have to wait for another day.

CHAPTER THREE Culture

1. The idea that there exists a culture of poverty is old. One can find a version of it articulated in W. E. B. Du Bois's *The Philadelphia Negro* (1899), with its emphasis on the cultural deficits of newly urbanized blacks, especially the so-called submerged tenth. The phrase "culture of poverty" came into popular use because of the influence of Oscar Lewis's *Five Families* (1959), which focused on Mexican urban communities. The theory is developed in relation to the black urban poor in such well-known texts as Michael Harrington's *The Other America* (1962), Kenneth Clark's *Dark Ghetto* (1965), and Daniel Patrick Moynihan's "The Negro Family: The Case for National Action" (1965).

2. See, e.g., Jack L. Roach and Orville R. Gursslin, "An Evaluation of the Concept 'Culture of Poverty,'" *Social Forces* 45, no. 3 (1967): 383–392; Charles Valentine, *Culture and Poverty: Critique and Counter-Proposals* (Chicago: University of Chicago Press, 1968); Mary Corcoran et al., "Myth and Reality: The Causes and Persistence of Poverty," *Journal of Policy Analysis and Management* 4 (Summer 1985): 515–536; William Julius Wilson, *The Truly Disadvantaged* (Chicago: University of Chicago Press, 1987); J. David Greenstone, "Culture, Rationality, and the Underclass," in *The Urban Underclass*, ed. Christopher Jencks and Paul E. Peterson (Washington, DC: Brookings Institution, 1991), 399–408; Rachel K. Jones and Ye Luo, "The Culture of Poverty and African-American Culture," *Sociological Perspectives* 42 (Autumn 1999): 439–458; Michèle Lamont and Mario Luis Small, "How Culture Matters for the Understanding of Poverty:

Enriching Our Understanding," in *The Color of Poverty: Why Racial and Ethnic Disparities Exist*, ed. David Harris and Ann Lin (New York: Sage Foundation, 2006), 76–102; and Orlando Patterson and Ethan Fosse, eds., *The Cultural Matrix: Understanding Black Youth* (Cambridge, MA: Harvard University Press, 2015).

3. See especially Orlando Patterson, "Taking Culture Seriously: A Framework and an Afro-American Illustration," in *Culture Matters: How Values Shape Human Progress*, ed. Lawrence E. Harrison and Samuel P. Huntington (New York: Basic Books, 2000), 202–218; and Van. C. Tran, "More Than Just Black: Cultural Perils and Opportunities in Inner-City Neighborhoods," in *The Cultural Matrix: Understanding Black Youth*, ed. Orlando Patterson and Ethan Fosse (Cambridge, MA: Harvard University Press, 2015), 252–280.

4. David Harding, Michèle Lamont, and Mario Luis Small, eds., "Reconsidering Culture and Poverty," *Annals of the American Academy of Political and Social Science* 629 (2010): 6–29.

5. Orlando Patterson, "The Social and Cultural Matrix of Black Youth," in Patterson and Fosse, *The Cultural Matrix*, 45–135.

6. The substantive differences between the new cultural analysts and Oscar Lewis (the originator of the concept "culture of poverty") may not be so stark. For a defense of the view that the classic culture-of-poverty theory, as articulated by Lewis, has been subject to gross distortion and misrepresentation, by those on the left and the right, see David L. Harvey and Michael H. Reed, "The Culture of Poverty: An Ideological Analysis," *Sociological Perspectives* 38 (Winter 1996): 465–495.

7. Katherine S. Newman, *No Shame in My Game: The Working Poor in the Inner City* (New York: Russell Sage, 1999); Elijah Anderson, *Code of the Street: Decency, Violence, and the Moral Life of the Inner City* (New York: Norton, 1999); Kathryn Edin and Maria Kefalas, *Promises I Can Keep: Why Poor Women Put Motherhood before Marriage* (Berkeley: University of California Press, 2005); Alford A. Young, *The Minds of Marginalized Black Men: Making Sense of Mobility, Opportunity, and Future Life Chances* (Princeton: Princeton University Press, 2006); Sandra S. Smith, *Lone Pursuit: Distrust and Defensive Individualism among the Black Poor* (New York: Russell Sage, 2007).

8. Patterson, "Social and Cultural Matrix."

9. Stephen Vaisey, "What People Want: Rethinking Poverty, Culture, and Educational Attainment," *Annals of the American Academy of Political and Social Science* 629 (May 2010): 75–101.

10. It is worth noting that there are advocates of the suboptimal cultural divergence thesis who do not believe that this set of cultural characteristics is, or ever was, an adaptation to poverty, slavery, Jim Crow, or any other unjust social conditions. For example, Thomas Sowell has argued that black ghetto culture is actually the remnants of southern white "redneck" culture, which has its origins in those regions of the British Isles from which white American southerners came. The cultural traits that Sowell attributes to blacks in the ghetto (and to poor rural whites) are much the same as those that culture-of-poverty theorists attribute to poor blacks. See Thomas Sowell, *Black Rednecks and White Liberals* (San Francisco: Encounter Books, 2005). Charles Murray, by contrast, has argued that a culture of poverty, in both black ghettos and white slums, arose as a response to

liberal welfare policies that encouraged the poor to depend on federal aid rather than strive to be economically self-sufficient. These antipoverty policies, he claims, created perverse incentives that led to a dramatic rise in nonmarital births, family breakdown, crime, and other social ills. See Murray, *Losing Ground: American Social Policy, 1950–1980* (New York: Basic Books, 1984). I will not discuss these variants of the cultural divergence thesis.

11. William Julius Wilson, *When Work Disappears: The World of the New Urban Poor* (New York: Knopf, 1996), 63–64; see also William Julius Wilson, *More Than Just Race: Being Black and Poor in the Inner City* (New York: Norton, 2009).

12. Michael Harrington, *The Other America: Poverty in the United States* (1962; repr., New York: Touchstone, 1997); Kenneth Clark, *Dark Ghetto: Dilemmas of Social Power* (New York: Harper and Row, 1965); Daniel Patrick Moynihan, "The Negro Family: The Case for National Action," in *The Moynihan Report and the Politics of Controversy*, ed. Lee Rainwater and William L. Yancey (Cambridge, MA: MIT Press, 1967), 41–124; Lee Rainwater, "The Problem of Lower-Class Culture," *Journal of Social Issues* 26 (1970): 133–148; Signithia Fordham and John Ogbu, "Black Students' School Success: Coping with the Burden of 'Acting White,'" *Urban Review* 18 (1986): 176–206; Mercer L. Sullivan, *"Getting Paid": Youth Crime and Work in the Inner City* (Ithaca, NY: Cornell University Press, 1989); Richard Majors and Janet Billson, *Cool Pose* (Lexington, MA: Heath, 1992); Anderson, *Code of the Street*; Patterson, "Taking Culture Seriously"; Annette Lareau, *Unequal Childhoods: Class, Race, and Family Life* (Berkeley: University of California Press, 2003); John McWhorter, *Winning the Race: Beyond the Crisis in Black America* (New York: Gotham Books, 2006); Martín Sánchez-Jankowski, *Cracks in the Pavement: Social Change and Resilience in Poor Neighborhoods* (Berkeley: University of California Press, 2008); and Patterson, "Social and Cultural Matrix."

13. Tommy L. Lott, "Marooned in America: Black Urban Youth Culture and Social Pathology," in *The Underclass Question*, ed. Bill E. Lawson (Philadelphia: Temple University Press, 1992), 71–89; Tricia Rose, *Black Noise: Rap Music and Black Culture in Contemporary America* (Hanover, NH: Wesleyan University Press, 1994); Tricia Rose, *The Hip Hop Wars* (New York: Basic Books, 2008); Robin D. G. Kelley, *Yo' Mama's Disfunktional! Fighting the Culture Wars in Urban America* (Boston: Beacon Press, 1997); Imani Perry, *Prophets of the Hood: Politics and Poetics in Hip Hop* (Durham, NC: Duke University Press, 2004).

14. Rose, *Black Noise*.

15. Veronica Miller, "Bourgie R Us," *The Root*, August 4, 2008, http://www.theroot.com/views/bourgie-r-us; Paul Farhi, "'Hot Ghetto' Leaves Some Blacks Cold," review of *Hot Ghetto Mess* (BET television), *Washington Post*, July 22, 2007.

16. Pew Forum, *Blacks See Growing Values Gap between Poor and Middle Class* (Washington, DC: Pew Research Center, 2007).

17. For discussions and critiques of black elite advocacy of cultural reform, see Michael Eric Dyson, *Is Bill Cosby Right? Or Has the Black Middle Class Lost Its Mind?* (New York: Basic Books, 2005); Mary Pattillo, *Black on the Block: The Politics of Race and Class in the City* (Chicago: University of Chicago Press, 2007), chap. 2; Cathy Cohen, *Democracy Remixed: Black Youth and the Future of American Politics* (New York: Oxford University Press, 2010), chaps. 2–3.

18. Tamar Schapiro, "What Is a Child?," *Ethics* 109 (1999): 715–738.

19. Despite having the right to vote and to enlist in the military, eighteen- to twenty-year-olds do not have the right to buy alcoholic beverages in the United States. I leave this controversial exception aside.

20. For defenses of such measures, see the essays in Lawrence M. Mead, ed., *The New Paternalism: Supervisory Approaches to Poverty* (Washington, DC: Brookings Institution, 1997). Also see Mickey Kaus, *The End of Equality* (New York: Basic Books, 1992).

21. Some of these measures have been instituted through the Personal Responsibility and Work Opportunity Reconciliation Act (1996). However, moral reform is not the only type of justification or rationale offered in their defense. The same could be said about the Moving to Opportunity experiment sponsored by the U.S. Department of Housing and Urban Development.

22. For a careful analysis of church–state collaborations in poor black neighborhoods, see Michael Leo Owens, *God and Government in the Ghetto: The Politics of Church–State Collaboration in Black America* (Chicago: University of Chicago Press, 2007).

23. Kwame Anthony Appiah, *The Ethics of Identity* (Princeton: Princeton University Press, 2005), chap. 5.

24. John Rawls, *A Theory of Justice*, rev. ed. (Cambridge, MA: Harvard University Press, 1999), 386–391.

25. Stephen L. Darwall, "Two Kinds of Respect," *Ethics* 88 (October 1977): 36–49; Laurence Thomas, "Rawlsian Self-Respect and the Black Consciousness Movement," *Philosophical Forum* 9 (1978): 303–314; David Sachs, "How to Distinguish Self-Respect from Self-Esteem," *Philosophy and Public Affairs* 10 (Autumn 1981): 346–360; Bernard R. Boxill, *Blacks and Social Justice*, rev. ed. (Lanham, MD: Rowman and Littlefield, 1992), 186–199.

26. Some people have lower self-esteem than they otherwise would because of clinical depression, which can sometimes be effectively treated. Government could enable those who need it to get access to such treatment. But this is not the same as distributing self-esteem; it is a way of repairing damaged self-esteem.

27. Thomas Hill Jr., *Autonomy and Self-Respect* (Cambridge: Cambridge University Press, 1991), chap. 1; Boxill, *Blacks and Social Justice*, 186–199; Sachs, "Distinguish Self-Respect from Self-Esteem."

28. The conception of self-respect discussed here differs from the one defended in Michael Walzer, *Spheres of Justice: A Defense of Pluralism and Equality* (New York: Basic Books, 1983), 272–280. While Walzer also distinguishes self-respect from self-esteem, he ties the idea of self-respect closely to group membership and conventional social roles, including membership in a democratic polity and the role of citizen. He thinks that the idea of a self-respecting *person* or *human being* is too vague and abstract to be of much normative use. I hope to show that this judgment is mistaken.

29. Hill, *Autonomy and Self-Respect*, chap. 1; Boxill, *Blacks and Social Justice*, 186–199.

30. Samuel Scheffler, *The Rejection of Consequentialism* (Oxford: Oxford University Press, 1982).

31. Howard McGary, "The Black Underclass and the Question of Values," in Lawson, *The Underclass Question*, 57–70.

32. The argument of this paragraph and the previous one are offered on the assumption that not all ghetto identities are the product of false consciousness, rationalization, or bad faith. That is, I am assuming that these identities have not all been formed as an unconscious psychological defense mechanism against a debilitating sense of personal failure and individual incompetence. I take it that some ghetto identities are consciously adopted in light of the sincere and justified judgment that U.S. society is unjust and that the ghetto poor in particular do not have a fair shot in life as a result. For a classic defense of the view that some ghetto identities are rationalizations that stave off a sense of failure and incompetence, see Elliot Liebow, *Tally's Corner: A Study of Negro Street Corner Men* (New York: Little and Brown, 1967).

33. Glenn C. Loury, *One by One from the Inside Out: Essays and Reviews on Race and Responsibility in America* (New York: Free Press, 1995); Bill Cosby and Alvin F. Poussaint, *Come On, People: On the Path from Victims to Victors* (Nashville: Thomas Nelson, 2007).

34. See Tommie Shelby, *We Who Are Dark: The Philosophical Foundations of Black Solidarity* (Cambridge, MA: Belknap Press of Harvard University Press, 2005), chap. 2.

35. See Daryl Michael Scott, *Contempt and Pity: Social Policy and the Image of the Damaged Black Psyche, 1880–1996* (Chapel Hill: University of North Carolina Press, 1997); Khalil Gibran Muhammad, *The Condemnation of Blackness: Race, Crime, and the Making of Modern Urban America* (Cambridge, MA: Harvard University Press, 2010).

36. It might be thought that a race-neutral moral reform policy that targets *all* poor people would not run into this problem. But this is not so clear. There is a long history of "race-neutral" policies with racist intent—from policies that concern voting rights to the criminal justice system to welfare—and most blacks would seem to be aware of this history.

37. Lawrence Bobo, James R. Klugel, and Ryan A. Smith, "Laissez-Faire Racism: The Crystallization of a Kinder, Gentler, Antiblack Ideology," in *Racial Attitudes in the 1990s*, ed. Steven A. Tuch and Jack K. Martin (Westport, CT: Praeger, 1997), 15–41; Thomas C. Holt, *The Problem of Race in the Twenty-First Century* (Cambridge, MA: Harvard University Press, 2000); Tali Mendelberg, *The Race Card: Campaign Strategy, Implicit Messages, and the Norm of Equality* (Princeton: Princeton University Press, 2001); Michael K. Brown et al., *Whitewashing Race: The Myth of a Color-Blind Society* (Berkeley: University of California Press, 2003).

38. See Rawls, *A Theory of Justice*, 273.

39. John Rawls, *Political Liberalism* (New York: Columbia University Press, 1996), 18–20, 72–77.

40. For a defense of a conception of self-respect along these lines, see Michele M. Moody-Adams, "Race, Class, and the Social Construction of Self-Respect," in *African-American Perspectives and Philosophical Traditions*, ed. John P. Pittman (New York: Routledge, 1997), 251–266; and Carol Hay, "The Obligation to Resist Oppression," *Journal of Social Philosophy* 42 (2011): 21–45.

41. There are other circumstances under which it may be permissible for a public official (e.g., a social worker or police officer) to intervene paternalistically to help those who, because of unjust treatment by the state, have become incapable of helping themselves. For instance, this may be acceptable when the would-

be benefactor is acting as a private citizen rather than in his or her official capacity as a representative of the state.

42. Bernard R. Boxill, "The Culture of Poverty," *Social Philosophy and Policy* 11 (Winter 1994): 249–280.

43. Adolph Reed Jr., *Stirrings in the Jug: Black Politics in the Post-Segregation Era* (Minneapolis: University of Minnesota Press, 1999), chap. 6.

44. Carol B. Stack, *All Our Kin: Strategies for Survival in a Black Community* (New York: Harper and Row, 1974); Stephen Steinberg, "Poor Reason: Culture Still Doesn't Explain Poverty," *Boston Review*, January 13, 2011, http://www .bostonreview.net/BR36.1/steinberg.php.

45. Cathy J. Cohen and Michael C. Dawson, "Neighborhood Poverty and African American Politics," *American Political Science Review* 87 (1993): 286–302.

CHAPTER FOUR Reproduction

1. See Vonnie C. McLoyd, "Socioeconomic Disadvantage and Child Development," *American Psychologist* 53, no. 2 (1998): 185–204; Rebekah Levine Coley and P. Lindsay Chase-Lansdale, "Adolescent Pregnancy and Parenthood: Recent Evidence and Future Directions," *American Psychologist* 53, no. 2 (1998): 152–166; Greg J. Duncan and Jeanne Brooks-Gunn, "Family Poverty, Welfare Reform, and Child Development," *Child Development* 71, no. 1 (2000): 188–196; and Gary W. Evans, "The Environment of Childhood Poverty," *American Psychologist* 59, no. 2 (2004): 77–92.

2. See Matthew Desmond, *Evicted: Poverty and Profit in the American City* (New York: Crown Publishers, 2016).

3. For an overview of such programs, see Theodora Ooms, Mary Parke, and Stacey Bouchet, *Beyond Marriage Licenses: Efforts in States to Strengthen Marriage and Two-Parent Families* (Washington, DC: Center for Law and Social Policy, 2004). Also see Andrew Clarkwest, Alexandra A. Killewald, and Robert G. Wood, "Stepping Up or Stepping Back: Highly Disadvantaged Parents' Responses to the Building Strong Families Program," in *The Cultural Matrix: Understanding Black Youth*, ed. Orlando Patterson and Ethan Fosse (Cambridge, MA: Harvard University Press, 2015), 444–470.

4. For an evaluation of the effectiveness of child support enforcement for reducing nonmarital births, see Anne Case, "The Effects of Stronger Child Support Enforcement on Nonmarital Fertility," in *Fathers under Fire: The Revolution in Child Support Enforcement*, ed. Irwin Garfinkel, Sara S. McLanahan, Daniel R. Meyer, and Judith A. Seltzer (New York: Russell Sage, 1998), 191–215.

5. Because the person who is the physical source of the ovum from which a fetus is created need not be the same person as the one who carries the fetus to term, there are, strictly speaking, two types of biological mothers—gamete parents and gestational parents. However, because gamete donors and surrogates aren't relevant to our questions, we can ignore the distinction.

Peter Vallentyne also makes a useful distinction between *biological parents* (the man and woman who provide the sperm and egg and thus have genetic links to a child) and *procreative parents* (those who are ultimately responsible for the child's existence though they may have provided no genetic material). Again, the distinction doesn't matter for our purposes, because when it comes to the ghetto poor, the relevant procreative parents are always the biological parents. I'll therefore simply speak of "biological parents." See Peter Vallentyne, "Equality and the Duties of Procreators," in *The Moral and Political Status of Children*, ed. David Archard and Colin M. Macleod (Oxford: Oxford University Press, 2002), 195–211.

6. This dwelling-centered account of the family might seem to be biased against the legitimate interests of extended family, particularly grandparents, who often are deeply invested in and take care of children who are not, strictly speaking, their children and with whom they do not share a residence. I do not mean to deny that adult members of extended families have moral rights and responsibilities with respect to children with whom they don't live. But for our purposes here, it is necessary to define family in terms of who has *primary* responsibility for children's care and who is *ultimately* accountable for failures to see to children's day-to-day needs. Moreover, the concept *householder* does not set the bounds of parental rights, only the right to determine cohabitation.

7. See Kathryn Edin and Timothy J. Nelson, *Doing the Best I Can: Fatherhood in the Inner City* (Berkeley: University of California Press, 2013).

8. See, for example, William A. Galston, *Liberal Purposes: Goods, Virtues, and Diversity in the Liberal State* (Cambridge: Cambridge University Press, 1991), 283–288.

9. In developing the argument for this section, I have benefitted greatly from discussions with Johann Frick and from reading drafts of two papers of his, "Conditional Reasons and the Procreation Asymmetry" and "Future Persons and Victimless Wrongdoing."

10. Some think that all procreation harms and is therefore wrong. See, for example, Seana Valentine Shiffrin, "Wrongful Life, Procreative Responsibility, and the Significance of Harm," *Legal Theory* 5, no. 2 (1999): 117–148; and David Benatar, "Why It Is Better Never to Come into Existence," *American Philosophical Quarterly* (1997): 345–355. Even if they are correct, some procreation may be much worse morally speaking. Procreating when one knows or can foresee that the newly created person is highly likely to have a miserable childhood or life is worse than procreating when one's offspring will likely have, on balance, a good childhood and a life that they consider worthwhile. So the state might be justified in deterring only this worse wrongful procreation.

11. The problem is discussed in Derek Parfit, *Reasons and Persons* (Oxford: Oxford University Press, 1984), pt. 4.

12. Vallentyne, "Equality and the Duties of Procreators."

13. Elizabeth Harman, "Can We Harm and Benefit in Creating?," *Philosophical Perspectives* 18 (2004): 89–113.

14. See Shiffrin, "Wrongful Life."

15. Harman considers the "Teenage Mother" case (which is due to Parfit): "A 14-year-old girl decided to conceive now and raise a child. Because she is so young, she gives her child a bad start in life: her child suffers from inadequate parental stability and support. If she had not conceived now, she would have waited and had a different child later, to whom she would have given a good start in life" (94). The relevant comparison for harm is not the state of the person had the action not been performed but a "healthy bodily state," which includes a normal human life span.

16. One might violate Harman's principle by passing on known genetic defects or some debilitating disease, but I leave this case aside.

17. One might think that creating a child who will have to live in a violent neighborhood can't be wrongful procreation because the mother isn't responsible for the neighborhood environment in the way that she is for the household environment. But that can't be right. One would be wrong to procreate (assuming one could avoid doing so) if one's child would be born a slave and thus vulnerable to unspeakable violence and torture, brutal and relentless exploitation, and the vicissitudes of the commercial traffic in human bodies.

18. James Woodward, "The Non-Identity Problem," *Ethics* 96 (1986): 804–831.

19. Harman argues that this approach doesn't allow the harm to the child to play a role in the explanation of the impermissibility of teenage childbearing. But I don't think that's true. The rights in question are ultimately justified in terms of basic interests, including our interest in mental and physical health and an ordinary life span. However, she may be right that Woodward's account can't explain the Temporary Condition case, given that the parent of the deaf child doesn't appear to violate the child's rights.

20. Judith Jarvis Thomson, "A Defense of Abortion," *Philosophy and Public Affairs* 1, no. 1 (1971): 47–66.

21. See Michael D. Bayles, "Limits to a Right to Procreate," in *Having Children: Philosophical and Legal Reflections on Parenthood*, ed. Onora O'Neill and William Ruddick (New York: Oxford University Press, 1979), 13–24; and Sarah Conly, "The Right to Procreate: Merits and Limits," *American Philosophical Quarterly* 42 (2005): 105–115.

22. See, for example, Hugh LaFollette, "Licensing Parents," *Philosophy and Public Affairs* 9, no. 2 (1980): 182–197; and Carter Dillard, "Child Welfare and Future Persons," *Georgia Law Review* 43 (2008): 367–445.

23. Bayles points out that any technique for limiting the number of children born (for the sake of the public good) that involves taking away financial benefits or providing financial incentives will affect the poor more, because the income gained or lost has a bigger impact on their lives than on the lives of the affluent. The poor would thus have less reproductive freedom than the affluent, which would be unfair. Bayles thinks this problem could be solved by making the gain or loss proportional to the affected person's income (on the assumption that then the burden would be the same). See Bayles, "Limits to a Right to Procreate," 20.

24. Anna Marie Smith argues that the requirement on poor single mothers that they help identify the biological fathers of their children (through paternity tests if necessary) violates their right to privacy, because it forces these women to reveal intimate details about their sexual lives and reproductive decisions, information that they should be free to keep private. For this and other reasons, Smith favors an unconditional "caregivers' entitlement" that single mothers (indeed, any custodial parent) could receive without having to reveal this personal information. See her *Welfare Reform and Sexual Regulation* (Cambridge: Cambridge University Press, 2007).

25. Dorothy Roberts, *Killing the Black Body: Race, Reproduction, and the Meaning of Liberty* (New York: Vintage Books, 1997).

26. Ibid., 8–18. Also see Angela Y. Davis, *Women, Race, and Class* (New York: Vintage Books, 1983), chap. 12; and Patricia Hill Collins, *Black Feminist Thought: Knowledge, Consciousness, and the Politics of Empowerment* (New York: Routledge, 1991), chap. 4.

27. See, for example, Annette Lareau, *Unequal Childhoods: Class, Race, and Family Life* (Berkeley: University of California Press, 2003).

CHAPTER FIVE Family

1. See Orlando Patterson, *Rituals of Blood: Consequences of Slavery in Two American Centuries* (New York: Civitas/Counterpoint, 1998), 4.

2. For a review of the evidence on the impact of father involvement on child welfare, see Timothy J. Nelson, "Low-Income Fathers," *Annual Review of Sociology* 30 (2004): 427–451; also see Rebekah Levine Coley, "(In)visible Men: Emerging Research on Low-Income, Unmarried, and Minority Fathers," *American Psychologist* 56 (2001): 743–753; and Sara McLanahan and Christine Percheski, "Family Structure and the Reproduction of Inequalities," *Annual Review of Sociology* 34 (2008): 257–276.

3. See, for example, Dorothy Roberts, "The Absent Black Father," in *Lost Fathers: The Politics of Fatherlessness in America*, ed. Cynthia R. Daniels (New York: St. Martin's Press, 1998), 145–161; Imani Perry, *More Beautiful and More Terrible: The Embrace and Transcendence of Racial Inequality in the United States* (New York: NYU Press, 2011), 63–70; and Kathryn Edin and Timothy J. Nelson, *Doing the Best I Can: Fatherhood in the Inner City* (Berkeley: University of California Press, 2013).

4. Archard points out that the case of the rapist shows that one can have parental responsibilities (financial child support) without parental rights to decide how the child will be raised. He says the same thing about the abusive or negligent parent who loses custody of his child. A similar thing could be said about the biological father who deserts his child. See David Archard, "The Obligations and Responsibilities of Parenthood," in *Procreation and Parenthood: The Ethics of Bearing and Rearing Children*, ed. David Archard and David Benatar (Oxford: Clarendon Press, 2010), 103–127.

5. Munoz-Dardé suggests that the parties in the Rawlsian original position would not choose generalized orphanages over families because they would prize equal liberty over equal socioeconomic prospects. In particular they would seek to preserve individuality, which the abolition of the family would threaten. See Véronique Munoz-Dardé, "Rawls, Justice in the Family and Justice of the Family," *Philosophical Quarterly* 48 (1998): 335–352; and Munoz-Dardé, "Is the Family to Be Abolished Then?," *Proceedings of the Aristotelian Society* 99 (1999): 37–56.

6. This view might seem to require parental licensing, as there would be no assumption that biological parents have natural or preinstitutional parenting rights. They would be on a par with adoptive or foster parents. Engster does an excellent job showing that parental licensing of biological parents is administratively unfeasible and unfair to women. He also explains why there are relevant differences between licensing adoptive parents and licensing biological parents. See Daniel Engster, "The Place of Parenting within a Liberal Theory of Justice: The Private Parenting Model, Parental Licenses, or Public Parenting Support?," *Social Theory and Practice* 36 (2010): 233–262.

7. It might also seem to conflict with the Declaration of the Rights of the Child, adopted by the United Nations General Assembly on November 20, 1989.

The Declaration's principles (particularly principles 6 and 7) assert that parents have primary responsibility for children's care and guidance.

8. John Rawls, *The Law of Peoples; with "The Idea of Public Reason Revisited"* (Cambridge, MA: Harvard University Press, 1999), 156–164; and John Rawls, *Justice as Fairness: A Restatement*, ed. Erin Kelly (Cambridge, MA: Harvard University Press, 2001), 162–168.

9. Claudia Card, "Against Marriage and Motherhood," *Hypatia* 11, no. 3 (1996): 1–23.

10. John Rawls, *A Theory of Justice*, rev. ed. (Cambridge, MA: Belknap Press of Harvard University Press, 1999), 405–413; and Susan Moller Okin, *Justice, Gender, and the Family* (New York: Basic Books, 1989), 97–101.

11. See Martha Nussbaum, "Rawls and Feminism," in *The Cambridge Companion to Rawls*, ed. Samuel Freeman (Cambridge: Cambridge University Press, 2003), 504–506; Samuel Scheffler, "Is the Basic Structure Basic?," in *The Egalitarian Conscience: Essays in Honor of G. A. Cohen*, ed. Christine Sypnowich (Oxford: Oxford University Press, 2006), 102–129; and Blain Neufeld, "Coercion, the Basic Structure, and the Family," *Journal of Social Philosophy* 40, no. 1 (2009): 37–54.

12. This is a partial reply to Cohen's claim that the inclusion of the family in the basic structure makes it unclear what the basic structure is, in particular whether we should emphasize its coercive or conventional dimensions. See G. A. Cohen, *Rescuing Justice and Equality* (Cambridge, MA: Harvard University Press, 2008), 132–140.

13. Samuel Scheffler, *Boundaries and Allegiances: Problems of Justice and Responsibility in Liberal Thought* (Oxford: Oxford University Press, 2001), chap. 6. Also see Eva Feder Kittay, *Love's Labor: Essays on Women, Equality, and Dependency* (New York: Routledge, 1999), chap. 2.

14. Colin M. Macleod, "Parental Responsibilities in an Unjust World," in *Procreation and Parenthood: The Ethics of Bearing and Rearing Children*, ed. David Archard and David Benatar (Oxford: Clarendon Press, 2010), 128–150.

15. The same can be said of marriage—it serves the interests of justice and is intrinsically valuable to those in the union.

16. John Rawls, *Political Liberalism* (New York: Columbia University Press, 1996), 137.

17. Susan Moller Okin, "Justice and Gender: An Unfinished Debate," *Fordham Law Review* 72 (2003): 1537–1567. Also see Nussbaum, "Rawls and Feminism"; and Ruth Abbey, "Back toward a Comprehensive Liberalism? Justice as Fairness, Gender, and Families," *Political Theory* 35, no. 1 (2007): 5–28.

18. Okin says: "Families are not voluntary associations readily entered and exited. Families of origin are not entered at all voluntarily. And though families one forms are usually entered voluntarily, they are by no means always exited voluntarily; moreover, even when they are, typically such exit does not come without considerable struggle or loss." Okin, "Justice and Gender," 1566.

19. See, for example, Harry Brighouse and Adam Swift, "Legitimate Parental Partiality," *Philosophy and Public Affairs* 37 (2009): 43–80; and Niko Kolodny, "Which Relationships Justify Partiality: The Case of Parents and Children," *Philosophy and Public Affairs* 38 (2010): 37–75.

20. Michael O. Hardimon, "Role Obligations," *Journal of Philosophy* 91 (1994): 333–363.

21. As Brake rightly notes, different societies (and even the same society in past eras) organize the care and upbringing of children in different ways, distributing its burdens across different types of individuals, kinship relations, and social groups; and there is no reason to think that rearing children in a two-parent, monogamous, heterosexual family is somehow more "natural" than other forms of organization or that there is only one type of childrearing arrangement that is consistent with morality and justice. See Elizabeth Brake, "Willing Parents: A Voluntarist Account of Parental Role Obligation," in *Procreation and Parenthood: The Ethics of Bearing and Rearing Children*, ed. David Archard and David Benatar (Oxford: Clarendon Press, 2010), 151–177.

22. Brake, "Willing Parents."

23. Ibid., 156.

24. Perhaps they should, though. bell hooks puts forward this provocative position: "Women need to know that it is important to discuss child care with men before children are conceived or born. There are women and men who have made either legal contracts or simply written agreements that spell out each individual's responsibility. Some women have found that men verbally support the idea of shared parenting before a child is conceived or born and then do not follow through. Written agreements can help clarify the situation by requiring each individual to discuss what they feel about parental care, who should be responsible, etc. Most women and men do not discuss the nature of child-rearing before children are born because it is simply assumed that women will be caretakers." bell hooks, *Feminist Theory: From Margin to Center*, 2nd ed. (Cambridge, MA: South End Press, 2000).

25. Joseph Millum, "How Do We Acquire Parental Responsibilities?," *Social Theory and Practice* 34 (2008): 71–93.

26. Claudia Mills, "What Do Fathers Owe Their Children?," in *Fact and Value: Essays on Ethics and Metaphysics for Judith Jarvis Thomson*, ed. Alex Byrne, Robert Stalnaker, and Ralph Wedgwood (Cambridge, MA: MIT Press, 2001), 183–198.

27. Condoms (unlike vasectomy) function to prevent the spread of sexually transmitted diseases, and so their use does not strictly imply that the sexual partners are attempting to avoid pregnancy. But as a conventional method for settling parental liability in the absence of explicit verbal communication, it seems adequate, as no one can reasonably assume that reproduction is intended when condoms are being used.

28. The points made in this paragraph rely heavily on Scanlon's account of the value of choice and its contrast with so-called forfeiture accounts of consent and responsibility. See T. M. Scanlon, *What We Owe to Each Other* (Cambridge, MA: Belknap Press of Harvard University Press, 1998), chap. 5.

29. See Tom Dougherty, "Sex, Lies, and Consent," *Ethics* 123, no. 4 (2013): 717–744.

30. In embracing this conclusion, I am not endorsing Brake's parity argument for parental obligations. (See Elizabeth Brake, "Fatherhood and Child Support: Do Men Have a Right to Choose?," *Journal of Applied Philosophy* 22, no. 1 [2005]: 55–73.) She argues that because the fact of pregnancy does not commit a pregnant woman to parenting the child (as she may permissibly choose abortion or adoption), neither should it commit the man who impregnated her. However, a pregnant woman may choose to terminate her pregnancy even if she did not use contraception and even if, at the time of the sexual encounter, she made it clear that

she wanted to have a baby. We may criticize her for not using birth control and maybe even for changing her mind after becoming pregnant. But we may not hold her liable to parent the child or force her to carry the fetus to term. So the fact that she does not use contraception should not be construed as her implied acceptance of the maternal role. For the woman, giving birth to a child without arranging for adoption constitutes assuming the role of mother, providing the public with a defensible basis for holding her responsible for the child's care.

By contrast, I think it reasonable to regard the nonuse of contraception as implying acceptance of the paternal role (unless he has otherwise made it explicit that he does not want to be a father). The lack of parity is accounted for by the liberty that women have to control over their bodies. With respect to bodily integrity, men's and women's situations are relevantly different. Women have the right to choose whether to bear a child because of the distinctive way in which pregnancy affects women's bodies. There is no analogous liberty for men. If we were to insist on strict parity, then men should be free to decline parental obligations up to the point of birth (assuming adoption arrangements have not been made) and this freedom should not be conditional on the use of birth control.

31. James Lindemann Nelson, "Parental Obligations and the Ethics of Surrogacy: A Causal Perspective," *Public Affairs Quarterly* 5 (1991): 49–61.

32. Ibid., 50–51. Bayne and Kolers offer what they regard as a "pluralist" account of parenthood that treats gestation and intentions as individually sufficient for parenthood. But these sufficiency conditions are ultimately explained in terms of causal responsibility for the creation of a dependent child. See Tim Bayne and Avery Kolers, "Toward a Pluralist Account of Parenthood," *Bioethics* 17, no. 3 (2003): 221–242.

33. Scanlon, *What We Owe to Each Other*, chap. 5.

34. Brake, "Fatherhood and Child Support."

35. Mills, "What Do Fathers Owe Their Children?"

36. Brake, "Willing Parents."

37. Archard, "Obligations and Responsibilities of Parenthood."

38. Given that the failure rate for condoms and the withdrawal method are high, that reversible vasectomy is less than sure, and that no effective male pill is available, perhaps contraception for women should be free. For discussion, see Emmalon Davis, "What Is It to Share Contraceptive Responsibility," *Topoi* (2015): 1–11.

39. Scott Altman construes child support payments as penalties. (See Altman, "A Theory of Child Support," *International Journal of Law, Policy and the Family* 17, no. 2 [2003]: 173–210.) But he thinks these penalties should be imposed for parental wrongs that harm children—the failure to demonstrate love for the child (by not sharing resources with the child) and the failure to establish or maintain a loving relationship with the child's other parent (by divorcing, leaving, or not marrying him or her). Child support, on his account, is understood as punishment and compensation for harms to children caused by parental wrongdoing. Some of these harms are psychological—the sense of betrayal and abandonment kids feel when a parent withdraws and refuses to provide support. Altman notes, though, that some psychological harms that children experience depend on the social meaning attached to nonsupport from biological parents. If these meanings were to change (e.g., if it were widely understood that accidental biological

fathers don't have parental duties), then perhaps most kids wouldn't experience biological-father absence as harm. Altman regards it as a virtue of his account that it explains the "condemnatory attitude" often taken toward noncustodial parents who do not pay child support.

40. Mills, "What Do Fathers Owe Their Children?," 191.

41. hooks, *Feminist Theory*, 142–147. Also see Patricia Hill Collins, *Black Feminist Thought: Knowledge, Consciousness, and the Politics of Empowerment* (New York: Routledge, 1991), 119–123.

42. The principle embedded here has deep roots in liberal thought. Here, from *On Liberty*, is John Stuart Mill: "It still remains unrecognized, that to bring a child into existence without a fair prospect of being able, not only to provide food for its body, but instruction and training for its mind, is a moral crime, both against the unfortunate offspring *and against society;* and that if the parent does not fulfill this obligation, the State ought to see it fulfilled, *at the charge, as far as possible, of the parent"* (emphasis added). Quoted in James S. Fishkin, *Justice, Equal Opportunity, and the Family* (New Haven, CT: Yale University Press, 1983), 40.

43. Robert S. Taylor, "Children as Projects and Persons: A Liberal Antinomy," *Social Theory and Practice* 35 (2009): 555–576.

44. Rolf George, "Who Should Bear the Cost of Children?," *Public Affairs Quarterly* 1, no. 1 (1987): 1–42; and George, "On the External Benefits of Children," in *Kindred Matters: Rethinking the Philosophy of the Family*, ed. Diana T. Meyers, Kenneth Kipnis, and Cornelius F. Murphy (Ithaca, NY: Cornell University Press, 1993), 209–217.

45. In more stringent accounts, *nonrivalry*—that one person benefiting does not reduce another's opportunity to benefit—would also be a condition. The law and order that comes from compliance with social norms and legal requirements would satisfy nonrivalry.

46. Serena Olsaretti, "Children as Public Goods?," *Philosophy and Public Affairs* 41, no. 3 (2013): 226–258.

47. Freeman, while acknowledging that the basic structure has a pervasive impact on our lives and involves coercive enforcement of public rules, believes that what makes the basic structure "basic" is that these are the social institutions necessary for a societal scheme of cooperation over time. See Samuel Freeman, *Rawls* (New York: Routledge, 2007), 101–102.

48. In this way, the institutions that make up the basic structure contrast sharply with Nozick's public address system. See Robert Nozick, *Anarchy, State, and Utopia* (New York: Basic Books, 1974), 90–95.

49. Some might argue that if children become unhealthy, criminal, and non-productive adults, then they should be considered *public bads* (negative externalities) and the public should penalize their parents for their inept parenting or compel their parents to compensate the public for the burdens they have imposed. I would agree that some parenting practices should be subject to moral criticism, and the sanctions inherent in public disapproval of poor parenting is sometimes justified. But the conduct and character of adults is not due solely to the parenting they received, and so we cannot infer from the fact that an adult is a bad citizen that his or her parents are to blame.

50. Onora O'Neill argues that because the public has a stake in children becoming independent and responsible citizens, the state must ensure that parents

carry out their duties; and when parents cannot or will not, the state must help with the rearing of their children and provide any care that the parents cannot (e.g., education and medical care). She sees the state's role in childrearing as essentially a matter of supplementing parents' work or compensating for the failures or absence of parents. (See O'Neill, "Begetting, Bearing and Rearing," in *Having Children: Philosophical and Legal Reflections on Parenthood*, ed. Onora O'Neill and William Ruddick [Oxford: Oxford University Press, 1979], 25–38.) It appears that in the background of O'Neill's account there is an assumption that parenthood is a natural duty of procreators. I want to distance myself from any such assumption. Taking an institutional approach, I see the public and parents as sharing the responsibility for childcare and childrearing in accordance with just public rules. I too would emphasize the fact that children are citizens and accordingly have civil rights, but I also want to emphasize that the public benefits from the creation of new human beings and so should share in the burdens of raising them to adulthood if the social scheme as whole is to be just.

51. See J. David. Velleman, "The Gift of Life," *Philosophy and Public Affairs* 36, no. 3 (2008): 245–266.

52. See, for example, J. David. Velleman, "Family History," *Philosophical Papers* 34, no. 3 (2005): 357–378.

53. For helpful discussions of this issue, see Lionel K. McPherson, "The Moral Insignificance of 'Bare' Personal Reasons," *Philosophical Studies* 110, no. 1 (2002): 29–47; and Sally Haslanger, "Family, Ancestry and Self: What Is the Moral Significance of Biological Ties?," *Adoption and Culture* 2 (2009).

54. For a thoughtful discussion of the pros and cons of open adoption, see Anita L. Allen, *Why Privacy Isn't Everything: Feminist Reflections on Personal Accountability* (Lanham, MD: Rowman and Littlefield, 2003), 78–93.

55. David T. Ellwood and Christopher Jencks, "The Spread of Single-Parent Families in the United States since 1960," Faculty Research Working Papers Series (Harvard John F. Kennedy School of Government, 2004).

56. William Julius Wilson, *The Truly Disadvantaged: The Inner City, the Underclass, and Public Policy* (Chicago: University of Chicago Press, 1987).

57. McLanahan and Percheski, "Family Structure and the Reproduction of Inequalities."

58. See Kathryn Edin and Maria Kefalas, *Promises I Can Keep: Why Poor Women Put Motherhood before Marriage* (Berkeley: University of California Press, 2005); and Ellwood and Jencks, "Spread of Single-Parent Families."

59. See, for example, hooks, *Feminist Theory*, chap. 10.

60. As Rawls points out in *A Theory of Justice:* "the principle of fair opportunity can be only imperfectly carried out, at least as long as some form of the family exists. The extent to which natural capacities develop and reach fruition is affected by all kinds of social conditions and class attitudes. Even the willingness to make an effort, to try, and so to be deserving in the ordinary sense is itself dependent upon happy family and social circumstances. It is impossible in practice to secure equal chances of achievement and culture for those similarly endowed, and therefore we may want to adopt a principle which recognizes this fact and also mitigates the arbitrary effects of the natural lottery itself" (64; also see pages 265, 447–448). Compare Fishkin, *Justice, Equal Opportunity, and the Family.*

61. See Kittay, *Love's Labor*, chap. 5; and Anna Marie Smith, *Welfare Reform and Sexual Regulation* (Cambridge: Cambridge University Press, 2007), 130–136.

62. See Ferdinand Schoeman, "Rights of Children, Rights of Parents, and the Moral Basis of the Family," *Ethics* 91, no. 1 (1980): 6–19; and Harry Brighouse and Adam Swift, "Parents' Rights and the Value of the Family," *Ethics* 117, no. 1 (2006): 80–108.

CHAPTER SIX Work

1. See Ron Haskins, *Work over Welfare: The Inside Story of the 1996 Welfare Reform Law* (Washington, DC: Brookings Institution Press, 2006); and Marisa Chappell, *The War on Welfare: Family, Poverty, and Politics in Modern America* (Philadelphia: University of Pennsylvania Press, 2010).

2. William Julius Wilson has defended an account that systematizes these various factors into a compelling explanation of ghetto poverty. See Wilson, *When Work Disappears: The World of the New Urban Poor* (New York: Knopf, 1996).

3. Booker T. Washington, *Up from Slavery: An Autobiography* (New York: Doubleday, Page, 1901); W. E. B. Du Bois, *The Philadelphia Negro: A Social Study* (Philadelphia: University of Pennsylvania Press, 1899).

4. See Howard McGary, "The Black Underclass and the Question of Values," in *The Underclass Question*, ed. Bill E. Lawson (Philadelphia: Temple University Press, 1992), 57–70.

5. See Robin D. G. Kelley, *Yo Mama's Disfunktional! Fighting the Culture Wars in Urban America* (Boston: Beacon Press, 1997).

6. For important exceptions, see Elijah Anderson, *Code of the Street: Decency, Violence, and the Moral Life of the Inner City* (New York: Norton, 1999); Alford A. Young Jr., *The Minds of Marginalized Black Men: Making Sense of Mobility, Opportunity, and Future Life Chances* (Princeton: Princeton University Press, 2004); Kathryn Edin and Maria Kefalas, *Promises I Can Keep: Why Poor Women Put Motherhood before Marriage* (Berkeley: University of California Press, 2005); and Sandra Susan Smith, *Lone Pursuit: Distrust and Defensive Individualism among the Black Poor* (New York: Russell Sage Foundation, 2007).

7. See Christopher Jencks, *Rethinking Social Policy: Race, Poverty, and the Underclass* (New York: HarperPerennial, 1993), 120–130; and Stephen M. Petterson, "Are Young Black Men Really Less Willing to Work?," *American Sociological Review* 62 (1997): 605–613.

8. For an exception, see Lawrence M. Mead, *Beyond Entitlement: The Social Obligations of Citizenship* (New York: Free Press, 1986), 78–79.

9. See John McWhorter, *Winning the Race: Beyond the Crisis in Black America* (New York: Gotham Books, 2005), chap. 5.

10. See Susan Moller Okin, *Justice, Gender, and the Family* (New York: Basic Books, 1989); Patricia Hill Collins, *Black Feminist Thought: Knowledge, Consciousness, and the Politics of Empowerment* (New York: Routledge, 1991), chap. 3; Iris Marion Young, "Mothers, Citizenship, and Independence: A Critique of Pure Family Values," *Ethics* (1995): 535–556; Eva Feder Kittay, *Love's Labor: Essays on Women, Equality and Dependency* (New York: Routledge, 1999); and Virginia Held, *The Ethics of Care: Personal, Political, and Global* (New York: Oxford University Press, 2006).

11. There are some libertarians who allow that the needy do have an enforceable justice claim (and not just a claim of beneficence) against the public for material support. See, for example, Thomas C. Grey, "Property and Need: The Welfare State and Theories of Distributive Justice," *Stanford Law Review* 28 (1976): 877–902.

12. Forceful criticisms of libertarianism can be found in G. A. Cohen, *Self-Ownership, Freedom, and Equality* (Oxford: Oxford University Press, 1995); Samuel Freeman, "Illiberal Libertarians: Why Libertarianism Is Not a Liberal View," *Philosophy and Public Affairs* 30 (2001): 105–151; and Liam Murphy and Thomas Nagel, *The Myth of Ownership: Taxes and Justice* (Oxford: Oxford University Press, 2002).

13. See Robert Nozick, *Anarchy, State, and Utopia* (New York: Basic Books, 1974), 150–153.

14. Ibid., 153–167.

15. See Melvin L. Oliver and Thomas M. Shapiro, *Black Wealth/White Wealth: A New Perspective on Racial Inequality* (New York: Routledge, 1995); Dalton Conley, *Being Black, Living in the Red: Race, Wealth, and Social Policy in America* (Berkeley: University of California Press, 1999); and David Lyons, "Corrective Justice, Equal Opportunity, and the Legacy of Slavery and Jim Crow," *Boston University Law Review* 84 (2004): 1375–1404.

16. For a sophisticated defense of reparations for African Americans, one that relies on principles that many libertarians accept, see Bernard R. Boxill, "A Lockean Argument for Black Reparations," *Journal of Ethics* 7 (2003): 63–91.

17. See Philippe Van Parijs, *Real Freedom for All: What (if Anything) Can Justify Capitalism* (Oxford: Oxford University Press, 1995); and Bruce Ackerman and Anne Alston, *The Stakeholder Society* (New Haven, CT: Yale University Press, 1999).

18. Trudy Govier, "The Right to Eat and the Duty to Work," *Philosophy of the Social Sciences* 5 (1975): 125–143.

19. John Rawls, *Political Liberalism* (New York: Columbia University Press, 1996).

20. For a discussion of the historical origins of this ideology, see Judith Shklar, *American Citizenship: The Quest for Inclusion* (Cambridge, MA: Harvard University Press, 1991). The racial, gender, and class dimensions of this worldview are examined in Michelle Lamont, *The Dignity of Working Men: Morality and the Boundaries of Race, Class, and Immigration* (New York: Russell Sage, 2000).

21. See Karl Marx, "Economic and Philosophic Manuscripts of 1844," 66–125; "Wage Labor and Capital," 203–218; and "Critique of the Gotha Program," 525–541, all in *The Marx-Engels Reader*, 2nd ed., ed. Robert C. Tucker (New York: Norton, 1978).

22. See A. D. M. Walker, "Political Obligation and the Argument from Gratitude," *Philosophy and Public Affairs* 17 (1988): 191–211. But also see George Klosko, "Four Arguments against Political Obligations from Gratitude," *Public Affairs Quarterly* 5 (1991): 33–48; and Barbara Herman, "Being Helped and Being Grateful: Imperfect Duties, the Ethics of Possession, and the Unity of Morality," *Journal of Philosophy* 109 (2012): 391–411.

23. Though Rawls does not defend a civic obligation to work, the relevant conception of reciprocity is developed in *Political Liberalism*, 15–18.

24. This form of argument is advanced by Lawrence C. Becker, "The Obligation to Work," *Ethics* 91 (1980): 35–49; Mead, *Beyond Entitlement;* Amy Gutmann and Dennis Thompson, *Democracy and Disagreement* (Cambridge, MA: Harvard University Press, 1996), chap. 7; Mickey Kaus, *The End of Equality* (New York: New Republic/Basic Books, 1996); and Stuart White, *The Civic Minimum: On the Rights and Obligations of Economic Citizenship* (Oxford: Oxford University Press, 2003).

25. Some have made a convincing case that universal basic income and unconditional welfare benefits are compatible with the principle of reciprocity. See Catriona McKinnon, "Basic Income, Self-Respect, and Reciprocity," *Journal of Applied Philosophy* 20 (2003): 143–158; and Shlomi Segall, "Unconditional Welfare Benefits and the Principle of Reciprocity," *Politics, Philosophy, and Economics* 4 (2005): 331–354.

26. Klosko's account, with its emphasis on "presumptive benefits," takes this form. See George Klosko, *The Principle of Fairness and Political Obligation* (Lanham, MD: Rowman and Littlefield, 1992), chap. 2.

27. Segall rightly points out that even if a civic obligation to work is enforceable, it does not follow that the penalty for nonwork should be the withholding of welfare benefits or basic income. See Segall, "Unconditional Welfare Benefits," 340.

28. Becker, "Obligation to Work," 43–46.

29. Jonathan Wolff, "Fairness, Respect, and the Egalitarian Ethos," *Philosophy and Public Affairs* 27 (1998): 97–122; and McKinnon, "Basic Income, Self-Respect, and Reciprocity," 151–152.

30. See David Schmidtz, *Elements of Justice* (Cambridge: Cambridge University Press, 2006), 100–101.

31. See Richard J. Arneson, "Is Work Special? Justice and the Distribution of Employment," *American Political Science Review* 84 (1990): 1127–1147.

32. I leave aside the interesting question of whether citizens have a duty to take up particular kinds of work or specific occupations if this would advance the cause of justice. But see Lucas Stanczyk, "Productive Justice," *Philosophy and Public Affairs* 40 (2012): 144–164.

33. See Mary Jo Bane and David T. Ellwood, *Welfare Realities: From Rhetoric to Reform* (Cambridge, MA: Harvard University Press, 1994), 143–150.

34. See Robert Michael Smith, *From Blackjacks to Briefcases: A History of Commercialized Strikebreaking and Unionbusting in the United States* (Athens: Ohio University Press, 2003); and Edna Bonacich, "Advanced Capitalism and Black/White Relations in the United States: A Split Labor Market Interpretation," *American Sociological Review* 41 (1976): 34–51.

35. For a helpful discussion of matters of fairness in regard to socially necessary "hard work," see Michael Walzer, *Spheres of Justice: A Defense of Pluralism and Equality* (New York: Basic Books, 1983), chap. 6.

36. See Elizabeth Anderson, "Welfare, Work Requirements, and Dependent-Care," *Journal of Applied Philosophy* 21 (2004): 243–256.

37. Some defenders of a civic obligation to work acknowledge this point and build in appropriate qualifications. See White, *The Civic Minimum*, 86–94.

38. See Gary Orfield, Susan E. Eaton, and The Harvard Project on School Desegregation, *Dismantling Desegregation: The Quiet Reversal of Brown v. Board of*

Education (New York: New Press, 1996); Jean Anyon, *Ghetto Schooling: A Political Economy of Urban Educational Reform* (New York: Teachers College Press, 1997); Jennifer L. Hochschild and Nathan Scovronick, *The American Dream and the Public Schools* (New York: Oxford University Press, 2004); and Kathryn M. Neckerman, *Schools Betrayed: Roots of Failure in Inner-City Education* (Chicago: University of Chicago Press, 2007).

39. Oliver and Shapiro, *Black Wealth/White Wealth;* Conley, *Being Black, Living in the Red;* Michael K. Brown et al., *Whitewashing Race: The Myth of a Color-Blind Society* (Berkeley: University of California Press, 2003).

40. See Paul Gomberg, *How to Make Opportunity Equal: Race and Contributive Justice* (Malden: Blackwell, 2007).

41. See A. John Simmons, "The Principle of Fair Play," *Philosophy and Public Affairs* 8 (1979): 307–337.

42. Jeremy Moss, "'Mutual Obligation' and 'New Deal': Illegitimate and Unjustified?," *Ethical Theory and Moral Practice* 9 (2006): 87–104.

43. Piven and Cloward go even further, arguing not only that the work regime is exploitative, but that it has the often intended effect of imposing discipline on and instilling fear in the rest of the workforce, making them more docile and easily exploitable. In response to the dehumanizing effects of the work regime, workers will often accept lower compensation, fewer benefits, and less job security to avoid sharing the degraded status of the ghetto poor. See Frances Fox Piven and Richard A. Cloward, *Regulating the Poor: The Functions of Public Welfare* (New York: Vintage, 1993).

44. See Patrick Sharkey, *Stuck in Place: Urban Neighborhoods and the End of Progress toward Racial Equality* (Chicago: University of Chicago Press, 2013).

45. Some might object that because the ghetto poor also benefit from the new work regime, the social arrangement cannot be exploitative. For instance, some theorists attempt to explain what it means for an exploiter to benefit at the expense of the exploited in *distributive* terms. They claim, for example, that a relationship is exploitative only if the benefits of the relationship are such that the exploiter has (much) more to gain from the relationship than the exploitee, or such that the exploitee stands only to lose from it. However, the severely disadvantaged are often made better off, materially speaking, by an exploitative arrangement. An exploitative relationship need not be zero-sum in character and may even be a Pareto-optimal improvement for the two parties. The fact is, exploitees often have a lot to gain from their relationship with their exploiters, sometimes even more than the exploiters themselves. Indeed, the benefits of being exploited often explain (at least partially) why the exploitee enters into the relationship. For a development of this point, see Allen W. Wood, "Exploitation," *Social Philosophy and Policy* 12 (1995): 147–148; and Alan Wertheimer, *Exploitation* (Princeton: Princeton University Press, 1996), 14–19. For a general critique of the distributive approach to exploitation, see Julius Sensat, "Exploitation," *Noûs* 18 (1984): 21–38.

46. This account is developed and defended in Tommie Shelby, "Parasites, Pimps, and Capitalists: A Naturalistic Conception of Exploitation," *Social Theory and Practice* 28 (2002): 381–418.

47. Sandra Danziger, Mary Corcoran, Sheldon Danziger, and Colleen M. Heflin, "Work, Income, and Material Hardship after Welfare Reform," *Journal of Consumer Affairs* 34 (2000): 6–30.

48. For an account of what it means to be "black" in America, see Tommie Shelby, *We Who Are Dark: The Philosophical Foundations of Black Solidarity* (Cambridge, MA: Harvard University Press, 2005), chap. 6. See also Tommie Shelby and Lionel K. McPherson, "Blackness and Blood: Interpreting African American Identity," *Philosophy and Public Affairs* 32 (2004): 171–192.

49. For a defense of the claim that the stigma of blackness remains intact, see Glenn C. Loury, *The Anatomy of Racial Inequality* (Cambridge, MA: Harvard University Press, 2002).

50. See Douglas S. Massey and Nancy A. Denton, *American Apartheid: Segregation and the Making of the Underclass* (Cambridge, MA: Harvard University Press, 1993); Mary Pattillo-McCoy, *Black Picket Fences: Privilege and Peril among the Black Middle Class* (Chicago: University of Chicago Press, 1999); and William Julius Wilson and Richard P. Taub, *There Goes the Neighborhood* (New York: Knopf, 2006).

51. Or maybe it is a "neighborhood in transition," if it is undergoing the process of gentrification and the poor are being priced out. But I will set this case aside.

52. See Collins, *Black Feminist Thought*, 70–74.

53. Ibid., 63.

54. See Jill Quadagno, *The Color of Welfare: How Racism Undermined the War on Poverty* (New York: Oxford University Press, 1994); Herbert J. Gans, *The War against the Poor: The Underclass and Antipoverty Policy* (New York: Basic, 1995); and Martin Gilens, *Why Americans Hate Welfare: Race, Media, and the Politics of Antipoverty Policy* (Chicago: University of Chicago Press, 1999).

55. Though I do not develop it further here, there is a fourth reason some among the ghetto poor may refuse to work. They may reasonably complain that they have been denied a fair opportunity to secure *meaningful* work—e.g., work that they find intrinsically satisfying or interesting, that exercises and allows them to develop their most basic human capacities, or that suits them given their abilities and fundamental aims. See Adina Schwartz, "Meaningful Work," *Ethics* 92 (1982): 634–646; Russell Muirhead, *Just Work* (Cambridge, MA: Harvard University Press, 2004); and Jeffrey Moriarty, "Rawls, Self-Respect, and the Opportunity for Meaningful Work," *Social Theory and Practice* 35 (2009): 441–459.

CHAPTER SEVEN Crime

1. See Judith R. Blau and Peter M. Blau, "The Cost of Inequality: Metropolitan Structure and Violent Crime," *American Sociological Review* 47 (1982): 114–129; Robert J. Sampson and William Julius Wilson, "Toward a Theory of Race, Crime, and Urban Inequality," in *Crime and Inequality*, ed. John Hagan and Ruth D. Peterson (Palo Alto: Stanford University Press, 1995), 37–54; Douglas S. Massey, "Getting Away with Murder: Segregation and Violent Crime in Urban America," *University of Pennsylvania Law Review* 143 (1995): 1203–1232; Lauren J. Krivo and Ruth D. Peterson, "Extremely Disadvantaged Neighborhoods and Urban Crime," *Social Forces* 75 (1996): 619–648; Elijah Anderson, *Code of the Street: Decency, Violence, and the Moral Life of the Inner City* (New York: W. W. Norton, 1999); Jody Miller, *Getting Played: African American Girls, Urban Inequality, and Gendered Violence* (New York: NYU Press, 2008); and Jill Leovy, *Ghettoside: A True Story of Murder in America* (New York: Spiegel and Grau, 2015).

2. Mary Pattillo-McCoy, *Black Picket Fences: Privilege and Peril among the Black Middle Class* (Chicago: University of Chicago Press, 1999).

3. Bruce Western, *Punishment and Inequality in America* (New York: Russell Sage Foundation, 2006); and Loïc Wacquant, *Punishing the Poor: The Neoliberal Government of Social Insecurity* (Durham, NC: Duke University Press, 2009), chap. 6.

4. Devah Pager, *Marked: Race, Crime, and Finding Work in an Era of Mass Incarceration* (Chicago: University of Chicago Press, 2008); and Michelle Alexander, *The New Jim Crow: Mass Incarceration in the Age of Colorblindness* (New York: New Press, 2010).

5. Katherine S. Newman, *No Shame in My Game: The Working Poor in the Inner City* (New York: Vintage and Russell Sage, 1999).

6. William Julius Wilson, *When Work Disappears: The World of the New Urban Poor* (New York: Knopf, 1996), 67–70.

7. See Jennifer L. Hochschild, *Facing Up to the American Dream: Race, Class, and the Soul of the Nation* (Princeton: Princeton University Press, 1995), chap. 4.

8. See Anderson, *Code of the Street;* David J. Harding, *Living the Drama: Community, Conflict, and Culture among Inner-City Boys* (Chicago: University of Chicago Press, 2010); and Orlando Patterson, "The Social and Cultural Matrix of Black Youth," in *The Cultural Matrix: Understanding Black Youth*, ed. Orlando Patterson and Ethan Fosse (Cambridge, MA: Harvard University Press, 2015), 45–135.

9. By "illegitimate" I do not mean "unjustified." That would beg the question. Rather, these are means, should one use them, that would violate widely recognized behavioral norms, whether legal, moral, or traditional. These norms can be "legitimate," in the relevant sense, without being fully justified.

10. See Sudhir Alladi Venkatesh, *Off the Books: The Underground Economy of the Urban Poor* (Cambridge, MA: Harvard University Press, 2006).

11. It is just this distinction between having committed criminal acts and being habitually disposed to criminal behavior that is elided in Michael Levin, "Responses to Race Differences in Crime," *Journal of Social Philosophy* 23 (1992): 5–29.

12. The "gangster" and the "hustler" are familiar social identities in poor urban communities, and these terms are generally associated with male personas and activities. In adopting these urban vernacular expressions, I do not mean to imply that only men and boys perform these roles or accept their associated ethics. Moreover, both men and women, boys and girls, use street capital and deploy the tactics and strategies of gangsters and hustlers, though not always in the same ways, for the same reasons, or with the same frequency. See Jody Miller, *One of the Guys: Girls, Gangs, and Gender* (New York: Oxford University Press, 2001).

13. See my "Parasites, Pimps, and Capitalists: A Naturalistic Conception of Exploitation," *Social Theory and Practice* 28 (2002): 381–418.

14. See Randall Kennedy, *Race, Crime, and the Law* (New York: Vintage Books, 1997), chap. 10; Western, *Punishment and Inequality*, chap. 3; and Lawrence D. Bobo and Devon Johnson, "A Taste for Punishment: Black and White Americans' Views on the Death Penalty and the War on Drugs," *Du Bois Review* 1 (2004): 151–180.

15. Sudhir Alladi Venkatesh and Steven D. Levitt, "'Are We a Family or a Business?' History and Disjuncture in the Urban American Street Gang," *Theory*

and Society 29 (2000): 427–462; and Laurence Ralph, *Renegade Dreams: Living through Injury in Gangland Chicago* (Chicago: University of Chicago Press, 2014).

16. Loïc Wacquant, "Deadly Symbiosis: When Ghetto and Prison Meet and Mesh," *Punishment and Society* 3 (2001): 95–133.

17. Western, *Punishment and Inequality*, chap. 5.

18. Venkatesh, *Off the Books;* Wilson, *When Work Disappears*, 59–72; Anderson, *Code of the Street*, chap. 3; and Peter Rosenblatt, Kathryn Edin, and Queenie Zhu, "'I Do Me': Young Black Men and the Struggle to Resist the Streets," in Patterson and Fosse, *The Cultural Matrix*, 229–280.

19. Jeffrey Fagan and Deanna L. Wilkinson, "Guns, Youth Violence, and Social Identity in Inner Cities," in *Crime and Justice*, vol. 24, ed. Michael Tonry and Mark H. Moore (Chicago: University of Chicago Press, 1998), 104–188.

20. Anderson, *Code of the Street;* and Patterson, "Social and Cultural Matrix," 78–92, 105–120.

21. See, for example, Lawrence Bobo, James R. Klugel, and Ryan A. Smith, "Laissez-Faire Racism: The Crystallization of a Kinder, Gentler, Antiblack Ideology," in *Racial Attitudes in the 1990s*, ed. Steven A. Tuch and Jack K. Martin (Westport, CT: Praeger, 1997), 15–41; Thomas C. Holt, *The Problem of Race in the Twenty-First Century* (Cambridge, MA: Harvard University Press, 2000); Tali Mendelberg, *The Race Card: Campaign Strategy, Implicit Messages, and the Norm of Equality* (Princeton: Princeton University Press, 2001); and Michael K. Brown, Martin Carnoy, Elliot Currie, Troy Duster, David B. Oppenheimer, Marjorie M. Shultz, and David Wellman, *Whitewashing Race: The Myth of a Color-Blind Society* (Berkeley: University of California Press, 2003).

22. Joleen Kirschenmen and Kathryn M. Neckerman, "'We'd Love to Hire Them, But . . .': The Meaning of Race for Employers," in *The Urban Underclass*, ed. Christopher Jencks and Paul E. Peterson (Washington, DC: Brookings Institution, 1991), 203–232; and Wilson, *When Work Disappears*, chap. 5.

23. William Julius Wilson, *The Truly Disadvantaged: The Inner City, the Underclass, and Public Policy* (Chicago: University of Chicago Press, 1987), 39–46; and John D. Kasarda, "Urban Industrial Transition and the Underclass," in *The Ghetto Underclass: Social Science Perspectives*, updated edition, ed. William Julius Wilson (Newbury Park: Sage, 1993), 43–64.

24. Douglas S. Massey and Nancy A. Denton, *American Apartheid: Segregation and the Making of the Underclass* (Cambridge, MA: Harvard University Press, 1993); Pattillo-McCoy, *Black Picket Fences;* Camille Zubrinsky Charles, *Won't You Be My Neighbor? Race, Class, and Residence in Los Angeles* (New York: Russell Sage Foundation, 2006); and William Julius Wilson and Richard P. Taub, *There Goes the Neighborhood* (New York: Knopf, 2006).

25. It is worth noting that the ghetto poor do sometimes manage to exit poor neighborhoods but then only to return to the same or a similar neighborhood shortly thereafter. Indeed, some are able to move to nonpoor neighborhoods, and then these new neighborhoods become poor later, as more poor people move in and the nonpoor move out. For many poor urban blacks, the problem is not so much getting out of the ghetto but staying out. See Lincoln Quillian, "How Long Are Exposures to Poor Neighborhoods? The Long-Term Dynamics of Entry and Exit from Poor Neighborhoods," *Population Research and Policy Review* 22 (2003): 221–249.

26. E. Ann Carson, "Prisoners in 2013," Bureau of Justice Statistics, NCJ 247282 (September 2014).

27. Todd D. Minton and Zhen Zeng, "Jail Inmates at Midyear 2014," Bureau of Justice Statistics, NCJ 248629 (June 2015).

28. Erinn J. Herberman and Thomas P. Bonczar, "Probation and Parole in the United States, 2013," Bureau of Justice Statistics, NCJ 248029 (October 2014).

29. See David Cole, *No Equal Justice: Race and Class in the American Criminal Justice System* (New York: New Press, 1999); Marc Mauer, *Race to Incarcerate* (New York: New Press, 1999); Loïc Wacquant, "From Slavery to Mass Incarceration: Rethinking the 'Race Question' in the U.S.," *New Left Review* 13 (2002): 41–60; Western, *Punishment and Inequality;* Jonathan Simon, *Governing through Crime* (New York: Oxford University Press, 2007); Todd R. Clear, *Imprisoning Communities: How Mass Incarceration Makes Disadvantaged Neighborhoods Worse* (New York: Oxford University Press, 2007); Glenn C. Loury, *Race, Incarceration, and American Values* (Cambridge, MA: MIT Press, 2008); Alexander, *The New Jim Crow;* and Michael Tonry, *Punishing Race: A Continuing American Dilemma* (New York: Oxford University Press, 2011).

30. Alexander, *The New Jim Crow;* and Tonry, *Punishing Race.* For an important discussion of the limits of this argument, see James Forman Jr., "Racial Critiques of Mass Incarceration: Beyond the New Jim Crow," *NYU Law Review* 87 (2012): 101–146.

31. Vesla M. Weaver, "Frontlash: Race and the Development of Punitive Crime Policy," *Studies in American Political Development* 21 (2007): 230–265.

32. Cole, *No Equal Justice;* and Loury, *Race, Incarceration, and American Values.*

33. Clear, *Imprisoning Communities;* and Loury, *Race, Incarceration, and American Values.*

34. Lincoln Quillian and Devah Pager, "Black Neighbors, Higher Crime? The Role of Racial Stereotypes in Evaluations of Neighborhood Crime," *American Journal of Sociology* 107 (2001): 717–767.

35. Cole, *No Equal Justice;* and Jeffrey Reiman, *The Rich Get Richer and the Poor Get Prison: Ideology, Class, and Criminal Justice,* 8th ed. (Boston: Allyn and Bacon, 2007).

36. Wacquant, *Punishing the Poor.*

37. Angela Y. Davis, *Are Prisons Obsolete?* (New York: Seven Stories Press, 2003); and Ruth Wilson Gilmore, *Golden Gulag: Prisons, Surplus, Crisis, and Opposition in Globalizing California* (Berkeley: University of California Press, 2007).

38. Carson, "Prisoners in 2013."

39. Mark A. R. Kleiman, *When Brute Force Fails: How to Have Less Crime and Less Punishment* (Princeton: Princeton University Press, 2009).

40. Paul Butler, *Let's Get Free: A Hip-Hop Theory of Justice* (New York: New Press, 2009).

41. Tom Robbins, "Attica's Ghosts," *The Marshall Project* (filed February 28, 2015). https://www.themarshallproject.org/2015/02/28/attica-s-ghosts.

42. Stuart Grassian, "Psychopathological Effects of Solitary Confinement," *American Journal of Psychiatry* 140 (1983): 1450–1454; and Lisa Guenther, *Solitary Confinement: Social Death and Its Afterlives* (Minneapolis: University of Minnesota Press, 2013).

43. George P. Fletcher, "Disenfranchisement as Punishment: Reflections on the Racial Uses of *Infamia*," *UCLA Law Review* 46 (1999): 1895–1907; Pamela S. Karlan, "Convictions and Doubts: Retribution, Representation, and the Debate over Felon Disenfranchisement," *Stanford Law Review* 56 (2004): 1147–1170; and Jeff Manza and Christopher Uggen, *Locked Out: Felon Disenfranchisement and American Democracy* (New York: Oxford University Press, 2006).

44. For a discussion of the distinction between the rational and the reasonable in practical affairs, see John Rawls, *Political Liberalism* (New York: Columbia University Press, 1996), 48–54. Also see T. M. Scanlon, *What We Owe to Each Other* (Cambridge, MA: Harvard University Press, 1998), 189–194. A similar distinction, between cognitive-instrumental rationality and communicative rationality, is elaborated in Jürgen Habermas, *The Theory of Communicative Action*, vol. 1: *Reason and the Rationalization of Society* (Boston: Beacon Press, 1984), 8–42.

45. In elaborating this distinction I draw on Rawls's distinction between social obligations and natural duties, though perhaps not in the way he intended. See John Rawls, *A Theory of Justice*, rev. ed. (Cambridge, MA: Belknap Press of Harvard University Press, 1999), 93–101.

46. Rawls, *Political Liberalism*, 227–230.

47. For a defense, within a broadly Rawlsian framework, of constitutionally guaranteed and robust welfare rights, see Frank I. Michelman, "In Pursuit of Constitutional Welfare Rights: One View of Rawls' Theory of Justice," *University of Pennsylvania Law Review* 121 (1973): 962–1019.

48. Jeffrie G. Murphy, "Marxism and Retribution," *Philosophy and Public Affairs* 2 (1973): 239.

49. But perhaps not. For compelling considerations in favor of treating fair equality of opportunity as a constitutional essential, see Seana Valentine Shiffrin, "Race, Labor, and the Fair Equality of Opportunity Principle," *Fordham Law Review* 72 (2004): 1643–1675.

50. See G. A. Cohen, "The Structure of Proletarian Unfreedom," *Philosophy and Public Affairs* 12 (1983): 3–33.

51. This point is developed, within a broadly Rawlsian framework, in Howard McGary, "The Black Underclass and the Question of Values," in *The Underclass Question*, ed. Bill E. Lawson (Philadelphia: Temple University Press, 1992), 57–70.

52. Rawls, *A Theory of Justice*, 312.

53. Ibid., 98–100.

54. This is a point I failed to emphasize in earlier work on the subject. For discussion, see Shatema Threadcraft, "Intimate Injustice, Political Obligation, and the Dark Ghetto," *Signs* 39 (2014): 735–760. Also see Miller, *Getting Played*.

55. See Venkatesh, *Off the Books*.

56. For a helpful discussion of this latter issue, see Mark A. R. Kleiman, "Neither Prohibition nor Legalization: Grudging Toleration in Drug Control Policy," *Daedalus* 121 (1992): 53–83; Douglas N. Husak, "Liberal Neutrality, Autonomy, and Drug Prohibitions," *Philosophy and Public Affairs* 29 (2000): 43–80; and Anita L. Allen, *Why Privacy Isn't Everything: Feminist Reflections on Personal Accountability* (Lanham, MD: Rowman and Littlefield, 2003), 56–78.

57. See Robin D. G. Kelley, *Race Rebels: Culture, Politics, and the Black Working Class* (New York: Free Press, 1996).

58. See Frances Fox Piven and Richard A. Cloward, *Poor People's Movements: Why They Succeed, How They Fail* (New York: Vintage, 1979), 18–23. For insightful reflections on the significance of a recent urban riot, see the essays in *Reading Rodney King/Reading Urban Uprising*, ed. Robert Gooding-Williams (New York: Routledge, 1993).

59. Rawls, *A Theory of Justice*, 308–310.

60. There is a variant of this point of view that would appear to have traction in some urban black communities. On this alternative view, the United States is thoroughly corrupt and cannot be redeemed. Given that mass emigration would be impossible for the poor, the only viable option is to build self-reliant ghetto communities without any expectation that justice will someday prevail throughout the whole of the society. Even if this pessimistic prognosis were correct (although I do not believe it is, or, rather, hope it is not), the duty of justice would still need to be honored in this black nation within a nation. However, I will not explore the practical implication of the duty in this context. For my response to this brand of black nationalism, see my *We Who Are Dark: The Philosophical Foundations of Black Solidarity* (Cambridge, MA: Harvard University Press, 2005), chaps. 3–4.

61. I owe this point to Tim Scanlon.

CHAPTER EIGHT Punishment

1. The distinction between legitimate authority and enforcement rights is widely recognized among political philosophers, though there is much disagreement about just how to understand these prerogatives of states and about which if any states have, or ever could have, legitimate authority. See, for example, A. John Simmons, *Moral Theory and Political Obligation* (Princeton, NJ: Princeton University Press, 1979); Joseph Raz, *The Morality of Freedom* (Oxford: Clarendon Press, 1986), chaps. 2–4; David Copp, "The Idea of a Legitimate State," *Philosophy and Public Affairs* 28 (1999): 3–45; Allen Buchanan, "Political Legitimacy and Democracy," *Ethics* 112 (2002): 689–719; Arthur Isak Applbaum, "Legitimacy without the Duty to Obey," *Philosophy and Public Affairs* 38 (2010): 215–239.

2. John Rawls, *A Theory of Justice*, rev. ed. (Cambridge, MA: Harvard University Press, 1999), 236–238.

3. If this point doesn't immediately strike you as obvious, then consider this analogy to parental authority. Parents' right to demand obedience from their children depends on parents caring for their children's needs. If a parent abuses his children or neglects his kids' needs, then he can't complain if they refuse to comply with his wishes. Parental authority is retained only on condition that pertinent parental duties are carried out to a sufficient degree. An analogous thing can be said about the state: if the state fails to maintain a reasonably just basic structure, then it cannot expect compliance from those who are burdened by the injustices it perpetrates or fails to prevent. The state would lack the authority to penalize their criminal deviance.

4. Ibid., 99–100; John Rawls, *Political Liberalism* (New York: Columbia University Press, 1996), 15–18. Also see Jeremy Waldron, "Special Ties and Natural Duties," *Philosophy and Public Affairs* 22 (1993): 3–30; and George Klosko, *The Principle of Fairness and Political Obligation* (Lanham, MD: Rowman and Littlefield, 1992).

5. See Daniel M. Farrell, "The Justification of General Deterrence," *Philosophical Review* 94 (1985): 367–394; and Warren Quinn, "The Right to Threaten and the Right to Punish," *Philosophy and Public Affairs* 14 (1985): 327–373. Also see Erin Kelly, "Criminal Justice without Retribution," *Journal of Philosophy* 106 (2009): 440–462.

6. For an insightful general account of the moral underpinnings of due process, see T. M. Scanlon, *The Difficulty of Tolerance: Essays in Political Philosophy* (Cambridge: Cambridge University Press, 2003), chap. 3.

7. It might be thought that if the state lacks the authority to criminalize drugs, then it can't have the enforcement right to penalize even violent drug dealing. After all, such violence wouldn't be necessary if the drugs weren't criminalized to begin with. However, even if the state wrongly criminalizes drugs, it would not be permissible to carry out the drug trade using violent means, even under unjust conditions.

8. See Herbert Morris, "Persons and Punishment," *Monist* 52 (1968): 475–501; Jeffrie Murphy, "Marxism and Retribution," *Philosophy and Public Affairs* 2 (1973): 217–243; George Sher, *Desert* (Princeton: Princeton University Press, 1987), chap. 5; and Jeffrey Reiman, "The Moral Ambivalence of Crime in an Unjust Society," *Criminal Justice Ethics* (2007): 3–15.

9. I take it that there is no increase in the burden on the law-abiding—they continue to have the same burden of self-restraint. That is, they shouldn't interfere with others' legitimate sphere of freedom.

10. One thing the benefits-and-burdens theory explains that other theories generally don't is the widespread sense that the offender owes a "debt" to society that, absent forgiveness, he should pay or be made to pay. He has taken something from us that he shouldn't have taken, and he must therefore make amends. One feels that if he doesn't pay, he would get away with something he shouldn't get away with. Simply condemning his act seems inadequate. It doesn't quite set things right. Punishing him to deter others or to prevent him from future wrongdoing doesn't seem to get at what we're seeking in holding him accountable for what he has done. He must answer for his crimes and an apology is insufficient. I'm not sure whether we should try to account for this sentiment or dismiss it as an unfortunate and perverse desire for retaliation.

11. Robert Nozick, *Anarchy, State, and Utopia* (New York: Basic Books, 1974), pt. 1.

12. Liam Murphy and Thomas Nagel, *The Myth of Ownership: Taxes and Justice* (Oxford: Oxford University Press, 2002).

13. See Joel Feinberg, "The Expressive Function of Punishment," *Monist* 49 (1965): 397–423; R. A. Duff, *Punishment, Communication, and Community* (Oxford: Oxford University Press, 2001); Andrew von Hirsch, *Censure and Sanctions* (Oxford: Oxford University Press, 1993); and Uma Narayan, "Appropriate Responses and Preventive Benefits: Justifying Censure and Hard Treatment," *Oxford Journal of Legal Studies* 13 (1993): 166–182.

14. It might be conceded that the state, in convicting the offender, has condemned the criminal *act* and the *person* for committing the prohibited act. But some would insist that there is a further condemnatory function of the criminal justice system: namely, to condemn the offender for being the *kind of person* who would do such reprehensible things. To carry out this function, the state must punish

the offender. However, I do not see why it is a legitimate state function to condemn *offenders* over and above condemning their wrongful *acts*. Why must the state render a judgment on the wickedness of offenders, and is the state really best positioned to make such assessments? But even if condemning criminal offenders is a legitimate state function, I don't see why the familiar rituals surrounding conviction wouldn't suffice.

15. Feinberg, "Expressive Function of Punishment," 402.

16. If legitimacy comes in degrees, we can say that the authority of some unjust states is compromised but not entirely void. We might even say that an unjust state has authority over some (e.g., the affluent members of society) but not others (e.g., those most directly affected and burdened by the injustices of the basic structure). We might also say that a state wields legitimate authority generally speaking, but that it lacks the authority to punish particular crimes or particular classes of people who commit them.

17. Victor Tadros, "Poverty and Criminal Responsibility," *Journal of Value Inquiry* 43 (2009): 391–413.

18. See Judith R. Blau and Peter M. Blau, "The Cost of Inequality: Metropolitan Structure and Violent Crime," *American Sociological Review* 47 (1982): 114–129; Robert J. Sampson and William Julius Wilson, "Toward a Theory of Race, Crime, and Urban Inequality," in *Crime and Inequality*, ed. John Hagan and Ruth D. Peterson (Palo Alto: Stanford University Press, 1995), 37–54; and Douglas S. Massey, "Getting Away with Murder: Segregation and Violent Crime in Urban America," *University of Pennsylvania Law Review* 143 (1995): 1203–1232.

19. G. A. Cohen discusses an interesting kind of complicity in wrongdoing. He argues that the standing to condemn can be lost if the complicit agent has caused a legitimate grievance that the wrongful act is a response to and the complicit agent has closed off the morally permissible practical means of gaining redress. See G. A. Cohen, "Casting the First Stone: Who Can, and Who Can't, Condemn the Terrorists," *Royal Institute of Philosophy Supplement* 58 (2006): 113–136.

20. Tadros also makes the interesting point that under conditions of distributive injustice, the poor have reason to not submit to being held accountable for their crimes (to distance themselves from official practices of being held responsible): because the state has shown insufficient concern for their welfare, they have reason to believe that the state's criminal justice system will also show insufficient concern for their interests and may thus treat them unfairly.

21. It might be thought that judges in a fair criminal justice system can also *condemn* serious wrongdoing in an otherwise unjust society. If they are fit to judge whether a person has committed a prohibited *malum in se*, then they should have the standing to condemn as well. Much will depend here on the extent to which judges in an unjust society are tainted by their association with an unjust legal order. As representatives of the state whose function it is to apply state law, they would be appropriately regarded as speaking for the state when they condemn, and so don't have the standing to condemn, at least not in their official capacity as legal administrators.

22. See David Cole, *No Equal Justice: Race and Class in the American Criminal Justice System* (New York: New Press, 1999); and Paul Butler, *Let's Get Free: A Hip-Hop Theory of Justice* (New York: New Press, 2009).

23. For an insightful set of reflections on this problem that attempts to resolve (or at least mitigate) it without rejecting penal expressivism, see Gary Watson, "A Moral Predicament in the Criminal Law," *Inquiry* 58 (2015): 168–188. Watson argues that punishment can be permissible in such circumstances when the state openly acknowledges its complicity (effectively canceling its condemnatory message) and attempts to reconcile with the oppressed through effective remedial measures. He also argues that violent criminal offenders cannot complain of being prevented from wrongly attacking others, as they must acknowledge the right of their prospective victims to protect themselves even when they do so by relying on state power.

24. See Khalil Gibran Muhammad, *The Condemnation of Blackness: Race, Crime, and the Making of Modern Urban America* (Cambridge, MA: Harvard University Press, 2010).

25. See Robert J. Sampson, *Great American City: Chicago and the Enduring Neighborhood Effect* (Chicago: University of Chicago Press, 2012), 157–159, 173–177.

26. See Tracey L. Meares, "Norms, Legitimacy and Law Enforcement," *Oregon Law Review* 79 (2000): 391–415.

27. See George P. Fletcher, "Disenfranchisement as Punishment: Reflections on the Racial Uses of *Infamia*," *UCLA Law Review* 46 (1999): 1895–1907; Pamela S. Karlan, "Convictions and Doubts: Retribution, Representation, and the Debate over Felon Disenfranchisement," *Stanford Law Review* 56 (2004): 1147–1170; and Jeff Manza and Christopher Uggen, *Locked Out: Felon Disenfranchisement and American Democracy* (New York: Oxford University Press, 2006).

CHAPTER NINE   Impure Dissent

1. Martin Luther King Jr., *Stride toward Freedom: The Montgomery Story* (New York: Harper, 1958); Jo Ann Gibson Robinson, *The Montgomery Bus Boycott and the Women Who Started It: The Memoir of Jo Ann Gibson Robinson*, ed. David J. Garrow (Knoxville: University of Tennessee Press, 1987).

2. Tommy L. Lott, "Marooned in America: Black Urban Youth Culture and Social Pathology," in *The Underclass Question*, ed. Bill E. Lawson (Philadelphia: Temple University Press, 1992); Tricia Rose, *Black Noise: Rap Music and Black Culture in Contemporary America* (Hanover, NH: University Press of New England, 1994); and Chuck D with Yusuf Jah, *Fight the Power: Rap, Race, and Reality* (New York: Delta Books, 1997).

3. This theme is explored in the documentary *Uprising: Hip Hop and the L.A. Riots*, directed by Mark Ford (Los Angeles: Creature Films, 2012), DVD.

4. These diametrically opposed, even Manichaean, assessments of hip hop are helpfully reviewed and incisively critiqued in Tricia Rose, *The Hip Hop Wars* (New York: Basic Books, 2008).

5. For more nuanced discussions of the meaning of urban riots, see Robert Gooding-Williams, ed., *Reading Rodney King/Reading Urban Uprising* (New York: Routledge, 1993).

6. For brief overviews of this debate, see Michael C. Dawson, *Black Visions: The Roots of Contemporary African-American Political Ideologies* (Chicago: University of Chicago Press, 2001), 74–82; and Michael P. Jeffries, *Thug Life: Race, Gender, and the Meaning of Hip Hop* (Chicago: University of Chicago Press, 2011), 10–15.

7. See Todd Boyd, *The New H.N.I.C.: The Death of Civil Rights and the Reign of Hip Hop* (New York: NYU Press, 2003).

8. For further reflections on the limits of the civil rights paradigm of political dissent, see Cristina Beltrán, "'Undocumented, Unafraid, and Unapologetic': DREAM Activists, Immigrant Politics, and the Queering of Democracy," in *From Voice to Influence: Understanding Citizenship in a Digital Age*, ed. Danielle Allen and Jennifer S. Light (Chicago: University of Chicago Press, 2015), 80–104.

9. For a discussion of some of the ways adults have historically sought to supervise and shape youths' political development and civic engagement, see Jennifer S. Light, "Putting Our Conversation in Context: Youth, Old Media, and Political Participation, 1800–1971," in Allen and Light, *From Voice to Influence*, 19–34.

10. Murray Forman, *The 'Hood Comes First: Race, Space, and Place in Rap and Hip-Hop* (Middletown, CT: Wesleyan University Press, 2002); and Imani Perry, *Prophets of the Hood: Politics and Poetics in Hip Hop* (Durham, NC: Duke University Press, 2004).

11. Danielle Allen elaborates this point in "Reconceiving Public Spheres: The Flow Dynamics Model," in Allen and Light, *From Voice to Influence*, 178–209. Also see Iris Marion Young, *Inclusion and Democracy* (Oxford: Oxford University Press, 2000).

12. Jane Mansbridge, "Using Power, Fighting Power," *Constellations* 1 (1994): 53–73; Nancy Fraser, *Justice Interruptus: Critical Reflections on the "Postsocialist" Condition* (New York: Routledge, 1997), chap. 3.

13. Lester Spence, *Stare in the Darkness: The Limits of Hip-Hop and Black Politics* (Minneapolis: University of Minnesota Press, 2011), 8–11.

14. Michael Warner, *Publics and Counterpublics* (Cambridge, MA: MIT Press, 2002).

15. Danah Boyd, "Social Network Sites as Networked Publics: Affordances, Dynamics, and Implications," in *A Networked Self: Identity, Community, and Culture on Social Network Sites*, ed. Zizi Papacharissi (New York: Routledge, 2010), 39–58; Kazys Varnelis, ed., *Networked Publics* (Cambridge, MA: MIT Press. 2008).

16. See S. Craig Watkins, *The Young and the Digital* (Boston: Beacon Press, 2009); Cathy J. Cohen and Joseph Kahne, *Participatory Politics: New Media and Youth Political Action* (Oakland, CA: Youth and Participatory Politics Survey Project, 2012), http://ypp.dmlcentral.net; and Joseph Kahne, Ellen Middaugh, and Danielle Allen, "Youth, New Media, and the Rise of Participatory Politics," in Allen and Light, *From Voice to Influence*, 35–55.

17. See, for example, the websites Rap Genius (http://rap.genius.com) and RapPad (http://www.rappad.com).

18. Wayne Marshall, "Hip-Hop's Irrepressible Refashionability: Phases in the Cultural Production of Black Youth," in *The Cultural Matrix: Understanding Black Youth*, ed. Orlando Patterson and Ethan Fosse (Cambridge, MA: Harvard University Press, 2015), 167–197.

19. Jeffrey O. G. Ogbar, *Hip Hop Revolution: The Culture and Politics of Rap* (Lawrence: University Press of Kansas, 2007), chap. 5.

20. For discussion of this issue, see Jody Dean, "Why the Net Is Not a Public Sphere," *Constellations* 10 (2003): 95–112.

21. Wendy Chun explores the concerns connected to the monetizable status of culture products that circulate digitally in "The Dangers of Transparent Friends: Crossing the Public and Intimate Spheres," in Allen and Light, *From Voice to Influence*, 105–129.

22. The difference between a motive and an intention can be distinguished in terms of two questions: What is the agent trying to achieve (intention) and why is he or she trying to achieve this objective (motive)?

23. Robin D. G. Kelley, *Race Rebels: Culture, Politics, and the Black Working Class* (New York: Free Press, 1994); Michael Hanchard, *Party/Politics: Horizons in Black Political Thought* (New York: Oxford University Press, 2006); and Kahne, Middaugh, and Allen, "Youth, New Media."

24. See James C. Scott, *Domination and the Arts of Resistance: Hidden Transcripts* (New Haven, CT: Yale University Press, 1990), chap. 7. Impure hip hop dissent within repressive regimes does often take the form of infrapolitics, as dissidents can be jailed, raped, maimed, or killed for open dissent.

25. Cornel West, *Race Matters* (Boston: Beacon Press, 1993), chap. 1.

26. Wenn, "Reverend Jackson Blasts Nas for Controversial Album Title," *Contactmusic.com*, October 17, 2007, http://www.contactmusic.com/news/reverend-jackson-blasts-nas-for-controversial-album-title_1046952.

27. Nas, *The Nigger Tape*, June 17, 2008, http://www.datpiff.com/Nas-The-Nigger-Tape-mixtape.15983.html.

28. https://www.youtube.com/watch?v=jYfB-wossac.

29. See, for example, reviews of Nas's *Untitled* by Jeff Weiss, *Los Angeles Times*, July 12, 2008, Entertainment section; by Katie Hintz, *Village Voice*, July 16, 2008, http://www.villagevoice.com/music/nass-untitled-6390608; and by Jon Caramanica, *New York Times*, July 14, 2008.

30. Adolph Reed Jr., *Class Notes: Posing as Politics and Other Thoughts on the American Scene* (New York: New Press, 2000), 167–170.

31. Reed, *Posing as Politics*, 170. For a similar point of view, see Yvonne Bynoe, *Stand and Deliver: Political Activism, Leadership, and Hip Hop Culture* (Brooklyn: Soft Skull Press, 2004).

32. Amiri Baraka, "The Black Arts Movement," in *The LeRoi Jones/Amiri Baraka Reader*, ed. William J. Harris (New York: Thunder's Mouth Press, 1999), 495–506.

33. Albert O. Hirschman, *Exit, Voice, and Loyalty: Responses to Decline in Firms, Organizations, and States* (Cambridge, MA: Harvard University Press, 1970).

34. See, for example, Gordon J. Schochet, "From Dissent to Disobedience: A Justification of Rational Protest," *Politics and Society* 1 (March 1971): 235–256.

35. See Marcyliena Morgan, *The Real Hiphop: Battling for Knowledge, Power, and Respect in the L.A. Underground* (Durham, NC: Duke University Press, 2009).

36. Thomas Hill Jr., "Symbolic Protest and Calculated Silence," *Philosophy and Public Affairs* 9 (Autumn 1979): 83–102.

37. See Hirschman, *Exit, Voice, and Loyalty*.

38. Bill E. Lawson argues that political rap artists, in light of continuing injustices against blacks, view the social contract in America as voided. See "Microphone Commandos: Rap Music and Political Philosophy," in *Hip Hop and Philosophy: Rhyme 2 Reason*, ed. Derrick Darby and Tommie Shelby (Peru, IL: Open Court, 2005), 161–172.

39. In her insightful discussion of the ethics of symbolic communication, Danielle Allen emphasizes sincerity as a condition for just "culture jamming." See Allen, "Political Equality and Communicative Action" (unpublished manuscript).

40. For a helpful analysis of the role of personas in hip hop and the challenge this poses for extracting the meaning of rap messages, see Stephen Lester Thompson, "'Knowwhatumsaying'? How Hip-Hop Lyrics Mean," in Darby and Shelby, *Hip Hop and Philosophy*, 119–132.

Epilogue

1. The "Ten Point Program" is reprinted in Huey Newton, *To Die for the People*, ed. Toni Morrison (San Francisco: City Lights Books, 2009), 3–6.

2. Newton, *To Die for the People*, 26–30.

3. "Ten Point Program," 4.

4. In *The Philadelphia Negro*, Du Bois works largely within a liberal medical model of social reform. And it is striking how much his reflections on ghetto poverty (what he calls "black slums") resemble contemporary social-scientific work on the subject. His principal aims were to understand the underlying causes of black urban poverty, joblessness, family disorganization, and crime and, on the basis of these scientific findings, to suggest ways that disadvantaged blacks (many of whom were only a generation out of slavery) could be integrated into modern industrial life on just terms. He emphasized the social class differences between blacks in these neighborhoods (distinguishing four strata: educated elite, stable working-class families, the poor who struggle to make ends meet, and the criminal class), and he complained that race prejudice led whites to judge the group as whole by the conduct of the worst elements within it (the "submerged tenth"). He argued that the white American elite should abandon this irrational prejudice and work with the black elite (the "aristocracy" of the race) to alleviate problems within the group (developing its potential and reforming bad habits acquired under slavery) and to prevent discrimination in employment, education, housing, and voting. Because race prejudice negatively affected black life chances and political power, blacks strongly resented it, and some, having become bitter, choose to rebel against their society through crime and other vices. What explains much of this deviance, according to Du Bois, is unrecognized merit and thwarted ambition.

5. Kenneth B. Clark, *Dark Ghetto: Dilemmas of Social Power*, 2nd ed. (Hanover: Wesleyan University Press, 1989).

6. Kenneth B. Clark, *The Negro Protest: James Baldwin, Malcolm X, Martin Luther King talk with Kenneth B. Clark* (Boston: Beacon Press, 1963), 51–52.

7. Daniel Patrick Moynihan, "The Negro Family: The Case for National Action," in *The Moynihan Report and the Politics of Controversy*, ed. Lee Rainwater and William L. Yancey (Cambridge, MA: MIT Press, 1967), 41–124.

8. Clark's reflections on blacks' distaste for (what they regard as) liberalism is instructive: "One of the dangers in the present white liberal ambivalence towards the Negro is that it has caused many Negroes to reject the 'liberal' label as a designation for themselves. For a number of Negroes 'liberal' has come to mean 'white.' They, too, are ambivalent, for they do not wish to feel alien to the liberal tradition with which they associate the concept of justice." *Dark Ghetto*, 232.

9. Ibid., 48.

10. Moynihan, "The Negro Family," 48–51, 65–73, 93.
11. Clark, *Dark Ghetto*, 79.
12. Ibid., 51, 54.
13. Ibid., 66, 67, 200, 196–198, 127–129, 101.
14. Ibid., 34–38, 77, 173–174.
15. Ibid., 11, 28, 74–77, 154–168.
16. Ibid., xxxix.
17. Ibid., xxviii.

Acknowledgments

I have worked on this book for a long time and so have incurred many debts. Parts of the book develop ideas I have explored initially elsewhere. Two sections of Chapter 1 incorporate excerpts from "Race" in *The Oxford Handbook of Political Philosophy*, ed. David Estlund (Oxford: Oxford University Press, 2012). Copyright © 2012 Oxford University Press. Four sections from Chapter 2 include portions from "Inequality, Integration, and Imperatives of Justice: A Review Essay," *Philosophy and Public Affairs* 42 (Summer 2014): 253–285. Copyright © 2014 by Wiley Periodicals, Inc. Chapter 3 is a slightly revised version of "Liberalism, Self-Respect, and Troubling Cultural Patterns in Ghettos," in *The Cultural Matrix: Understanding Black Youth*, ed. Orlando Patterson and Ethan Fosse (Cambridge, MA: Harvard University Press, 2015). Copyright © 2015 by the President and Fellows of Harvard College. Chapter 6 is a slightly revised and expanded version of "Justice, Work, and the Ghetto Poor," *Law and Ethics of Human Rights* 6 (2012): 69–96. Copyright © 2012 by Walter de Gruyter GmbH. Chapter 7 revises and augments elements in "Justice, Deviance, and the Dark Ghetto," *Philosophy and Public Affairs* 35 (Spring 2007): 126–160. Copyright © 2007 by Blackwell Publishing, Inc. Chapter 9 is an updated version of "Impure Dissent: Hip Hop and the Political Ethics of Marginalized Black Urban Youth," in *From Voice to Influence: Understanding Citizenship in a Digital Age*, ed. Danielle Allen and Jennifer Light (Chicago: University of Chicago Press, 2015). Copyright © 2015 by the University of Chicago.

I first started work on this project while a faculty fellow at Princeton University's Center for Human Values in 2005–2006. I also made significant progress on the manuscript while a fellow at Harvard's Safra Center for Ethics in 2009–2010. I thank these two invaluable centers for their generous financial support, stimulating intellectual environment, and wonderful camaraderie. I have also presented work in progress at numerous universities and colleges and at conferences in North America and abroad, and I'm grateful for the helpful comments and constructive criticism I received on those occasions.

While countless individuals have aided me through their comments and criticism over the years, a few have provided extensive feedback on chapters or have been unusually generous in discussing the book's arguments with me. They include Danielle Allen, Eric Beerbohm, Melina Bell, Harry Brighouse, Emmalon Davis, Ethan Fosse, Johann Frick, Christopher Jencks, Erin Kelly, Christopher Lebron, Christopher Lewis, Jennifer Light, Wendy Salkin, Laurie Shrage, Lucas Stanczyk, Brandon Terry, Andrew Valls, Erik Olin Wright, and Naomi Zack. Ronni Gura Sadovsky provided editorial and research assistance. The students in a number of my courses (Race and Social Justice, Punishment and Social Justice, and Justice and the Family) read chapters and offered thoughtful critical commentary.

Lindsay Waters, executive editor for the humanities at Harvard University Press, was excited about the project from the time I first pitched it to him back in 2006 and never wavered in his enthusiasm. Amanda Peery, assistant editor at HUP, provided excellent editorial advice and much-needed encouragement. Louise Robbins and Kim Giambattisto oversaw the book's editing and production and were patient despite its author's delays toward the end. Wendy Nelson, who also copyedited my first book, was terrific yet again. I also want to thank Justin Bua for allowing the Press to use his "Bronx Tree" painting for the cover.

I have the tremendous good fortune to be part of a reading group in Cambridge, Massachusetts, that, for more than fifteen years, has met regularly to discuss contemporary philosophical work on race and racism. As I was developing the ideas for this book, I benefited enormously from these discussions and from feedback on written work from its individual members, who include Lawrence Blum, Jorge Garcia, Sally Haslanger, Lionel McPherson, Jose Mendoza, and Megan Mitchell.

William Julius Wilson and Orlando Patterson have provided advice, inspiration, and critical feedback from the start of this project to its completion. I have learned an enormous amount from each, and in many ways this book represents my side of a running debate with them. No one could reasonably hope for better colleagues and guides to the sociological literature on black urban poverty.

Robert Gooding-Williams and Ronald Sundstrom each read the penultimate draft of the book and offered numerous suggestions for improvement and saved me from embarrassing errors and omissions. Tim Scanlon not only gave feedback on the manuscript as a whole but has been discussing its questions with me, suggesting ideas, and offering encouragement as necessary, for many years now. For those who know Tim's work, his influence on my thinking will be evident. Derrick Darby has the most intimate acquaintance with the ideas in this book, as we have been reflecting together on the ghetto since we first met in graduate school back in 1990. We grew up in such neighborhoods and have grown up together in academic philosophy, so he "gets" *Dark Ghettos* in a way that no one else can.

My largest debt is to my family. Ella and Christopher, my beloved children, were tolerant and loving throughout, even though they no doubt wish their father would work less and play more. My spouse, Jessie, listened patiently while I explained and defended every argument in this book *many times over* and offered steadfast support when self-doubt threatened my resolve to see the project through. I am also grateful for her superb editorial work on the manuscript and her many suggestions for increasing its accessibility. Gratitude is insufficient, though. I owe my family something akin to an apology. The mood swings, impatience, and obsessive focus that accompanied my working through the ideas of this book made me, let us say, less than an ideal parent and spouse. I hope they can forgive me for the collective sacrifice I imposed and take at least a little pride in the work that only we, as a family, could have accomplished together.

Index

paternal liability, 160; and paternity conception of moral fatherhood, 168; strict liability penalties for, 159–160, 168. *See also* Family; Parental obligations; Parents

Feinberg, Joel, 240

Fiss, Owen, 64–66, 76–78

Freedom of association, 43, 63, 67, 69, 226, 278

Gangs, 203, 206, 220, 226

Gangster-hustler ethic, 206, 207, 219, 224, 226

Gangsters, 205–206, 207, 219, 224, 226

Gender, 5, 14, 36, 199, 281; discrimination, 35, 176; and equality, 5, 125, 159; gender-based violence, 220; ideologies, 23, 139, 179, 199; and inequality, 163; stereotypes, 139, 162

George, Rolf, 164

Ghetto, defined, 38, 41

Ghetto abolitionism, 275–284

Ghetto identity, 87–88; distinguished from black identity, 87; suboptimal, 101

Ghetto poor, defined, 82–83

Guaranteed basic income, 181, 182–184, 277. *See also* Work

Hardimon, Michael, 149

Harman, Elizabeth, 129–131

Harm Principle, 129–131; and family, 130; and gestation, 130; and neighborhood, 130–131

Hill, Thomas, 99, 266

Hip hop (rap), 81, 87, 253–273, 276; celebration of lawlessness, 269–270; gangsta rap, 271; personas, 271; political rap, 253–273; political rap as political speech, 255; standards of coherence, 271–272. *See also* Dissent; Impure dissent; Nas

Hirschman, Albert, 265, 267–268

hooks, bell, 162

Housing, 41, 44, 208; affordable, 44, 77, 78, 256, 277; assistance (vouchers, subsidies), 77, 78, 250; discrimination, 43–45, 46, 62, 64, 71, 176, 193, 208, 279; and householders, 124, 130; mortgage discrimination, 43; prima facie race-neutral housing policies with negative impacts on blacks, 44, 46;

projects for low-income persons, 44; substandard, 256, 277; unjust housing policies, 44–45; urban housing policies, 46. *See also* Integration

Hustlers, 205–206, 207, 219, 224, 226; gangster-hustler ethic, 206, 207, 219, 224, 226

Ideal theory, 11–13. *See also* Nonideal theory

Ideology, 22–23, 275; definition of, 22; political, 56; postracial, 29; racist, 23–25, 28–29, 139, 275; sexist, 23, 139, 179, 199; social sciences as source of antiblack ideology, 103

Impure dissent, 252–273, 276; aesthetic impurities of, 257; as avenue to avoid complicity with injustice, 266; cognitive impurities of, 257; as declaration of unwillingness to submit to society's unfair expectations, 269; as denunciation of structural injustice, 268; expressive function of, 268–270; and hip hop, 259–273; moral impurities of, 257; as normatively transgressive political dissent, 257; as not recognizing state's authority, 269; political impurities of, 257; as political speech, 265; as positive expression of association with those burdened by injustice, 268; relationship to activism, 265; sincerity condition on dissent, 271–272; as speaking truth to power, 269; as symbolic exit, 269, 272; varieties of, 256–257; as voicing lack of respect for society's unfair rules, 269. *See also* Condemnation; Dissent; Exit; Hip hop; Nas; Voice

Incarceration, 8, 9, 203–204, 218; convicted felons, 203–204, 206; felon disenfranchisement, 212, 250; formerly incarcerated, 204, 206; racialized mass incarceration, 209–212, 279

Individuals, 10, 12, 21, 166, 167; and choice, 9, 31, 67, 181; and colorblindness argument, 31; as the primary unit of moral concern, 10

Inequality, 8, 36, 49; correlation with violent crime, 251; economic, 38–39, 46, 47, 72, 193, 210, 228, 256, 282; group, 64; racial, 23, 43, 46, 64–66, 74, 210, 281; socioeconomic, 67, 77, 214, 215, 282. *See also* Equality; Gender